Oxford Studies in European Law

General Editors: Paul Craig and Gráinne de Búrca

THE ENFORCEMENT OF EC ENVIRONMENTAL LAW

The Enforcement of EC Environmental Law

PÅL WENNERÅS

OXFORD
UNIVERSITY PRESS

OXFORD
UNIVERSITY PRESS

Great Clarendon Street, Oxford OX2 6DP

Oxford University Press is a department of the University of Oxford.
It furthers the University's objective of excellence in research, scholarship,
and education by publishing worldwide in

Oxford New York

Auckland Cape Town Dar es Salaam Hong Kong Karachi
Kuala Lumpur Madrid Melbourne Mexico City Nairobi
New Delhi Shanghai Taipei Toronto

With offices in

Argentina Austria Brazil Chile Czech Republic France Greece
Guatemala Hungary Italy Japan Poland Portugal Singapore
South Korea Switzerland Thailand Turkey Ukraine Vietnam

Oxford is a registered trade mark of Oxford University Press
in the UK and in certain other countries

Published in the United States
by Oxford University Press Inc., New York

First published 2007

British Library Cataloguing in Publication Data

Data available

Library of Congress Cataloging-in-Publication Data

Wenneras, Paul.
The enforcement of EC environmental law / Paul Wenneras.
p. cm.
Includes bibliographical references and index.
ISBN 978-0-19-922901-7 (hardback: alk. paper)
1. Environmental law—European Union countries. 2. Environmental policy—European Union countries. 3. Offenses against the environment—European Union countries. I. Title
KJE6242.W46 2007
344.2404'6—dc22 2007018617

Typeset by Newgen Imaging Systems (P) Ltd., Chennai, India
Printed in Great Britain
on acid-free paper by
Biddles Ltd., King's Lynn

ISBN 978-0-19-922901-7

10 9 8 7 6 5 4 3 2 1

GENERAL EDITORS' PREFACE

It is axiomatic that the effectiveness of legal norms will depend in part at least on the extent to which they are effectively enforced. This may be through public enforcement via an established arm of government, such as the Commission. It may alternatively be through private enforcement, where individuals are accorded the power and incentive to bring actions. The duality in this regard lies at the heart of EU law. The original EEC Treaty provided an explicit mechanism for public enforcement in Article 169, now Article 226 EC, but it rapidly became clear to the ECJ that this, while valuable, could not serve as the only method for the enforcement of Community law. The potential case load could not plausibly be borne by the Commission alone, more especially when one factored in the need to enforce regulations, directives and decisions as well as primary Treaty articles. The remedies available under Article 169 were moreover limited to say the least prior to the TEU. Direct effect served therefore not only to bring individuals into the very heart of the Community legal order. It also had the distinct practical advantage of fostering the more effective enforcement of Community law, by spreading the burden and benefit of such enforcement through all the citizens of the EU, provided that the conditions for direct effect were met. Small wonder then that the ECJ, when concluding that directives could have vertical direct effect, focused, *inter alia*, on the functional argument that the application of direct effect to directives would enhance their enforcement and hence their effectiveness.

This addition to the series is therefore especially welcome. Wenneras provides an in-depth study of the enforcement regime that applies in EC Environmental Law. The author considers the role played be judicial review before national courts, the use made of the preliminary reference procedure and indirect review by the ECJ, direct actions for judicial review before the Community courts and enforcement by the Commission under Article 226. The application of these enforcement mechanisms is especially interesting in the context of environmental law and the insightful analysis by Wenneras casts interesting new light on the relative efficacy of these enforcement mechanisms in this area.

Paul Craig
Gráinne de Búrca

PREFACE

This book is a revised version of my doctoral thesis, which I wrote during 2002–2006 at the Centre of Environmental Law, University of Amsterdam. There are many people to whom I owe great gratitude for inspiring me to undertake this work and supporting its conclusion. I should first of all like to thank all my colleagues for providing a warm and stimulating environment in these years. Hanna Sevenster has been a great supervisor. Han Somsen's arrival in Amsterdam gave me invaluable academic and social impetus. Floor Fleurke has been the best colleague and friend one could hope for. Jos Janssen endured endless monologues on my part and always gave sound advice. I should also like to thank professors Geelhoed, Jans, Krämer and Prechal for valuable and instructive comments. Last but not least, my family and friends deserve much credit for putting up with me during the writing of this book, and they have certainly supported its conclusion.

Pål Wennerås
Oslo, January 2007

CONTENTS

Abbreviations xii
Table of Cases xiii

1. Introduction 1

1 Enforcement 1
2 Rights 6
3 Evolution 9

2. EC Environmental Law in the National Legal Order 14

1 Introduction 14
2 Direct effect 15
2.1 Rights 15
2.2 Conditions 25
2.3 Horizontal effect 44
3 Consistent interpretation 55
3.1 Introduction 55
3.2 Substance 55
3.3 Added value 57
4 Duties on national courts and authorities 68
5 Conclusion 71

3. Judicial Review Before National Courts 75

1 Introduction 75
2 Jurisprudential harmonization of procedural law 76
2.1 Introduction 76
2.2 The principles 77
2.3 Relevance for EC environmental law 84
2.4 Rule of reason and proportionality 88
3 The Aarhus Convention and implementing EC legislation 90
3.1 The Aarhus Convention 90
3.2 Community implementation 91
3.3 Jurisprudential harmonization v the Aarhus Convention and implementing legislation 91

4 Procedural requirements 93
4.1 Introduction 93
4.2 Passive role of judges 93
4.3 Time limits 96
4.4 *Res judicata* 98
4.5 Legal costs 100
5 Acts susceptible to review 104
5.1 Introduction 104
5.2 Case law 105
5.3 The Aarhus Convention and implementing legislation 107
6 Standing 108
6.1 Introduction 108
6.2 Case law 109
6.3 The Aarhus Convention and implementing legislation 114
6.4 Standing in matters concerning information and public participation 117
6.5 Standing in proceedings against private parties 118
7 Grounds and intensity of review 120
7.1 Introduction 120
7.2 Case law 120
7.3 The Aarhus Convention and implementing legislation 123
8 Legal consequences and basic remedies 124
8.1 Introduction 124
8.2 Legal consequences of procedural infringements 125
8.3 Remedies against illegal acts 130
8.4 Remedies against illegal failures to act 134
9 Interim relief 137
9.1 Introduction 137
9.2 Case law 138
10 Reparation on the basis of direct effect 141
10.1 Introduction 141
10.2 Directive 2004/35/EC and other liability legislation 142
10.3 Specific performance 143
10.4 Nullify unlawful consequences 145
10.5 Nullify unlawful consequences v state liability 146
10.6 Reparation by private parties 147
11 State liability 149
11.1 Introduction 149
11.2 Rights and damage 150

11.3 Sufficiently serious breach 157
11.4 Causation 160
11.5 Acts and omissions by the judiciary 163
12 Sanctions 167
13 Conclusion 169

4. Preliminary References 171

1 Introduction 171
2 General conditions 172
2.1 Competence 172
2.2 Obligations 173
2.3 Admissibility 175
2.4 *Ex officio* 176
3 Interpretation 177
3.1 Introduction 177
3.2 Acts susceptible to interpretation 178
3.3 Consequences 180
4 Judicial review 183
4.1 Introduction 183
4.2 Time limits 184
4.3 Reviewable acts 185
4.4 Grounds of review 189
4.5 Consequences 202
4.6 Interim relief 204
5 Sanctions 211
6 Conclusion 212

5. Judicial Review Before Community Courts 215

1 Introduction 215
2 Direct and individual concern 216
2.1 Introduction 216
2.2 Decision addressed to the plaintiff 216
2.3 Community acts of direct and individual concern 217
3 Internal review 226
3.1 Introduction 226
3.2 Personal scope 227
3.3 Time limits 229
3.4 Substantive scope 230
3.5 Grounds and nature of review 237

4 Judicial review 238
4.1 Introduction 238
4.2 Standing 239
4.3 Time limits 240
4.4 Grounds of review 241
4.5 Consequences 243
5 Interim relief 244
6 Community liability 246
6.1 Grant of rights 246
6.2 Causation 247
6.3 Sufficiently serious breach 248
7 Conclusion 249

6. Enforcement by the Commission 251
1 Introduction 251
2 Article 226 EC 252
2.1 Introduction 252
2.2 Monitoring 253
2.3 Prejudicial stage 256
2.4 Judicial stage 256
3 General and persistent (GAP) infringements 262
3.1 Introduction 262
3.2 Substantive conditions 263
3.3 Procedural conditions 266
3.4 Added value 268
3.5 Futher development 272
4 Article 228 EC 274
4.1 Introduction 274
4.2 Legal framework and ECJ's discretion 275
4.3 Penalty payments 277
4.4 Lump sums 286
5 Structural deficits 290
5.1 Duration 291
5.2 Independence 293
6 Rights of private parties 295
6.1 Introduction 295
6.2 Access to information 296
6.3 Right to participation 299

6.4 Access to judicial review 299
6.5 Community liability 301
7 Horizontal enforcement 302
8 The complementary role of private enforcement 304

7. Conclusion 309
1 Introductory remarks 309
2 Private enforcement against national authorities and private parties 309
2.1 Rights and remedies 309
2.2 Effectiveness 313
3 Private enforcement against Community institutions and bodies 316
4 The Aarhus Convention 320
5 Recommendations 322
6 Final conclusion 323

Bibliography 326
Index 337

ABBREVIATIONS

CLJ	Cambridge Law Journal
CMLRev	Common Market Law Review
EBLR	European Business Law Review
ECR	European Court Reports
EJCL	Electronic Journal of Comparative Law
EELR	European Environmental Law Review
EJIL	European Journal of International Law
EL	Environmental Liability
ELJ	European Law Journal
ELR	European Law Review
EnvLR	Environmental Law Reports
EPL	European Public Law
JEEPL	Journal of European Environmental & Planning Law
JEL	Journal of Environmental Law
JEPL	Journal of Planning & Environment Law
LIEI	Legal Issues of Economic Integration
MLR	Modern Law Review
YEEL	Yearbook of European Environmental Law
YEL	Yearbook of European Law
WLR	Weekly Law Reports

TABLE OF CASES

European Court of Justice

Joined Cases 32 and 33/58 SNUPAT [1959] ECR 136 240
Case 6/60 Humblet [1960] ECR 559.............................. 145–6, 149, 153, 315
Joined Cases 9 to12/60 Vloebergs [1961] ECR 197 244
Joined Cases 14, 16, 17, 20, 24, 26 to 27/60, and 1/61 Meroni [1961] ECR 161 193
Joined Cases 16 and 17/62 Producteurs de Fruits v Council [1962] ECR 478............. 235
Case 25/62 Plaumann v Commission [1963] ECR 95 ...... 209–10, 218–219, 222–3, 235, 316
Case 26/62 Van Gend & Loos [1963] ECR 1 .... 3, 15, 57, 79, 304
Joined Cases 28 to 30/62 Da Costa [1963] ECR 31 174
Joined Cases 73/63 and 74/63 Internatio [1964] ECR 1 .... 177, 189
Case 6/64 Costa Enel [1964] ECR 592.............................. 130, 174
Case 16/65 Schwarze [1965] ECR I–877 177
Case 18/65 R Gutman v Commission [1996] ECR 135 245
Case 48/65 Luetticke and Others v Commission [1966] ECR 19 242
Case 61/65 Vaassen [1966] ECR 272.............................. 173
Case 8/66 Cimenteries and Others v Commission [1967] ECR 93 243
Case 13/67 Becher [1968] ECR 197.............................. 179
Case 28/67 Molkerei-Zentrale [1968] ECR 143.............................. 32, 35, 181
Case 34/67 Lück [1968] ECR 245 130
Case 13/68 Salgoil [1968] ECR 453.............................. 32, 107, 138, 189
Case 9/70 Grad [1970] ECR 825 16
Case 15/70 Chevalley [1970] ECR 975.............................. 216
Case 25/70 Köster [1970] ECR 1170.............................. 236
Joined Cases 41 to 44/70 International Fruit [1971] ECR 411.............................. 235
Joined Cases 21 to 24/72 International Fruit [1972] ECR 1226 .... 189, 196
Case 70/72 Commission v Germany [1973] ECR 813 260
Case 2/73 Geddo [1973] ECR 685.............................. 300
Case 9/73 Schlüter [1973] ECR 1135 179
Case 166/73 Rheinmuhlen v Einfuhr- und Vorratsstelle Getreide [1974] ECR 33.......... 68
Case 167/73 Commission v France [1974] ECR 359 258
Case 181/73 Haegeman [1974] ECR 449.............................. 179
Case 185/73 König [1974] ECR 617 177
Case 8/74 Dassonville [1974] ECR 837.............................. 189
Case 41/74 van Duyn [1974] ECR 1337 .... 16, 34
Case 23/75 Rey Soda [1975] ECR 1279.............................. 203, 235
Case 60/75 Russo [1976] ECR 45.............................. 149
Case 113/75 Frescasetti [1976] ECR 1983 179
Case 28/76 Milac [1976] ECR I–1653.............................. 177
Case 33/76 Rewe [1976] ECR 1989 .... 76–8, 111
Case 45/76 Comet [1976] ECR 2043 .... 77, 85
Case 80/76 R Ditterich v Commission [1976] ECR 1586 245

Joined Cases 117/76 and 16/77 Ruckdeschel [1977] ECR 1753 203
Joined Cases 124/76 and 20/77 Moulins [1977] ECR 1795 203
Case 66/77 Kuyken [1977] ECR 2311 181
Case 106/77 Simmenthal [1978] ECR 629 .... 79, 107, 130, 138, 189
Case 14/78 Denkavit [1978] ECR 2497 301–2
Case 148/78 Ratti [1979] ECR 1629 .... 16, 31
Case 244/78 French Dairy [1979] ECR 2663 180
Case 68/79 Hans Just [1980] ECR 501 77
Case 104/79 Foglia v Novello [1980] ECR 745 175
Case 105/79 Hayange [1979] ECR 2257 175
Case 145/79 Roquette [1980] ECR 2917 203
Case 804/79 Commission v United Kingdom [1981] ECR 1045 203
Case 66/80 International Chemical Corporation [1981] ECR 1191 202
Case 158/80 Rewe II [1981] ECR 1805 .... 76, 130, 138
Case 203/80 Casati [1981] ECR 2595 167
Case 8/81 Becker [1982] ECR 53 .... 16, 20, 28, 35, 45
Case 283/81 CILFIT [1982] ECR 3415 .... 10, 163, 175, 181, 213
Case 11/82 Piraiki-Patraiki v Commission [1985] ECR 207 223
Joined Cases 75 and 117/82 Razzouk v Commission [1984] ECR 1509 244
Case 199/82 San Giorgio [1983] ECR 3595 77
Case 231/82 Spijker v Commission [1983] ECR 2559 218
Case 264/82 Timex [1985] ECR 849 203
Case 14/83 Von Colson [1984] ECR 1891 .... 52, 56, 59, 82, 156
Case 112/83 Produits de Mais [1985] ECR 719 183
Case 152/83 Demouche [1987] ECR 3833 180
Case 229/83 Leclerc [1985] ECR 1 27
Case 240/83 ADBHU [1985] ECR 531 .... 10, 89
Case 294/83 Les Verts [1986] ECR 1339 .... 84, 221, 240
Case 131/84 Commission v Italy [1985] ECR 3531 275
Case 152/84 Marshall I [1986] ECR 723 .... 38, 45
Case 160/84 R Kavallas [1984] ECR 3217 245
Case 192/84 Commission v Greece [1985] ECR 3967 254
Case 222/84 Johnston [1986] ECR 1651 .... 45, 81, 87
Joined Cases 67, 68, and 70/85 Van der Kooy and Others v Commission [1988] ECR 219 223
Case 69/85 Wunsche [1986] ECR 947 185
Case 71/85 FNV [1986] ECR 3855 38
Case 97/85 Deutsche Lebensmittelwerke and Others v Commission [1987] ECR 2265 218
Joined Cases 281 and 283 to 285/85 Germany v Commission [1987] ECR 3203 191
Case 293/85 Commission v Belgium [1988] ECR 305 256
Case 309/85 Barra [1988] ECR 355 97
Case 311/85 Vlaamse Reisbureaus [1987] ECR 3801 27
Case 314/85 Foto-Frost [1987] ECR 4199 .... 84, 173, 183, 207
Joined Cases 331, 376, and 378/85 Bianco and Girard [1988] ECR 1099 77
Case 12/86 Demirel [1987] ECR 3719 26
Case 14/86 Pretore de Salo [1987] ECR 2545 .... 66, 175

Case 80/86 Kolpinghuis Nijmegen [1987] ECR 3969 . . . . . 61, 66
Joined Cases 97, 99, 193, and 215/86 Asteris [1988] ECR 2181 243
Case 117/86 UFADE v Council and Commission [1986] ECR 3255 220
Case 157/86 Murphy [1988] ECR 673 56–7
Joined Cases 166 and 220/86 Irish Cement [1988] ECR 6473 239
Case 199/86 BALM [1988] ECR 1169 203–4
Case 222/86 Heylens [1987] ECR 4097 . . . . . 80, 87
Case 267/86 Van Eycke [1988] ECR 4769 27
Case 300/86 MERA [1988] ECR 3443 203
Case 302/86 Commission v Denmark [1988] ECR 4607 . . . . . 10–1, 89, 195
Case 169/87 Commission v France [1988] ECR 4093 275
Case 240/87 Deville [1988] ECR 3513 97
Case 247/87 Star Fruit v Commission [1989] ECR 291 . . . . . 232, 300
Case C–287/87 Commission v Greece [1990] ECR I–125 258
Case 377/87 EP v Council [1988] ECR 4017 241
Case 380/87 Enichem Base [1989] ECR 2491 . . . . . 15, 18, 19, 125, 126
Case 16/88 Commission v Council [1989] ECR 291 234
Case 22/88 Vreugdenhil and Others [1989] ECR 2049 . . . . . 195, 236
Case C–64/88 Commission v France [1991] ECR I–2727 . . . . . 271, 292
Case 68/88 Commission v Greece [1989] ECR 2965 167
Case 103/88 Costanzo Fratelli [1989] ECR 1839 . . . . . 45, 48, 69–70
Joined Cases C–143/88 and 92/89 Zuckerfabrik [1991] ECR I–415 . . . . . 80, 83, 139–40, 205–7, 211
Case C–152/88 Sofrimport v Commission [1990] ECR I–2477 223
Case C–177/88 Dekker [1990] ECR I–3941 . . . . . 50, 67
Case C–221/88 Busseni [1990] ECR I–495 . . . . . 34, 45, 48
Case C–322/88 Grimaldi [1989] ECR 4407 . . . . . 58, 105, 179, 185–6, 233
Case C–331/88 Fedesa [1990] ECR I–4023 245
Case C–361/88 Commission v Germany [1990] ECR I–2567 . . . . . 18, 85, 112
Case C–57/89 Commission v Germany (Leybucht) [1991] ECR I–883 . . . . . 34–5, 261
Case C–58/89 Commission v Germany [1991] ECR I–4983 . . . . . 18, 85, 112,113
Case C–59/89 Commission v Germany [1991] ECR I–2607 . . . . . 18, 85, 112
Case C–69/89 Nakajima v Council [1991] ECR I–2069 233
Case C–96/89 Commission v Netherlands [1991] ECR I–2461 257
Joined Cases C–100 and 101/89 Kaefer and Proccai [1990] ECR I–4647 36
Case C–106/89 Marleasing [1990] ECR I–1799 . . . . . 56, 63
Case C–188/89 Foster [1990] ECR I–3313 . . . . . 45–7, 70
Case C–213/89 Factortame [1991] ECR I–3905 . . . . . 79, 80, 103, 107, 135–6, 138–40, 178, 189, 211
Case C–244/89 Foglia v Novello II [1991] ECR 3045 175
Case C–246/89 Commission v UK [1991] ECR I–4585 178
Case C–260/89 ERT [1991] ECR I–2925 180
Case C–300/89 Commission v Council (Titanium Dioxide) [1991] ECR I–2867 . . . . . 192, 303
Case C–309/89 Codorniu v Council [1994] ECR I–1853 . . . . . 192, 303
Case C–340/89 Vlassopoulou [1991] ECR I–2357 106
Case C–345/89 Stockel [1991] ECR I–4047 110
Case C–358/89 Extramet Industrie v Council [1991] ECR I–2501 219

Case C–370/89 SCEEM [1992] ECR I–6211 240
Case C–2/90 Commission v Belgium (Wallon Waste) [1992] ECR I–4431 .... 11, 200
Joined Cases 6 and 9/90 Francovich and Others [1991] ECR I–5357 .... 35–6, 77–8, 80, 135, 150, 155
Case C–7/90 Vandevenne and Others [1991] ECR I–4371 167
Case C–33/90 Commission v Italy [1991] ECR I–5987 254
Joined Cases C–38 and 151/90 Lomas [1991] ECR I–1781
Case C–56/90 Commission v UK [1993] ECR I–4109 .... 39, 41
Case C–72/90 Asia Motor [1990] ECR I–2189 302
Joined Cases C–87, 88, and 89/90 Verholen [1991] ECR I–3757 .... 22, 78, 80
Case C–155/90 Commission v Council [1991] ECR I–2867 303
Case C–208/90 Emmot [1991] ECR I–4269 97
Case C–237/90 Commission v Germany [1992] ECR I–5973 151
Case C–313/90 CIRFS and Others v Commission [1993] ECR I–1125 223
Case C–355/90 Commission v Spain [1993] ECR I–4221 .... 34, 37, 39, 123
Joined Cases C–15 and 108/91 Buckl and Others [1992] ECR I–6061 241
Case C–45/91 Commission v Greece [1991] ECR I–2509 .... 1, 262
Case C–97/91 Borelli [1992] ECR I–6313 .... 80–2, 87, 103–4, 113
Case C–101/91 Commission v Italy [1993] ECR I–191 69
Case C–107/91 ENU [1993] ECR I–6 241
Joined Cases C–134 and 135/91 Kerafina [1992] ECR I–5699 180
Case C–155/91 Commission v Council [1993] ECR I–939 192
Case C–158/91 Levy [1993] ECR I–4827 110
Case C–165/91 Munster [1994] ECR I–4661 56
Case C–169/91 Stoke-on-Trent (Sunday Trading) [1992] ECR–6635 195
Case C–188/91 Shell [1993] ECR I–363 179
Case C–200/91 Russell [1994] ECR I–4389 113
Case C–297/91 Marshall II [1993] ECR I–4367 156
Case C–314/91 Weber v Parliament [1993] ECR I–1093 233
Case C–9/92 Dr Tretter [1993] ECR I–3569 56
Case C–91/92 Faccini Dori [1994], ECR I–3325 .... 45, 63
Case C–128/92 Banks v British Coal Corporation [1994] ECR I–1209 29
Case C–188/92 TWD Textilwerke Deggendorf v Germany [1994] ECR I–833 184
Case C–228/92 Roquette Frères [1994] ECR I–1445 201
Case C–236/92 Comitato [1994] ECR I–483 .... 15, 20, 33, 40, 59, 61
Case C–317/92 Commission v Germany [1994] ECR I–2093 257
Case C–334/92 Wagner Miret [1993] ECR I–6911 62
Case C–360/92 P Sytraval [1995] ECR I–23 241
Case C–379/92 Peralta [1994] ECR I–3453 .... 26, 161, 197
Case C–382/92 Commission v UK [1994] ECR I–2435 167
Case C–412/92 P Parliament v Meskens [1994] ECR I–3757 244
Case C–422/92 Commission v Germany [1995] ECR I–1097 .... 200, 232, 257–8, 302
Case C–431/92 Commission v Germany (Grosskrotzenburg) [1995] ECR I–2189 .... 30, 69, 257–8
Joined Cases C–46 and 48/93 Brasserie du Pêcheur [1996] ECR I–1029 .... 78, 83, 150–3, 156–9, 161, 179
Case C–130/93 Lamaire [1994] ECR I–3215 180

Case C–156/93 Parliament v Commission [1995] ECR I–2019 303
Case C–187/93 Parliament v Council [1994] ECR I–2857 .... 192, 303
Case C–312/93 Peterbroeck [1995] ECR I–4599 .... 77–8, 86, 88–9, 97
Joined Cases C–367 to 77/93 Roders [1995] ECR I–2229 182
Case C–392/93 British Telecom [1996] ECR I–1631 .... 151, 158–9, 165, 181, 248
Case C–415/93 Bosman [1995] ECR I–4921 .... 176, 182
Joined Cases C–430 and 431/93 van Schijndel ECR [1995] I–4705 ... 69, 78, 86, 88–9, 93, 125
Case C–441/93 Pafitis [1996] ECR I–1347 50
Case C–465/93 Atlanta [1995] ECR I–3761 .... 83, 139–40, 205–11
Case C–5/94 Hedley Lomas [1996] ECR I–2553 .... 61, 158, 160
Case C–36/94 Siesse v Director da Alfândega de Alcântara [1995] ECR I–3573 167
Case C–61/94 Commission v Germany [1996] ECR I–3989 .... 55, 235
Case C–90/94 Hahr Petroleum [1997] ECR I–4085 97
Case C–127/94 Ecroyd [1996] ECR I–2731 203
Case C–129/94 Ruis Bernáldez [1996] ECR I–1829 50
Case C–133/94 Commission v Belgium [1996] ECR I–2623 228
Case C–177/94 Perfili [1996] I-161 180
Joined Cases C–178 to 179 and 188 to 190/94 Dillenkofer [1996] ECR I–4845 ... 113, 150–1, 155
Case C–194/94 CIA-Security [1996] ECR I–2201 .... 19, 48, 50, 125–6, 129, 150
Case C–201/94 Smith & Nephew and Primecrown [1996] ECR I–5819 48
Joined Cases C–283, 291, and 292/94 Denkavit [1996] ECR I–5063 158
Case C–297/94 Bruyère and Others [1996] ECR I–1551 172
Case C–303/94 Parliament v Council [1996] ECR I–2943 .... 195, 236, 303
Case C–334/94 Commission v France [1996] ECR I–1307 275
Case C–10/95 P Asocarne v Council [1995] ECR I–4149 219
Case C–44/95 Royal Society for the Protection of Birds (Lappel Banks) [1996]
ECR I–3805 .... 103, 204
Joined Cases C–58 and 75/95 Galloti and Others [1996] ECR I–4345 167
Case C–66/95 Sutton [1997] ECR I–2163 146
Case C–68/95 T Port & Co [1996] ECR I–6065 .... 186, 205
Case C–72/95 Kraaijeveld [1996] ECR I–5403 .... 17, 20, 23, 28–30, 33, 69,
85, 153, 176, 228
Joined Cases C–94 and 95/95 Bonifaci and Others [1997] ECR I–3969 156
Case C–142/95 Rovigo [1996] ECR I–6669 .... 186, 224, 232
Case C–168/95 Arcaro [1996] ECR I–1531 .... 63, 66–7
Case C–188/95 Fantask [1997] ECR I–6783 147
Case C–241/95 Accrington Beef [1996] ECR I–6699 184
Case C–261/95 Palmisani [1997] ECR I–4025 .... 97, 146, 172
Case C–265/95 Commission v France [1997] ECR I–6959 265
Case C–284/95 Safety Hi-Tech [1998] ECR I–4301 .... 26, 193, 197
Case C–321/95 Greenpeace and Others v Commission [1998] ECR I–1651 .... 84, 219–21
Case C–338/95 Wiener [1997] ECR I–6495 175
Case C–341/95 Bettati v Safety Hi-Tech [1998] ECR I–4355 .... 55, 235
Case C–373/95 Maso v INPS [1997] ECR I–4051 156
Case C–390/95 P Antillean Rice Mills and Others v Commission [1999] ECR I–769 223
Case C–399/95 R Germany v Commission [1996] ECR I–2441 245
Case C–3/96 Commission v Netherlands [1998] ECR I–3031 39

Case C–92/96 Commission v Spain [1998] ECR I–505 143
Case C–95/96 URSSAF [1996] ECR I–12 175
Case C–97/96 Daihatsu Deutschland [1997] ECR I–6843 46
Case C–129/96 Inter-Environment [1997] ECR I–7411 .... 31, 107, 161
Case C–147/96 Netherlands v Commission [2000] ECR I–4723 .... 217, 239
Case C–159/96 Portugal v Commission [1998] ECR I–7379 233
Case C–180/96 UK v Commission [1998] ECR I–2265 .... 198, 201, 208
Case C–203/96 Dusseldorp [1998] ECR I–4075 11
Case C–213/96 Outokumpu [1998] ECR I–1777 .... 10, 89
Case C–246/96 Maggorian [1997] ECR I–7153 .... 97, 133
Joined Cases C–253 to 258/96 Kampelmann [1997] ECR I–6907 46
Case C–319/96 Brinkman [1998] ECR I–5255 .... 158, 161, 181
Case C–326/96 Levez [1998] ECR I–7835 88
Case C–336/96 Gilly [1998] ECR I–2739 .... 26, 32
Case C–386/96 P Dreyfus v Commission [1998] I-2309 218
Case C–389/96 Aher-Waggon [1998] ECR I–4473 11
Case C–393/96 R Antonissen [1997] ECR I–441 245
Case C–416/96 Nour Eddline El-Yassini [1999] ECR I–1209 173
Joined Cases C–10 to 22/97 INCOGE [1998] ECR I–6307 131
Case C–67/97 Bluhme [1998] ECR I–8033 .... 11, 161
Case C–77/97 Smithkline Beecham [1999] ECR I–431 51
Case C–120/97 Upjohn [1999] ECR I–223 .... 83, 120–3, 160
Case C–126/97 Eco-Swiss [1999] ECR I–3055 .... 94–5, 173
Case C–130/97 Giloy v Hauptzollamt Frankfurt am Main-Ost [1997] ECR I–4291 176
Case C–131/97 Carbonari [1999] ECR I–1103 .... 56, 59–60, 63
Case C–140/97 Rechberger [1999] ECR I–3499 161
Joined Cases C–164 and 165/97 Parliament v Council [1999] ECR I–1139 .... 192, 303
Case C–166/97 Commission v France [1999] ECR I–1719 39
Case C–185/97 Coote [1998] ECR I–5199 82
Case C–198/97 Commission v Germany [1999] ECR I–3257 41
Case C–207/97 Commission v Belgium [1999] ECR I–275 257
Case C–209/97 Commission v Council [1999] ECR I–8067 191
Case C–215/97 Bellone [1998] ECR I–2191 .... 57, 62, 64
Case C–224/97 Ciola [1999] ECR I–2517 130
Case C–226/97 Lemmens [1998] ECR I–3711 .... 23, 167
Case C–265/97 Commission v France [1997] ECR I–6959 265
Case C–293/97 Standley [1999] ECR I–2603 .... 194, 199
Case C–302/97 Konle [1999] ECR I–3099 .... 150, 153
Case C–319/97 Kortas [1999] ECR I–3143 34
Case C–321/97 Andersson [1999] ECR I–3551 161
Case C–346/97 Braathens [1999] ECR I–3419 35
Case C–358/97 Commission v Ireland [2000] ECR I–6301 300
Case C–365/97 Commission v Italy (San Rocco) [1999] ECR I–7773 ... 28, 40–1, 259–63, 265
Case C–387/97 Commission v Greece [2000] ECR I–5047 ..... 1, 276, 278–80, 283, 285, 292
Joined Cases C–418 and 419/97 ARCO Chemie and Others [2000]
ECR I–4475 .... 12, 27
Case C–424/97 Haim [2000] ECR I–5123 150

Case C–435/97 WWF [1999] ECR I–5613 .... 17, 28–9, 48, 127, 145
Case C–78/98 Preston and Others [2000] ECR I–3201 .... 77, 88, 97
Case C–81/98 Alcatel [1999] ECR I–7671 57
Case C–212/98 Commission v Ireland [1999] ECR I–8571 .... 300, 302
Joined Cases C–240 to 244/98 Océano [2000] ECR I–4491 .... 64, 95–6, 101
Case C–254/98 TK-Heimdienst [1998] ECR I–151 176
Case C–256/98 Commission v France [2000] ECR I–2487 29
Case C–260/98 Commission v Greece [2000] ECR I–6537 300
Case C–287/98 Linster [2000] ECR I–6717 .... 17, 19, 28–9, 145
Joined Cases C–300 and 392/98 Dior [2000] ECR I–11307 179
Case C–303/98 Simap [2000] ECR I–7963 34
Case C–307/98 Commission v Belgium [2000] ECR I–3933 41
Case C–343/98 Collino [2000] ECR I–6659 46
Case C–352/98 P Bergaderm and Goupil v Commission [2000] ECR I–5291 246–7
Case C–372/98 Cooke [2000] ECR I–8683 182
Case C–374/98 Commission v France [2000] ECR I–10779 .... 37, 39, 113, 123
Case C–377/98 Netherlands v Parliament and Council [2001] ECR I–7079 26
Case C–379/98 Preussen Elektra [2001] ECR I–2099 .... 11–12, 195
Case C–393/98 Gomes [2001] ECR I–1327 178
Joined Cases C–397 and 410/98 Metallgessellschaft and Others [2001]
ECR I–1727 162
Case C–443/98 Unilever [2000] ECR I–7535 48
Case C–451/98 Antillean Rice Mills v Council [2001] ECR I–8949 218
Case C–456/98 Centrosteel [2000] ECR I–6007 .... 57, 61, 64, 67
Case C–473/98 Toolex [2000] ECR I–5681 11
Case C–1/99 Kofisa [2000] ECR I–207 176
Case C–74/99 The Queen v Secretary of State for Health and Others, ex parte Imperial
Tobacco Ltd and Others [2000] ECR I–8599 188
Case C–150/99 Stockholm Lindöpark [2001] ECR I–493 .... 141, 162
Case C–239/99 Nachi [2001] ECR I–1197 184
Case C–292/99 Commission v France [2002] ECR I–4097 40
Case C–441/99 Ghareveran [2001] ECR I–7687 .... 36, 59
Case C–453/99 Courage [2001] ECR I–6297 .... 79–80, 85, 131, 148
Case C–459/99 MRAX [2002] ECR I–6591 .... 110, 113
Case C–472/99 Clean Car Auto [2001] ECR I–9687 100
Case C–510/99 Tridon [2001] ECR I–7777 12
Joined Cases C–515, 519 to 524/99, and 526 to 540/99
Reisch and Others [2002] ECR I–2157 176
Case C–3/00 Commission v Denmark [2003] ECR I–2643 .... 195, 200–1, 236
Case C–50/00 P UPA [2002] ECR I–6677 .... 56, 80, 83, 183, 186, 188, 221–2
Case C–62/00 Marks & Spencer [2002] ECR I–6325 .... 28, 97, 119, 142, 148
Case C–99/00 Lyckeskog [2002] ECR I–4839 174
Case C–103/00 Commission v Greece (the Greek turtles case) [2002] ECR I–1147 28
Case C–118/00 Larsy [2001] ECR I–5603 69
Case C–129/00 Commission v Italy [2003] ECR I–14637 162
Case C–133/00 Commission v Greece [2002] ECR I–1147 254
Case C–159/00 Sapod Audic [2002] ECR I–5031 .... 131, 182

Case C–240/00 Commission v Finland [2003] ECR I–2187 ... 263
Case C–253/00 Munoz [2002] ECR I–7289 ... 24, 79, 111–3, 118–19, 135
Case C–258/00 Commission v France [2002] ECR I–5959 ... 34, 40, 123
Joined Cases C–260 to 263/00 LohmanandMedi Bayreuth [2002] ECR I–10045 ... 180
Case C–268/00 Commission v Netherlands [2002] ECR I–2995 ... 41
Case C–287/00 Commission v Germany [2002] ECR I–5811 ... 257
Case C–304/00 Shawson and Gagg & Sons [2002] ECR I–10737 ... 177
Case C–312/00 P Camar and Tico v Commission and Council [2002] ECR I–11355 ... 246–7
Case C–327/00 Santex [2003] ECR I–1877 ... 97
Case C–336/00 Huber [2002] ECR I–7699 ... 192
Case C–378/00 Commission v Parliament and Council (LIFE) [2003] ECR I–937 ... 196, 203
Case C–445/00 R Austria v Council [2001] ECR-1461 ... 208
Case C–445/00 Austria v Council [2003] ECR I–8549 ... 190, 202, 206
Case C–453/00 Kühne [2004] ECR I–837 ... 77–8, 99, 133, 145
Case C–466/00 Kaba [2003] ECR I–2219 ... 172
Case C–472/00 P Commission v French Marine [2003] ECR I–7541 ... 248
Case C–473/00 Cofidis [2002] ECR I–10875 ... 97–8, 101
Case C–13/01 Safalero [2003] ECR I–8679 ... 80, 114
Case C–60/01 Commission v France [2002] ECR I–5879 ... 38–9, 41, 55, 129, 144, 146, 270
Case C–63/01 Evans [2003] ECR I–14447 ... 101–2
Case C–159/01 Netherlands v Commission [2004] ECR I–4461 ... 190
Case C–160/01 Mau [2003] ECR I–4791 ... 56
Case C–167/01 Inspire Art [2003] ECR I–10155 ... 175
Case C–171/01 Wählergruppe Gemeinsam [2003] ECR I–4301 ... 26
Case C–186/01 R Dory v Germany [2001] ECR I–7823 ... 138, 204
Case C–211/01 Commission v Council [2003] ECR I–8913 ... 192
Case C–224/01 Köbler [2003] ECR I–10239 ... 98–9, 150, 158, 162, 181
Case C–236/01 Monsanto Agricoltura Italia and Others [2003] ECR I–8105 ... 199
Case C–278/01 Commission v Spain [2003] ECR I–14141 ... 275–6, 279, 281–5, 287, 290, 292
Case C–281/01 Commission v Council [2002] ECR I–12049 ... 192, 303
Case C–299/01 Commission v Luxembourg [2002] ECR I–5899 ... 145
Case C–300/01 Salzmann [2003] ECR I–4899 ... 176
Case C–304/01 Spain v Commission [2004] ECR I–7655 ... 190
Case C–326/01 Commission v Ireland [2002] ECR I–11433 ... 256
Case C–378/01 Commission v Italy [2003] ECR I–2857 ... 263
Joined Cases C–397 to 403/01 Pfeiffer [2004] ECR I–08835 ... 52, 56, 61, 63, 65–7
Case C–439/01 Kvasnicka [2003] ECR I–745 ... 177, 179
Case C–446/01 Commission v Spain [2003] ECR I–6053 ... 257, 263, 267
Case C–491/01 British American Tobacco [2002] ECR I–11453 ... 84, 107, 188
Case C–494/01 Commission v Ireland [2005] ECR I–3331 ... 27–8, 171, 252, 255, 258, 262, 265–72
Case C–1/02 Borgmann [2004] ECR I–3219 ... 92
Case C–14/02 ATRAL [2003] ECR I–4431 ... 31
Joined Cases C–53 and 217/02 Commune de Braine-le Château [2004] ECR I–3251 ... 128

Case C–127/02 Waddenzee [2004] ECR I–7405 .. 12, 17, 18, 20, 22, 27–9, 49, 85–6, 114, 127, 134, 176, 181, 198–9, 208
Case C–157/02 Rieser [2004] ECR I–1477 46
Case C–174/02 Streekgeweest [2005] ECR I–85 111
Case C–201/02 Wells [2004] ECR I–723 .... 17, 28–9, 46, 78, 85–6, 114, 127, 132–4, 145, 155
Case C–216/02 Zuchtverband für Ponys [2004] ECR I–10683 .... 20, 114
Case C–222/02 Peter Paul [2004] ECR I–9425 .... 24, 26, 150, 154–5
Case C–234/02 Médiateur Européen v Lamberts [2004] ECR I–2803 .... 246, 248
Case C–263/02 P Commission v Jego Quere [2004] ECR I–3425 221
Case C–304/02 Commission v France (French Fisheries) [2005] ECR I–6263 .... 28, 159, 251, 271, 273, 275–83, 285–9, 292
Case C–309/02 Radlberger [2004] ECR I–11763 181
Case C–350/02 Commission v Netherlands [2004] ECR I–6213 257
Case C–387/02 Berlusconi [2005] ECR I–3655 66
Case C–420/02 Commission v Greece [2004] ECR I–11175 .... 42, 262, 265
Case C–1/03 Van de Walle [2004] ECR I–7613 .... 12, 27, 144, 148
Case C–6/03 Deponiezweckwerband Eiterkφpfe [2005] ECR I–2753 12
Case C–53/03 Syfait [2005] ECR I–4609 173
Case C–82/03 Commission v Italy [2004] ECR I–6035 254
Case C–94/03 Commission v Parliament and Council [2006] ECR I–1 .... 192, 303
Case C–105/03 Puppino [2005] ECR I–5285 .... 56, 58, 63, 179
Case C–117/03 Dragaggi [2005] ECR I–167 .... 18, 22, 38–9, 86
Case C–121/03 Commission v Spain [2005] ECR I–7569 .... 264, 266, 271
Case C–136/03 Dörr and Ünal [2005] ECR I–4759 122
Case C–173/03 Traghetti [2006] ECR I–5177 165
Case C–176/03 Commission v Parliament and Council [2005] ECR I–7879 .... 10, 58, 89, 168, 179, 191, 303
Case C–177/03 Commission v France [2004] ECR I–1167 257
Case C–178/03 Commission v Parliament and Council [2006] ECR I–107 .... 192, 303
Case C–210/03 Swedish Match [2004] ECR I–11893 193
Joined Cases C–211, 299, and 316 to 318/03 HLH and Others [2005] ECR I–5141 121
Case C–213/03 Pêcheurs de l'Étang de Berre [2004] ECR I–7357 .... 25–6, 36,
Case C–291/03 My Travel [2005] ECR I–8477 180
Case C–301/03 Italy v Commission [2005] ECR I–10217 233
Case C–320/03 R Commission v Austria [2003] ECR I–7929 261
Case C–320/03 R Commission v Austria [2003] ECR I–11665 .... 90, 208, 211, 261
Case C–320/03 R Commission v Austria [2004] ECR I–3593 161
Case C–320/03 Commission v Austria [2005] ECR I–9871 11
Case C–342/03 Spain v Council [2005] ECR I–1975 190
Case C–376/03 D [2005] ECR I–5821 101
Case C–402/03 Bilka [2006] ECR I–199 182
Joined Cases C–453/03 , C–11, C–12, and C–194/04 ABNA and Others [2005] ECR I–10423 .... 193–4, 202, 205, 207
Case C–461/03 Gaston Schul [2005] ECR I–10513 174
Case C–495/03 Intermodal [2005] ECR I–8151 175

Case C–502/03 Commission v Greece unpublished 1
Joined Cases C–23 to 25/04 AEVE [2006] ECR I–1265 80
Case C–119/04 Commission v Italy [2006] ECR I–6885 . . . . 288, 292
Case C–122/04 Commission v Parliament and Council (Forest Focus) [2006] ECR I–2001 196
Case C–125/04 Denuit [2005] ECR I–923 173
Case C–144/04 Mangold [2005] ECR I–9981 . . . . 31, 52–4, 61–2, 175
Case C–177/04 Commission v France [2006] ECR I–2461 . . . . 257, 276, 278, 280–3, 285, 287, 289, 292
Case C–180/04 Vassallo [2006] ECR I–7251 . . . . 145, 156
Case C–212/04 Adeneler and Others [2006] ECR I–6057 . . . . 62, 145
Case C–234/04 Kapferer v Schank and Schick [2006] ECR I–2585 100
Case C–259/04 Emanuel [2006] ECR I–3089 173
Joined Cases C–295 to 298/04 Manfredi and Others [2006] ECR I–6619 . . . . 148–9, 157
Case C–344/04 International Air Transport Association [2006] ECR I–403 173
Case C–368/04 Transalpine [2006] ECR I–9957 111
Case C–470/04 N [2006] ECR I–7409 158
Case C–499/04 Werhof [2006] ECR I–2397 92
Case C–500/04 Proxxon [2006] ECR I–1545 172
Case C–523/04 Commission v Netherlands [2007] OJ C96/6 . . . . 257, 300
Case C–135/05 Commission v Italy [2007] OJ C96/8 272
Case C–168/05 Mostaza Claro [2006] ECR I–10421 . . . . 95–6, 101
Case C–222/05 van der Weerd and Others [2005] OJ C193/12 94–5
Case C–244/05 Bund Naturschutz [2006] ECR I–8445 . . . . 38, 86
Case C–356/05 Farrell [2005] OJ C96/10 46–7
Case C–432/05 Unibet [2006] OJ C36/23 . . . . 81, 106, 138, 141
Case C–441/05 Roquette Frères [2006] OJ C36/25 106
Case C–45/06 Campina, not yet reported 177

Court of First Instance

Joined Cases T–17/90, 28/91, and 17/92 Alloisio and Others v Commission [1993] ECR II–841 203
Case T–84/91 Meskens v Parliament [1992] ECR II–2335 244
Case T–435/93 ASPEC and Others v Commission [1995] ECR II–1281 301
Joined Cases T–447 to 449/93 AITEC and Others v Commission [1995] ECR II–1971 220
Joined Cases T–480 and 483/93 Antillean Rice Mills and Others v Commission [1995] ECR II–2305 223
Joined Cases T–528, 542 to 543, and 546/93 Métropole Télévision and Others v Commission [1996] ECR II–649 223
Case T–585/93 Greenpeace and Others v Commission [1995] ECR II–2205 . . . . . 219–20, 223
Case T–99/94 Asocarne v Council [1994] ECR II–871 218
Case T–117/94 Rovigo and Others v Commission [1995] ECR II–455 234
Case T–194/94 Guardian Newspaper [1995] ECR II 2765 . . . . 217, 239
Case T–290/94 Kaysersberg v Commission [1997] ECR II–2137 191
Case T–298/94 Roquette [1996] ECR II–1153 . . . . 217, 235

Joined Cases T–369/94 and T–85/95 International Film and Others [1998] ECR II–357 . . . 240
Case T–105/95 WWF v Commission [1997] ECR II–313 . . . 296
Case T–126/95 Dumez v Commission [1995] ECR II–2863 . . . 232, 300–1
Case T–174/95 Svenska Journalistförbundet v Council [1998] ECR II–2289 . . . 217, 239
Joined Cases T–198/95, T–171/96, T–230/97, T–174/98, and T–255/99 Comafrica and Dole Fresh Fruit Europe v Commission [2001] ECR II–1975 . . . 218
Case T–17/96 TF1 v Commission [1999] ECR II–1757 . . . 301
Case T–124/96 Interporc v Commission [1998] ECR II–231 . . . 217, 239, 241
Case T–125/96 Boehringer [1999] ECR II–4342 . . . 242
Case T–149/96 Coldiretti [1998] ECR II–3841 . . . 240
Case T–39/97 T Port [1997] ECR II–2125 . . . 241
Case T–188/97 Rothmans [1999] ECR II–2463 . . . 240
Case T–220/97 Ecroyd [1999] ECR II–1677 . . . 203
Case T–309/97 Bavarian Lager v Commission [1999] ECR II–3217 . . . 297
Case T–43/98 Emesa Sugar v Council [2001] ECR II–3519 . . . 218, 235, 246
Case T–13/99 Pfizer [2002] ECR II–3305 . . . 198, 208, 210, 223
Cases T–38 to 50/99 Sociedade Agrícola dos Arinhos and Others v Commission [2001] ECR II–585 . . . 223
Case T–191/99 Petrie and Others v Commission [2001] ECR II–3677 . . . 297
Case T–17/00 Willi Rothley v Parliament [2002] ECR II–579 . . . 233
Case T– 47/00 Rica Foods v Commission [2002] ECR II–113 . . . 223
Joined Cases T–74, 76, 83 to 85, 132, 137, and T–141/00 Artegodan and Others [2002] ECR I–4945 . . . 121, 200
Case T–179/00 Menarini [2002] ECR II–2879 . . . 121
Case T–344/00 CEVA-Santé [2003] ECR II–229 . . . 248
Case T–84/01 Association contre l'heure d'été v Parliament and Council [2002] ECR II–99 . . . 217
Case T–177/01 Jego-Quere [2002] ECR II–2365 . . . 218, 223, 225
Joined Cases T–195/01 and T–207/01 Gibraltar v Commission [2001] ECR I–3915 . . . 204
Case T–76/02 Messina [2003] ECR II–3203 . . . 217, 239
Case T–168/02 IFAW v Commission [2004] ECR II–4135 . . . 297
Case T–321/02 Vannieuwenhuyze-Morin v Parliament and Council [2003] II-1997 . . . 218
Case T–84/03 Turco v Commission [2004] ECR II–4061 . . . 297, 299
Case T–110, 150 and 450/03 Sison v Council [2005] ECR II–1429 . . . 237, 242
Case T–187/03 Scippacercola v Commission [2005] ECR II–1029 . . . 237
Case T–366/03 and T–235/04 Austria v Commission [2005] ECR II–4005 . . . 191
Case T–415/03 San Pedro [2005] ECR II–4355 . . . 246–7
Case T–37/04 R The Autonomous Region of the Azores v Council [2004] ECR II–2153 . . . 206–7, 210, 229
Case T–94/04 EEB and Stichting Natuur en Milieu [2005] ECR II–4919 . . . 206, 222–3, 324
Joined Cases T–236 and 241/04 EEB and Others [2005] ECR II–4945 . . . 222
Case T–229/04 Sweden v Commission [2004] OJ C106/24 . . . 201, 225, 245

Pending Cases

Case C–334/04 Commission v Greece [2004] OJ C239/8 . . . 272
Case C–64/05 P Sweden v Commission [2005] OJ C115/9 . . . 298

Case C–440/05 Commission v Council [2006] OJ C22/10 . . . . 58, 168, 179, 192, 303
Case C–14/06 Parliament v Commission [2006] OJ C86/11 . . . . 199, 243, 304
Case C–112/06 Commission v Greece [2006] OJ C121/4 . . . . 1, 285
Case T–139/06 France v Commission [2006] OJ C131/8 284

National Cases

United Kingdom

Associated Provincial Houses v Wednesbury Corporation [1948] 1 KB 223 [1947] All ER 680 121–2
R v Inspectorate of Pollution, ex p Greenpeace Limited [1994] 1 WLR 570 103
R v Secretary of State for the Environment, ex p the Royal Society for the Protection of Birds [1997] Env LR 430 103
Bowden v South West Water and Another [1998] 3 CMLR 330 151
Bowden v South West Water and Another [1999] 3 CMLR 180 151
Three Rivers District Council v Bank of England [2000] 2 WLR 1220–76 154
Berkeley v Secretary of State for the Environment [2001] 13 JEL 89 134
Belize Alliance of Conservation Non-Governmental Organisations v Department of the Environment and Belize Electricity Company Limited (Privy Council Appeal no 47, 2003) 103
R v London Borough of Lewisham [2003] Env LR 28 123

The Netherlands

Hoge Raad, 21 March 2003 (Waterpakt) JB 2003 nr 120, NJ 2003 nr 691 136

1

Introduction

1 Enforcement

The mouth of the Greek river Kouroupitos was once a beautiful and scenic place, unspoiled by man. That was before the location was deemed well-suited as a rubbish-tip, and the accumulation of waste, including toxic and dangerous waste, started growing fast. In a letter of January 1988 the European Commission (the Commission) asked the Greek Government to explain why the site was still not in conformity with the applicable EC waste legislation, which had entered into force in Greece in January 1981. Four years after the initial letter from the Commission, in April 1992, the European Court of Justice (the ECJ) ruled that Greece had infringed two EC waste directives by not ensuring that waste was disposed of without endangering human health and without harming the environment.[1] That judgment had still not been complied with eight years later, and Greece was subsequently ordered by the ECJ to pay penalty payments until the situation had been rectified.[2] The unlawful disposal of waste eventually stopped, but the site at Kouroupitos has according to the Commission not been decontaminated and still poses risks to human health and the environment. Nearly 20 years after its first letter of complaint, on 24 February 2006, the Commission brought its third case against Greece concerning Kouroupitos. The case is currently pending before the ECJ.[3]

This example illustrates what has long been recognized in the field of EC environmental law:[4] the most tenacious problem is not the absence of adequate

[1] Case C–45/91 *Commission v Greece* [1992] ECR I–2509.

[2] Case C–387/97 *Commission v Greece* [2000] ECR I–5047.

[3] Case C–112/06 *Commission v Greece* [2006] OJ C121/4.

[4] One might add that the case of Kouroupitos is by no means unique. The ECJ found in a recent judgment that there were 1125 landfills operating illegally in Greece; see Case C–502/03 *Commission v Greece*, unpublished.

laws, but flawed and belated Member State transposition (of directives), as well as insufficient application and enforcement of those rules.[5] In the mid-1980s, following an EP resolution in the aftermath of the *Seveso* accident which accused the Commission of 'having failed to perform fully and properly its role as guardian of the Treaty', focus shifted from law-making to effective enforcement of the environmental *acquis communautaire*.[6] The Commission started more actively to pursue Member States in infringement proceedings and the ECJ routinely found in favour of the Commission in a steadily growing body of case law pursuant to Article 226 EC.[7] The deterrent effect of these judgments was bolstered by the Maastricht Treaty, which introduced economic sanctions for Member States failing to comply with Article 226 EC judgments.[8] The Commission's efforts nevertheless paid relatively scarce dividend for various reasons. Whilst it enjoyed some success in tackling instances concerning untimely or incorrect implementation of environmental directives, the Commission failed to address adequately the problem of lacking application and enforcement of EC environmental law.[9] This was owing to, inter alia, lack of monitoring powers, slowness of the infringement procedure, scarce resources, and – most likely – political considerations.[10] The latter seems evidenced by the fact that economic sanctions were hardly ever requested by the Commission.[11] Furthermore, the Commission has never brought cases against other Community institutions for failing to protect the environment. The few legal challenges it has tabled mostly concerned choice of legal basis and correct decision-making procedures, and reflected inter-institutional power struggles rather than environmental concerns.[12]

The limited impact of Commission enforcement on compliance therefore suggested an important complementary role for private enforcement – judicial actions driven by individuals or environmental organizations in response to infringements of EC environmental law by national authorities or Community institutions. But the potential of this line of enforcement has never fully materialized, as indicated by the very modest body of cases brought before the ECJ by individuals or NGOs – either through the preliminary reference procedure

[5] Hattan 2003, 276–77.

[6] Resolution of the Parliament on the treatment of waste in the EC [1984] OJ C127/67.

[7] Macrory 2006, 385 notes that this shift coincided with Ludwig Krämer's headship of the legal unit of DG Environment, and that it was during his stay that the enforcement procedures were 'significantly re-invigorated'.

[8] Chapter 6, section 4.

[9] Krämer 2006, 574 comments that the application and enforcement of EC environmental law has been, and still is, the most serious legal and political problem of environmental policy. In the same vein, Macrory 2006.

[10] Macrory 1996, 16.

[11] Chapter 6, section 4.

[12] ibid section 7.

or in direct actions before the court.[13] The meagre results become particularly striking when considering that private enforcement has been instrumental in promoting the effectiveness of EC law and ensuring closer integration in many other areas, such as the internal market, competition and social protection.

So why has not 'the vigilance of individuals to protect their rights [amounted] to an effective supervision in addition to the supervision entrusted by Articles 169 and 170 [Articles 226 and 227 EC] the Commission and the Member States'[14] in the field of environment? One reason is that individuals mostly are simply not vigilant when it comes to protecting their environmental rights. Most environmental rules protect diffused and non-economic interests, and there are normally no financial incentives to bring suits. Coupled with the high costs of legal proceedings and the risk of having to bear the other party's costs, environmental litigation becomes a much less attractive proposition than is the case for most other fields of Community law.[15] Another reason is that it is difficult and demanding to be environmentally vigilant. EC environmental law has over the years become a highly regulated and complex field of law, which is hard to penetrate even for experts.[16] There are in addition practical difficulties associated with the collection and subsequent presentation of scientific evidence underpinning legal claims.[17]

Lastly, environmental legislation typically does not confer rights on individuals, and the legal procedures and remedies for enforcement of EC environmental law in national and Community courts are consequently less accessible to them compared with other areas of Community law. As Prechal and Hancher have commented:

Environmental law is different from other areas of law. The diffuse interests which environmental law often represents cannot easily be captured in the language of individual rights. Therefore, the category of environmental rules which may be potentially

[13] See statistics in chapter 4, section 1; and chapter 5, section 1.

[14] Case 26/62 *Van Gend & Loos* [1963] ECR 263.

[15] This fact is also reflected in the type of environmental cases that are brought. Of the mere 46 preliminary referrals concerning EC environmental law that had been made until the mid 1990s, more than half related to the internal market and the waste sector, whilst most of the remaining cases (24) revolved around criminal proceedings, ie individuals invoking EC environmental law as a defence; see Somsen 2000, 327.

[16] The Commission has in recent years therefore submitted several proposals aimed at simplifying the existing environmental framework and championing better legislation, see eg the White Paper on European Governance COM(2001) 248; Commission Action Plan on Improving and Simplifying the Regulatory Environment, COM(2002) 278; and Commission Staff Working Paper Annex to the Communication on the 2004 Environmental Policy Review (SEC(2005) 97, 36–37). Some have claimed, however, that the slogan of better regulation in reality amounts to deregulation; see Krämer 2006, 567.

[17] Somsen 2000, 337.

enforced through the concept of protection of individual rights is limited . . . [There is a] need to develop realistic alternatives for the sake of effective environmental protection.[18]

This quote captures widespread agreement in legal circles that EC environmental law is, indeed, 'different' from other sectors of EC law in terms of rights and remedies.[19] According to this view, several of the judicial tools devised by the ECJ to ensure that individuals can enforce Community law in national courts are of limited application in the field of environmental law. This is the main hypothesis tested in this book, which can be split into two questions: do environmental plaintiffs have access to the basic judicial means for enforcing EC environmental law (1) and, if so, are these instruments effective in practice (2)?[20] The first issue provokes several interconnected questions: does environmental legislation confer rights on individuals, what is the content of those rights, are rights indeed a prerequisite for access to justice and, if so, does the content of that condition vary according to the nature of the claim and remedies sought? The second question concerns whether the procedures and remedies applicable to private enforcement of EC environmental law are suitable and effective in light of the particular features of this area of Community law. These distinguishing factors include inter alia the legal instruments employed and drafting techniques used, the balancing of competing interests, the emphasis on factual rather than legal results, the nature of environmental litigation and the actors involved, as well as the realities of environmental damage and practical possibilities pertaining to its remediation.

The bulk of this book concerns enforcement by private parties vis-à-vis national authorities in national courts, but possibilities for individuals and environmental organizations to bring actions against Community institutions will also be addressed. This holistic approach is needed to address the question whether, as the ECJ has repeatedly stated, the EC Treaty ensures a 'complete system of procedures and remedies'.[21] This will in turn allow for an

[18] Prechal and Hancher 2002, 109.

[19] See eg Edwards 1997; Hilson 1997, 51 – although he concedes in Hilson and Downes 1999, 131 fn 63, that his views 'have changed somewhat'; Scott 1998, 124; van Gerven 2000, 507; Craig and de Búrca 2003, 181; and Krämer 2003, 386.

[20] Effectiveness is here understood in a strictly legal and functional sense: to what extent do the applicable procedural rules ensure that plaintiffs can judicially enforce material environmental rules and, vice versa, to what extent do the material rules lend themselves to judicial enforcement? Whether environmental litigation as such is effective or efficient when seen from socio-legal or 'law and economics' perspectives, for instance, is not addressed in any detail.

[21] See references and comment in chapter 3, section 2.2.4.

assessment of the assertion that the Community provides for a coherent judicial system, according to which the legal protection of individuals 'must remain the same, irrespective of whether they contest the compatibility of national legal provisions with Community law or the validity of secondary Community law, in view of the fact that the dispute in both cases is based on Community law itself'.[22] It should be added that only brief reference will be had to the Treaty Establishing a Constitution for Europe in this respect,[23] given that it has not yet been ratified by the Member States and its future looks highly uncertain. The same applies to the European Charter of Fundamental Rights, which will become binding once, or if, the Constitution is ratified.[24]

A focus on private enforcement of EC environmental law is also opportune now that the legislative paralysis within the field of harmonization of procedures and remedies in environmental matters appears to have ended following the Community's ratification of the Aarhus Convention.[25] This caused a flurry of legislative activity in various areas, the most important being the Community's recent adoption of Regulation 1367/2006 on the application of the Aarhus Convention on Access to Information, Public Participation in Decision-making and Access to Justice in Environmental Matters to Community Institutions and Bodies (Regulation 1367/2006).[26] This regulation may alter the dynamics of private enforcement by permitting direct legal actions before the Community courts. There is also a proposal for a Directive on Access to Justice in Environmental Matters pending, which would implement the third pillar of the Aarhus Convention in relation to the Member States, but unfortunately it appears that this proposal has been put on hold.[27]

The book is not exclusively concerned with enforcement by private parties, however. Amidst the current emphasis on private enforcement in the wake of the Community's ratification of the Aarhus Convention, one should not lose sight of the fact that the Commission is still the most important actor for supervision of EC environmental law.[28] The effectiveness of the Commission in monitoring and enforcing environmental law is therefore considered. In order to tie this part with the main body of the book, I pay heed to the interplay between enforcement by the Commission and private parties. Our findings in this respect will subsequently allow for the identification

[22] ibid. [23] [2004] OJ C310/1.
[24] For an extensive analysis on the Charter of Fundamental Rights, see Craig 2006, ch 14.
[25] Decision 2005/370/EC [2005] OJ L124/1. [26] [2006] OJ L264/13.
[27] COM(2003) 624. [28] Chapter 6, section 1.

of areas of EC environmental policy in which claims by individuals and environmental organizations may most usefully complement the Commission's efforts.

2 Rights

The notion of individual rights is a recurring topic in the context of judicial actions in courts. It is therefore necessary first to provide some guidance on how this concept is understood in Community law.

The ECJ has never provided a clear definition of 'rights'.[29] Rather, it has used the notion indiscriminately to cover a wide range of different meanings – sometimes seemingly referring to rights as a precondition for a given remedy, whilst on other occasions labelling rights as the result of a remedy.[30] Recourse to the abundant legal literature on rights in domestic systems provides little relief as well. The notion of rights is an autonomous concept of Community law and its meaning varies in any event significantly according to the different legal traditions in which it operates. It is therefore something of a misnomer to refer to 'a right'; there exist as many models of rights as there are legal systems. Prechal for these reasons has repeatedly criticized and dismissed the concept of rights as a viable judicial term for analysing the ECJ's case law.[31] I agree with this criticism and the position that the notion of individual environmental rights represents 'conceptual pollution in EU Environmental law'.[32] Although this book will necessarily have to tackle the notion of individual rights, I will as far as possible avoid being drawn into abstract discussions on the concept of rights, and for that reason refrain from in-depth comparisons of how the ECJ's usage of the concept compares with different national legal systems.

Nonetheless, since the rights terminology has persisted in the ECJ's case law and academic debate, it is necessary briefly to present some of the doctrinal discussion relating to 'rights'. This does not mean that the court's case law reflects such distinctions – or the same distinctions – but will at least allow us to label what the court is doing, and helps us understand and comment on the vast academic literature in this field. With the caveat that it is 'mission

[29] Eg Eilmansberger 2004, 1200–1201; Prechal 2005, 97 et seq.

[30] See analysis in chapters 2 and 3.

[31] Prechal 2000, 1040–1058; Prechal 2001, 54–56.

[32] Prechal and Hancher 2002, 109.

impossible' to give an authoritative definition of the notion of rights, van Gerven has submitted the following description:

> The concept of *right* refers, in my view, to a legal position which a person recognized as such by the law – thus a legal 'subject' (hence the name 'subjective' right) – may have and which in its normal state can be enforced by that person against (some or all) others before a court of law by means of one or more *remedies*, those are classes of action, intended to make good infringements of the rights concerned, in accordance with *procedures* governing the exercise of such classes of action and intended to make the remedy concerned operational.[33]

This does not us bring us much closer to the meaning of rights since it provides no guidance about the constitutive conditions for a right, nor does it clarify the remedies which a particular right may give rise to. This is perfectly understandable, since the answers to both questions depend on the individual legal system in which 'rights' operate. As far as the first issue is concerned, it may be generally said that a person qualifies for a right if he has a relevant interest. What amounts to a relevant interest differs considerably, however. Under the classical interest theory, a person has a subjective right if he is the intended addressee of a duty.[34] The German *Schutznorm* doctrine is a manifestation of this view.[35] Ruffert provides an example of how this doctrine applies in practice.[36] A provision in the German Federal Emission Protection Act of 1974 stipulates that industrial plants have to operate without causing environmental nuisance to the neighbourhood. This provision has been interpreted so as to confer neighbours of such plants with rights to sue authorities that fail to ensure compliance with the requirement of the Act. Another provision of the same Act obliges operators to take precautionary measures to protect the environment. Since it is assumed that this provision is intended to protect the public at large, individuals may not enforce this obligation in legal proceedings. Other countries operate less stringent requirements. In France, for instance, it is not necessary that the legislature intended to confer an enforceable right on individuals. Instead of judicial protection of rights, the focus is on review of legality, and for these purposes it suffices that the individual is factually concerned.[37] In this context one often talks about objective rights. Thus, a rule of precaution as

[33] Van Gerven 2000, 502.
[34] Hilson and Downes, 123; Eilmansberger 2004, 1238.
[35] For an overview of the *Schutznorm* doctrine, see Ruffert 1997, 310–312.
[36] ibid.
[37] Prechal and Hancher 2002, 97.

contained in the German Protection Act of 1974 could probably have been invoked by individuals in a French court for the purposes of judicially reviewing whether national authorities have failed to ensure compliance with the applicable requirements.[38]

Differences as to the stringency of the conditions for individuals to plead environmental provisions in courts in turn may influence the remedies available for plaintiffs. In countries that require subjective rights, plaintiffs are generally afforded a broader arsenal of remedies than countries where mere interests suffice.[39] Noting the ambiguity of the notion of rights, van Gerven has commented that it:

> [r]efers to the general right, and accompanying remedy to have a court set aside national measures which conflict with the requirements of a directive, but may also refer to a specific right which a directive grant to private parties, and which together with other conditions, gives rise . . . to a right and accompanying remedy for compensation in respect of harm sustained.[40]

As this brief *tour d'horizon* demonstrates, the notion of rights has many different connotations. Consequently, this book will have to discuss the role and content of rights in Community law in various contexts. Chapter 2 examines the notion of rights in relation to direct effect, and the possibility of invoking environmental rules in national courts. Chapter 3 looks at rights in three different settings: the link between rights and access to the ECJ's judicial protection doctrine, the general right and accompanying remedy of having illegal national measures set aside, and the specific right of reparation. Chapter 5 analyses rights from the perspective of, inter alia, 'individual and direct concern', and chapter 6 examines rights of individuals when lodging private complaints with the Commission in the context of the infringement procedure of Article 226 EC. For the reasons explained above it ought to be stressed that the notion of rights will necessarily vary depending on the context, however, and it is used here as an umbrella term.[41]

[38] Another matter is that the suit would be likely to fail due to the margin of discretion enjoyed by the national authorities; see chapter 2, section 2.2.5.

[39] de Sadeleer, Roller, and Dross 2005, 193.

[40] Van Gerven 2000, 502. This seems commensurable with the Hohfeld distinction between immunity-rights and claim-rights; see Hilson and Downes 1999.

[41] The same reservation was made by Prechal and Hancher 2002, 91 in their seminal article on the notion of rights in EC environmental law.

3 Evolution

Since this book attempts to tackle the question whether the environment is – and should be considered – a distinct field of Community law in terms of enforcement, it is helpful briefly to outline the characteristic features of EC environmental law on a more general level, in particular as concerns its status in the Treaty and the ECJ's role in its development. This will not only help put the book in perspective, but also provides the background against which the ECJ's case law on harmonization of procedures and remedies should be assessed.

The original text of the EEC Treaty did not contain any provisions obliging the Member States or the Community to protect the environment, apart from Article 36 EEC (now Article 30 EC) which stipulated that the Member States should not be precluded from restricting the free movement of goods for reasons justified by the protection of health and life of humans, animals, or plants. At the time when the Treaty was signed, in 1957, the political agenda was altogether concerned with economic growth and integration, which in turn would ensure a politically stable and secure Europe. The environmental costs of industrialization had not yet become fully apparent, and few Member States had well-developed environmental legislation. Not much would change before the 1972 European Council instructed the Commission to elaborate an environmental policy, which today is seen as the start of EC environmental law.[42] This was followed by recognition of environmental protection as a Community objective in the *ADBHU* case,[43] and subsequent inclusion in Articles 130r, s and t of the Treaty by virtue of the Single European Act (SEA) 1986. The Treaty of Maastricht moved environment up the Treaty hierarchy, which culminated in the Treaty of Amsterdam conferring environmental policy-making quasi-constitutional status by including references to environmental protection in Part One of the EC Treaty entitled 'principles'. Article 2 EC now provides that the Community shall promote a high level of protection and improvement of the environment, which is complemented by the requirement of an environmental policy in Article 3(l) EC. Furthermore, Article 6 EC stipulates that environmental protection requirements shall be integrated in the Community's other policies

[42] [1967] OJ L196/1. For a thorough analysis of the evolution of EC environmental law, see Krämer 2002b.

[43] Case 240/83 *ADBHU* [1985] ECR 531. See criticism by Bengoetxea, MacCormick, and Moral Soriano 2001, 67–78.

and activities. On the basis of the aforementioned Treaty provisions the ECJ has on several occasions declared that protection of the environment constitutes one of the essential objectives of the Community.[44] With the help of the Commission, the Community legislature has meanwhile elaborated an ever more comprehensive body of secondary legislation that now covers most issues with an environmental dimension. In sum, it is safe to say that, measured by its substance, EC environmental law is now a mature policy field.[45]

The ECJ has played a vital role in the development of EC environmental law, and may in fact be seen as its founding father through its 1983 ruling in the mentioned *ADBHU* case. At that time the Treaty did not contain any provisions providing a legal basis for environmental legislation, yet the Commission had in response to the 1972 Council instructions started to flesh out Community directives concerning environmental protection. One of these, a directive providing for environmental requirements concerning the disposal of waste oils, was subsequently challenged by a French association for the interests of waste oil burners on the grounds that the directive was incompatible with principles of free movement of goods and competition. The ECJ rebutted the challenge with a remarkably brief justification:

> The directive must be seen in the perspective of environmental protection, which is one of the Community's essential objectives.[46]

The judgment has been given short shrift by many for lacking the grounds (and effort to identify such grounds) justifying this conclusion.[47] Others have described it as a process of judicial anticipation.[48] Work on the Single European Act 1986 was underway, and the court most likely was confident that it would contain an explicit legal basis for environmental policy-making. The ruling should also be seen in context with the previously rendered *CILFIT* judgment,[49] in which the court held that Community law should be interpreted in light of its evolution. At the time of the *ADBHU* judgment the environmental movement had gained momentum as the detrimental effects of unchecked exploitation of natural resources became more evident, and in the same year Germany became the first major Member State to have significant representation in parliament by an environmental party.[50]

[44] Case 302/86 *Commission v Denmark* [1988] ECR 4607, para 8; Case C–213/96 *Outokumpu* [1998] ECR I–1777, para 32; and Case C–176/03 *Commission v Council* [2005] ECR I–7879, para 41.

[45] Another matter, which will be dealt with further in chapter 2, section 2.2.6, is that there has recently been a negative tendency of deregulation, and increased reliance on flexible and differentiated tools.

[46] Para 13.

[47] Bengoetxea, MacCormick, and Moral Soriano 2001, 67–78.

[48] Jacobs 2006, 187.

[49] Case 283/81 *CILFIT* [1982] ECR 3415, para 20.

[50] Jacobs 2006, 186.

Having established a legal basis for Community environmental legislation, the ECJ three years later provided a similar service to the Member States. Following the *Cassis de Dijon* judgment,[51] any national restrictions on imports of goods lawfully produced in another Member State was unlawful unless justified by so-called mandatory requirements. Based on its judgment in the *ADBHU* case and the subsequent adoption of the Single European Act 1986, the ECJ declared in *Danish Bottles* that environmental protection was a mandatory requirement capable of justifying restrictions to trade.[52] Although hailed as an environmental landmark ruling, the result would have been better from an environmental perspective if the ECJ had been bold enough to interpret Article 36 EEC (now Article 30 EC) as a general derogation clause for environmental protection measures. Whilst even discriminatory national measures may be justified for the specific reasons listed in Article 30 EC (protection of animals and plants), the mandatory requirement doctrine requires that the national measures are indistinctly applicable. In order to circumvent the ensuing limitation, the ECJ has in several cases construed national environmental acts as non-discriminatory even though this was clearly not the case,[53] or simply ignored their discriminatory nature and proceeded to examine whether the acts could be justified for reasons of environmental protection.[54] Interestingly, two Advocates General have on the basis of this case law, and with reference to the principle of integration in particular, invited the ECJ to come clean and explicitly state that discriminatory restrictions to trade can also be justified on environmental grounds.[55] The ECJ did not accept the invitations, but in both cases the court came to the same conclusion as the Advocates General.

Another striking feature of the court's case law is the relatively lenient proportionality test applied in the environmental sphere.[56] There are even some cases suggesting that, provided the measures are genuinely aimed at environmental justification and suitable to achieve that aim, the ECJ will uphold

[51] Case 120/78 *Rewe (Cassis de Dijon)* [1979] ECR 649.

[52] Case 302/86 *Commission v Denmark* [1988] ECR 4607, paras 8–9.

[53] Case C–2/90 *Commission v Belgium* [1993] ECR I–4431, para 34.

[54] Eg Case C–203/96 *Dusseldorp* [1998] ECR I–4075; Case C–389/96 *Aher-Waggon* [1998] ECR I–4473; Case C–379/98 *Preussen Elektra* [2001] ECR I–2099; and Case C–320/03 *Commission v Austria* [2005] ECR I–9871.

[55] Opinion by Advocate General Jacobs in Case C–379/98 *Preussen Elektra* [2001] ECR I–2099, paras 230–33; and Opinion of Advocate General Geelhoed in Case C–320/03 *Commission v Austria* [2005] ECR I–9871, paras 105–107.

[56] Eg Case C–67/97 *Bluhme* [1998] ECR I–8033, paras 36–37; Case C–473/98 *Toolex* [2000] ECR I–5681, paras 41–46; and by implication Case C–320/03 *Commission v Austria* [2005] ECR I–9871, paras 87–89.

those measures without further ado, whilst in other cases the ECJ left the national court to carry out the proportionality test itself.[57] Former Advocate General Jacobs has thus suggested that the intensity of review of domestic environmental acts has been the same as that applicable to Community measures in this field, ie merely a test of whether the acts are manifestly inappropriate to achieve their aims.[58]

The ECJ has brought with it the same green credentials when interpreting secondary Community environmental legislation, often providing far-reaching teleological interpretations in light of environmental principles such as the precautionary principle, the polluter pays principle, and the principle of a high level of environmental protection.[59] This line of case law has in turn led to charges by some academics of invention in the guise of interpretation.[60]

In sum, it appears that the ECJ has ventured far in order to place environmental policies on an equal footing with other essential Community policies, and in the balancing act often favouring environmental interests. On the constitutional and substantive level it appears therefore that the environment has gained the same weight as the original building blocks of the Community, ie the internal market, competition, and state aid. The situation is different in the field of procedural law. Although the ECJ has provided several landmark rulings concerning enforcement of environmental law, most of the harmonization of the Member States' procedural autonomy has occurred in the areas of the internal market, competition and gender discrimination as a consequence of the much higher number of cases brought in these fields of law. When examining in the following chapters whether this case law may be transposed to environmental law it should be borne in mind that the ECJ has consistently sought to balance the requirements of free movement and competition with environmental concerns, and that equal possibilities for effective enforcement is a necessary corollary of this aim. This follows arguably also from the principle of integration in Article 6 EC.

As a final preliminary observation it is noteworthy that public support for environmental protection has reached new heights. In recent years most Europeans have become aware of the adverse effects which today's society has

[57] Eg Case C–379/98 *Preussen Elektra* [2001] ECR I–2099, paras 73–81; Case C–510/99 *Tridon* [2001] ECR I–7777, paras 58–59; and Case C–6/03 *Deponiezweckwerband Eiterkøpfe* [2005] ECR I–2753, paras 57–63.

[58] Jacobs 2006, 198.

[59] Eg Joined Cases C–418 and 419/97 *ARCO Chemie Nederland and Others* [2000] ECR I–4475, paras 36–40; Case C–127/02 *Waddenzee* [2004] ECR I–7405, paras 58–59; and Case C–1/03 *Van de Walle* [2004] ECR I–7613, paras 45 and 57 et seq.

[60] Eg Rasmussen 1998, 237–57; Bengoetxea, MacCormick, and Moral Soriano 2001, 67–78; and Bergkamp 2004, 177.

on the environment, and many have witnessed the rapid loss of biodiversity and the effects of global warming through recurrent floods and shorter winters. The scientific community has meanwhile provided increasingly compelling evidence on causation and the state of the environment.[61] As a consequence of increased environmental awareness, Eurobarometer polls now show that a large majority of Europeans (more than 70 per cent) want decision-makers to give equal weight to environmental matters as those of economic and social issues.[62] This is not only important news for policy-makers, but is also legally relevant since the ECJ has held that that every provision of Community law must be interpreted in light of its state of evolution at the date on which the provision in question is to be applied. As we shall see, the ECJ has strayed far in order to interpret Article 10 EC and the notions of rights and effectiveness liberally in order to ensure enforcement of Community law, and specifically EC environmental law.

[61] The European Environment Agency 2005 report indicated for instance that the temperature is expected to rise by 2–6°C in this century, whilst the OECD has reported that 6.4 per cent of deaths and illnesses in European children are caused by outdoor pollution; see European Environment Agency 2006, 2–3. The report also states that European wildlife is under serious threat, and that this concerns 42 per cent of mammals, 15 per cent of birds, 45 per cent of butterflies, 45 per cent of reptiles, and 52 per cent of freshwater fish, whereas the Food and Agriculture Organization of the United Nations estimates that 75 per cent of the world's fish stocks are over-fished; see European Environment Agency 2006, 5.

[62] European Environment Agency 2006, 1.

2

EC environmental law in the national legal order

1 Introduction

Although the ECJ introduced the concept of direct effect in the 1960s which has given rise to a wealth of case law on the issue, and despite an abundance of academic comment, the limits of direct effect, especially within the field of environmental law, remain uncertain.[1] One judge has thus written extra-judicially that 'the Court's jurisprudence on direct effect is not readily transposable to the general and sometimes vague concepts used in environmental legislation'.[2] Other commentators have claimed that environmental provisions typically do not confer rights on individuals and therefore lack direct effect.[3] Still others have argued that the prohibitions on reverse and horizontal direct effect of directives, coupled with the general interpretative difficulties of establishing direct effect, make this doctrine of rather restricted use for environmental purposes.[4]

Section 2 below will shed light on this grey area of the direct effect doctrine, and seeks to answer the question to what extent individuals can invoke EC environmental directives in national courts. Three fundamental questions are: who can invoke directives (section 2.1), under what conditions (section 2.2), and against whom (section 2.3)? Next, we examine to what extent the principle of consistent interpretation offers added value for the purposes of enforcement of environmental directives (section 3). The subsequent section shifts the focus to the extent to which national courts and

[1] Craig and de Búrca 2003, 181. [2] Edward 1997.

[3] Scott 1998, 124; Hilson 1997, 51; cf Hilson and Downes 1999, 131 fn 63.

[4] Krämer 2003, 386.

authorities are under a Community obligation to ensure effective implementation and application of environmental law (section 4).

2 Direct effect

2.1 *Rights*

2.1.1 *Introduction*

The relationship between direct effect and rights has been the subject of one of the longest running debates in EC legal literature. The court sparked off this discussion by linking rights with direct effect in the seminal *Van Gend & Loos* judgment.[5] In one of the better-known paragraphs, the ECJ stated that Article 12 EEC laid down a clear and unconditional prohibition, thus producing direct effects and creating individual rights. This caused some uncertainty whether individual rights were a condition for direct effect, or rather its result. This is particularly significant in the field of environment, where rules are generally not perceived as conferring rights on individuals but the public at large. In the following sections we will attempt to answer this question on the basis of the ECJ's case law. First, it will be necessary to revisit *Van Gend & Loos* and its progeny for the purpose of grasping the justification for direct effect.

2.1.2 *Raison d'être*

There are several reasons why the ECJ chose to employ rights terminology in *Van Gend & Loos*. First, the reference from the Dutch court itself was phrased in rights language, which may have triggered an answer in the same fashion.[6] More fundamentally, according to Dutch constitutional law (and other Member States' constitutional law), provisions of international law could only have direct applicability to the extent that they conferred rights on individuals. Although the ECJ had stressed in a preceding paragraph that the EEC Treaty was a *sui generis* international legal order, it might thus have felt that linking direct effect[7] to protection of individual rights would ease the

[5] Case C–26/62 *Van Gend & Loos* [1963] ECR 1.

[6] See also Case C–380/87 *Enichem Base* [1989] ECR 2491 and Case C–236/92 *Comitato* [1994] ECR I–483, commented upon in sections 2.1.4.2–3.

[7] Although the question from the Dutch court concerned the issue of direct application, the court also dealt with the conditions for direct effect and framed its answer in direct effect terminology, which for some time caused confusion; see Winter 1972, 425 and section 2.2.2.

inception of Community law into the Member States' legal order, and mobilize the cooperation of national courts.[8] It is also noteworthy that the ECJ stressed that individuals should be able to rely on Community law in national courts not only to protect their rights, but also to complement the effective supervision powers granted by the Commission and the Member States.

The ECJ grew bolder in later judgments, and increasingly emphasized the binding nature of Community law and the need to ensure its effectiveness as the primary *raison d'être* for direct effect. When confirming that decisions and directives could also have direct effect in *Grad*[9] and *Van Duyn*,[10] the ECJ emphasized that the *effet utile* of Community measures would be weakened if individuals could not invoke binding obligations in national courts. The estoppel argument in *Ratti* added another dimension to this line of reasoning: 'A Member State should not be able to rely on – and take advantage of – its failure to fulfil binding obligations as against individuals.'[11] In short, all of these judgments indicate that the ECJ construed the direct effect doctrine primarily as an instrument to ensure effective implementation and application of Community law.[12]

2.1.3 *Clarifications*

Some clarification of the relationship between direct effect and rights came after the *Becker* ruling, which presented a consolidated definition of direct effect that has been consistently repeated thereafter:

> [W]herever the provisions of a directive appear, as far their subject matter is concerned, to be unconditional and sufficiently precise, those provisions may... be relied upon as *against any national provision which is incompatible with the directive or in so far as the provisions define rights which individuals are able to assert against the state*.[13]

Becker appeared to clarify two issues. First, for a provision to have direct effect it sufficed that it was unconditional and sufficiently clear. Secondly, individuals derived rights from directly effective provisions and not vice versa. These rights were of a procedural nature, ie the right for individuals to rely on provisions that were sufficiently precise and unconditional. The separation between direct effect and rights became even more pronounced after *Kraaijeveld*, where the ECJ held that individuals could also rely on provisions

[8] Eilmansberger 2004, 1202–1203. [9] Case C–9/70 *Grad* [1970] ECR 825, para 5.
[10] Case C–41/74 *Van Duyn* [1974] ECR 1337, para 23.
[11] Case C–148/78 *Ratti* [1979] ECR 1629, para 22. [12] Ruffert 1997, 316.
[13] Case 8/81 *Becker* [1982] ECR 53, para 25 (emphasis added).

of Directive 85/337/EEC (the EIA Directive),[14] which (a) was not thought to confer rights on individuals and (b) were not sufficiently precise and unconditional.[15] The ECJ justified this judgment as follows:

> As regards the right of an individual to invoke a directive and of the national court to take it into consideration [...] it would be incompatible with the binding effect attributed to a directive by Article 189 [now Article 249 EC] to exclude, in principle, the possibility that the obligation which it imposes may be invoked by those concerned. In particular, where the Community authorities have, by directive, imposed on Member States the obligation to pursue a particular course of conduct, the useful effect of such an act would be weakened if individuals were prevented from relying on it before their national courts [...].[16]

The *Kraaijeveld* doctrine has since been repeated by the ECJ in a series of environmental cases, and is now settled case law.[17] Leaving aside for now the question whether the *Kraaijeveld* jurisprudence amounts to direct effect in the classical *Becker* sense,[18] most commentators seem to agree that rights are not a precondition for direct effect but its effect.[19]

2.1.4 *Exceptions?*

This seemingly clear picture has, however, been blurred by some (environmental) cases in which the ECJ denied individuals from relying on Community provisions on the basis that they did not confer rights. These cases have led some commentators and Advocates General to argue that direct effect still presupposes some sort of conferral of rights or protected interest vested in the plaintiff. It is therefore necessary to examine these claims, and the cases upon which they are based, before reaching a final conclusion on the relationship between rights and direct effect.

2.1.4.1 Are purely environmental provisions capable of direct effect?

Some commentators have argued that provisions dealing strictly with environmental protection do not confer rights on individuals, and are thus not capable of producing direct effect.[20] These views have been based on the ECJ's case law on implementation of environmental directives, in which it

[14] [1985] OJ L175/40, as amended by Directive 97/11 [1997] OJ L73/5 and Directive 2003/35 [2003] L156/17.

[15] Edward 1997.

[16] Case C-72/95 *Kraaijeveld* [1996] ECR I-5403, para 56.

[17] Case C-435/97 *WWF* [1999] ECR I-5613; Case C-287/98 *Linster* [2000] ECR I-6717; Case C-201/02 *Wells* [2004] ECR I-723; and Case C-127/02 *Waddenzee* [2004] ECR I-7405.

[18] Section 2.2.2.

[19] Eg Ruffert 1997, 315; and van Gerven 2000, 507.

[20] Eg Hilson 1997, 53 et seq.

ruled that Member States must implement in law provisions *intended to grant rights to individuals* so that they can rely on their rights before national courts. The ECJ has held in this context that environmental provisions which (also) seek to protect public health confer rights on individuals.[21] Hilson therefore reasoned that, conversely, 'pure' environmental protection provisions do no confer rights on individuals, and cannot therefore be relied upon before national courts under the direct effect doctrine. This argument is not directly contradicted by *Kraaijeveld* and its progeny, since those cases concerned the EIA Directive,[22] which according to its preamble seeks to protect public health and thereby confers rights on individuals. But there is a logical flaw in such attempts to transpose the case law on implementation to direct effect. The point the ECJ is making in its implementation case law is that provisions that are *not* sufficiently precise and unconditional, ie those that are not directly effective, must be implemented in such a way that individuals can predict their legal situation and if necessary rely on the provision before national courts where they confer individual rights. Hence, the ECJ is merely stipulating preferential treatment for rules that confer rights on individuals and requires that Member States make such provisions 'directly effective'. This of course does not mean that individuals are prevented from relying on rules that can be made operational without such transposition. This conclusion in recent years has been confirmed in cases concerning Directives 79/409/EEC (Birds Directive)[23] and 92/43/EC (Habitats Directive)[24] – which do not have a public health dimension – in which the ECJ has allowed individuals to invoke relevant provisions against national authorities.[25]

2.1.4.2 Are provisions governing the relationship between Member States and Community institutions capable of direct effect? The *Enichem Base* case[26] concerned an attempt by Italian producers of plastic bags to set aside a local ban on non-biodegradable bags because the Commission had not been notified of the Italian act pursuant to Article 3(2) of Directive

[21] See eg Case C–361/88 *Commission v Germany* [1990] ECR I–2567, para 16; Case C–59/89 *Commission v Germany* [1991] ECR I–2607, para 19; and Case C–58/89 *Commission v Germany* [1991] ECR I–4983, para 14.

[22] [1985] OJ L175/40, as amended by Directive 97/11 [1997] OJ L73/5 and Directive 2003/35 [2003] L156/17.

[23] [1979] OJ L103/18 as amended by Directive 94/24/EC [1994] OJ L641/9.

[24] [1992] OJ L206/7 as amended by Directive 97/62/EC [1997] OJ L305/42.

[25] See sections 2.2.4–5 and eg Case C–127/02 *Waddenzee* [2004] ECR I–7405 and, by implication, Case C–117/03 *Dragaggi* [2005] ECR I–167.

[26] Case C–380/87 *Enichem Base* [1989] ECR 2491.

75/442/EEC (on waste).[27] The court rejected their claim, ruling that the matter concerned 'relations between the Member States and the Commission and [did] not give rise to any right for individuals which might be infringed by a Member State's breach of its obligation to inform the Commission in advance of draft rules'.[28] This prompted some commentators to argue that a precondition for direct effect was that obligations laid down in the Community provisions were directly owed to individuals.[29]

However, in *CIA-Security* traders were allowed to invoke a breach of Directive 83/139/EEC[30] on notification of technical standards in order to set aside national regulations, even though this concerned the relationship between the Member States and the Commission.[31] In reaching this conclusion the ECJ did not query whether the provisions conferred subjective rights on the plaintiffs, but focused on the legal consequences stemming from the failure to notify. Distinguishing the case from *Enichem Base*, the ECJ held that 'in the present case, however, the aim of the directive is not simply to inform the Commission [...]. Articles 8 and 9 of Directive 83/189 [...] provide for a procedure for Community control of draft national regulations and the date of their entry into force is made subject to the Commission' s agreement or lack of opposition'.[32] *CIA-Security* thus illuminates that the reason why the plaintiffs in *Enichem Base* could not rely on the EC provisions was not informed by the issue of subjective rights, but by the *legal consequences* of failures to notify. As poignantly commented in the opinion in *Linster*:

> In such proceedings [judicial review of national measures] which are simultaneously 'vertical' and 'objective' (non-personal), in which the pleas put forward by a party against a public body do not seek directly to obtain recognition of an individual right, the question of direct effect tends to be eclipsed by that of primacy.[33]

Since the failure to notify under Directive 75/442/EEC[34] did not render the national legislation unlawful, the principle of primacy did not dictate the setting aside of the national measures and the plaintiffs did accordingly not have a right to demand this.

[27] [1975] OJ L194/9 as amended by Directive 75/442/EEC [1991] OJ L78/37.

[28] Para 23.

[29] Krämer 1996, 108–10; Ruffert 1997, 317 with references to German academic debate; Hilson and Downes 1999, 132–34.

[30] [1983] OJ L109/8, as amended by Council Directive 88/182/EEC [1988] OJ L81/75.

[31] Case C–194/94 *CIA-Security* [1996] ECR I–2201.

[32] Paras 49–50.

[33] Opinion of AG Léger in Case C–287/98 *Linster* [2000] ECR I–6917, para 73.

[34] [1975] OJ L194/9 as amended by Directive 75/442/EEC [1991] OJ L78/37.

2.1.4.3 Do claims based on Community provisions require rights?

As indicated by the passage quoted, the justification for allowing individuals to rely on Community provisions for the purposes of challenging the legality of national measures mainly resides in the principle of supremacy. Conversely, if individuals are seeking specific performance of a positive obligation, the justification for allowing such suits must be found elsewhere. The *Becker* ruling was understood by some as justifying direct effect for such purposes in the protection of individual rights:

> [W]herever the provisions of a directive appear, as far as their subject matter is concerned, to be unconditional and sufficiently precise, those provisions may... be relied upon as against any national provision which is incompatible with the directive *or in so far as the provisions define rights which individuals are able to assert against the state.*[35]

Whereas direct effect invoked for the purpose of review of legality existed irrespective of rights, a literal reading of the second limb of the judgment – in so far as the provisions define rights – could suggest that the plaintiffs had to demonstrate that the relevant obligation was specifically intended to afford them protection. Indeed, two of the ECJ's Advocates General have adopted such an interpretation of *Becker*.[36] This view also gains prima facie support from other judgments. A group of concerned individuals and two non-governmental organizations (NGOs) attempted in *Comitato* to invoke Article 4 of Directive 75/442/EEC[37] and claimed that the Italian authorities should implement that obligation through waste recovery rather than waste tipping. The ECJ rejected their claim on the basis that Article 4 did not confer rights on individuals.[38] The recent *Zuchtverband für Ponys* judgment was phrased in similar fashion.[39] The case was brought by an Austrian pony breeder association – the only one in existence – which claimed on the basis of Decision

[35] Case C–8/81 *Becker* [1982] ECR 53, para 25 (emphasis added). According to *Hohfeldian* rights terminology, the individual derives an 'immunity' right from Community law in the first situation, which is coupled with a negative obligation, eg to disapply national measures incompatible with Community law – whereas the latter is a 'claim' right, which jural correlative is a positive obligation to fulfil a certain duty, cf Hilson and Downes 1999, 131. This distinction appears to be commensurate with the German construction of 'objective' direct effect and 'subjective direct effect'; see Prechal and Hancher 2002, 97.

[36] Opinion by AG Elmer in Case C–72/95 *Kraaijeveld* [1996] ECR I–5403, paras 69–72; and Opinion of AG Kokott in Case C–127/02 *Waddenzee* [2004] ECR I–7405, para 140.

[37] [1975] OJ L194/9 as amended by Directive 75/442/EEC [1991] OJ L78/37.

[38] Case C–236/92 *Comitato* [1994] ECR I–483, para 15.

[39] Case C–216/02 *Zuchtverband für Ponys* [2004] ECR I–10683.

92/353/EC[40] that the national authorities should refuse recognition of a new association on the basis that doing so would endanger the preservation of the breed. Article 2(2) of Decision 92/353/EC did indeed provide that recognition could be denied on this basis, but the ECJ nevertheless ruled that the provision did not confer on the plaintiffs 'a personal right to demand of the competent authorities concerned that they should refuse recognition of a new association [of pony breeders]' even if the grounds for doing so were fulfilled.[41] A literal reading of these judgments could suggest that the ECJ is actually requiring that Community provisions lay down personal rights before they may be invoked for the purposes of claims. However, upon closer scrutiny of the *ratio decidendi* of the judgments, it appears that the ECJ was actually referring to the fact that the relevant provisions were not sufficiently clear and unconditional to allow for such claims, which is why the plaintiffs could not derive rights from the provisions for these purposes. Article 4 of Directive 75/442/EEC did not require state authorities to favour waste recovery over waste tipping, whilst Article 2(2) of Decision 92/353/EC afforded national authorities discretion in deciding whether to refuse recognition of new pony associations.

Hence, the distinction between judicial review and claims proceedings in terms of rights is not relevant in relation to direct effect.[42] The rights language permeating the ECJ's case law in the latter type of proceedings merely reflects the nexus between a claim and a right. A successful claim gives the individual the right to a specific result – fulfilment of a positive duty – whereas judicial review does not secure the individual a specific result.[43] But in neither of these relations is conferral of rights a precondition for direct effect.

2.1.5 *Interests*

Although the rights discussion in relation to direct effect seems to have subsided, it has been replaced by a closely related debate whether direct effect presupposes that the relevant Community rules protect the plaintiff's individual interests. All legal systems operate with some form of interest requirement – legitimate interest, sufficient interest, public concerned etc – in order to

[40] Decision 92/353/EC laying down the criteria for the approval or recognition of organizations and associations which maintain or establish stud-books for registered equidæ [1992] OJ L192/63.

[41] Para 36.

[42] Similarly Ruffert 1997, 314–15; van Gerven 2000, 507. For a different view, see Lenaerts and Corthaut 2006, 290–92.

[43] Edward 1997.

separate plaintiffs with valid law suits from meddling busybodies. The issue is therefore not so much whether there is an interest requirement in order to invoke Community provisions, but what the content of that requirement is. The second question is whether the issue of legal interest is governed by Community law or national law. It appears from the ECJ's case law that direct effect indeed presupposes that the plaintiff has a certain legitimate interest. The content of this interest requirement will be discussed below, whilst the issue of whether national procedural law may further delimitate the legal interest in this respect is dealt with in the next chapter.[44]

It should be noted from the outset that where plaintiffs fall within a delimited personal scope, it becomes unnecessary for purposes of direct effect to query further about whether the plaintiffs have a relevant interest. Hence, when Directive 85/337/EEC[45] confers certain procedural rights on the 'public concerned' in respect of access to information and public participation, the classification of the plaintiffs who have legal interest to invoke those obligations hinges in principle on an interpretation of this term, albeit the vagueness of this term confers some discretion on the Member States.[46] Another matter is that the ECJ has occasionally held that plaintiffs falling outside the personal scope of a directive might also invoke the relevant provisions if they have a direct interest.[47] The matter is more complicated where the personal scope of a directive is not defined, and the plaintiff is merely relying on the fact that the Community rules can be made operational in national courts. However, it appears that the ECJ has applied very lenient interest requirements in such cases with a view to promote the effectiveness of the Community rules. The cases where plaintiffs have been allowed to invoke provisions of Directives 79/409/EEC (Birds)[48] and 92/43/EC (Habitats)[49] confirm that it is neither necessary for Community rules to protect economic interests, nor for them to protect plaintiffs' individual interests.[50] This fact is also evidenced by the *Kraaijeveld* case in which the plaintiff was allowed to invoke Directive 85/337/EEC[51] to challenge a decision permitting the construction of a dyke, even though the relevant

44 Chapter 3, section 6.2.

45 [1985] OJ L175/40, as amended by Directive 97/11 [1997] OJ L73/5 and Directive 2003/35 [2003] L156/17.

46 See chapter 3, section 6.3.

47 Joined Cases C–87 to 89/90 *Verholen* [1991] ECR I–3757.

48 [1979] OJ L103/18.

49 [1992] OJ L206/7.

50 See sections 2.2.4–5 and eg Case C–127/02 *Waddenzee* [2004] ECR I–7405 and, by implication, Case C–117/03 *Dragaggi* [2005] ECR I–167.

51 [1985] OJ L175/40, as amended by Directive 97/11 [1997] OJ L73/5 and Directive 2003/35 [2003] L156/17.

provisions clearly did not protect his economic interests which would be affected by the dyke.[52]

However, the ruling in *Lemmens* could be understood as sharpening the interest requirement in so far as the Community rules must have been designed for the protection of plaintiffs' individual interests.[53] This was a criminal case concerning drink-driving in which the defendant – relying on the previous judgment in *CIA-Security* – sought to refute evidence based on a breathalyzer test. The argument was that the law regulating the equipment had not been notified to the Commission in accordance with Directive 83/139/EEC.[54] But unlike the plaintiffs in *CIA-Security*, Mr Lemmens was not allowed to rely on the directive. Some commentators have explained the different outcomes on the basis of interests: Directive 83/139/EEC protected the interests of commercial traders, but not the general public.[55] However, closer reading of the judgment suggests that the ECJ did not in fact distinguish the cases on the basis of protected interests. Instead, it focused on the different consequences of the infringements in the two situations. Lacking notification only rendered national regulation inapplicable if it hindered the use or marketing of the product in question, whereas use of a product by the public authorities for purposes of enforcing criminal law was not liable to create an obstacle to trade.[56]

Even if there was an element of a 'protected interest' rationale underpinning the judgment in *Lemmens*, it was clearly not very stringent. The elaborate opinion by AG Fennelly is noteworthy in this respect. In his view, direct effect presupposed that the plaintiff had a relevant interest in invoking the Community rule, but it sufficed for this purpose that the suit 'will assist in the result sought to be achieved in the directive',[57] ie free trade of goods. In the case of Mr Lemmens, he argued, the interest arose exclusively as a matter of national law and the plaintiff consequently did not have a right to invoke the provisions.[58] Hence, even if *Lemmens* is construed as requiring an 'effective interest'[59] for plaintiffs to rely on directly effective provisions, it will not stand in the way for plaintiffs to invoke an environmental directive where this will assist in the achievement of the result sought to be achieved by the rules.

A seemingly more stringent approach was suggested by AG Geelhoed in *Muñoz*. In this case he argued that there must be a link between the interest

[52] Case C–72/95 *Kraaijeveld* [1996] ECR I–5403.

[53] Case–226/97 *Lemmens* [1998] ECR I–3711.

[54] Para 36.

[55] To this effect, van Gerven 2000, 508–509.

[56] Paras 35–37.

[57] Opinion, paras 28 and 32.

[58] Opinion, para 30.

[59] Hilson and Downes 1999, 132–35.

invoked by the person concerned and the protection afforded by the relevant Community provision.[60] But he argued at the same time that the interest criterion should not be applied too stringently, as otherwise it would jeopardise the effectiveness of the direct effect doctrine.[61] The ECJ yet again refrained from commenting specifically on protection of interests, and simply held that direct effect of the provision was warranted by its binding nature and the need to ensure effectiveness of Community law.[62] It therefore appears that the ECJ is 'pragmatically granting' interests – or presuming their existence.[63] Its rationale is to further the *effet utile* of directives.

A shift towards a more restrictive approach may appear to follow from the court's ruling in *Peter Paul*, however.[64] In order to understand the legal reasoning, it is first necessary to provide the factual and legal background. The plaintiffs in the case had lost their deposits following bankruptcy of their bank, and claimed compensation in a national court. They asserted that German authorities had failed to implement Directive 94/19/EC[65] regarding a Community deposit-guarantee scheme for credit institutions. The national court awarded compensation in the sum of €20,000, which was the sum provided for in Article 7(1) of Directive 94/19/EC. This did not cover their full loss, however, and they claimed compensation for the remaining loss on the basis of failure to fulfil the supervisory obligations stipulated in Article 3(2)–(5) of the Directive 94/19/EC, as well as obligations laid down in Directives 77/780/EEC,[66] 89/299/EEC,[67] and 89/646/EEC,[68] or based on *Francovich* liability in the alternative. AG Stix-Hackl held that the plaintiffs could not invoke these directives, since the supervisory obligations articulated were not exclusively concerned with the protection of their interests.[69] The ECJ, on the other hand, merely pointed out that the purpose of the supervisory obligations in Article 3(2)–(5) in Directive 94/19/EC was to ensure depositors' right to compensation under Article 7(1). Since the plaintiffs had already obtained the guarantee sum of €20,000 laid down in that provision, they could accordingly not invoke Article 3(2)–(5) for the purpose of seeking additional compensation.[70] As for the supervisory obligations

[60] Opinion in Case C–253/00 *Muñoz* [2002] ECR I–7289, para 47.
[61] ibid.
[62] See also comment by Eilmansberger 2004, 1227–28.
[63] Hilson and Downes 1999, 133.
[64] Case C–222/02 *Peter Paul* [2004] ECR I–9425.
[65] [1994] OJ L135/15 as amended by Directive 2005/1/EC [2005] OJ L79/9.
[66] [1977] OJ L322/30.
[67] [1989] OJ L239/33 as amended by Directive 92/16/EEC [1992] OJ L75/48.
[68] [1989] OJ L386/1 as amended by Directive 95/26/EC [1995] OJ L168/7.
[69] Opinion, paras 75–77 and paras 123 et seq.
[70] Paras 29–30.

in Directives 77/780/EEC, 89/299/EEC, and 89/646/EEC, the ECJ held similarly that protection of individuals was ensured by the compensation based on Directive 94/19/EC. The plaintiffs could therefore not derive additional rights on the basis of the other directives.[71] Hence, the ruling in *Peter Paul* in essence did not concern the conditions for direct effect, but the substance of the relevant Community rules.

On the basis of the case law it follows that, although the requirement of the existence of an interest is a condition for the direct effect of provisions of (environmental) directives, the ECJ will readily find this condition fulfilled for the sake of ensuring the effectiveness of those Community rules. Often, it will not even review the interest requirement, but presume the existence of a relevant interest. This is illustrated by the recent ruling in *Pêcheurs de L'Étang de Berre*,[72] in which the plaintiffs sought to invoke the Protocol for the Protection of the Mediterranean Sea against Pollution from Land-based Sources, against Éléctricité de France, for damage caused to the aquatic environment of the Étang de Berre. The ECJ briefly noted that the relevant provisions were unconditional and sufficiently precise, and concluded on that basis they had 'direct effect, so that any interested party is entitled to rely on those provisions before the national courts'.[73] The question remains, however, whether national law may impose additional requirements in relation to the legal interest of plaintiffs invoking directly effective provisions. This matter is discussed in chapter 3.

2.2 *Conditions*

2.2.1 *Introduction*

Prechal has defined the concept of direct effect as 'the obligation of a court or another authority to apply the relevant provision of Community law, either as a norm which governs the case or as a standard for legal review'.[74] This obligation revolves around two formally distinct issues – that the source of law applies directly in the national legal order without further implementing measures (direct applicability) and that the wording of the relevant provision allows it to be made operational by the national court (direct effect). Article 249 EC provides that regulations are directly applicable whilst directives and decisions are not, and one would therefore think that the latter two could a fortiori not have direct effect. However, as we saw in the previous

[71] Para 45, cf 29–30. [72] Case C–213/03 *Pêcheurs de l'Étang de Berre* [2004] ECR I–7357.
[73] ibid para 47. [74] Prechal 1995, 276.

section, the ECJ has found that directives and decisions are also capable of direct effect where they contain provisions which do not require further implementing measures.[75] Conversely, provisions in regulations (and Treaty provisions) may lack direct effect where they require implementing measures.[76] In my view, it is therefore opportune to treat both these issues under the umbrella of direct effect.[77]

Most Community legislation in the field of environment comes in the form of directives, and we will therefore focus on the conditions for direct effect of environmental directives (section 2.2.2). However, the conditions for direct effect are largely the same for all Community acts, and the ensuing analysis will therefore hold general relevance. Some preliminary comments in relation to other Community acts should be made, however. First, unlike directives, Treaty provisions and regulations take effect from the moment they enter into force, unless otherwise specified (section 2.2.3).[78] Secondly, unlike directives, Treaty provisions and regulations are in principle capable of horizontal direct effect, as they may address individuals and Member States (section 2.3). Thirdly, with regard to direct effect of international agreements which the Community has entered into, it appears that the ECJ will first examine whether the aim and purpose of an agreement favour its direct effect, before examining if the wording allows it to be made operational by national courts.[79] The ECJ has confirmed the direct effect of environmental agreements in the *Biotechnology* case, and more recently in *Pêcheurs de l'Étang*.[80]

The final preliminary observation concerns the interplay between the environmental principles of Article 174 EC and (directly effective) obligations laid down in directives. Although Article 174 EC is primarily addressed to the Community institutions, they do not assume sole responsibility for the achievement of the environmental objectives stipulated therein.[81] Responsibility and

[75] See references in section 2.1.2.

[76] See eg Case C–336/96 *Gilly* [1998] ECR I–2739, para 15.

[77] Similar opinion in Case C–222/02 *Peter Paul* [2004] ECR I–9425, para 57. See also Lauwaars and Timmermans 2003, 107–108; cf Winter 1972, 425. See, for further references, Prechal 2005, 228.

[78] See eg Articles 13 and 14 of Regulation 1367/2006 [2006] OJ L264/13.

[79] See eg Case 12/86 *Demirel* [1987] ECR 3719, para 14; and Case C–171/01 *Wählergruppe Gemeinsam* [2003] ECR I–4301, para 54.

[80] Case C–377/98 *Netherlands v Parliament and Council* [2001] ECR I–7079; and Case C–213/03 *Étang de Berre* [2004] ECR I–7357.

[81] Case C–284/95 *Safety Hi-Tech* [1998] ECR I–4301, para 49. This is in my view not in contradiction with Case C–379/92 *Peralta* [1994] ECR I–3453, para 57 in which the ECJ commented that Article 130r (Article 174 EC) conferred responsibility for environmental policy to the Council.

competence is shared with the Member States.[82] Therefore, Article 174 EC is in principle capable of producing direct effect, although the discretion inherent in these obligations undermines their effectiveness as grounds for claims or review of legality.[83] More important is the indirect effect these principles have on the interpretation of directives. In competition law the ECJ has held that Articles 85 and 86 EC (now 81 and 82 EC) must be read in conjunction with Articles 3 and 5 EC (now 10 EC), and that these articles together impose (discrete) obligations on Member States.[84] The same should apply analogously to Articles 3(l), 6, 10, and 174 EC in respect of environmental obligations laid down in directives.[85] The environmental principles in Article 174(2) EC have for instance inspired the ECJ's progressive interpretation of the requirements in Directive 75/442/EEC on Waste[86] as well as Directive 92/43/EC on Habitats,[87] which in turn enhances the effectiveness of the obligations laid down in these directives.[88]

2.2.2 *Directives and the notion of direct effect*

Article 249(3) EC provides that 'a directive shall be binding, as to the result to be achieved, upon each Member State to which it is addressed, but shall leave to the national authorities the choice of forms and methods'. The duty to implement directives may be divided into transposition and operationalisation.[89] The former concerns the obligation to transpose the substantive content of a directive into national law in a clear and precise manner, as well as to set up a legal and administrative framework to ensure application and

The reason why the ECJ found that Article 130 r did not preclude the Italian legislation in question was because it found that the national measures in fact promoted the objectives in that article.

[82] Doyle and Carney 1999, 45.

[83] Chapter 4, section 4.4.4. For a more restrictive view, also related to a more narrow usage of the notion of direct effect, see Krämer 1996, 113–15 and Somsen 2000, 321.

[84] See eg Case C–267/86 *Van Eycke* [1988] ECR 4769, para 16; Case C–229/83 *Leclerc* [1985] ECR 1; and Case C–311/85 *Vlaamse Reisbureaus* [1987] ECR 3801.

[85] Doyle and Carney 1999, 46. For a general comment of the direct effect of principles, see Witte 1999, 187. For a general overview of principles in EC environmental law, see de Sadeleer 2002.

[86] Joined Cases C–418 and 419/97 *ARCO Chemie Nederland and Others* [2000] ECR I–4475, paras 36–40; and Case C–1/03 *Van de Walle* [2004] ECR I–7613, paras 45 and 57 et seq.

[87] Case C–127/02 *Waddenzee* [2004] ECR I–7405, paras 58–59.

[88] The impact these principles have had is perhaps best discerned by the outrage which the recent ruling in Case C–1/03 *Van de Walle* [2004] ECR I–7613, paras 45 and 57 et seq provoked in some quarters: 'It [*Van de Walle*] illustrates how politically unaccountable judges can use abstract and selective "principles" in statutory interpretation to create entirely new rules that the legislature did not intend'; see Bergkamp 2004, 177.

[89] See opinion in Case C–494/01 *Commission v Ireland (Irish Waste)* [2005] ECR I–3331, paras 23–27.

enforcement of the provisions. The operational phase concerns actual application and enforcement of the Community provisions as incorporated into national law.

Direct effect is usually seen as a remedy for errors in the transposition phase, in the sense that individuals can invoke obligations enshrined in a directive which have not been implemented in law, or implemented incorrectly. However, the ruling in *Marks & Spencer* shows that individuals may also rely on the direct effect of Community provisions where national measures correctly transposing the directive are not being applied in a way as to achieve the required result.[90] The same applies to insufficient enforcement by national authorities.[91]

Hence, plaintiffs may rely on directly effective provisions either to review the legality of national measures which are in conflict with relevant Community rules, or invoke those rules with a view to obtaining the factual result required. This distinction was as aforementioned articulated in *Becker*, where the ECJ noted that 'wherever provisions of a directive appear, as far as their subject matter is concerned, to be unconditional and sufficiently precise, those provisions may... be relied upon *as against any national provision which is incompatible with the directive or in so far as the provisions define rights which individuals are able to assert against the state*.'[92] However, in a string of later cases (the *Kraaijeveld* case law) concerning review of legality of national measures (the first limb of *Becker*), the ECJ rephrased the national courts' questions concerning direct effect to questions as to whether those provisions may serve as a basis for a review of the exercise of discretion by national authorities.[93] Some Advocates General[94] and scholars[95] have inferred from this that Community provisions need not be sufficiently precise and unconditional in order to be invoked for purposes of judicial review of national measures, and that this usage of the Community rules is fundamentally different from direct effect.

[90] Case C–62/00 *Marks & Spencer* [2002] ECR I–6325, para 27.

[91] See by implication eg Case C–365/97 *Commission v Italy (San Rocco)* [1999] ECR I–7773; Case C–103/00 *Commission v Greece (Greek Turtles)* [2002] ECR I–1147; Case C–494/01 *Commission v Ireland (Irish Waste)* [2005] ECR I–333; and Case C–304/02 *Commission v France (French Fisheries)* [2005] ECR I–6263.

[92] Case C–8/81 *Becker* [1982] ECR 53, para 25 (emphasis added).

[93] Case C–72/95 *Kraaijeveld* [1996] ECR I–5403; Case C–435/97 *WWF* [1999] ECR I–5613; Case C–287/98 *Linster* [2000] ECR I–6717; Case C–201/02 *Wells* [2004] ECR I–723 and Case C–127/02 *Waddenzee* [2004] ECR I–7405.

[94] See in particular opinion by AG Léger in Case C–287/98 *Linster* [2000] ECR I–6717, paras 69–90.

[95] See eg Krämer 1996, 105; Edward 1997, 424; Edward 1998; Scott 1998, 123–24; Hilson and Downes 1999, 125; and Lenaerts and Corthaut 2006, 290–92. See also Timmermans 1979, 555.

This, in my view, is not entirely correct. The relevant provisions in these cases, Article 4(2) read in conjunction with Article 2(1) of Directive 85/337/EEC,[96] placed national authorities under an unconditional obligation to specify types, criteria or thresholds for the projects likely to have significant effects and which for that reason must be made subject to an environmental impact assessment,[97] whilst Directive 92/43/EC[98] prohibits authorisations of projects that will adversely affect the integrity of Special Areas of Conservation (SACs).[99] Another matter is that the question as to what projects are 'likely to have significant effects on the environment' or 'likely to affect the integrity of the site concerned' – involves a margin of discretion on the part of national authorities. But this obviously did not prevent these provisions from being 'sufficiently precise' for the purposes of reviewing the legality of the national measures. The provisions in these cases were therefore unconditional and sufficiently precise, a matter pointed out by the Advocates General in some of the opinions.[100] The requisite level of precision will of course differ, depending on whether the plaintiff is merely seeking review of the legality of national measures, or whether he is seeking to obtain positive performance of an obligation of Community law, but this difference is catered for in the condition that the Community rules must be 'sufficiently precise' for the purposes of the proceedings. There is hence no need to distinguish between the 'two types' of direct effect, and it would in fact be misleading to do so. As opined by AG van Gerven in *Banks*:

> [P]rovided and in so far as a provision of Community law is sufficiently operational in itself to be applied by a court, it has direct effect. The clarity, precision, unconditional nature, completeness or perfection of the rule and its lack of dependence on discretionary implementing measures are in that respect merely aspects of one and the same characteristic feature which that rule must exhibit, namely it must be capable of being applied by a court to a specific case.[101]

[96] [1985] OJ L175/40, as amended by Directive 97/11 [1997] OJ L73/5 and Directive 2003/35 [2003] L156/17.

[97] Case C–72/95 *Kraaijeveld* [1996] ECR I–5403; Case C–435/97 *WWF* [1999] ECR I–5613; Case C–287/98 *Linster* [2000] ECR I–6717; and Case C–201/02 *Wells* [2004] ECR I–723.

[98] [1992] OJ L206/7.

[99] Case C–127/02 *Waddenzee* [2004] ECR I–7405. In Case C–256/98 *Commission v France* [2000] ECR I–2487, para 39, it was flatly refused that the notion 'likely to have a significant effect' in Article 6(3) of Directive 92/43 conferred discretion on the Member States in terms of exempting projects from environmental impact assessments.

[100] See opinion in C–72/95 *Kraaijeveld* [1996] ECR I–5403, paras 72–74; and opinion in Case C–127/02 *Waddenzee* [2004] ECR I–7405, paras 128–31.

[101] Opinion in Case C–128/92 *Banks v British Coal Corporation* [1994] ECR I–1209, para 27.

Hence, the doctrine of direct effect does not need to be redefined, merely because some rules of EC law cannot be directly applied in specific cases because they are vague, or too incomplete to allow for judicial application.[102] If anything, some have argued, it seems more sensible to do away with the notion of direct effect altogether.[103]

For similar reasons, it is difficult to see how the question as to whether a given Community provision imposes obligations for the purpose of infringement proceedings 'is quite separate' from the question as to whether individuals can rely on provisions in national courts which are unconditional and sufficiently precise.[104] If the ECJ in the context of infringement proceedings has found that a given provision puts Member States under a certain obligation, it must follow that individuals may under the same terms invoke that provision in national courts.[105] Indeed, when AG Elmer in his opinion in *Kraaijeveld* examined whether Article 2(1) of Directive 85/337/EEC[106] was directly effective, he invoked the ECJ's ruling in the *Grosskrotzenburg* case in respect of the unconditional nature of this provision.[107]

After these general but fundamental observations, we shall now turn to the various conditions for the direct effect of environmental directives. For this purpose, I will also deal with judgments rendered in the context of infringement proceedings. This will shed light on how different Community provisions can be made operational in courts. It might seem inconsistent with the position taken above to examine the conditions under which Community provisions have direct effect in the abstract. After all, we have argued that this depends on the context and the facts of the case. Whilst this is true, an abstract analysis serves to articulate the base-line for provisions of environmental directives to produce direct effect. Focus will be placed on the extent to which environmental directives, despite levels of discretion that often characterize them, lend themselves to claims for fulfilment of obligations of result.

2.2.3 *Temporal effect*

Environmental directives become directly effective, subject to the other conditions discussed below, at the expiry of the deadline for implementation.[108] Some directives contain provisions stipulating specific measures which must

[102] Pescatore 1983, 176–77. [103] Eg Prechal 2000 and 2002.

[104] Case C–431/92 *Commission v Germany (Grosskrotzenburg)* [1995] ECR I–2189.

[105] Similarly, Prechal 2005, 313.

[106] [1985] OJ L175/40, as amended by Directive 97/11 [1997] OJ L73/5 and Directive 2003/35 [2003] L156/17. [107] Opinion in C–72/95 *Kraaijeveld* [1996] ECR I–5403, para 72.

[108] Case C–148/78 *Ratti* [1979] ECR 1629.

be implemented at a later point in time, which consequently only become directly effective after that deadline has expired.[109] Furthermore, it would seem that provisions specifying general environmental objectives, as opposed to more specific obligations of result, may only become directly effective after a 'protracted period' after the deadline for implementation, an issue which shall be discussed in more detail below.[110]

Prior to the deadline of implementation, directives cannot be relied upon directly by individuals and national legislation remains applicable.[111] The ECJ has, however, implicitly acknowledged exceptions to this rule. In the *Inter-Environnement* case, it held that after a directive has been notified in accordance with Article 191 EC, Member States must not, by virtue of Treaty Articles 5(2) (10(2) EC) and 189 (249 EC), take measures 'liable seriously to compromise the result prescribed'.[112] National courts must therefore review the legality of such measures against this standard.[113] When performing that review, the court must consider in particular whether the national provisions at issue are meant to constitute full transposition of a directive.[114] The ECJ must have had cases in mind particularly in which there is a strong likelihood of insufficient or flawed implementation, which might be coined as a form of 'precautionary direct effect'. But the ruling in *ATRAL* confirms that also rules of domestic law which are not intended to transpose a directive must similarly be disapplied.[115] Moreover, it is noteworthy that the ECJ refers to measures liable to compromise the intended *result* of a directive. Hence, not only (legal) measures that may impede formal implementation of directives may be reviewed and, if necessary set aside, but also measures that are likely to jeopardize factual implementation of directives.

The threshold of this standard appears to have been lowered in the *Mangold* ruling.[116] In that case, the fact that a national rule infringing Directive 2000/78/EC[117] was due to expire one month after expiry of the deadline for implementation of the Directive did not preclude it from seriously impeding the result prescribed.[118] However, some reserve is appropriate as regards the

[109] See examples in section 2.2.5. [110] ibid.

[111] Case C–148/78 *Ratti* [1979] ECR 1629.

[112] Case C–129/96 *Inter-Environnement* [1997] ECR I–7411, para 45. [113] Para 46.

[114] Paras 47–49. [115] Case C–14/02 *ATRAL* [2003] ECR I–4431, paras 58 and 59.

[116] *Mangold* also implies that the *Inter-Environnement* doctrine applies in proceedings between private parties; see discussion below in section 3.3.2.

[117] Directive 2000/78/EC establishing a general framework for equal treatment in employment and occupation [2000] OJ L303/16.

[118] Case 144/04 *Mangold* [2005] ECR I–9981, paras 70 et seq. For criticism of this case, see Editorial, 'Horizontal Direct Effect – A Law of Diminishing Coherence' 43 CMLR (2006) 1–8.

general applicability of this ruling. First, the effect of the national rule would in fact continue to affect Mr Mangold and other mature workers after expiry of the national rule.[119] Secondly, particularly stringent conditions applied in this case since the defaulting Member State had already obtained an extension of three years to implement the directive.[120] Thirdly, the ECJ also based its ruling on the principle of equal treatment laid down in Article 12 EC,[121] which is directly applicable and thus binds Member States regardless of expiry of the deadline for implementation of the directive expressing this principle.

2.2.4 *Unconditional*

The condition that the relevant Community provision must be unconditional is a multifaceted notion made up of various sub-requirements.

The first and most fundamental requirement is that the obligation is binding on national authorities. Sometimes it is unclear whether Community law merely confers competence to do something, or whether the authorities are obliged to act. Examples of obligations that are not legally binding include those containing the notion that Member States must 'encourage' certain measures. Article 3 of Directive 75/442/EEC[122] (the Waste Directive), for instance, instructs Member States to encourage recovery of waste over waste disposal. However, the Commission has not brought any cases, and has not considered doing so, in respect of Member States failing to prioritize waste prevention.[123] The same probably applies to Article 14 of Directive 2004/35/EC[124] (the Environmental Liability Directive) which stipulates that Member States must take measures to encourage development of financial security instruments in the field of environmental liability. Although Member States are obliged to take certain measures, the provision is not binding as to the result to be achieved, and therefore probably lacks direct effect. In an analogous case concerning the second indent of Article 220 EC, which requires Member States to enter into negotiations with a view to avoiding double taxation, the ECJ rejected direct effect on the grounds that the provision did not oblige Member States to reach a certain result.[125]

Secondly, with regard to positive obligations the ECJ originally required that Member States must not be granted any discretion in terms of their implementation.[126] This assertion must, however, be qualified by distinguishing

[119] [2000] OJ L303/16, para 73. [120] ibid para 72. [121] ibid para 74–76.

[122] [1975] OJ L194/39 as amended by Directive 75/442/EEC [1991] OJ L78/37.

[123] Krämer 2003, 320. [124] [2004] OJ L143/56.

[125] Case C–336/96 *Gilly* [1998] ECR I–2739, para 15.

[126] See eg Case 28/67 *Molkerei-Zentrale* [1968] ECR 143; and Case 13/68 *Salgoil* [1968] ECR 453.

between two types of discretion.[127] There exist countless 'indefinite legal concepts', where several alternative interpretations are possible, but where only one is ultimately correct. In contrast, in cases of genuine 'discretion' there are multiple possible interpretations, all of which are correct or acceptable. Discretion of the first sort does not prevent an obligation from being directly effective, whereas the latter does stand in the way of direct effect. The difference between the two types of discretion is whether the room for manoeuvre left to Member States is of a legal or political nature. If discretion flows from the vagueness of a legal term, it is the task of the judiciary to ascertain the correct interpretation among several alternatives, and the provision thereby becomes directly effective. If, on the other hand, the provision explicitly or implicitly confers discretion on Member States to choose between different regulatory alternatives, the judiciary should not place itself in the position of the legislature or the administration, and make that choice. The opinion in *Kraaijeveld* applies a similar distinction between legal and policy discretion when interpreting the notion of 'significant effect' in the EIA Directive:[128]

> The decision as to whether an effect is to be designated as significant is a discretionary one. It is not, however, an unfettered discretion or discretion the exercise of which is conditional upon the Member States' laying down further provisions. It is, rather, a legal discretion the exercise of which is entirely suitable for judicial review in the light of all the specific circumstances affecting the individual project[129]

Sometimes it is clear that authorities have been granted 'policy discretion'. Hence, Article 4 of Directive 75/442/EEC[130] clearly implies that national authorities are free to choose between different methods of waste disposal, as long as they ensure that their policy does not endanger human health or the environment. Accordingly, the ECJ held in *Comitato* that a plaintiff may not claim priority of any particular waste disposal method.[131]

But the nature of discretion is at times unclear. In particular, it may be difficult to be sure whether use of a vague term is meant to confer 'policy discretion' or not. Thus, it was long uncertain whether the obligation to designate 'suitable' areas under Directive 79/409/EEC[132] (the Birds Directive)

[127] Kapteyn and Themaat 1998, 530.

[128] Directive 85/337/EEC [1985] OJ L175/40, as amended by Directive 97/11 [1997] OJ L73/5 and Directive 2003/35 [2003] OJ L156/17.

[129] Opinion of AG Elmer in Case C–72/95 *Kraaijeveld* [1996] ECR I–5403.

[130] [1975] OJ L194/39, as amended by Council Directive 91/156/EEC [1991] OJ L78/32.

[131] Case C–236/92 *Comitato di Coordinamento per la Difesa della Cava* [1994] ECR I–483.

[132] [1979] OJ L103/1.

referred solely to ornithological criteria, or whether Member States enjoyed discretion to take other factors into account. The *Leybucht* case[133] indicated that Member States enjoyed 'political' discretion to determine areas most suitable for conservation.[134] However, in *Santoña Marshes* the ECJ ruled that Member States' discretion was confined to the application of ornithological criteria.[135] The obligation to designate areas fulfilling these criteria is therefore unconditional. The ECJ similarly held in *French Nitrates*[136] that, although the obligation to designate waters under Directive 91/676/EC[137] confers significant discretion on national authorities, the decisive criterion is whether waters are 'eutrophoric'. The obligation to designate nitrate sensitive zones under the directive as such is therefore again unconditional.

For the same reason, the fact that a directive provides for exceptions or derogations does not render the basic obligation conditional in cases where the discretion to invoke such derogations is legally circumscribed, on the basis of which national courts can review whether those conditions have been fulfilled. The ECJ for instance has ruled that the possibility for derogation in Article 48(3) EC (Article 39(3) EC) does not undermine the direct effect of the basic obligation to ensure free movement of workers, because application of these exceptions is subject to judicial control.[138] The same applies a fortiori if the possibility to derogate from a given obligation is conditional on the discretion of a Community institution. This is especially relevant in respect of derogations which require the Commission's approval. Thus, the possibility for Member States to derogate from Community legislation under Article 95(4)–(6) EC does not prevent obligations therein from being directly effective until the national measures have been notified and approved by the Commission.[139]

Conversely, if Community rules confer on Member States 'policy' discretion in respect of the choice to derogate from certain obligations, the provision is conditional and thus in principle not capable of direct effect. However, the basic obligation may still remain unconditional if it is possible to determine its minimum content.[140] Directive 2004/35/EC[141] on Environmental

133 Case C–57/89 *Commission v Germany* [1991] ECR I–883, para 20.

134 See also Jans 2000, 181.

135 Case C–355/90 *Commission v Spain* [1993] ECR I–4221, para 26.

136 Case C–258/00 *Commission v France* [2002] ECR I–5959. Another matter, to which we shall return in the next section, is that the direct effect of these obligations may fail because the terms used are not sufficiently precise.

137 [1991] OJ L375/1.

138 Case 41/74 *van Duyn* [1974] ECR 1337 at 1374, para 7. See also Case C–221/88 *Busseni* [1990] ECR I–495.

139 Case C–319/97 *Kortas* [1999] ECR I–3143, paras 24–38.

140 See eg Case C–303/98 *Simap* [2000] ECR I–7963, para 69.

141 [2004] OJ L143/56.

Liability, for instance, allows national authorities to exempt the operator responsible for environmental damage from providing full remediation in favour of a more limited restoration, ie ensuring that the area does not pose a 'significant risk of adversely affecting human health, water or protected species and natural habitats'.[142] The obligation of national authorities to ensure remediation by the responsible operator is thus in any event unconditional as far as this minimum option is concerned.

In some cases the ECJ has applied a type of estoppel reasoning to the effect that the plaintiff may nevertheless require fulfilment of the full obligation. In *Becker*, *Francovich* and *Braathens* the ECJ held that national authorities could not plead their own omissions to reduce the rights of the plaintiffs, which it otherwise could have done had it implemented the necessary measure in time.[143] Hence, if a Member State has designated a special protection area under Directive 79/409/EEC,[144] and later fails to take the necessary protective measures in respect of certain parts, it may not in its defence plead that it could have designated a smaller area, and thus have excluded these parts at the time of designation.[145] Similarly, if individuals invoke Directive 85/337/EEC[146] in order to challenge a development permit issued without the requisite environmental impact assessment, the national authorities may not dispute the unconditional nature of that obligation with reference to the fact that, prior to the consent, they could have exempted the project under Article 2(3) of that directive.[147]

Another requirement that may be subsumed under the heading 'unconditional' is that the relevant Community rule is not subject, in its implementation or effects, to the taking of any measure either by the institutions of the Community or by the Member States.[148] This definition is slightly misleading as directives, by definition, require implementation. The case law therefore concerns 'further' implementation, over and above the basic obligation laid down in Article 249 EC. For instance, in *Francovich*, Directive 80/987/EC[149]

[142] Annex II, Point 1.3.3.

[143] Case 8/81 *Becker* [1982] ECR 53, para 34; Joined Cases 6 and 9/90 *Francovich and Others* [1991] ECR I–5357, para 21; Case C–346/97 *Braathens* [1999] ECR I–3419, paras 31–32.

[144] [1979] OJ L103/18 as amended by Directive 94/24/EC [1994] OJ L641/9.

[145] See, by implication, Case 57/89 *Commission v Germany (Leybucht)* [1991] ECR I–883, para 20.

[146] [1985] OJ L175/40, as amended by Directive 97/11 [1997] OJ L73/5 and Directive 2003/35 [2003] L156/17.

[147] Similarly, Jans 2000, 196.

[148] Case C–28/67 *Molkerei-Zentrale* [1968] ECR 143.

[149] [1980] OJ L283/23 as amended by Directives 87/164/EEC [1987] OJ L66/11 and 2002/74/EC [2002] OJ L270/10.

was not held directly effective until the Member State had implemented the provisions pertaining to the organization, operation, and financing of the guarantee institutions.[150] Once Member States have taken the necessary implementing measures, the obligation becomes directly effective.[151]

Moreover, whether an obligation becomes conditional because of the need for further implementing measures depends on the context of the case. The ECJ's ruling in *Étang de Berre*[152] is illustrative in this respect. The case concerned the Protocol for the Protection of the Mediterranean Sea against Pollution from Land-based Sources. Article 6 of the protocol requires that discharges of certain pollutants listed in Annex II must be subject to authorization, whilst Article 7 provides that contracting parties must stipulate criteria concerning the conditions under which authorization may be given, eg quantities of substances that may be discharged and methods for their discharge. The facts leading up to the proceedings involved several power stations that had discharged substances listed in Annex II of the protocol into the Étang de Berre without authorization. Local fishermen attempted to halt this activity by relying on the direct effect of Article 6. The defendants submitted in turn that Article 6 was conditional upon adoption of the implementing measures stipulated in Article 7.[153] The ECJ noted that, in the absence of further criteria, Member States enjoyed discretion as to the terms under which authorization could be issued. However, it pointed out that Article 6 contained an unconditional prohibition on discharges *without prior authorization*.[154] Conversely, if the power stations had operated in accordance with national authorizations, and the plaintiffs had then invoked Article 6 for the purposes of challenging the conditions attached to the permit, the ECJ would probably have found that that provision could not be directly invoked, as in this context it is conditional on further implementing measures.

It is important to underline that it is only if Member States are afforded genuine discretion in the choice of implementing measures that the obligation becomes conditional.[155] Alternatively, courts may conduct judicial control and the obligations are directly effective. An interesting question in this respect is whether the obligation common in environmental directives to take protective measures in relation to special protection areas (SPAs) is conditional upon prior designation. Such obligations are found in, inter alia,

150 Joined Cases C–6 and 9/90 *Francovich* [1991] ECR I–5357, para 25.
151 Case C–441/99 *Gharehveran* [2001] ECR I–7687, paras 39–43.
152 Case C–213/03 *Étang de Berre* [2004] ECR I–7357. 153 Paras 33–34.
154 Para 42.
155 Joined Cases C–100 and 101/89 *Kaefer and Procacci* [1990] ECR I–4647, para 26.

Directives 75/442/EEC (Directive on Waste),[156] 79/409/EEC (Birds Directive),[157] Directive 91/767/EEC (Nitrates Directive),[158] 92/43/EC (Habitats Directive),[159] and 2000/60 (Water Framework Directive).[160] The *Santoña Marshes* case mentioned above established in respect of the Birds Directive that the obligation in Article 4(4) to protect designated areas also applied where an area had erroneously not been designated.[161] This was because it was possible for the ECJ to establish, on the basis of the ornithological criteria referred to in Directive 79/409/EEC, that the Santoña Marshes – one of the most important ecosystems on the Iberian peninsula for many aquatic birds – should have been designated as a special protection area. Once this preliminary finding had been established, it followed that national authorities were obliged to take requisite protective measure pending its designation as a SPA.[162] Furthermore, the court ruled in the *Basses Corbières* case[163] that, although Article 6 of Directive 92/43/EC[164] regulates the conditions under which Member States have to take protective measures for SPAs designated under Directive 79/409/EEC,[165] until such designation has actually occurred, the more stringent requirements in Article 4 of Directive 79/409/EEC[166] should apply. This is reminiscent of the estoppel line of reasoning discussed above.

The issue is more complicated for areas that have erroneously not been designated under Directive 92/43/EC. In contrast to Directive 79/409/EEC, the procedure under Directive 92/43/EC is that the Member States must draw up a list of nominated areas, which become designated areas following approval by the Commission. Since it is the Commission that draws up the list of nominated areas that are to be designated, it would appear that the obligation to take protective measures under Article 6(2)–(3) is conditional upon a Commission decision, prior to which the obligation is not enforceable.[167] The ECJ ruled in *Dragaggi* that the Commission has discretion to leave out a site proposed by the Member States on the draft list, but it went on to say that 'this does not mean that the Member States are not to protect

[156] [1975] OJ L194/39 as amended by Directive 75/442/EEC [1991] OJ L78/37.
[157] [1979] OJ L103/18 as amended by Directive 94/24/EC [1994] OJ L641/9.
[158] [1991] OJ L375/1.
[159] [1992] OJ L206/7 as amended by Directive 97/62/EC [1997] OJ L305/42.
[160] [2000] L327/1.
[161] Case C–355/90 *Commission v Spain* [1993] ECR I–4221, paras 33 et seq.
[162] Paras 33 et seq. [163] Case C–374/98 *Commission v France* [2000] ECR I–10779, para 45.
[164] [1992] OJ L206/7 as amended by Directive 97/62/EC [1997] OJ L305/42.
[165] [1979] OJ L103/18 as amended by Directive 94/24/EC [1994] OJ L641/9.
[166] ibid. [167] Jans 2000, 181.

sites as soon as they propose them'.[168] In order to achieve the objectives of the directive, Member States were 'by virtue of the Directive' (for lack of any specific provision to which to tie this obligation) required to take protective measures appropriate for the purpose of safeguarding the ecological interest which warranted nomination of the area.[169] This conclusion was recently reaffirmed in *Bund Naturschutz*, in which the ECJ further specified that the national authorities could not authorize interventions which might 'seriously compromise the ecological characteristics' of the site in question.[170] Since the project at hand involved the construction of a Bavarian motorway running through forest containing priority natural habitat types listed in Annex I of Directive 92/43/EC, one might hope that the national court did not find the assessment too difficult. Interestingly, the Advocate General opined that Article 6(4) of the directive should be applicable by analogy,[171] so that inter alia economic reasons could warrant an exception from the obligation to protect sites under the aforementioned terms, but the ECJ did not follow his lead.

2.2.5 *Sufficiently precise*

The content of Community provisions must also be of a certain degree of clarity in order for them to be directly effective. A provision was traditionally only deemed sufficiently precise if the obligation was set out in 'unequivocal terms'.[172] The ECJ's application of this notion has gradually softened,[173] however, and the mere fact that the wording is vague, or requires complex evaluations does not exclude that the obligation is sufficiently precise to be justiciable.[174]

It should be recalled that directives, according to Article 249(3) EC, 'shall be binding, as to the result to be achieved, upon each Member State to which it is addressed, but shall leave to the national authorities the choice of forms and methods'. Hence, one of the principal characteristics of directives is that they are intended to achieve a specified result. However, there are great differences in the types of obligations which directives impose and the results which must be achieved.[175]

Least problematic are directives that require Member States to achieve precisely circumscribed results. Chief among these are directives containing

168 Case C–117/03 *Dragaggi* [2005] ECR I–167, para 29.
169 Para 29.
170 Case C–244/05 *Bund Naturschutz* [2006] ECR I–8445, para 46.
171 Opinion, ibid para 34.
172 Case C–152/84 *Marshall I* [1986] ECR 723; and Case C–71/85 *FNV* [1986] ECR 3855.
173 Jans 2000, 173.
174 Kapteyn and van Themaat 1998, 530.
175 Case C–60/01 *Commission v France* [2002] ECR I–5679, para 25.

numerically defined obligations. These may come in the form of technical requirements for the operation of various types of industrial plants,[176] emissions limit values, or quality limit values.[177] Such obligations have in common that they unequivocally require a clearly defined result to be achieved. If Member States fail in this respect, they may not plead in their defence that all necessary measures have been taken, or that it was 'practically impossible' to obtain these results.[178] Another matter is that also such precisely worded obligations may be difficult to enforce in practice. Somsen has emphasized that quality values are inherently difficult to verify factually, whilst emission limits may only be effectively enforced if the directive provides for a system of prior authorizations stipulating the limit standards.[179]

Other directives contain obligations of result that hinge on scientific terms which, although perhaps semantically precise, actually require complex scientific assessments. One example is the obligation under the Birds and Habitats directives to designate special areas of protection on the basis of ornithological criteria. The ECJ has managed to render these obligations justiciable by finding a breach where a Member State has designated manifestly fewer special protection areas than the number and total area of sites considered suitable for conservation.[180] Furthermore, the ECJ has found these obligations based on ornithological criteria sufficiently precise to establish that specific areas should have been designated as special protection areas.[181] An interesting aspect of these cases is that the ECJ has accepted the relevance of an inventory list of important bird habitats, drawn up by the International Council of Bird Preservation. It was this list that effectively rendered the obligation to designate the 'most suitable areas' operational.

Similar reasoning has been applied to the complex assessments necessary for the designation of 'vulnerable zones' under Directive 91/767/EEC, and this time without the help of guidelines. Although conceding that the operative criteria for 'eutrophoric' water granted a margin of discretion, the ECJ found in *French Nitrates* that that discretion had been exceeded, since large

[176] See eg Case C–60/01 *Commission v France* [2002] ECR I–5679.

[177] See eg Case C–56/90 *Commission v UK* [1993] ECR I–4109.

[178] ibid. [179] Somsen 2000, 337–38.

[180] Case C–3/96 *Commission v Netherlands* [1998] ECR; and Case C–166/97 *Commission v France* [1999] ECR I–1719.

[181] Case C–355/90 *Commission v Spain* [1993] ECR I–4221; and Case C–374/98 *Commission v France* [2000] ECR I–10779. See also Case C–117/03 *Dragaggi* [2005] ECR I–167.

sections of waters in French territory had not been designated as nitrate vulnerable zones, and even found the criteria sufficiently precise to identify specific waters that should have been designated.[182]

In other instances, the substance of the obligations of result is precisely worded, whilst the temporal aspect of the obligations leave a margin of discretion. Environmental directives often contain provisions requiring the drawing up of plans and programmes, but the time period within which this must happen is not always clearly defined. *Commission v France*[183] centred on the question whether a long-running failure to draw up waste management plans breached the obligation in Article 7(1) of Directive 75/442/EEC to prepare waste management plans 'as soon as possible'. The ECJ conceded that that provision allowed Member States a 'reasonable time' to act, but noted that the obligation to draw up such plans was necessary for the attainment of the directive's objectives, chief among which were protection of public health and the environment. Thus, any infringement of that obligation had to be considered 'serious', which led the ECJ to conclude that inactivity stretching over a period of seven years went beyond the discretion conferred by the directive.[184]

Yet other directives contain objectives formulated in even more general terms, whilst leaving national authorities with discretion regarding the concrete measures to be taken. This is a common feature of environmental framework directives in particular, which often contain provisions of the type found in Article 4 of Directive 75/442/EEC:

> Member States shall take the necessary measures to ensure that waste is disposed of without endangering human health and without harming the environment.

Such provisions indicate a programme to be followed, and set out the parameters which Member States must observe in their performance of more specific obligations in other provisions. They articulate the framework within which Member State action is to be taken without requiring, in itself, the adoption of specific measures or a particular method of implementation. Following the ruling in *Comitato*, it was generally believed that such rules were not sufficiently precise (nor unconditional) to be justiciable.[185]

Some years later came the *San Rocco* case.[186] The case concerned the question whether Italian authorities had breached Article 4 of the Waste Directive

[182] Case C-258/00 *Commission v France* [2002] ECR I-5959.

[183] Case C-292/99 *Commission v France* [2002] ECR I-4097.

[184] Para 44.

[185] C-236/92 *Comitato* [1994] ECR I-483, para 14.

[186] Case C-365/97 *Commission v Italy* [1999] ECR I-7773.

by failing to stop fly-tipping of waste in the San Rocco valley, which endangered human health and the environment in that area. It was common ground that Italy had taken measures to stop the pollution of the San Rocco valley, but it had nevertheless not managed to prevent the continuing occurrence of illegal fly-tipping. The opinion, relying on the *Comitato* ruling,[187] concluded that Article 4 was not sufficiently clear independently to serve as the basis for finding an infringement of the directive without establishing violation of other, more specific provisions.[188] The court ruled that Article 4 is 'none the less binding on the Member States as to the objective to be achieved, whilst leaving to the Member States a margin of discretion'.[189] It continued, 'although the fact that a situation is not in conformity with the objectives of a directive did not allow for the direct interference of failure to take the necessary measures, if this situation continues over a protracted period without any action being taken, it may be an indication that the Member States have exceeded the discretion conferred on them by Article 4'.[190]

Since Italy had been made aware of the waste disposal problems in the San Rocco valley in 1988 and the problem was still not resolved by 1996, the ECJ concluded that Italy had failed to take the necessary measures required by Article 4. It must follow that framework obligations of the type found in Article 4 of Directive 75/442/EEC may under similar terms be sufficiently precise to be invoked by individuals.

Despite the progressive nature of *San Rocco* compared with *Comitato*, the judgment still lent itself to a certain degree of doctrinal criticism. With regard to failures to fulfil clearly defined obligations of result, eg failure to comply with bathing water quality objectives in *Blackpool*, the ECJ automatically draws the conclusion that Member States have failed to take all necessary measures, and consequently find that a breach of the relevant directive has occurred.[191] However, the ECJ was only prepared to draw the same conclusion in *San Rocco* after the omission to act had persisted for a protracted period of time.

This dichotomy was touched upon in passing in a later case – *French Nitrates*[192] – where France argued that the ECJ could not directly infer from its

[187] See section 2.2.

[188] Opinion C–365/97 *Commission v Italy* [1999] ECR I–7773, para 92.

[189] Para 67.

[190] Para 68.

[191] Case C–56/90 *Commission v UK* [1993] ECR I–4109. See also Case C–198/97 *Commission v Germany* [1999] ECR I–3257; Case C–307/98 *Commission v Belgium* [2000] ECR I–3933; and Case C–268/00 *Commission v Netherlands* [2002] ECR I–2995.

[192] Case C–60/01 *Commission v France* [2002] ECR I–5679.

failure to ensure that all waste incinerator plants fulfilled the technical requirements in Directives 83/369/EEC and 89/429/EEC that the authorities had not taken all the necessary measures, in particular since the situation had not 'persisted for a protracted period of time'. The Advocate General distinguished the case from *San Rocco* on the basis that in the latter case the Italian authorities had to deal with a large number of unknown operators who were unlawfully disposing of waste. 'It was therefore impossible on practical grounds alone for the national authorities to put a stop to every infringement of Community law.'[193] The ECJ instead underlined the difference between directives laying down very precise and specific results, and directives containing objectives formulated in general and non-quantifiable terms. A failure in the first situation allowed the direct conclusion that a Member State had failed to take all the necessary measures (*Blackpool*), whilst such a finding could only be drawn in the second situation if it had persisted for a protracted period of time (*San Rocco*).[194]

It seems to me, however, that such a formalistic distinction between 'obligations of result' and 'objectives' is logically flawed. Objectives are nothing but loosely phrased obligations of result, and whilst their lack of precision might raise the threshold for when an infringement can be established, there is no reason why, once such a finding has been made, the unlawful situation should be allowed to persist for a protracted period of time before an infringement can be formally established. The corollary of the ECJ's argument would otherwise be that the direct effect of provisions such as Article 4 of Directive 75/442/EEC is effectively suspended until a 'protracted period of time has passed'. This runs counter to Article 249(3) EC.

It is encouraging to see that the ECJ in *Pera Galini*[195] – which is a mirror case of *San Rocco* – found four years to constitute a 'protracted period of time', as compared to eight years in *San Rocco*. At the same time, it shows that the ECJ is still not prepared to draw the direct conclusion from a failure to achieve environmental objectives that a Member State has failed to fulfil its obligations. This is serious, since there is a clear trend in EC environmental policy to move away from harmonized limit values in favour of environmental objectives, a matter that is discussed further in the next section.

2.2.6 *General observations*

The general picture emerging from this *tour d'horizon* has revealed that the ECJ has gone to great lengths to construe obligations in environmental directives in

[193] Opinion, para 79. [194] See, by implication, paras 28–33.
[195] Case C–420/02 *Commission v Greece* [2005] ECR I–11175.

a manner as to make them operational. Despite the fact that provisions are not always strictly unconditional or very precise, the ECJ has been able effectively to review the authorities' margin of discretion as well as establishing failures to act in specific cases. These findings are equally relevant for purposes of suits brought by environmental litigants in national courts. However, the effectiveness of environmental directives and the purposes for which they may be invoked differ greatly depending on the type of obligations they contain, and the precision with which the results to be achieved are formulated. It falls outside the ambit of this study to provide a general analysis of environmental directives from this perspective, but an unwelcome development can be discerned in recent years where environmental directives are increasingly vague, open-ended, and conditional.[196] This is largely due to slogans such as subsidiarity, flexibility, and differentiation, which have gained favour in Brussels. There is increased reliance on environmental framework directives, and a move away from uniform emission standards and limit values set at Community level in favour of standards determined at national, regional, or local levels can also be witnessed.[197] In some cases, limit values are even forgone altogether in favour of general technical requirements.

EC environmental policy on air pollution provides a good example of this paradigm shift. Community legislation on air pollution was traditionally centred on directives containing emission standards for individual plants,[198] or quality limit values.[199] This changed with the adoption of Directive 96/61/EC (IPPC Directive).[200] Instead of fixing uniform Community emissions standards, Article 9(4) delegates responsibility for prescribing emissions standards to the Member States, ie state, regional, and local authorities. Such standards must be based on best available techniques (BAT), which requires a complex assessment of the notion of 'best techniques' as well as cost-benefit evaluations aimed at the 'availability' of any given technique. Article 9(4) also stipulates that the emission standards must be fixed taking into account 'technical characteristics of the installation concerned, its geographical location and the local environmental conditions'.[201] In addition, Article 9(3) allows Member States

[196] Somsen 2003. [197] See Krämer, 2000, 136 *et seq.*

[198] See eg Directive 87/217 on emission of asbestos; Directive 88/609 on the limitation of emissions of certain pollutants into the air from large combustion plants; and Directive 94/67 on the incineration of hazardous waste. [199] Somsen 2000, 337; and Krämer 2006, 569–70.

[200] For a thorough analysis of the discretion inherent in the IPPC Directive, see Scott 2000 and Doppelhammer 2000.

[201] Doppelhammer 2000, 203: 'This provision [Article 9.4] has a crucial impact. It enables national authorities to derogate from the BATs, which are already economically qualified, and to

to supplement or replace emission standards by equivalent parameters or technical measures. Article 18(1) allows for the adoption of Community emission limit values, but the decentralized and integrated approach in the IPPC Directive is obviously based on the view that such uniform Community-wide standards should be an exception to the rule.[202] The Community's policy on water pollution and management is going through a similar transformation in the name of subsidiarity, flexibility, and differentiation, and finds expression in Directive 2000/60/EC (Water Framework Directive).[203]

These changes will make compliance with EC environmental law increasingly difficult to monitor and ultimately undermines effective enforcement of EC environmental law. Indications to this effect appeared in the Commission's first report on the IPPC Directive, which failed to assess whether the Member States had correctly implemented the directive:

> The reason is not that Member States have not made a real effort, but rather that they all use very different ways of expressing limits, which they are perfectly allowed to do, since the [IPPC] Directive does not require harmonisation of these diverse practices.[204]

It is small wonder that the Commission warned that it might be necessary to introduce Community emission limit values.[205]

In sum, whilst the recent trend of flexible and differentiated environmental policy-making may provide cost-efficiency benefits, and in theory tailor-made and thus enhanced environmental protection, it does so at the expense of the direct effect of environmental directives and effective enforcement of EC environmental law.[206] Time will tell whether the end has justified the means.[207]

2.3 *Horizontal effect*

2.3.1 *Introduction*

The ECJ denied horizontal effect of directives in its *Marshall* ruling on the basis that according to Article 189 (now 249 EC), they are addressed to

impose less stringent permit conditions whenever they consider this justified by the local environmental conditions.'

202 Krämer 2000, 137. 203 See Grimeaud 2001.

204 Commission Communication 'On the Road to a Sustainable Production' (COM(2003) 354) 10. 205 ibid 23.

206 The IPPC Directive may in turn also undermine the effectiveness of other directives, eg Directive 2004/35 on environmental liability; see Wennerås 2005a, 175–78.

207 Somsen 2000, 343 argues that 'if the *acquis communautaire* is to be preserved, new instruments should only be used in instances where this does not disadvantage individuals wishing to invoke EC environmental law in their national courts'.

Member States and not individuals. Directives which have not been transposed can therefore not impose obligations directly on individuals, and may consequently not be invoked against private parties in national courts.[208] The matter was brought up again in *Faccini Dori*, where the Advocate General urged the ECJ to review its position on horizontal effect of directives.[209] The ECJ dismissed this invitation on three grounds. First, referring to its *Marshall* ruling, it held that directives are only binding on Member States according to Article 189 (249 EC).[210] Secondly, it held that the case law recognizing direct effect of directives as against state entities was based on the estoppel principle, which did not apply in relations between individuals.[211] Thirdly, acknowledging horizontal direct effect would be tantamount to accepting that the Community had competence to enact obligations for individuals in directives, whereas it had only competence to do so (according to Article 249 EC) in areas where it is empowered to adopt regulations.[212]

It would thus appear that environmentally concerned individuals or NGOs are prevented from bringing suits directly against individuals or companies acting in breach of environmental directives. However, in practice there are important exceptions to this seemingly clear-cut principle, which will be given attention in the following sections.

2.3.2 *Emanations of state*

Since direct effect is prima facie limited to vertical application – individuals asserting obligations as against national authorities – it is of crucial importance to determine the concept of state. The ECJ in several cases has extended the concept to 'public entities' or 'emanations of the state', notions which in turn have been afforded a broad meaning by the ECJ.[213] The issue was raised in the *Foster* case,[214] where the public company serving as a respondent – British Gas – had been privatized. The House of Lords asked whether British Gas had to be considered a public entity at the 'material time', ie prior to privatization.

[208] Case 152/84 *Marshall* [1986] ECR 723, para 48.

[209] Case C–91/92 *Faccini Dori* [1994] ECR I–3325. [210] Para 22. [211] ibid.

[212] Para 24. To this it may be objected, as criticized already in 1992 by the House of Lords Select Committee, that neither the Commission nor the Council has articulated clear principles or criteria concerning choice of legal instruments; see Macrory 1996, 10.

[213] The court has accordingly held that provisions of a directive could be relied on against tax authorities (Case C–8/81 *Becker* [1982] ECR 3057 and in Case C–221/88 *Busseni* [1990] ECR I–495), local or regional authorities (Case C–103/88 *Costanzo* [1989] ECR 1839), constitutionally independent authorities responsible for the maintenance of public order and safety (Case 222/84 *Johnston* [1986] ECR 1651), and public authorities providing health services (Case 152/84 *Marshall* [1986] ECR 723). [214] Case C–188/89 *Foster* [1990] ECR I–3313.

Drawing on earlier case law, the ECJ presented the following, broad definition of a 'public entity':

> [A] body, whatever its legal form, which has been made responsible, pursuant to a measure adopted by the State, for providing a public service under the control of the State and has for that purpose special powers beyond those which result from the normal rules applicable in relations between individuals is in any event among the bodies against which the provisions of a directive capable of having direct effect may be relied upon.[215]

The introductory limb of the ruling 'a body, whatever its legal form' is significant, as it indicates that private subjects may under certain circumstances also be regarded a 'public entity'. This has now been confirmed in *Rieser*.[216] Furthermore, the caveat 'in any event' suggests that the requirements outlined are not necessarily cumulative. Four conditions may be discerned:

1) the body must fulfil a public service,
2) it must have been made responsible for that service pursuant to a measure adopted by the State,
3) it must be under control of the State, and,
4) it must have special powers beyond those which result from the normal rules applicable in relations between individuals.

The ruling in *Kampelmann* suggested that conditions 3) and 4) were alternatives,[217] but the ECJ applied all four conditions in the *Rieser* judgment. The background to the case was that Asfinaq, a body governed by private law and in which Austria was sole shareholder, had been entrusted by the national authorities to operate motorways and levy user charges. The plaintiffs in the proceedings argued that Asfinaq had charged tolls in violation of certain Community directives, and the question was whether the plaintiffs could rely on the direct effect of the relevant provisions against Asfinaq. The ECJ answered affirmatively, focusing on the fact that Asfinaq's activities constituted a public service and that the state had extensive rights of supervision, eg as concerned the fixing of the amounts of tolls to be paid. Although the ruling in *Rieser* suggests that the *Foster* criteria are cumulative, it seems that emphasis is placed on the notions of public service and state control.

The opinion in the pending *Farrell* case indicates, moreover, that the notion of state control may be given far-reaching teleological interpretations.[218]

215 Para 20. See also Case C–343/98 *Collino* [2000] ECR I–6659.
216 See Case C–157/02 *Rieser* [2004] ECR I–1477, paras 24–28.
217 Joined Cases C–253 to 258/96 *Kampelmann* [1997] ECR I–6907, para 46.
218 Opinion in Case C–356/05 *Farrell* [2005] OJ C96/10: 46–7.

The question referred to the ECJ concerns whether the Motor Insurers' Bureau of Ireland (MIBI), consisting of private insurance companies, may be seen as an emanation of state. The MIBI has, according to an agreement with the state, been entrusted to administer a compensation scheme for victims of motor vehicle accidents in accordance with Article 1(4) of Directive 84/57EEC. This provision confers discretion on the Member States concerning the organization of the scheme, and whether to choose a private or public entity to manage the compensation fund. Considering the limited information submitted by the national court, Advocate General Stix-Hackl found it questionable whether MIBI was subject to state control as well as uncertain whether it had any special powers beyond those which result from the normal rules applicable to relations between individuals. However, the responsibility of MIBI was found to be public in nature, since it carried out the task laid down in Article 1(4) of the directive, and state control was deemed exercised by means of the authorization contained in the agreement between MIBI and the state.[219] As an argument of more general application, the Advocate General pointed out that it would ensure uniform application of Community law if individuals could rely on the direct effect of secondary legislation, whatever the nature of the body chosen by the state for the purpose of performing a public duty provided for in Community directives.[220] For these reasons she concluded that MIBI should be put on the same footing as the state. Although the logic is compelling, it is appears that *Farrell* would represent a broadening of the scope of emanations of state if the ECJ confirms the opinion. The notion of state control is found to be fulfilled if the entity is acting according to appointment of the state, which essentially renders the meaning of the third condition in *Foster* nugatory, whilst little attention is paid to the condition of special powers. In fact, the essence of the opinion in *Farrell* is that an undertaking which carries out a public service obligation stipulated in a directive, according to appointment by the state, will automatically be deemed an emanation of state.

It would seem that the *Foster* doctrine is gaining increased relevance in the environmental sector, where many public utilities have been privatized over the last decade, such as energy and gas supply, waste management, collective transport, and water and sewage management. Furthermore, most environmental activities are subject to authorization and national authorities typically have control functions to ensure compliance with permit conditions. Pending the ruling in *Farrell*, it should be added that others have

[219] Para 71. [220] ibid; see footnote 48.

interpreted the notion of state control more restrictively, in that the public service provider must be subject to supervision going beyond ordinary control through permits and authorizations. Burnett-Hall has suggested that public services constituting a monopoly or oligopoly, which are usually tightly regulated, eg gas and electricity industries, rail-track services etc, fall within the scope of *Foster*, whereas subjects not subject to any 'particular public services controls', eg a privatized mining industry would presumably not be held as emanations of the state.[221]

2.3.3 *Inverse vertical direct effect*

The ECJ has imposed certain restrictions on the possibility for individuals to invoke directives against the state where this has direct adverse legal consequences for third parties. The ECJ offered a succinct overview of this issue in the *Wells* case.[222] The principle of legal certainty and the prohibition on horizontal direct effect hinder individuals from relying on a directive against the authorities where 'it is a matter of a State obligation directly linked to the performance of another obligation falling, pursuant to that directive, on a third party'.[223] At the same time, 'mere adverse repercussions' on the rights of third parties, even if those are certain, do not prevent an individual from invoking obligations articulated in a directive against the state.[224] The concrete question in *Wells* was whether the plaintiff, a neighbour of Conygar Quarry, could rely on the direct effect of Directive 85/337/EEC in order to challenge an authorization for mining activities in the quarry on the grounds that no prior environmental impact assessment had been conducted. The ECJ ruled that the obligation to carry out an environmental impact assessment rested on the authorities and was not directly linked to performance of any obligation falling on the mining operators. The fact that the mining operations would have to be halted pending an environmental impact assessment was a mere adverse repercussion which could not be seen as 'inverse direct effect' that would prevent Mrs Wells from invoking Directive 85/337/EEC.[225]

[221] Burnett-Hall 1995, 44. [222] Case C–201/02 *Wells* [2004] ECR I–723.

[223] ibid para 56. See references to Case C–221/88 *Busseni* [1990] ECR I–495, paras 23–26, and Case C–97/96 *Daihatsu Deutschland* [1997] ECR I–6843, paras 24 and 26.

[224] Case C–201/02 *Wells* [2004] ECR I–723, para 57; see references to Case 103/88 *Costanzo* [1989] ECR 1839, paras 28–33; Case C–435/97 *WWF* [1999] ECR I–5613, paras 69 and 71; Case C–194/94 *CIA Security International* [1996] ECR I–2201, paras 40 to 55; Case C–201/94 *Smith & Nephew and Primecrown* [1996] ECR I–5819, paras 33–39; and Case C–443/98 *Unilever* [2000] ECR I–7535, paras 45–52. [225] Para 58.

There is a delicate distinction between imposing a new obligation on individuals and mere adverse repercussions.[226] Although an environmental impact assessment is conducted by the authorities, it also involves certain obligations for the operators of the relevant site, namely to furnish information, which often is quite an extensive task.[227] By relying on Directive 85/337/EEC to force the authorities to conduct an environmental impact assessment, Mrs Wells did in fact impose new obligations on the mining operators. The ECJ acknowledged this fact, as is illustrated by the somewhat awkward comment that the obligation to conduct an environmental impact assessment was not 'directly linked' to performance of any obligation falling on the mining operators.

Furthermore, 'mere adverse consequences' may not necessarily be less detrimental to the legal position of third parties than being subject to a 'new obligation'. Such obligations may be minor ones, eg reporting duties or small modifications to a permit, whereas mere adverse repercussions can evidently include suspension or revocation of a permit.

In sum, the ECJ considers that the prohibition on inverse direct effect only applies to specific obligations laid down in directives, and not to indirect obligations flowing from government intervention. Verschuuren has therefore wondered whether 'there is any environmental directive [to] which the *Wells* considerations are applicable?'[228] This is an exaggeration – there are various directives which contain obligations directed at private parties, eg Directive 2004/35/EC on Environmental Liability – but the majority of environmental directives indeed contain indirect obligations which can be enforced without falling foul of the 'inverse direct effect' test. It is interesting in this respect to note that in the *Waddenzee* case the ECJ did not even bother to address the issue of 'inverse direct effect' in respect of a challenge brought on the basis of Article 6(3) of Directive 92/43/EC against permits for cockle fishing issued without environmental impact assessments, although this issue was raised by the parties and was analysed at some length in the opinion of the Advocate General.[229]

2.3.4 *Incidental horizontal direct effect*

To blur even further the scope of the *Marshall/Dori* rulings, the ECJ has in some cases allowed individuals to invoke directives against other individuals,

[226] Dougan 2000a, 605.

[227] See Article 5(3) of Directive 85/337 [1985] OJ L175/40, as amended by Directive 97/11 [1997] OJ L73/5.

[228] Verschuuren 2005, 282.

[229] See opinion of AG Kokott in Case C–127/02 *Landelijke Vereniging tot Behoud van de Waddenzee* [2004] ECR I–7405, paras 145–50.

thus sparking an abundant amount of academic debate as to whether the ban on horizontal direct effect still applies.[230] The first important case was *CIA Security*,[231] which concerned claims by a competing firm, Signalson, that CIA Security should be restrained from marketing alarm systems that had not been approved according to national law. CIA Security claimed in defence that the national law was incompatible with Directive 83/189/EEC on Notification of Technical Standards and Regulations. The question was whether CIA-Security could invoke the provisions of that directive in the proceedings as this would prima facie amount to horizontal direct effect. Focusing on the effectiveness of Community law, the ECJ held that CIA Security could indeed do so in order to render the national law inapplicable.[232] This ruling was confirmed in the *Unilever* case, in which the ECJ again allowed Directive 83/189/EEC to be invoked in proceedings between private entities in order to set aside national law that had not been notified.

There have also been cases in which the ECJ has allowed individuals to invoke other directives as against private parties. *Decker*[233] concerned an action for compensation brought against a private employer for breaching Directive 76/207/EEC by refusing the plaintiff's job application on the grounds of pregnancy. The respondent pointed out that under national law liability presupposed fault attributable to the employer, and the claim would therefore fail. The ECJ held that making liability conditional upon fault would weaken the practical effect of the directive, and therefore ruled that 'any breach of the prohibition of discrimination must, in itself, be sufficient to make the employer liable, without there being any possibility of invoking the grounds of exemption provided by national law'.[234] In *Ruiz Bernáldez* the ECJ held that Article 3(1) of Directive 72/166/EEC[235] precluded a national law that exempted an insurance company from compensating third party victims in case of accidents caused by an intoxicated driver.[236] *Panagis Pafitis*[237] concerned a decision to increase bank capital by issuing new shares without holding a shareholder meeting. The old shareholders were adversely affected by this move, and brought proceedings against the bank as well as the

[230] Eg Tridimas 1994, 621; Craig 1997, 519; Schermers 1997, 527; Ward 2000.

[231] Case C–194/94 [1996] ECR I–2201. [232] Para 48.

[233] Case C–177/88 *Dekker* [1990] ECR I–3941. See also Timmermans 1998, 1 at 23.

[234] Paras 24–25.

[235] Directive 72/166 on the approximation of the laws of the Member States relating to insurance against civil liability in respect of the use of motor vehicles, and to the enforcement of the obligation to insure against such liability; see OJ English Special Edition 1972(II) p 360.

[236] Case C–129/94 *Ruis Bernáldez* [1996] ECR I–1829, para 20.

[237] Case C–441/93 *Pafitis* [1996] ECR I–1347.

new shareholders, arguing that the national law allowing for such a decision without informing shareholders was in breach of Directive 77/91/EEC,[238] which the ECJ confirmed.[239] Finally, in *Unilever v Smithkline Beecham*, the ECJ allowed Article 6 of Directive 76/768[240] to be invoked in proceedings between two competing companies, with the result that national laws which prohibited advertisements of certain cosmetics products had to be set aside.[241]

This case law begs the question whether the ECJ has changed its view on horizontal direct effect, or alternatively, how this case law may be differentiated from the cases where horizontal direct effect was denied, eg *Marshall* and *Faccini Dori*. The ECJ addressed some of these issues in *Unilever*:

> Whilst it is true that a directive cannot of itself impose obligations on an individual and cannot therefore be relied on as such against an individual ... that case-law does not apply where non-compliance with Article 8 or Article 9 of Directive 83/189, which constitutes a substantial procedural defect, renders a technical regulation adopted in breach of either of those articles inapplicable. In such circumstances, and unlike the case of non-transposition of directives with which the case-law cited by those two Governments is concerned, Directive 83/189 does not in any way define the substantive scope of the legal rule on the basis of which the national court must decide the case before it. It creates neither rights nor obligations for individuals.

This may explain the rulings under Directive 83/189/EEC – *CIA Security* and *Unilever* – but it does not explain why the ECJ allowed horizontal effect in the other cases mentioned above. The quote nevertheless gives hint at a more general explanation, reminiscent of the distinction between invoking directives for purposes of exclusion versus substitution of national law discussed above in the context of rights.[242] The point the ECJ was making in *Unilever* was that Directive 83/189/EEC does not contain substantive provisions which may give rise to rights and obligations, but may merely be invoked in order to exclude national provisions incompatible with that directive, ie technical regulations that have not been notified. The legal void thus created is not filled with provisions of the directive, but by other applicable national rules. Applying that line of reasoning in a general context, it follows that any directive which is invoked for purposes of setting aside a particular national rule may be applied horizontally, since it does not thereby impose obligations on individuals.[243] This may

[238] [1977] OJ L26/1. [239] Para 60. [240] [1976] OJ L262/169.
[241] Case C–77/97 *Smithkline Beecham* [1999] ECR I–431, para 37.
[242] See section 2.1.4.3.
[243] See Craig and de Búrca 2003, 226; and Lenz, Tynes, and Young 2000, 509.

obviously have adverse consequences for private parties but – as seen in respect of inverse vertical effect – 'mere adverse repercussions' do not conflict with Article 249 EC as interpreted in *Marshall* and *Faccini Dori*.

This theory is corroborated by cases where horizontal direct effect was recognized and those where it was denied.[244] The plaintiff in *Marshall* relied on the directive to impose obligations on the other party, namely to obtain compensatory measures for unlawful dismissal. In *CIA Security*, *Unilever*, *Decker*, *Ruis Bernaldez*, *Panagis Pafitis*, and *Smithkline Beecham*, however, the plaintiffs merely invoked Community law to exclude national provisions without, in addition, seeking to fill the gap with the respective directives, and therefore were not imposing new obligations on their adversaries in the proceedings. Thus, in *Decker* it was clearly stated by the ECJ that the plaintiff could only invoke the Equal Treatment Directive's obligation to ensure an adequate remedy to exclude incompatible national provisions once the Member State had exercised its discretion to choose the sanction applicable, in this case liability. It follows, conversely, that Mrs Decker could not have required compensation on the grounds of the Equal Treatment Directive if 'the sanction chosen by the Member States [was not] contained within the rules governing an employer's civil liability'.[245] The ruling in *Faccini Dori*, in contrast, is difficult to fit into the scheme suggested above, since the plaintiff was not permitted to rely on the directive in order to cancel a contract, which essentially turned on disapplication of certain provisions of national contract law and thus did not impose any direct obligation on the other party. However, this ruling in my view should be interpreted narrowly on the basis of the facts. The plaintiff attempted to avoid a contract because it had disregarded the seven-day standstill provision in the Consumer Directive. If the ECJ had allowed horizontal direct effect in such a situation, it could have called into question the binding quality of contracts in general, which may explain why the ECJ chose a different solution than in the other cases mentioned above.[246]

The distinction advanced above may be criticized for being unduly formal and arbitrary. Invoking Community provisions for the purposes of exclusion of a national rule may have equally detrimental effects for legal certainty as substitution.[247] But this arbitrariness in any event is pre-existing by virtue of the principle of consistent interpretation, the progressive application

[244] For a different view, see Dougan 2000a, 605.

[245] Para 25. See also Case C–14/83 *Von Colson* [1984] ECR 1891.

[246] Edward 2002, 3.

[247] See opinion in Case C–144/04 *Mangold* [2005] ECR I–9981, para 106.

of which by the ECJ has made the ban on horizontal effect often seem illusory.[248] This seemed set to change in *Pfeiffer*,[249] where the Grand Chamber reopened the oral procedure and referred to the full court to answer the question whether Directive 93/104/EC[250] (Working Time Directive) could be applied in proceedings between individuals. A hearing was arranged to discuss this point and the Member States were invited to give comments, in which they 'quite openly, show[ed] their dismay at the possibility of a change of direction in the case-law [on horizontal] direct effect'.[251] AG Colomer took this as a cue to propose to the ECJ that it should recognize a form of preclusive horizontal direct effect, while stressing that his intention was not to encroach on the ban on imposing obligations directly on individuals.[252] However, the ECJ fell back on the classic *Marshall* formula, and reiterated that directives could not be invoked so as to impose obligations directly on individuals. This being as it may, as we will discuss below, it applied the principle of consistent interpretation in its usual extensive manner, and the arbitrariness which *Pfeiffer* might have ended still lives on. At least it is now clear that the ECJ will not, at least not formally, recognize horizontal direct effect.

Nevertheless, the question of exclusionary horizontal direct effect is still relevant, in particular after the ECJ's recent ruling in *Mangold*.[253] Perhaps with *Pfeiffer* fresh in mind, AG Tizzano dismissed the possibility of applying the direct effect of Directive 2000/78/EC[254] (equal treatment in employment and occupation) in proceedings between individuals, and explicitly rejected the Commission argument that the ban on horizontal direct effect did not mean that it could not be invoked for the purposes of setting aside the national rule in question. The disapplication of the national rule in question 'would in reality constitute direct effect of the Community act and it would therefore in fact be the Community act that prevented the party concerned from relying on rights conferred on him by his own national law'.[255] The court relied on its reasoning in the line of cases prior to *Pfeiffer*, and concluded that Article 6 of the directive precluded the national rule in question. The national court was accordingly required to set the national provisions aside, even where the period prescribed for transposition of the

[248] See section 3. [249] Joined Cases C-397 to 403/01 *Pfeiffer* [2004] ECR I-08835.
[250] [1993] OJ L307/18.
[251] See opinion in Joined Cases C-397 to 403/01 *Pfeiffer* [2004] ECR I-08835, para 22.
[252] ibid paras 43–48. [253] Case 144/04 *Mangold* [2005] ECR I-9981.
[254] [2000] OJ L303/16.
[255] Opinion in Case C-144/04 *Mangold* [2005] ECR I-9981, para 106.

directive had not yet expired.[256] This provoked fury from scholars, who argued that the 'convoluted case law on direct effect had received a further twist' and queried whether 'in the light of the judgment in *Mangold* there [is] any real sense in which the no horizontal direct effect for rules of directives can be said to survive'.[257] However, it is noteworthy that the ECJ held that the principle of non-discrimination was a general principle of law, and could as such not 'be conditional upon the expiry of the period allowed to the Member States for the transposition of a directive intended to lay down a general framework [for the operation of this principle]... and the organisation of appropriate legal remedies'.[258] Hence, the *ratio decidendi* could be construed so as to concern the horizontal effect of the general principle of non-discrimination inherent in the Treaty, in particular Article 12 EC, which is directly applicable and may be enforced in horizontal proceedings. The problem with this reasoning, however, is that the ECJ held that 'Community law [ie the general principle of non-discrimination] *and more particularly Article 6 of Directive 2000/78* precluded the national rule in question'.[259] The discussion of exclusionary horizontal direct effect of directives is therefore likely to continue following the ruling in *Mangold*.

What are the practical consequences of this case law for private enforcement of environmental law? It would at least appear that the judgments in *CIA Security* and *Unilever* could be applied analogously to the environmental sphere. This means that failures by the authorities to notify national measures under environmental directives containing such obligations can be invoked in civil proceedings against private parties with a view to having the relevant acts set aside.[260] Every directive would have to be interpreted individually in order to determine whether the breach would render the national measure unlawful, but I submit that Article 2(3) of Directive 85/337/EEC provides an important example. If, for instance, a private development project has been exempted from an environmental impact assessment without the reasons for that decision having been notified to the Commission prior to approval, individuals or NGOs should be able to bring proceedings directly against the developer to have the authorization suspended, pending such notification.

The consequences would obviously be more far-reaching if the case law should be understood, as was suggested above, as allowing for a general right

[256] See section 2.2.3.
[257] Editorial, 'Horizontal Direct Effect – A Law of Diminishing Coherence' 43 CMLR (2006) 1–8.
[258] Paras 75–76.
[259] Para 78.
[260] See chapter 3, section 7.1.

to invoke horizontally directly effective provisions for purposes of setting aside incompatible national measures. In that event, individuals or NGOs would have an opportunity to challenge the validity of permits directly against operators in all cases where it is based on national provisions which are claimed to be incompatible with EC environmental law. However, plaintiffs could not fill the legal void created by invoking obligations directly against the operator. A NGO could for instance bring proceedings against the operator of a waste incinerator plant for the suspension of a permit incompatible with the technical requirements in the relevant Community directives,[261] but the plaintiff could not oblige the operator to take specific measures to comply with those requirements. In that case the NGO would instead have to bring a case against the proper authorities with the aim of obtaining an injunction ordering them to require such measures to be taken by the operator, taking into account the possible restrictions of such actions under the *Wells* doctrine.

3 Consistent interpretation

3.1 *Introduction*

The direct effect doctrine is complemented by the principle of consistent interpretation. It is necessary to clarify their relationship and in particular to examine the extent to which the latter offers any added value for the purposes of enforcement of EC environmental law.

3.2 *Substance*

The principle of consistent interpretation is a general principle of international law, which requires courts to interpret national law in conformity with a rule of international law, with a view to ensuring that that rule is given effect.[262] The ECJ has accordingly held that secondary EC legislation must be interpreted, as far as possible, in conformity with international agreements concluded by the Community.[263] Secondary legislation must in a

[261] See, for illustration, Case C–60/01 *Commission v France* [2002] ECR I–5879.

[262] Betlem and Nollkaemper 2003, 571.

[263] Case C–61/94 *Commission v Germany* [1996] ECR I–3989, para 52; and Case C–341/95 *Safety Hi-Tech* [1998] ECR I–4355, para 20.

similar vein be interpreted in conformity with the Treaty, and an implementing regulation must as far as possible be given an interpretation consistent with a basic regulation.[264]

We will now focus on the duty of national courts to interpret national law in conformity with Community law, a principle that was introduced in the *Von Colson* ruling.[265] As was the case with direct effect, the ECJ has held that the principle of consistent interpretation is inherent in the system of the Treaty.[266] More specifically, it is based on Article 249 EC in conjunction with Article 10 EC, according to which national authorities, including national courts, must take all appropriate measures, whether general or particular, to ensure the result envisaged by Community directives.[267] Hence, not only the wording of directives must be taken into account, but also '[their] purpose [...] in order to achieve an outcome consistent with the objective pursued by the directive'.[268]

The principle of consistent interpretation applies to Community law in general,[269] including the third pillar of the EU Treaty,[270] the EC Treaty itself,[271] secondary legislation,[272] general principles of Community law,[273] and even non-binding Community acts.[274] This obligation rests with all national authorities, eg administrative authorities, emanations of state, as well as national courts.[275] As for the scope of national law which must be interpreted in conformity with the Community rules, the ECJ has ruled that national courts must consider 'the whole body of rules of national law'.[276] Consequently, the principle of consistent interpretation concerns not only implementing legislation (in respect of directives), but 'any national law which may have a bearing on the result of the directive, whether adopted before or after the Community measure'.[277] National law includes, in addition

[264] Case C–9/92 *Dr Tretter* [1993] ECR I–3569, para 11.

[265] Case 14/83 *Von Colson* [1984] ECR 1891.

[266] Case C–160/01 *Mau* [2003] ECR I–4791, para 34; and Joined Cases C–397 to 403/01 *Pfeiffer* [2004] ECR I–08835.

[267] Case 14/83 *Von Colson* [1984] ECR 1891, para 26.

[268] Joined Cases C–397 to 403/01 *Pfeiffer* [2004] ECR I–08835, para 119.

[269] Case C–165/91 *Munster* [1994] ECR I–4661, para 34.

[270] Case C–105/03 *Puppino* [2005] ECR I–5285.

[271] Case 157/86 *Murphy* [1988] ECR 673.

[272] Case 14/83 *Von Colson* [1984] ECR 1891.

[273] Case C–50/00 P *UPA* [2002] ECR I–6677; and opinion in Case C–144/04 *Mangold* [2005] ECR I–9981.

[274] Case C–322/88 *Grimaldi* [1989] ECR I–4407, para 18.

[275] See section 4 below.

[276] Joined Cases C–397 to 403/01 *Pfeiffer* [2004] ECR I–08835, para 119. See also Case C–131/97 *Carbonari* [1999] ECR I–1103, paras 49–50.

[277] Case C–106/89 *Marleasing* [1990] ECR I–1799, para 8.

to legislation, 'settled domestic case law'[278] and probably administrative acts as well.

There are limitations to the principle of consistent interpretation, eg in its temporal applicability, interpretation of national law *contra legem*, and other factors pertaining to legal certainty. But rather than examining these limitations in the abstract, it seems more useful to assess these restrictions in conjunction with an analysis of the added value of the principle of consistent interpretation compared with direct effect, a matter discussed in the next section.

3.3 *Added value*

As point of departure, it is important to note that the principle of consistent interpretation has priority over direct effect. This applies generally in public international law,[279] and the ECJ has confirmed this for the purpose of Community law in *Mary Murphy*.[280] Hence, 'it is for the national court... to give [national law] an interpretation which accords with the requirements of the applicable Community law, and to the extent that this is not possible, to hold such domestic law inapplicable'.[281] Although perhaps instinctively reasonable, this may undermine legal certainty and ultimately the effectiveness of EC law to the extent that this results in the maintenance of national provisions that do not properly implement Community directives.[282] This state of affairs may then only be corrected by infringement proceedings under Article 226 EC, which leaves a certain tension in respect of the *raison d'être* of direct effect as articulated in *Van Gend & Loos*, ie to allow individuals to complement the supervision powers conferred on the Commission.[283] This being as it may, the next sections will examine situations where recourse to the direct effect doctrine is prima facie not possible, with a view to assessing the added value of the principle of consistent interpretation has for purposes of private enforcement of EC environmental law.

3.3.1 *Substantive application*

One benefit which can be quickly dispensed with for our purposes is that the principle of consistent interpretation applies to framework decisions and

[278] Case C–215/97*Bellone* [1998] ECR I–2191; and Case C–456/98 *Centrosteel* [2000] ECR I–6007, para 17.

[279] Betlem and Nollkaemper 2003, 572.

[280] Case 157/86 *Murphy* [1988] ECR 673.

[281] ibid para 11.

[282] See opinion in Case 81/98 *Alcatel* [1999] ECR I–7671, paras 99–100. For an interesting overview of Dutch court practice on this issue, see Jans 2002.

[283] Case 26/62 [1963] ECR 1.

decisions on police and judicial cooperation in criminal matters,[284] acts which according to Article 34 EU do not have direct effect. Following the ruling in *Commission v Council*,[285] if such acts are intended to protect the environment they must be adopted under Article 175 EC, so that this advantage becomes somewhat theoretical.[286]

A more significant issue pertains to the binding nature of Community acts. The direct effect doctrine is based on Article 249 EC and the principle of primacy of Community law, and applies therefore only to binding Community measures. Hence, on a preliminary question in *Grimaldi* whether Community recommendations had direct effect and could be relied upon by individuals before national courts, the ECJ answered in the negative. However, the fact that such measures are not binding does not mean that they are not capable of legal effects. The ECJ therefore concluded that national courts are bound to take recommendations into consideration in order to decide disputes submitted to them, 'in particular where they cast light on the interpretation of national measures adopted in order to implement them or where they are designed to supplement binding Community provisions'.[287] Since recommendations are addressed to Member States one might question whether the same obligation applies to non-binding acts which are not. However, it follows from the *ratio decidendi* that the significant issue is whether national measures in fact are intended to implement the Community act. Important examples in this respect are environmental action programmes adopted under Article 175(3) EC, which set out set a five year plan containing the objective, principles, and priorities of the Community in the environmental sector. It is generally agreed that such plans have influenced, in their own right, national environmental policies.[288]

Another issue, often emphasised in legal literature, is that the principle of consistent interpretation is a complementary tool in those instances where the relevant Community rules do not fulfil the conditions for direct effect, ie are not unconditional and sufficiently precise.[289] However, this assertion is questionable. On the one hand, as will be recalled from section 2.2, neither the fact that the Community rules require further implementing measures nor that they lack sufficient precision necessarily precludes judicial review

[284] See Case C–105/03 *Puppino* [2005] ECR I–5285.

[285] Case C–176/03 *Commission v Council* [2005] ECR I–7879, discussed in further detail in chapter 3, section 11.

[286] See also pending Case C–440/05 *Commission v Parliament and Council*.

[287] Case 322/88 *Grimaldi* [1989] ECR I–4407, para 18.

[288] Krämer 2003, 55.

[289] Eg Prechal 2005, 184 and 312.

of whether the national authorities have moved beyond their margin of discretion. On the other hand, where the relevant Community rules confer genuine discretion on the national authorities national courts are prevented from substituting their assessment with their own. It is irrelevant for this purpose whether they are approaching the matter from the perspective of direct effect or the principle of consistent interpretation.[290] With this in mind, it is necessary to examine cases in which the principle of consistent interpretation allegedly provided plaintiffs with remedies whilst the doctrine of direct effect would have left them empty handed.

The problem in *Von Colson*[291] was that Article 6 of Directive 76/07/EEC on Equal Treatment for Workers neither stipulated the nature nor the level of relief which Member States had to provide against acts of discrimination. Article 6 was thus found to lack direct effect, but the ECJ added with reference to the principle of consistent interpretation that '*if* a Member State chooses to penalise breaches [...] by the award of compensation [...] that compensation must in any event be adequate'.[292] In other words, if the national authorities have exercised discretion as to the choice of the requisite sanction, the national court is bound to secure the minimum result inherent in Article 6 as concerns 'adequate compensation'. Under these circumstances, one might as well say that Article 6 was capable of direct effect. This is analogous to the *Ghareveran* case,[293] where the ECJ held that once national authorities have exercised their discretion in respect of a conditional Community rule, that provision becomes directly effective and the plaintiff can claim performance of that obligation. The content of the relevant obligation was more precisely specified in *Ghareveran*, but the obligation to provide 'adequate compensation' must presumably have been sufficiently precise as to its minimum content for how else would the national court know how to 'interpret' its national law?

The *ratio decidendi* in *Carbonari*[294] may also be construed in terms of direct effect, rather than consistent interpretation. Directive 82/76/EEC provides that Member States must ensure that medical specialists in training receive 'appropriate remuneration', but fails to stipulate the competent body that must effectuate these payments, nor the levels of payment that are 'appropriate'. After having confirmed that the obligation was neither sufficiently precise nor unconditional, the ECJ held in a not particularly eloquent manner

[290] See opinion of AG Darmon in Case C–236/92 *Comitato* [1994] ECR I–483, para 26 cf para 38.

[291] Case 14/83 *Von Colson* [1984] ECR 1891.

[292] Para 23.

[293] Case C–441/99 *Ghareveran* [2001] ECR I–7687, paras 39–43.

[294] Case C–131/97 *Carbonari* [1999] ECR I–1103.

that 'it is therefore for the national court to [...] decide whether the level of appropriate remuneration and the institution on which is imposed the obligation to pay that remuneration may be determined on the basis of all provisions of national law'.[295]

Taken out of context, this statement does not make much sense, but it appears that the ECJ was referring to a national law which in fact did implement Directive 82/76/EEC, in which both levels of appropriate remuneration and the competent bodies liable to effectuate payments were specified.[296] The problem was that the legislation belatedly implemented the directive and did not apply to trainee medical specialists prior to 1991, thus excluding the plaintiffs. Against this background, it appears that the ECJ was essentially asking the national court to interpret the rule which hindered the implementing legislation from applying to trainee medical specialists admitted before 1991 restrictively. Again, this obligation can be construed as an issue of direct effect, since the ECJ basically required the national court to set aside a national rule which infringed the Community directive. This is no different from what the ECJ did in the cases on incidental horizontal direct effect examined above,[297] ie ordering the setting aside of a national rule incompatible with the directive it is intended to implement, thus paving the way for the plaintiff to make claims on the basis of the corrected national legislation.

In sum, the principle of consistent interpretation cannot logically provide any added value compared with the doctrine of direct effect if we concentrate on the way in which Community provisions are phrased – the question in both relations being whether the provisions can be made operational. The results in *Von Colson* and *Carbonari* could thus for better or worse have been based on direct effect. This is not to say that the principle of consistent interpretation has limited applicability, the point is that the direct effect doctrine has a very broad scope.

3.3.2 *Temporal application*

As mentioned above, the direct effect doctrine may only be relied upon once the deadline for transposition of a directive has expired, or even later if specific deadlines have been set for individual provisions. The *Inter-Environment Wallonie* case brought an exception to this rule, but this exception is nevertheless limited to cases where national measures are 'liable to seriously impede' the result to be achieved by the directive. The apparent relaxation in *Mangold*

295 Para 50. 296 Paras 14–18, cf para 35. 297 Section 2.3.4.

should probably be interpreted restrictively on the basis of the specific facts of that case. In contrast, Advocates General[298] and commentators[299] have argued that the principle of consistent interpretation requires the national courts to interpret national law in conformity with the aim and result of a directive as soon as such a directive enters into force. This view is often based on the *Kolpinghuis* judgment, in which the ECJ ruled as follows:

> As regards the third question concerning the limits which Community law might impose on the obligation or power of the national court to interpret the rules of its national law in the light of the directive, it makes no difference whether or not the period prescribed for implementation has expired.[300]

The limits referred to was that application of the principle of consistent interpretation would subject the defendant to criminal liability and the ECJ therefore concluded that the principle could not be applied. Commentators have therefore often acknowledged that the temporal application referred to was an *obiter dictum*, but still held that it indicated the position the ECJ might take in future case.

This in my view amounts to a misreading of the case. The point the ECJ made was that it was irrelevant whether the period prescribed for implementation had expired since the principle of consistent interpretation could either way *not* be relied upon where it would aggravate the liability of a private party.[301] Indeed, in more recent case law the ECJ has used the following formula for the temporal application of the principle of consistent interpretation:

> Where it is seized of a dispute falling within the scope of the Directive and *arising from facts postdating the expiry of the period for transposing the Directive*, the national court ... must as far as possible interpret the law in such a way that it is applied in conformity with the aims of the directive.[302]

However, these judgments cannot be taken as conclusive evidence that national courts are, conversely, not obliged to do so also in respect of facts predating expiry of the deadline for transposing the directive. As noted by

298 See eg opinion of AG Darmon in Case C–236/92 *Comitato* [1994] ECR I–483, para 27; opinion of AG La Pergola in Case C–5/94 *Hedley Lomas* [1996] ECR I–2553, para 64; and opinion of AG Colomer in Case C–144/04 *Mangold* [2005] ECR I–9981, para 115.

299 See eg Timmermans 1998, 11; and Betlem 2002, 79.

300 Case C–80/86 *Kolpinghuis Nijmegen* [1987] ECR 3969, para 15.

301 Similarly, Hartley 2003, 220.

302 See eg Case C–456/98 *Centrosteel* [2000] ECR I–6007, para 17; and Joined Cases C–397 to 403/01 *Pfeiffer* [2004] ECR I–8835, para 117.

Timmermans, 'when entered into force directives are not instruments of suspended validity pending the time-limit of its transposition', but are 'legally complete and form part . . . of the law of the books'.[303] National courts should therefore be obliged, he argues, to interpret national law as far as possible in conformity with directives from this point in time. Furthermore, it seems clear that the *Inter-Environment Wallonie* obligation must apply mutatis mutandis to consistent interpretation. This has now been confirmed in the *Adeneler* case, in which the court gave the following ruling:

From the date upon which a directive has entered into force, the courts of the Member States must refrain as far as possible from interpreting domestic law in a manner which might seriously compromise, after the period of transposition has expired, attainment of the objective pursued by that directive.[304]

The wording is not perfect as it imposes an obligation phrased in the double negative – to refrain from interpretations that would compromise the directive. Read in the context of the case it seems that the meaning was to require the national court positively to construe the national law in order to avoid that the objective pursued by the directive was jeopardized. But even so it is clear that the ECJ did not intend to subject the national court to the full application of the principle of consistent interpretation, but only insofar as was necessary to preclude that the objective of the directive was not 'seriously compromised'. Advocate General Kokott opined in contrast in favour of a regular application of the principle of consistent interpretation, for which there are good reasons in my view.[305] It should be recalled that national courts are already required to interpret national law in conformity with non-binding measures,[306] which suggests a fortiori that the same obligation should apply to a directive which has entered into force, but for which the deadline for implementation has not yet expired. One might perhaps argue that legal certainty militates in favour of the court's ruling, but the prohibition on interpretations *contra legem* would in any event be applicable.[307] It is therefore hard to see why national courts under such circumstances should not be obliged to interpret the national law as far as possible in order to ensure an outcome consistent with the directive, and not merely avoiding the serious disruption of the directive's objectives. Another matter is that the

[303] Timmermans 1998, 11.

[304] Case C–212/04 *Adeneler and Others* [2006] ECR I–6057, para 123.

[305] Opinion, ibid para 54.

[306] Similarly, opinion in Case C–144/04 *Mangold* [2005] ECR I–9981, paras 117 et seq; and opinion, ibid para 50.

[307] See section 3.3.3 below.

difference between the regular application of the principle of consistent interpretation and the *Adeneler* version is probably going to be difficult to apply in practice.

3.3.3 *Horizontal application*

Although the ECJ's case law on horizontal direct effect of directives raises many questions, after *Pfeiffer*[308] directives may in principle not impose obligations directly on private parties. This does not prevent plaintiffs from asking national courts to interpret national law in conformity with directives in proceedings against other private parties, since any such obligations stem from national law. The principle of consistent interpretation is therefore a significant complementary instrument for enforcement of EC environmental law against private parties. Exactly to what extent it offers added value, however, may only be fully appreciated by examining the restrictions which the ECJ has placed on the applicability of this principle in horizontal cases.

The most fundamental restriction, which is inherent in the nature of interpretation, is that national courts are not obliged – or even allowed under the principle of legal certainty – to interpret provisions of domestic law *contra legem*. This was implicit in *Marleasing*[309] in which the ECJ held that national courts must interpret national law *so far as possible* in the light of the wording and the purpose of EC directives. The ECJ has since clarified that national courts are, in accordance with the principle of legal certainty, not required to interpret national law *contra legem*,[310] and more specifically that 'there is no method of procedure in Community law allowing the national court to eliminate national provisions contrary to provisions of a directive which has not been transposed where those provisions may not be relied upon before the national court'.[311] The ECJ in such instances has regularly advised plaintiffs to seek damages on the basis of state liability instead, a point to which I shall return below.[312]

[308] Joined Cases C–397 to 403/01 *Pfeiffer* [2004] ECR I–8835.

[309] Case C–106/89 *Marleasing* [1990] ECR I–1799, para 8.

[310] Case C–334/92 *Wagner Miret* [1993] ECR I–6911, para 22.

[311] Case C–168/95 *Arcaro* [1996] ECR I–1531, para 43; Joined Cases C–397 to 403/01 *Pfeiffer* [2004] ECR I–08835; and, by analogy, Case C–105/03 *Puppino* [2005] ECR I–5285, para 47 (preliminary ruling under Article 35 EU).

[312] Case C–91/92 *Faccini Dori* [1994] ECR I–3325, para 27; Case C–334/92 *Wagner Miret* [1993] ECR I–0525; and Case C–131/97 *Carbonari* [1999] ECR I–1103.

It is therefore essentially in the context of vague or ambiguous national rules that national courts are obliged to apply the principle of consistent interpretation. Yet, such cases, too, may raise problems of legal certainty. Open-ended provisions are usually given more concrete meaning through judicial interpretation. Deviating from settled and clear case law may be as harmful from the point of legal certainty as interpreting *contra legem*.[313]

However, closer scrutiny of the case law reveals that although the ECJ has in principle held that national courts are not obliged to interpret national law *contra legem*, in practice it has often required them to do precisely that. Hence, after reciting the 'as far as possible' caveat in *Marleasing*, the ECJ ruled as follows:

> It follows that the requirement that national law *must* be interpreted in conformity with Article 11 of the Directive *precludes* the interpretation of provisions of national law related to public limited companies in such a manner that the nullity of a public limited company may be ordered on grounds other than those exhaustively listed in Article 11 of the directive in question.[314]

Out went 'as far as possible, in came 'must' and 'precludes'. The ECJ ruled similarly in *Bellone*.[315] After having verified that the Italian rules in question made agency contracts conditional upon registration, which was clearly conflicting with the relevant EC directive, the ECJ held that the directive must lead to an interpretation of national law which precludes such a condition.[316] One must concur with AG Saggio's (opinion in *Océano*) comment on *Bellone*:

> That statement can be construed in one sense only, given the procedural context, namely as requiring the national court not to apply the conflicting national legislation, which was incompatible with the Directive that had not been transposed within the prescribed period.[317]

In the *Océano* case, AG Saggio opined that the principle of consistent interpretation could not be relied upon since 'there is clearly no domestic legal

[313] This was illustrated by Case C–215/97*Bellone* [1998] ECR I–2191and Case C–456/98 *Centrosteel* [2000] ECR I–6007 in which the court required a fundamentally different interpretation of Italian rule pertaining to contact law, deviating from settled case law from the Italian Civil Supreme Court. In contrast, AG Jacobs did not find any problem linked to legal certainty in his opinion in *Centrosteel*. Quite the opposite, he argued that this case did not raise any difficulty with regard to the principle of consistent interpretation as there were no express conflicts with national law, only to settled case law (para 36).

[314] Para 9.

[315] Case C–215/97*Bellone* [1998] ECR I–2191.

[316] ibid paras 12 and 18.

[317] Opinion of AG Saggio in Joined Cases C–240 to 244/98 *Océano* [2000] ECR I–4491, para 35.

provision that can be interpreted in such a way as to attain the objectives required'.[318] But on the basis of the case law referred to, he argued that the ECJ should openly recognize what in his mind amounted to exclusionary horizontal direct effect. The ECJ did not do so, and sufficed to rule that the national court was required 'to favour' that very interpretation which AG Saggio held was impossible under national law.[319]

The last case to be mentioned, *Pfeiffer*,[320] is in many respects a mirror image of *Océano*. The national rule in question could clearly not be interpreted in conformity with the EC directive and the opinion (by Colomer) again argued along the lines of exclusionary horizontal direct effect, although employing more convoluted language than that of AG Saggio in *Océano*. The ECJ could not be swayed from the principle that horizontal direct effect of directives was precluded even in the case of exclusionary direct effect, however, and returned to the principle of consistent interpretation, adding the usual caveats 'as far as possible' and the more recent 'if national application of interpretative methods recognised by national law enables…'. However, in its final conclusions, the ECJ required the national court to ensure that the result laid down in the directive was achieved, ie 'to ensure that the maximum period of weekly working time, which is set at 48 hours by Article 6(2) of Directive 93/104, is not exceeded'.[321]

So, what are we to make of this dichotomy between principle and practice in this line of cases? One might say that, since the obligation of result to be achieved through consistent interpretation is preceded with the caveat 'as far as possible', there is no problem. However, as noted by AG Colomer in *Pfeiffer*, in all these cases (preceding *Pfeiffer*) the national courts have in fact followed the ECJ's 'advice' and they clearly took these rulings as laying down an obligation for them to ensure a directive's result, even if this meant interpretation *contra legem* in horizontal proceedings.[322] Hence, the ECJ has either adopted a very narrow interpretation of the notion of '*contra legem*' or a very broad interpretation of what 'is possible' under national law. Furthermore, *Pfeiffer* suggests that national courts are under a particularly strict obligation to push the legal envelope in cases where the rule to be interpreted is an exception to the main rule in the domestic legislation.[323]

Finally, the interesting observation of AG Colomer in respect of the relationship between directive-conform interpretation and state liability must be mentioned. As will be recalled, the ECJ in some cases has shied away

318 ibid para 28. 319 Para 32. 320 See commentary by Prechal 2005b.
321 Para 119. 322 Opinion, para 47. 323 See para 116.

from advocating interpretations *contra legem*, and instead advised plaintiffs to seek damages under the state liability doctrine. In his opinion in *Pfeiffer* Colomer noted that some of the plaintiffs' claims lacked economic content and were difficult to determine, which meant that the likelihood for obtaining compensation from state authorities was 'very limited'.[324] He therefore advocated that national courts under such circumstances have a particularly far-reaching obligation to uphold the plaintiff's claim through the principle of consistent interpretation. If this reasoning finds favour with the ECJ, which did not comment on this specific issue, it will have significant implications for environmental suits which often suffer from similar impediments.[325]

An undisputed limitation of the principle of consistent interpretation is that national law cannot be interpreted in such a way as to determine or aggravate liability in criminal law.[326] This applies primarily to criminal proceedings between state prosecutors and individuals, and is as such a vertical limitation. But the question may also arise indirectly in cases between private parties where the principle of consistent interpretation may result in the finding of a breach which is sanctioned by criminal law, and could thus lead to subsequent criminal proceedings. This is especially pertinent for breaches of environmental law, which in many Member States are considered criminal offences.

This begs the question whether, for instance, an NGO could require a national court to interpret national law regulating a certain activity in light of an EC environmental directive, even if this would result in finding an operator in breach of a permit, which at a later stage could lead to imposition of criminal sanctions? I would submit that the two issues should be distinguished: the NGO should be allowed to invoke the principle of consistent interpretation in order to enforce proper application of environmental directives, whereas the public authorities should be prevented from relying on this finding in a subsequent criminal proceeding. This solution ensures that the principle of consistent interpretation functions to enforce environmental law, and at the same time precludes individual criminal liability on the basis of an unimplemented EC directive. Any other solution would undermine the relevance of the principle of consistent interpretation in private proceedings

[324] Para 117.

[325] Although I do not subscribe to the notion that claims must have an economic content to qualify under the rule in *Francovich*; see chapter 3, section 10.

[326] Case 14/86 *Pretore di Salo* [1987] ECR 2545; Case 80/86 *Kolpinghuis Nijmegen* [1987] ECR 3986, paras 13–14; Case C–168/95 *Arcaro* [1996] ECR I–1531; and Case 387/02 *Berlusconi* [2005] ECR I–3655.

in Member States which sanction environment offences by criminal law, and could thus threaten the *effet utile* of Community environmental legislation. Paradoxically, this situation will only be exacerbated if the proposed Directive on the Protection of the Environment through Criminal Law will go ahead (following the annulment of the EU Framework Decision 2003/80 on the Protection of the Environment through Criminal Law).[327]

A final potential restriction to the doctrine of consistent interpretation stems from the *Arcaro* judgment, in which the ECJ went one step further, and held that courts are also precluded from applying the principle of consistent interpretation where it leads to the imposition of an *obligation* on an individual.[328] If taken literally, this would impose significant restrictions on the principle of consistent interpretation. After all, any choice between alternative interpretations of a national rule will typically result in novel obligations on individuals. In his opinion in the following *Centrosteel* case,[329] AG Jacobs argued that this statement had to be interpreted restrictively in the light of the facts of the *Arcaro* case, which involved criminal proceedings against an individual. He claimed, as was advocated in the opinion in *Pfeiffer*,[330] that the principle of consistent interpretation may well lead to the imposition upon an individual of civil liability or a civil obligation which would not otherwise have existed.[331]

This is in my view correct. Any obligations resulting from consistent interpretation that fall within the scope of a national rule, even if it results from a new interpretation, nevertheless flows from national law, and does therefore not conflict with Article 249 EC and the *Marshall* ruling. Given that the ECJ in practice allows for exclusionary horizontal direct effect of directives, but never accepts invocations of a directive for the purpose of directly imposing obligations on individuals, it is in this (latter) situation that the principle of consistent interpretation most significantly complements the direct effect doctrine.

The far-reaching implications can be illustrated through the following example. Let us assume that national law in a Member State contains a general obligation for industry to provide for information on the polluting

[327] See chapter 3, section 12. [328] Case C–168/95 *Arcaro* [1996] ECR I–4075, para 42.

[329] Opinion of AG Jacobs in Case C–456/98 *Centrosteel* [2000] ECR I–6007, para 34.

[330] Opinion in Joined Cases C–397 to 403/01 *Pfeiffer* [2004] ECR I–08835, paras 37–38. See also Timmermans 1998, 23 who argues that case law makes it 'abundantly clear that the instrument of consistent interpretation allows the imposition of obligations, on private parties also, which otherwise would not, or not necessarily have resulted from national law alone'. To support this view, he refers to Case C–177/88 *Dekker* [1990] ECR I–3941. [331] Para 35.

properties of their activities and products. At the same time it has failed to implement Directive 99/94/EC, which requires that all new passenger cars at the point of sale bear a label on the official fuel consumption and their average CO_2 emission. An environmental NGO should in such a situation be able to bring proceedings directly against a car producer, and require the national court to interpret national law in conformity with Directive 99/94/EC and order the company to label all new cars for sale, including their petrol-guzzling jeeps. This would obviously impose a significant obligation on the producer, but the obligation is nevertheless based on national law, the scope of which is sufficiently broad to allow for such an interpretation. The consequences for the producer may seem harsh, and perhaps questionable in light of the principle of legal certainty. However, this is not an argument which should preclude such suits since, to the extent that the company may claim legitimate expectations, which is not obvious, it should bring claims against the state under the *Francovich* doctrine.

4 Duties on national courts and authorities

The focus in the preceding sections has been on the ability for individuals to invoke EC environmental law in national courts. In the final section of this chapter, we shall briefly pay attention to obligations for national courts as well as public authorities to apply such law. The principle of loyalty enshrined in Article 10 EC requires Member States, including national courts and authorities, to take all necessary measures to achieve the results prescribed by directives. A particularly important question is whether this merely implies that national courts must respond to submissions made by parties to the proceedings or whether, alternatively, it means that national courts must raise issues pertaining to Community law on their own initiative.

From early case law regarding the duty of national courts to refer preliminary questions to the ECJ, it followed implicitly that these had the power to raise issues of their own motion.[332] However, it was not until the ruling in the *Verholen* case that the ECJ explicitly ruled that national courts have such a competence.[333] The ECJ took one step further in *Van Schijndel*, ruling that the non-discrimination principle in *Rewe* obliged national courts to raise

[332] Case 166/73 *Rheinmuhlen v Einfuhr- und Vorratsstelle Getreide* [1974] ECR 33, para 3.
[333] Joined Cases C–87, 88 and 89/90 *Verholen* [1991] ECR I–3757, para 15.

issues of binding Community law *ex officio* to the extent that this was also required under domestic law.[334] Furthermore, the position was 'the same' if domestic law laid down discretion to raise issues of law *ex officio*.[335] It was not entirely clear whether 'the same' meant that national courts similarly *may* raise issues of Community law when they have discretion to do so in respect of domestic law, or whether courts *had* to do so in such cases. The ECJ was more explicit in *Kraaijeveld*, where it held that, if a court *must or may* raise legal issues of its own motion under domestic law, it *must* examine *ex officio* whether the legislative or administrative authorities have remained within the limits of binding Community law.[336] In addition to the arguments advanced in *Van Schijndel* to justify such a duty, the ECJ added that national courts, like other national authorities, by virtue of Article 249(3) EC and the directive itself are obliged to take all measures necessary to achieve the result prescribed by the directive.[337] Finally, the ECJ stressed that the *effet utile* of a directive would be reduced if a court was prevented from taking into consideration issues of Community law under such circumstances.[338]

The next question is whether the obligations pertaining to national courts also rest on national authorities. The court held in *Fratelli Costanzo*, and confirmed in later case law, that all organs of the administration, including decentralized authorities such as municipalities, were under the 'same obligation' as national courts to apply directly effective provisions.[339] From this it appears to follow that, similar to national courts, administrative authorities must apply such provisions *ex officio*.[340] That seems to have been confirmed in the *Grossenkrutzburg* case,[341] in which Germany argued that it was under no obligation to conduct an environmental impact assessment in respect of a specific project, since that obligation was not directly effective and therefore incapable of being enforced by individuals against the national authorities. The ECJ dismissed that argument, holding that for the question whether national authorities were obliged to fulfil that duty it was irrelevant whether individuals could enforce it.[342] Hence, as implicitly confirmed by the *Kraaijeveld* case, authorities must *ex officio* conduct an environmental impact

334 Joined Cases C–430 and 431/93 *Van Schijndel* [1995] ECR I–4705, para 13.

335 Para 14.

336 Case C–72/95 *Kraaijeveld* [1996] ECR I–5403, para 60.

337 Paras 55–56.

338 Whether national courts in some instances may also raise issues of Community law where national law prevents this is dealt with in Chapter 3, section 4.2.

339 Case 103/88 *Fratelli Costanzo* [1989] ECR 1839, para 33. See also Case C–101/91 *Commission v Italy* [1993] ECR I–191, para 24; and Case C–118/00 *Larsy* [2001] ECR I–5063, para 52.

340 See also Krämer 1996, 131–32.

341 Case C–431/92 *Commission v Germany* [1995] ECR I–2189.

342 Para 26.

assessment in accordance with the EIA directive even if there is no legislation in place.[343] This obligation applies generally to environmental directives that are not transposed or erroneously implemented, but is tempered by the ban on reverse direct effect – authorities can act even though it has adverse consequences on private parties, but not where it would result in imposing obligations directly on companies and individuals.

However, it follows from *Fratteli Costanzo* that administrative authorities are also required to apply the principle of consistent interpretation so as to make obligations laid down in unimplemented directives effective, since they are under the 'same' obligation to apply Community law as national courts. This obligation also applies to emanations of state.[344] To the extent that national laws allow for flexible interpretations, national authorities are therefore competent to act, even where this imposes obligations on individuals. As mentioned above in section 3, this does not conflict with Article 249 EC and the *Marshall* case law because the obligations, although derived from Community law, are based on national law.[345] Admittedly, there is the difference that suits brought by individuals against other individuals are decided by national courts which, unlike administrative authorities, can refer preliminary questions to the ECJ. Although the ECJ was made aware of this problem by AG Lenz in his opinion in *Fratteli Costanzo*[346] it did not change its mind.[347]

The principle of consistent interpretation is therefore a most important tool for remedying the well-known problem of EC environmental law of late or insufficient transposition of directives. The 1998 Doñana accident may serve to illustrate how national authorities can make good use of the principle of consistent interpretation. The facts leading to this case were that the waste retention dam of the Aznalcollar mining complex collapsed, which led to significant environmental damage in the neighbouring Doñana National Park, including loss of biodiversity. Spanish authorities subsequently tried to hold the private company in charge of the Aznacollar mining complex liable for this damage.

Let us assume certain further facts for purposes of illustration. Suppose that, according to Spanish law, operators of industrial plants are liable for 'environmental damage'. We further assume that this notion has been interpreted as including costs of restoring contaminated land, but excludes

[343] Krämer 1991, 239. Cf Wyatt 1998, 18–19 who is critical of this aspect of *Kraaijeveld*, which seems misguided as that case merely spelled out the consequences stemming from Case C–103/88 *Costanzo* [1989] ECR 1839.

[344] By analogy Case C–188/89 *Foster* [1990] I–3313.

[345] Similarly, Krämer 1991, 240.

[346] Opinion in Case C–103/88 *Costanzo* [1989] ECR 1839, para 36.

[347] See criticism by Somsen 2000, 343–44.

loss of biodiversity. The authorities in this case therefore would be precluded from holding the operator responsible for the bulk of the environmental damage caused to the Doñana National Park. The operator could be held responsible for loss of biodiversity under Article 3 of Directive 2004/35/EC, but we assume that Spain has failed to implement the directive and that the deadline for transposition has expired.

Under such circumstances, I would argue that the national authorities and courts could interpret the national notion of environmental damage in conformity with Directive 2004/35 so that loss of biodiversity is included. The authorities can do this without interpreting national law *contra legem*. The additional obligation imposed on the operator therefore stems from national law, not community law.

A variation of this example serves to illustrate how the obligation to interpret national law in conformity with Community law *ex officio* can substitute obligations for non-binding rules. The scenario is now that under national law the operator of the Aznacollar mining complex is liable for all relevant damage, but that national authorities enjoy discretion whether to hold operators liable, and that in the end they choose not to do so. However, under Article 6(3) of Directive 2004/35 the authorities are required to act against the operator. Since the authorities are obliged to interpret national law in light of the directive, they are consequently obliged to use their discretionary powers and hold the operator responsible.

One might question whether the obligation to apply Community law *ex officio* in this way has any added value, since if the authorities fail to interpret national law in light of the directive and refrain from taking action against the operator, individuals must nevertheless bring proceedings against the authorities. However, this would constitute an infringement of Article 10 EC which could require the national authorities to nullify the consequences of the breach,[348] eg to undertake the remediation themselves. This provides incentives for the authorities to act of their own motion in such circumstances.

5 Conclusion

As the case law of the ECJ has developed and matured, it seems now safe to say that the subjective conditions for direct effect do not pose a significant restriction in the environmental sphere. Individuals and NGOs can invoke

[348] See chapter 3, section 10.

provisions in EC environmental legislation in national courts without having to demonstrate that those rules confer subjective rights. Although there is a requirement for the plaintiff to show a relevant interest, this condition is fulfilled where the suit is intended to promote the interests protected by the Community rules, regardless of whether the provisions protect the plaintiff's individual interests. In other words, 'the question is whether the provision has entered the province of the judiciary and can be judicially enforced, irrespective of who is asking for it to be enforced'.[349]

A more pressing question is indeed whether the provision can be 'judicially enforced'. This hinges on whether the relevant rule is unconditional and sufficiently precise, which in turn must be assessed in light of the facts of the case and the purpose of the proceedings, ie review of legality or claims of result. Whether the direct effect doctrine should properly be reserved to the latter situation is, in my opinion, immaterial. The question is always whether the relevant rule can be made operational in the context of the particular case, and where this is answered in the affirmative the rule has direct effect. Another matter is that environmental provisions will thus more seldom be deemed capable of direct effect in claims proceedings, where the fulfilment of a particular result is sought, compared with cases revolving around review of discretion.

There is no disputing that EC environmental legislation, typically in the form of directives, confers more discretion on national authorities than in many other areas of Community law. Environmental law is characterized by minimum harmonization and modest emphasis is placed on uniformity. Open-ended objectives are regularly favoured over clearly delimited result obligations, and the national authorities usually have significant discretion in selecting the appropriate means to achieve these aims.

It is therefore all the more striking that the ECJ has nevertheless been very successful in making environmental provisions operational in legal proceedings concerning erroneous or inadequate implementation of environmental directives. Several of the cases documented in this chapter concerned environmental provisions which were vague or even conditional, but this did not prevent the ECJ from effectively policing the applicable margin of discretion or establishing failures to fulfil obligations in specific cases. The tenet of this case law is that, albeit the Member States have discretion to choose the means necessary to implement the directives, they are nevertheless under an obligation to achieve the requisite results. A failure to achieve

[349] Edward 2002, 12.

certain results therefore allows the ECJ to conclude that the Member States have not taken the appropriate measures. Although most of this progressive case law has occurred in the context of infringement proceedings, there is no reason why individuals cannot require national courts to make environmental provisions operational under similar terms.

But there are limits to what the ECJ and national courts can do in order to make environmental rules operational. This chapter has documented several instances where the relevant provisions could not be judicially enforced owing to their non-binding character, or where they conferred 'policy discretion' which could not be censored by the judiciary. In other cases the relevant provisions only allowed for a modest review of discretion, making the plaintiffs unable to require fulfilment of a particular result. Another matter is that even precisely worded provisions can be difficult to enforce, eg quality limit values, since they are often inherently difficult to verify factually. Other provisions stipulate clearly the content of the relevant obligation, but leave significant discretion as to when they must be fulfilled. To make matters worse, it appears that there is now a growing trend in environmental policy to move away from specified result obligations towards open-ended, flexible, and differentiated objectives, as well as excessive reliance on technical requirements – so-called means obligations – instead of result obligations. It is questionable, in my view, whether the benefits of such 'efficient' legislation outweigh the costs in terms of enforcement deficits.

Although the ECJ should be congratulated on its progressive case law, there is one strand of cases which gives rise to certain criticism. Where environmental directives stipulate open-ended objectives, the ECJ will only find an infringement where there has been a failure to achieve the objectives over a 'protracted period of time'. It is of course clear that the courts will find it more difficult to establish a failure to achieve vaguely phrased objectives, and that the threshold for an infringement is higher in this relation than in respect of clearly delimited result obligations. But it is difficult to see why, once a failure to achieve such objectives has been established, it should be allowed to continue for a protracted period of time before an infringement can be found.

The frequent usage of directives as the favoured type of legislation also means that the effectiveness of EC environmental law is vulnerable to the prohibition on horizontal direct effect. But although the ECJ has not been willing to change its principled view that obligations in non-transposed directives may not be imposed directly on individuals, it has through different constructions modified this doctrine. The ECJ has for instance transferred some prima facie horizontal cases to the domain of vertical direct effect by a progressive interpretation of 'emanations of state'. Another significant development is a relatively narrow interpretation of what amounts to 'direct obligations' imposed on individuals. Actions brought against national authorities which in turn have adverse spill-over effects on third parties do not fall foul of this test, but will normally, it seems, be considered 'mere adverse effects'. The ECJ has even allowed for direct effect in cases between private parties, in which the provisions were invoked for purposes of excluding national provisions incompatible with EC directives. The logic which seems to underpin this case law is that, when directives are invoked for purposes of excluding national law and the void is not filled with Community law, any obligations imposed upon individuals stems from national law. This reasoning suggests that environmentally concerned individuals and NGOs could invoke environmental provisions by virtue of the principle of consistent interpretation even if that means imposing obligations on individuals and private companies, since these consequences still stem from national law. This presupposes of course that the national law can be construed in a manner compatible with the relevant provisions, but it appears that the ECJ in practice has gone far in requiring quite liberal interpretations.

The possibility for individuals to rely on Community law is mirrored by an obligation on national courts and authorities to apply and enforce obligations in EC environmental law *ex officio*. National courts and authorities are therefore under a duty to apply directly effective provisions and the principle of consistent interpretation of their own motion, subject to the limits examined above.

3

Judicial review before national courts

1 Introduction

The direct effect doctrine does not entail an absolute right for plaintiffs to have recourse to judicial review and the remedies necessary to enforce Community obligations in national courts. In the absence of harmonization, the rules on procedures and remedies in national courts are in principle governed by domestic law. The ECJ has nevertheless articulated certain minimum requirements which the procedural laws of the Member States must satisfy. The ECJ has also construed autonomous EC remedies which must be applied uniformly in the Member States. Furthermore, the Community legislature has in recent years enacted some directives, with others that are still in the pipeline, which lay down procedural requirements for judicial enforcement of EC environmental law. This flurry of legislative activity has been inspired by the Community's accession to the Aarhus Convention.[1] The aim of this chapter is to analyse to what extent the ECJ's case law, the Aarhus Convention, and secondary Community legislation, ensure effective judicial enforcement of EC environmental law in national courts.

The chapter is organized as follows. Section 2 provides a general analysis of the principles arising from the ECJ's case law on procedures and remedies with a view to determining their relevance for the enforcement of EC environmental law. What follows is an introduction to the Aarhus Convention and the secondary legislation implementing the Aarhus Convention (section 3). This section also contains an analysis of the relation between the judicial protection guarantees that follow from the ECJ's case law, and the requirements embodied in the legislation implementing the Aarhus Convention

[1] See section 3.

(section 3.3). In light of these findings, the subsequent sections (sections 4–12) examine the requirements Community law places on Member States as regards the distinct elements that make out the anatomy of access to justice in environmental matters.

2 Jurisprudential harmonization of procedural law

2.1 *Introduction*

The general rule was articulated in *Rewe*: in the absence of harmonization, procedural law is left for the Member States.[2] Furthermore, as held in *Rewe II*, 'it [the Treaty] was not intended to create new remedies in the national courts to ensure observance of Community law other than those already laid down by national law'.[3] The ECJ has since made several far-reaching inroads into procedural autonomy of Member States, which has caused some commentators to substitute the notion of 'autonomy' with 'competence'.[4] What is clear in any event is that rules on procedures and remedies in national proceedings are now governed by Community law as well as domestic law. This section presents an overview of the principles that have informed the ECJ in its harmonization efforts, the substance of the minimum requirements they impose on Member States, and how the different principles relate individually.

Two important concepts discussed below should first be explained: 'procedural rules' and 'remedial rules'. Academics afford different meanings to them, and sometimes use the terms indiscriminately, or at times merely refer to 'procedural rules'. However, arguably there is a fundamental difference between the two types of rules, which warrants the use of different terms.[5] According to van Gerven, 'remedial rules' are laws and practices that 'govern the conditions, and restrictions, under which individuals are enabled to bring and maintain actions before courts of law'.[6] This covers rules regulating acts susceptible to judicial review, standing, grounds for review, and remedies (sections 5–11). 'Procedural rules', on the other hand, 'refers to the practical rules according to which a remedy is to be pursued in a court of law'.[7] This includes rules governing the role of judges in national proceedings, time

[2] Case 33/76 *Rewe* [1976] ECR 1989. [3] Case 158/80 *Rewe II* [1981] ECR 1805, para 44.
[4] Kakouris 1997. [5] Van Gerven 2000, 524.
[6] ibid. [7] ibid.

limits, *res judicata* and costs (section 4). In summary, remedial rules essentially regulate *whether* a certain suit may be brought and the sanctions/remedies available, whereas procedural rules essentially govern how suits are dealt with. The stringency of the requirements Community law places on Member States may therefore differ, depending on whether there is a restrictive procedural rule or a remedial rule, the latter being subject to closer Community scrutiny.[8]

2.2 *The principles*

There are several discrete principles from which the ECJ has derived its judicial harmonization. These principles differ in many respects, eg as concerns their legal basis, *raison d'être*, material application, and the stringency of the requirements they impose. For these reasons, it is necessary to differentiate between these principles, even though the ECJ has not always consistently taken account of their distinguishing features.

2.2.1 *The* Rewe *doctrine*

The *Rewe* doctrine was derived from the principle of loyal cooperation laid down in Article 5 of the Treaty (Article 10 EC).[9] Referring to this provision, the ECJ stated that it was for national courts to ensure the legal protection which citizens derived from the direct effect of Community law. The ECJ accepted that, in the absence of Community rules governing the matter, it was for the domestic legal system of each Member State to designate the courts and tribunals having jurisdiction, and to lay down the detailed procedural rules, but nevertheless laid down two minimum requirements which had to be fulfilled. First, Member States are required to offer procedural conditions for actions based on Community law that are not less favourable than those governing domestic cases and, secondly, that they do not make it 'virtually impossible' to exercise Community rights.[10] The second limb has since been rephrased and strengthened by requiring that the application of Community law is not made 'virtually impossible *or excessively difficult*'.[11]

[8] See to this effect opinion in Case C–453/00 *Kühne* [2004] ECR I–837, paras 70–72. See also van Gerven 1995, 693. A good overview of the principles is provided in the recent decision in Case C–423/05 *Unibet* [2006] OJ C36/23, paras 37–44.

[9] Eg Case 33/76 *Rewe* [1976] ECR 1989, para 5; Case 45/76 *Comet* [1976] ECR 2043, para 12.

[10] Eg Case 33/76 *Rewe* [1976] ECR 1989, para 5; Case 45/76 *Comet* [1976] ECR 2043, para 14; Case 68/79 *Hans Just* [1980] ECR 501, para 25; Case 199/82 *San Giorgio* [1983] ECR 3595, para 14.

[11] Eg Joined Cases 331, 376 and 378/85 *Bianco and Girard* [1988] ECR 1099, para 12; Joined Cases C–6 and 9/90 *Francovich and Others* [1991] ECR I–5357, para 43; Case C–312/93 *Peterbroeck* [1995] ECR I–4599, para 12; and Case C–78/98 *Preston and Others* [2000] ECR I–3201, para 31.

These two *Rewe* conditions are often referred to as the principle of equivalence and the principle of effectiveness, respectively.[12] The *Rewe* principle of effectiveness should not be confused with the *Simmenthal* principle of full effectiveness of EC law, discussed in the next section.[13] To avoid confusion, this chapter will therefore mostly refer to the *Rewe* doctrine, or the principle of 'impossibility' when specifically referring to the second limb of the *Rewe* formula.

Reference to the *Rewe* doctrine is usually initiated with the caveat that it is in principle for Member States to lay down the 'detailed procedural rules' governing proceedings in national courts, which suggests, according to van Gerven's definition, that the scope of the *Rewe* doctrine is limited to 'procedural rules' as opposed to 'remedial rules'. That may have been the original usage intended by the ECJ, as it was construed in respect of domestic time limits. But it has since also been invoked by the ECJ to review remedial rules, eg rules on locus standi,[14] provisions on causality and rules on the notion of damage,[15] and must now be considered to apply generally to both procedural and remedial rules which may impede application of EC law.

The fact that it concerns 'detailed procedural rules', which typically are not absolute obstacles to bringing a case before the courts, has nevertheless influenced the content and the application of this principle in the sense that relatively lenient conditions are placed on the Member States. This is evident from the fact that the ECJ in *Peterbroeck* and *Van Schijndel*, which both concerned the legality of national time limits, held that restrictive rules that prima facie could make the application of EC law excessively difficult could still be justified if they promoted a legitimate purpose, eg legal certainty or procedural economy.[16] This balancing of interests is more difficult to accept in respect of restrictive remedial rules which are absolute obstacles to enforcing claims effectively under EC law.[17] Indeed, as will be shown below, as regards this situation the ECJ has sometimes used principles other than the *Rewe* doctrine in order to require the disapplication of the national rule.

[12] Eg Case C–201/02 *Wells* [2004] ECR I–723, para 67.

[13] See also Prechal 2001, 48.

[14] Joined Cases C–87, 88 and 89/90 *Verholen* [1991] ECR I–3757, para 24.

[15] Joined Cases C–6 and 9/90 *Francovich* [1991] ECR 5357, para 43; and Joined Case C–46 and 48/93 *Brasserie du Pêcheur* [1996] ECR I–1029, para 67.

[16] Case C–312/93 *Peterbroeck* [1995] ECR I–4599, para 14; Joined Cases C–430 to 431/93 *Van Schijndel* ECR [1995] I–4705, para 19.

[17] Similarly, opinion in Case C–453/00 *Kühne* [2004] ECR I–837, paras 70–72.

2.2.2 *The* (Simmenthal) *principle of effectiveness of Community law*

The principle of effectiveness (*effet utile*) is a general principle of Community law, which the ECJ has applied in many different contexts, including review of national procedural law. It was one of several arguments presented as justification for the direct effect of Community law in *Van Gend & Loos*.[18] Since the principle of effectiveness is inherent to the EC Treaty the ECJ has not explicitly presented a legal basis for this principle. The court has nevertheless indicated that the principle is an expression of 'those requirements which are the essence of Community law',[19] and it is clear that its *raison d'être* is closely related to direct effect and the supremacy of EC law.[20] The ECJ could also have derived a basis for this principle from Article 220 EC, which implores the ECJ to 'ensure that [...] the interpretation and application of this Treaty is observed'.

The principle of effectiveness was first invoked for purposes of reviewing the compatibility with EC law of a national procedural rule in *Simmenthal*, where the ECJ ruled as follows:

> Any provisions of a national legal system and any legislative, administrative or judicial practice which might impair the effectiveness of Community law by withholding from the national courts having jurisdiction to apply such law the power to do everything necessary at the moment of its application to set aside national legislative provisions which might prevent Community rules from having full force and effect are incompatible with those requirements which are the essence of Community law.[21]

The ECJ has since applied the principle of effectiveness in several cases where it sought to remove obstacles to the application and precedence of Community law, and the procedure of Article 234 EC in particular, eg concerning national rules on standing,[22] interim relief,[23] and compensation for loss caused by contracts incompatible with EC law.[24] The principle of

[18] Case C–26/62 *Van Gend & Loos* [1963] ECR 1.

[19] Case 106/77 *Simmenthal* [1978] ECR 629, para 22.

[20] Tridimas 1999, 277.

[21] Case 106/77 *Simmenthal* [1978] ECR 629, para 22. Craufurd Smith 1999, 299, argues that *Simmenthal*, also on the basis of the facts, represented a more intrusive level of review as the rule in question merely resulted in a delay in the exercise of the Community rights, which is different from the earlier standard of 'practical impossibility'. For a different view, see AG Jacobs's opinion in Case C–312/93 *Peterbroeck* [1995] ECR I–4599, para 43, where he commented that the rule adjudicated upon in *Simmenthal* did make the exercise 'virtually impossible'.

[22] Case C–253/00 *Muñoz* [2002] ECR I–7289, para 28.

[23] C–213/89 *Factortame and Others* [1990] ECR I–2433, para 20.

[24] Case C–453/99 *Courage* [2001] ECR I–6297, para 25.

effectiveness was also invoked as justification for the doctrine of state liability and interim relief against Community acts.[25]

The application and scope of the *Simmenthal* principle of effectiveness differs in several respects from the *Rewe* doctrine. In general, the *Simmenthal* principle is primarily invoked when reviewing 'remedial rules', whereas the *Rewe* doctrine is often left to regulate 'procedural rules', although there are exceptions to this general rule in the case law. A typical example of this division of labour was provided in *Courage*.[26] The ECJ required with reference to the principle of full effectiveness of Community law, Article 81 EC in this case, that a national rule prohibiting a party to an illegal contract to claim compensation against the contracting party had to be set aside,[27] whilst subsequently accepting that some restrictions to such suits would be acceptable, subject to the *Rewe* doctrine.[28]

Another distinguishing feature is that, whereas the ECJ in recent case law often leaves it to national courts to examine whether national law satisfies the *Rewe* doctrine,[29] it usually applies the principle of effectiveness itself.[30] Furthermore, the ECJ has used the principle of effectiveness to construe positive remedies, eg the principle of state liability and interim relief against Community measures, in contrast to negative minimum requirements as laid down in the *Rewe* doctrine.

2.2.3 *The principle of effective judicial protection and control*

The ECJ has used many different phrases when referring to this doctrine, eg the right to effective judicial protection,[31] the right to effective judicial control,[32] or the right to an effective judicial remedy.[33] The right to an effective judicial remedy has been codified in the non-binding Charter of Fundamental Rights in the Nice Treaty, as well as Article II–107 in the not yet

[25] Joined Cases C–6 and 9/90 *Francovich* [1991] ECR 5357, para 32; and Joined Cases 143/88 and C–92/89 *Zuckerfabrik* [1991] ECR I–415, para 19.

[26] Case C–453/99 *Courage* [2001] ECR I–6297, paras 25–31. See also, in this respect, Joined Cases C–6 and 9/90 *Francovich* [1991] ECR 5357, paras 32–33 cf paras 42–43.

[27] Paras 25–26. [28] Paras 29–31. [29] Similarly, Biondi 2005, 138.

[30] See cases referred to in section 2.2.2.

[31] Eg Case 222/84 *Johnston* [1986] ECR 1651, para 18; Joined Cases C–87, 88 and 89/90 *Verholen and Others* [1991] ECR I–3757, para 24; Case C–50/00 P *UPA* [2002] ECR I–6677, para 39; and Case 13/01 *Safalero* [2003] ECR I–8679, para 50.

[32] Eg Case 222/86 *Heylens* [1987] ECR 4097, para 14; and Case C–97/91 *Borelli* [1992] ECR I–6313, para 13.

[33] Eg Case 222/84 *Johnston* [1986] ECR 1651, para 18; Joined Cases 23 to 25/04 *AEVE* [2006] ECR I–1265, para 28. See also, to this effect, Case C–213/89 *Factortame* [1990] ECR I–2433, paras 20–21.

ratified Treaty Establishing a Constitution for Europe.[34] We will interchangeably refer to the principle of effective judicial protection or control, which linguistically are the two broadest notions.

Although the principle of effective judicial protection has now been established as a Community law principle, in contrast to the above-mentioned principles, it was not derived from the system of the Treaty. Instead the ECJ held that the principle followed constitutional traditions common to the Member States and Articles 6 and 13 of the European Convention on Human Rights.[35]

The principle of effective judicial control has been invoked by the ECJ in a wide range of cases in order to disapply national rules which in some way undermined proper and effective judicial review, eg rules on evidence, standing, and the duty to state reasons.[36] Perhaps the most far-reaching application was in evidence in the *Borelli* case, in which the ECJ held that the principle of effective judicial control required national courts 'to review any definitive measure... which is capable of adversely affecting third parties and consequently to regard an action brought for that purpose as admissible even if the domestic rules of procedure do not provide for this in such a case'.[37] This principle was recently confirmed and elaborated upon in *Unibet*.[38] The Member States need not provide for an abstract review of whether national provisions are compatible with Community law as long as they may be reviewed as a preliminary issue, eg in damages suits, in judicial review of individuals decisions, or in administrative or criminal proceedings. On the other hand, if individuals were forced to be subject to administrative or criminal proceedings as the sole legal remedy for disputing the compatibility of national regulations with Community law, that would not be sufficient to ensure effective judicial protection.

Although the core of the principle of effective judicial protection prima facie concerns the obligation for Member States to extend the remedies necessary for individuals effectively to enforce the rights conferred upon them by Community law, it also contains a punitive element that arguably is aimed less at protecting rights per se, but rather at preventing (future) infringements of EC law. Thus, in *Von Colson*, the ECJ held in respect of Article 6 of Directive 76/207/EEC (equal treatment),[39] which obliged the Member

[34] It is noteworthy that the Treaty Establishing a Constitution for Europe implements the Charter of Fundamental Rights as laying down binding obligations [2004] OJ C310/1.

[35] Case 222/84 *Johnston* [1986] ECR 1651, para 18.

[36] See references in footnotes 31–33.

[37] Case C–97/91 *Borelli* [1992] ECR I–6313, para 13.

[38] Case C–432/05 *Unibet* [2006] OJ C36/23, paras 48–65.

[39] [1976] OJ L39/40.

States to allow victims of discrimination to 'pursue their claims by judicial process', that that provision also entailed an obligation to impose *sanctions* that guaranteed real and effective judicial protection, as well as having a *deterrent* effect.[40] Hence, the ECJ interpreted the judicial protection ensured by Article 6 as having a two-fold aim: first, to protect victims of discrimination and, secondly, to prevent future infringements of the directive. Although the ECJ derived this from Article 6 of Directive 76/207/EEC, it has since held that that provision is an expression of the principle of judicial protection.[41] It follows that the obligation to provide adequate and deterrent sanctions should be seen as part of the principle of effective judicial protection.

The ECJ's use of the principle of effective judicial control is in many ways similar to that of the *Simmenthal* principle of effectiveness. It is regularly applied in respect of national rules which directly undermine effective judicial review, and where a conflict with this principle is established the ECJ requires the national court to disregard the national rules without further ado.[42] Detailed procedural rules, eg time limits and so forth, are usually examined in the light of the *Rewe* doctrine, and not the principle of effective judicial control. Furthermore, the ECJ often provides clear guidance on whether the relevant rule undermines judicial protection compared with the regularly more deferential application of the *Rewe* doctrine, where the matter is usually left to the national court to assess. However, this of course does not mean that national courts are not bound by this principle in areas where the ECJ has not rendered a ruling on national law. The principle of judicial control is derived from traditions common to the Member States, and national courts must therefore apply this principle, if necessary of their own motion.[43]

The similarities between the principle of effective judicial protection and the principle of effectiveness have led some authors not to differentiate between the two principles, but generally place them under the umbrella 'principle of effective judicial protection'.[44] However, the legal justification for the two principles is as seen different, and the ECJ formally distinguishes the two principles by its coherent reference to two distinct strands of case law.[45] Some commentators have suggested that the ECJ established the principle of effective judicial protection – instead of continuing to rely

[40] Case 14/83 *Von Colson* [1984] ECR 1891, paras 22–23.
[41] Case C–185/97 *Coote* [1998] ECR I–5199, para 21.
[42] Eg Case C–97/91 *Borelli* [1992] ECR I–6313, para 13.
[43] Chapter 2, section 4, and section 4.2. below.
[44] Prechal 2001, 42–43.
[45] Cf references in section 2.2.2 above.

on the principle of effectiveness or the *Rewe* doctrine – as a response to fears and criticism from national courts and Member States that the Community was obsessed with the well-functioning of the internal market to the detriment of fundamental human rights.[46] By construing a principle of effective judicial protection derived directly from traditions common to the Member States and the ECHR in particular, the ECJ sought to address such fears.

2.2.4 *The principle of coherence and the principle of a complete system of remedies*

The ECJ has on occasion justified inroads into Member States' procedural autonomy with reference to the need to ensure a coherent system of procedures and remedies in the EC. This pertains to the shared competence between national and Community courts to adjudicate on Community matters. The ECJ has held in several cases that EC law requires that the legal protection of individuals remains the same, irrespective whether they contest the compatibility of national measures with Community law or the legality of Community acts. This view is justified with reference to the fact that both cases are based on Community law.[47] This 'parallelist' form of argumentation has been employed, inter alia, in the fields of interim relief, state liability, and judicial review.[48] But although the words 'remain the same' indicate that the conditions must be uniform, the ECJ has indicated that national courts remain free to offer judicial relief under more lenient conditions than those applied by the Community courts.[49] The principle of coherence therefore is a reverse application of the principle of equivalence, in that national courts must, as a minimum, offer as effective judicial relief as that available before the Community courts.[50]

Closely related is the principle of a complete system of legal remedies and procedures. This principle essentially requires that Community acts can be made subject to judicial control, either through direct actions before the

[46] Jacobs 2004, 309.

[47] Joined Cases 143/88 and C–92/89 *Zuckerfabrik* [1991] ECR I–415, para 20; Case C–465/93 *Atlanta* [1995] ECR I–3761, para 24; and Joined Cases C–46 and 48/93 *Brasserie du Pêcheur* [1996] ECR I–1029, para 42.

[48] ibid, and Case C–120/97 *Upjohn* [1999] ECR I–223, paras 34–35.

[49] Joined Cases C–46 and 48/93 *Brasserie du Pêcheur* [1996] ECR I–1029, para 66; and Case C–120/97 *Upjohn* [1999] ECR I–223, para 35. With regard to interim relief against acts by the Community institutions, however, the court has seemingly enacted total harmonization in the sense that national courts cannot apply less stringent conditions than the court; see discussion in section 9.2 cf chapter 4, section 4.6.

[50] De Búrca and Ryall 2002, 155.

Community courts, or by virtue of preliminary references from national courts.[51] Whilst one would think that the principle of a complete system would require both Community courts and national courts to make efforts to ensure effective judicial control, the ECJ has nonetheless been more demanding as regards national courts' responsibilities. In *Greenpeace*, for instance, the ECJ indicated that it was not necessary to liberalize its own standing rules under Article 230 EC, since the plaintiffs were ensured judicial relief in national courts and could, if necessary, request a preliminary reference.[52] The *UPA* case demonstrated even more clearly that the principle of a complete system is a one-way street. Instead of liberalizing its standing conditions, the ECJ this time explicitly said that it was for the Member States to ensure a system of legal remedies and procedure which ensured the right of judicial protection.[53] It then compelled the national court, ironically with reference to the principle of sincere cooperation, to interpret, in as far as possible, its national law so as to allow for the law suit in question, and thus allow for a preliminary reference on the validity of the disputed Community act.[54]

2.3 *Relevance for EC environmental law*

Having examined the basic tenet of the principles concerning remedies and procedures in national courts, the fundamental question that remains to be answered is to what extent these principles are applicable in environmental cases.

The answer appears relatively straightforward in as far as the *Simmenthal* principle of effectiveness is concerned. This principle does not refer to the protection of individual rights, but seeks to ensure the full and effective application of Community law. It follows from the nature (and name) of that principle that its objective is to ensure effective enforcement of EC law, and that it is irrelevant whether the rules confer individual rights.

The situation is slightly more complex in respect of the *Rewe* doctrine, which calls upon Member States to ensure the legal protection of individuals'

[51] Eg Case 314/85 *Foto-Frost* [1987] ECR 4199, para 16; Case 294/83 *Les Verts* [1986] ECR 1339, para 23; Case C-50/00 P *UPA* [2002] ECR I-6677, para 40; and Case C-491/01 *British American Tobacco* [2002] ECR I-11453, para 39.

[52] Case C-321/95 *Greenpeace and Others v Commission* [1998] ECR I-1651, paras 32-33. See also chapter 5, section 2.3.

[53] Para 41. For a scathing criticism of the judgment on this point, see Arnull 2002.

[54] Case C-50/00 P *UPA* [2002] ECR I-667, paras 41-42. See further comment in chapter 5, section 2.3.

rights. This begs the question whether *Rewe* refers to subjective rights or procedural rights that individuals derive from direct effect. It is necessary in this respect to distinguish between the two limbs in the *Rewe* doctrine. The first limb, the principle of equivalence, is nothing but a specific use of the general principle of non-discrimination, which applies generally in EC law. Member States must therefore clearly extend the same procedures and remedies to environmental actions brought under Community law as under national environmental law, regardless of whether the provisions concern individual rights. The second limb, in contrast, prima facie revolves around individual rights, in the sense that their exercise may not be made excessively difficult. However, if the reference to rights should be understood in the narrow sense, the principle of impossibility in any event applies to actions brought to enforce environmental provisions that protect public health.[55] This has been confirmed in the jurisprudence concerning Directive 85/337/EEC which according to its preamble seeks to protect environment and public health – although, interestingly, the public health dimension was not an issue in these cases.[56]

The remaining question is therefore whether the principle of impossibility may also be invoked against national rules restricting enforcement of Community rules that protect pure environmental interests, eg protection of species and habitats. Advocate General Kokott opined in *Waddenzee* that the *Rewe* test could not be applied in relation to national standing rules in proceedings brought under Directive 92/43/EC, since that directive did not confer (subjective) rights on the plaintiffs.[57] The ECJ unfortunately omitted to comment on this specific issue.

But there are, in my view, several elements in the general body of case law that suggest a broader application of the *Rewe* doctrine than that favoured by AG Kokott. First, it is noteworthy that when the ECJ created the doctrine it referred to the need for legal protection of rights which individuals 'acquired from the direct effect of Community law'.[58] Later case law often refers to rights which individuals 'derive directly from Community law'[59] or

[55] See, by implication, eg Case C–361/88 *Commission v Germany* [1990] ECR I–2567, para 16; Case C–59/89 *Commission v Germany* [1991] ECR I–2607, para 19; and Case C–58/89 *Commission v Germany* [1991] ECR I–4983, para 14.

[56] Case C–72/95 *Kraaijeveld* [1996] ECR I–5403, paras 57–58; and Case C–201/02 *Wells* [2004] ECR I–723, para 67.

[57] Opinion in Case C–127/02 *Waddenzee* [2004] ECR I–7405, paras 142–42.

[58] Eg Case 45/76 *Comet* [1976] ECR 2043, para 12.

[59] Eg Case C–453/99 *Courage* [2001] ECR I–6297, para 29.

rights which are 'conferred by the Community legal order'.[60] The phrasing in these cases indicates that the notion of 'rights' should be understood in procedural fashion, ie those rights that individuals derive from the direct effect of the Community legal order. Since the ECJ in recent case law has made clear that provisions pertaining to pure environmental protection, eg Directive 92/43/EC, are also capable of producing direct effect from which individuals can derive rights,[61] it should follow that the *Rewe* doctrine must be extended to such cases. Secondly, the seminal *Peterbroeck* and *Van Schijndel* rulings on the interpretation of the *Rewe* doctrine rephrased the question as to whether national rules make the exercise of 'rights' excessively difficult to one whether national procedural provisions render *application of Community law* impossible or excessively difficult.[62] For these reasons, both limbs of the *Rewe* doctrine must be considered applicable in respect of any claim based on EC environmental law, regardless of whether the provision in question as to concerns human health or pure environmental protection, the only criterion being that the provision can be made operational in national courts.

This conclusion gains implicit support from the recent ruling in *Bund Naturschutz*, in which an environmental organization invoked Directive 92/43/EC with the aim of halting the construction of a highway through sensitive forest habitats.[63] The ECJ answered affirmatively that the national authorities had to take all necessary measures available under national law in order to prevent seriously compromising the habitats, and that that obligation was subject to the *Rewe* principles of equivalence and effectiveness.[64] The corollary of this ruling is that *Bund Naturschutz* can invoke the *Rewe* doctrine if the national authorities subsequently fail to adhere to the ECJ ruling,[65] and the same should apply if there are procedural restrictions for bringing such an action.

Perhaps the most difficult question is whether the principle of effective judicial protection applies to environmental actions in the absence of infringements

[60] Case C–201/02 *Wells* [2004] ECR I–723, para 29.

[61] Eg Case C–127/02 *Waddenzee* [2004] ECR I–7405, paras 66–69: and, by implication, Case C–117/03 *Dragaggi* [2005] ECR I–167; and Case C–244/05 *Bund Naturschutz* [2006] ECR I–8445. See chapter 2, section 2.1.4.2.

[62] Case C–312/93 *Peterbroeck* [1995] ECR I–4599, para 14; and Joined Cases C–430 and 431/93 *Van Schijndel* [1995] ECR I–4705, para 19.

[63] Case C–244/05 *Bund Naturschutz* [2006] ECR I–8445.

[64] ibid para 50.

[65] Subject to the assessment of the national court as to whether the highway would actually seriously compromise the habitats in question.

of individual rights. Since this principle was derived from ECHR, it could be argued that it primarily applies to suits based on the protection of human rights, excluding environmental provisions with a more distant relationship to protection of individual rights. And since the principle of effective judicial protection is based on principles common to the Member States, it might be argued that the notion of rights should in this context not be linked to direct effect in the fashion argued above in respect of the *Rewe* doctrine.

However, it is noteworthy that Article II–37 of the Charter of Fundamental Rights and Fundamental Freedoms includes environmental protection. Furthermore, there are aspects in the case law suggesting that the principle of effective judicial protection is in any event not limited to ensuring protection of individuals' rights. As was pointed out, the ECJ does not consistently refer to the principle of effective judicial protection, but sometimes refers to the principle of effective judicial control instead.[66] The notion of judicial control encompasses more than merely protecting individual rights. Instead, it pertains more generally to ensuring that Member States implement and apply Community law correctly. It is also important to recall that the principle of judicial control entails imposition of sanctions which have a deterrent effect,[67] which is focused less on the protection of individual rights than on ensuring the effectiveness of Community law.

This interpretation is supported by a recent extra judicial writing by AG Jacobs, in which he sums up the evolution of the legal order of the Community. At a general level, he argues that:

> The court's approach, historically at any rate, has not been to promote the rights of individuals for their own sake or as a matter of ideology; its approach has been essentially pragmatic and the recognition of individuals' rights has been almost instrumental, being necessary to ensure the effectiveness of the legal order.[68]

More specifically in respect of the principle of judicial protection, he notes:

> [I]n response to pressure from national courts [...] the court declares that a guarantee of fundamental rights can be derived from the Treaty, so that the court itself can determine the contours of protection within the EC legal order – and the effect is to reduce the risk of challenge to the primacy of EC law, so the court's approach might again be seen as inspired in part by concerns for effectiveness and pragmatic considerations.[69]

[66] Case 222/84 *Johnston* [1986] ECR 1651, para 18, and in Case 222/86 *Heylens* [1987] ECR 4097, para 14; Case C–97/91 *Borelli* [1992] ECR I–6313, para 14.
[67] Section 2.2.3.
[68] Jacobs 2004, 308.
[69] ibid 309.

For all these reasons, the conclusion must be that the principle of effective judicial protection/control applies to any suits where plaintiffs are seeking to enforce Community rules for the protection of the environment.

As regards the characteristics of the other principles mentioned above – the principle of coherence and the principle of a complete system of remedies and procedures – it is important that they are both concerned with safeguarding the system of judicial control ensured by the Treaty. It is therefore clear that these principles apply to the enforcement of Community law in general, including EC environmental law.

2.4 *Rule of reason and proportionality*

In respect of the *Simmenthal* principle of effectiveness and the principle of effective judicial control, in principle there are no exceptions. If a national rule is found to fall short of these standards, national courts are compelled to disapply it in the case at hand without further ado. This has traditionally been the situation in respect of the *Rewe* doctrine as well, but a more nuanced test was introduced by the *Peterbroeck* and *Van Schijndel* rulings.[70] In these cases, the ECJ held that when examining whether a domestic procedural rule makes the application of Community law 'excessively difficult', the national court must in particular take into account:

> [T]he role of that provision in the procedure, its progress and its special features, viewed as a whole, before the various national instances. In the light of that analysis the basic principles of the domestic judicial system, such as protection of the rights of the defence, the principle of legal certainty and the proper conduct of procedure, must, where appropriate, be taken into consideration.[71]

In the wake of these rulings, several commentators[72] have argued that the ECJ introduced a 'rule of reason' similar to the doctrine of mandatory requirements introduced in relation to Article 28 EC in *Cassis de Dijon*.[73] It could seem at first sight that the so-called rule of reason inherent in the *Peterbroeck* and *Van Schijndel* rulings represents a more deferential attitude from the ECJ, by conferring on Member States the possibility to justify provisions which otherwise

[70] Case C–312/93 *Peterbroeck* [1995] ECR I–4599; and Joined Cases C–430 and 431/93 *Van Schijndel* ECR [1995] I–4705.

[71] Case C–312/93 *Peterbroeck* ibid, para 14; and Joined Cases C–430 and 431/93 *Van Schijndel* ibid, para 19. A similar test has been devised for the principle of equivalence: see Case C–326/96 *Levez* [1998] ECR I–7835, paras 41–44 and Case C–78/98 *Preston* [2000] ECR I–3201, paras 61–62.

[72] Prechal 1998, 691; and van Gerven 2000, 533.

[73] Case 120/78 *Rewe (Cassis de Dijon)* [1979] ECR 649.

might be deemed in breach of the 'excessively difficult' test.[74] However, the corollary of a certain parallelism between the *Peterbroeck* and *Van Schijndel* judgments and the mandatory requirements doctrine seems to be that the threshold for prima facie infringements must be lowered, as happened mutatis mutandis in *Dassonville*[75] and *Cassis de Dijon*.[76] In other words, the scope of national rules that prima facie makes the application of Community law excessively difficult should be extended in a similar fashion as the notion of national measures having equivalent effects to quantitative restrictions was broadened by the court in relation to Article 28 EC, given that the national courts in both relations can uphold the national rules under the rule of reason test.

In addition, it has been argued that the ECJ is likely to scrutinize national procedural laws with different intensity, depending on the aim and importance of the Community right the exercise of which is being restricted by national procedural law.[77] However, nothing in the excerpt derived above from *Peterbroeck* suggests that the balancing formula places any relevance on the *right* in question. The balancing to be conducted by national courts amounts to weighing the restrictive impact of the procedural rule in question against any legitimate functions or purposes it promotes.[78]

Even if there is a weighing of different Community interests influencing the intensity of the ECJ's review of national procedural laws, it seems clear that environmental protection would carry as much weight as any other Community policy area. The ECJ has on several occasions stressed that protection of the environment constitutes one of the essential objectives of the Community.[79] Furthermore, Article 2 EC states that the Community has as its task to promote 'a high level of protection and improvement of the quality of the environment', whilst Article 6 EC provides that '[e]nvironmental protection requirements must be integrated into the definition and implementation of the Community policies and activities'. Indeed, the ECJ ruled recently that Article 6 'emphasises the fundamental nature of that objective [high level of protection] and its extension across the range of those policies and activities.[80] It is also noteworthy that in a recent order concerning

[74] In a plea in favour of deference to national procedural law, Biondi has commented that 'the Peterbroeck and Van Schijndel test should offer the ECJ a sensible "escape route" '; see Biondi 2005, 137.

[75] Case 8/74 *Dassonville* [1974] ECR 837.

[76] Case 120/78 *Rewe (Cassis de Dijon)* [1979] ECR 649.

[77] Craig and de Burca 2003, 252.

[78] Similarly, Prechal 1998, 690.

[79] Case 240/83 *ADBHU* [1985] ECR 531, para 13; Case 302/86 *Commission v Denmark* [1988] ECR 4607, para 8; Case C–213/96 *Outokumpu* [1998] ECR I–1777, para 32; and Case C–176/03 *Commission v Council* [2005] ECR I–7879, para 41.

[80] Case C–176/03 *Commission v Council* [2005] ECR I–7879, para 42.

interim relief the president of the court held that interests linked to environmental protection must as a rule prevail over economic considerations.[81]

3 The Aarhus Convention and implementing EC legislation

3.1 *The Aarhus Convention*

The United Nations Economic Commission for Europe (UNECE) Convention on Access to Information, Public Participation in Decision-making and Access to Justice in Environmental Matters was adopted on 25 June 1998 in the Danish City of Aarhus, from which it derives its popular name. The Aarhus Convention entered into force on 30 October 2001, and was approved by the Community on 17 February 2005 through Decision 2005/370/EC.[82] The Member States, except for Ireland, have also ratified Aarhus independently from the Community.[83]

As the title of the convention indicates, the Aarhus Convention consists of three distinct parts – often referred to as the three pillars. The first concerns information, the second relates to public participation, and the third pertains to access to justice. In line with the ambit of this study, I shall focus on the third pillar. Article 9, which regulates the conditions for access to justice, may be further divided into three mini-pillars. Article 9(1) concerns access to justice in relation to acts and omissions concerning information, Article 9(2) does the same for public participation, whilst Article 9(3) is the general provision regarding access to justice, which regulates all matters not falling within Article 9(1)–(2). In view of the specific examination of these provisions in the following sections, it suffices to note here that the most stringent requirements are found in Article 9(1), whilst Article 9(2) and in particular Article 9(3) offer a significant margin of discretion for the Community and the Member States. But this discretion is to some extent limited by virtue of Article 9(4), which requires that the procedures shall provide 'adequate and effective remedies, including injunctive relief as appropriate, and be fair, equitable, timely and not prohibitively expensive'.

81 Case C–320/03 R *Commission v Austria* [2003] ECR I–11665, para 58.
82 [2005] OJ L124/1. 83 By March 2007.

3.2 *Community implementation*

The first pillar of Aarhus is implemented through Directive 2003/4/EC on Public Access to Information,[84] whilst Community legislation concerning the second pillar is found in various directives, eg Directives 85/337/EEC[85] (EIA) and 96/61/EC (IPPC),[86] as well as Directive 2001/42/EC[87] (SEA) and 2000/60 (WFD).[88] A Commission proposal for a Directive on Access to Justice in Environmental Matters (the proposed directive on access to justice) was brought forward in 2003,[89] but the Council has not yet concluded its first reading, and its future looks uncertain.[90] Indeed, the declaration annexed to Decision 2005/370/EC concluding the Aarhus Convention on behalf of the Community stated that the 'legal instruments in force do not cover fully the implementation of the obligations resulting from Article 9(3) [...] and that, consequently, [the] Member States are responsible for the performance of these obligations'.[91] The declaration stated furthermore that the Member States will 'remain so [responsible] unless and until the Community [...] adopts provisions of Community law covering the implementation of its obligations'.[92] Provisions on access to justice are nevertheless found in some of the above-mentioned directives implementing Aarhus, eg Directives 85/337/EEC and 96/61/EC,[93] whilst other directives contain such provisions seemingly independently of Aarhus, eg Directive 2004/35/EC on Environmental Liability.[94] The Community has also recently adopted Regulation 1367/2006 on the Application of the Provisions of the Aarhus Convention to Community Institutions and Bodies,[95] which is examined in chapter 5 in relation to enforcement of EC environmental law at the Community level.

3.3 *Jurisprudential harmonization v the Aarhus Convention and implementing legislation*

As will be recalled from chapter 2, it follows from the primacy of international agreements concluded by the Community over provisions of secondary

84 [2003] OJ L41/26.

85 [1985] OJ L175/40, as amended by Directive 97/11 [1997] OJ L73/5 and Directive 2003/35 [2003] L156/17.

86 [1996] OJ L257/26.

87 [2001] OJ L197/30

88 [2000] OJ L327/1.

89 COM(2003) 624.

90 Similarly, Dross 2005, 22.

91 [2005] OJ L124/3.

92 ibid.

93 Section 6.3.

94 The preamble to Directive 2004/35 fails to mention the Aarhus Convention; see also analysis in section 10.2.

95 [2006] OJ L264/13.

Community legislation that such provisions must, as far as possible, be interpreted in conformity with those agreements.[96] The above-mentioned directives must accordingly be interpreted consistently with the Aarhus Convention. Where this is not possible, individuals may be able to invoke provisions in the Aarhus Convention directly, if the relevant provisions are found to have direct effect.[97]

The ECJ's case law on minimum requirements concerning procedures and remedies may similarly have to be interpreted in conformity with the Aarhus Convention, if this is necessary in order to fulfil the Community's obligations.[98] One might question, moreover, if the ECJ's case law remains applicable in areas where the Community has adopted legislation that harmonizes procedures and remedies in environmental matters. This is of course particularly relevant if the proposed directive on access to justice in environmental matters is adopted. One might instinctively draw this conclusion from the fact that the ECJ has fleshed out its judicial protection doctrine with the caveat of absence of Community harmonization.[99]

However, it is clear that the judicial protection principles laid down in the ECJ's case law will continue to apply if they provide a higher level of protection than harmonizing legislation in force. This follows from the fact that the procedural and remedial requirements imposed on Member States by the ECJ have been derived from the system of the Treaty and Article 10 EC, and these principles are *lex superior* to secondary legislation concerning harmonization of procedures and remedies.[100] It is noteworthy in this respect that the principle of coherence requires secondary Community legislation to be interpreted in accordance with the general principles of Community law.[101] This is important since, as we shall see, the jurisprudential harmonization of procedures and remedies in many respects is more progressive than the minimum requirements laid down in Community legislation.[102]

[96] Chapter 2, section 4.

[97] Chapter 2, section 2.2.1.

[98] Albeit this duty cannot be based on primacy; see below in this section.

[99] Section 2 above.

[100] On the relationship between the jurisprudential guarantees flowing from the ECJ's case law and the provisions on access to justice under Directive 2004/35 on environmental liability; see section 10.6 and Wennerås 2005, 264–65.

[101] Case C–1/02 *Borgmann* [2004] ECR I–3219, para 30; Case C–499/04 *Werhof* [2006] ECR I–2397, para 32.

[102] See conclusion in section 13.

4 Procedural requirements

4.1 *Introduction*

This section examines the requirements that Community law places on different types of national procedural rules, ie 'the practical rules according to which a remedy is pursued in a court of law'.[103] We shall first assess the compatibility of national rules preventing national judges to raise questions concerning Community law *ex officio* (section 4.2), followed by an analysis of the legitimacy of temporal restrictions (sections 4.3–4.4) as well as rules on costs in judicial proceedings (section 4.5).

4.2 *Passive role of judges*

Article 10 EC obliges national courts to raise issues pertaining to Community law of their own motion in so far as they have such powers under domestic law.[104] The question examined here is to what extent this obligation also applies in situations where domestic law does not afford courts such discretion. This is particularly relevant in civil proceedings between private parties, where principles of procedural law often dictate that national courts play a passive role. The compatibility of such a rule with the *Rewe* doctrine was at issue in the *Van Schijndel* case.[105] The ECJ first noted that the Dutch rule in question – according to which it was for the parties in civil proceedings to define the ambit of the dispute and the national court being able to act of its own motion only in exceptional cases where the public interest required its intervention – was common to most of the Member States, and served the purpose of safeguarding rights of the defence and ensuring proper conduct of proceedings.[106] The ECJ accordingly concluded that Community law did not preclude a national rule hindering the national court from raising an issue of EC law in civil proceedings 'where examination of that issue would oblige them to abandon the passive role assigned to them by going beyond the ambit of the dispute defined by the parties themselves and relying on facts and circumstances other than those on which the party with interest in application of those provisions bases his claim'.[107]

[103] Section 2.1. [104] Chapter 2, section 4.
[105] Joined Cases C-430 to 431/93 *Van Schijndel* [1995] ECR I-4705. [106] Para 21.
[107] Para 22.

Although the ECJ thus upheld the national rule, careful reading of the judgment reveals two implicit reservations. First, it would seem to follow, conversely, that Community law requires that national courts must still be allowed to raise issues of their own motion *within* the ambit of the dispute. Furthermore, it is arguable that it falls to Community law to delimit that motion. In the case at hand, it was obvious that the question of whether a collective pension fund was in breach of EC competition law was outside the ambit of the dispute, as the sole question discussed before the lower courts was whether the fund violated national law. But it is easy to imagine cases where it is more difficult to determine the ambit of the dispute. Take the example of a NGO challenging a permit on the grounds that it has been granted in breach of certain provisions in Directive 85/337/EEC. Is the ambit of the dispute EC environmental law, Directive 85/337/EEC, or the specific provisions on which the claim is based? These questions are not conclusively resolved by *Van Schijndel.* The matter has been raised more explicitly in the pending case *Van der Weerd*, which will give the ECJ an opportunity to provide further clarification.[108]

Secondly, the ECJ seemingly upheld the national rule in *Van Schijndel*, inter alia, because it allowed national courts to act of their own motion 'where the public interest requires its intervention'. This raises the question of what legal issues should be regarded as matters of 'public interest'. The Dutch Supreme Court subsequently asked for an interpretation of this concept in the *Eco-Swiss* case,[109] albeit in a different context from that of *Van Schijndel.* The case concerned an application for annulment of an arbitration award, which had been delivered without considering whether the agreement in question was in breach of Article 85 EC (ex Article 81 EC). According to Dutch law, a national court could only grant such an application on grounds of public policy, which according to domestic law did not include breaches of competition law. The ECJ pointed out, however, that 'according to Article 3(g) of the EC Treaty [Article 3(1)(g) EC], Article 85 of the Treaty [Article 81 EC] constitutes a fundamental provision which is essential for the accomplishment of the task entrusted to the Community' and it followed therefore that where domestic law required the national court to act on the basis of 'public policy', it had to act in response to breaches of Article 85 EC

[108] Case C–222/05, pending. The case concerns interpretation of certain provisions in Directive 85/111, and the question is whether the national court is obliged to examine grounds which are outside the specific terms of dispute, but which nevertheless are based on the directive.

[109] Case C–126/97 *Eco-Swiss* [1999] ECR I–3055.

(Article 81 EC).[110] The ruling begs the question whether the same line of reasoning may be applied as regards some of the Community policies listed in Article 3 EC. The question is controversial and some scholars have adopted a narrow interpretation of *Eco-Swiss* and the provisions in the EC Treaty which should properly be deemed 'fundamental' for these purposes.[111] However, the recent ruling in *Mostaza Claro* extended the *Eco-Swiss* principle to consumer protection, which constitutes 'according to Article 3(1)(t) EC, a measure which is essential to the accomplishment of of the tasks entrusted to the Community'.[112] This should apply mutatis mutandis to infringements of EC environmental law, which by virtue of Article 3(l)(l) EC is similarly considered one of the fundamental public polices entrusted to the Community. The fact that both cases concerned judicial review of awards by arbitration panels, which are not courts or tribunals for the purposes of Community law and which may therefore not refer preliminary questions to the ECJ, may nevertheless limit the judgments' general relevance – both as regards the principle of effectiveness and the principle of equivalence.[113]

Furthermore, the compatibility of national rules restricting national courts from raising issues based on Community law of their own motion are not only subject to the negative requirements flowing from the *Rewe* doctrine, but may also have to be scrutinized in the light of obligations in specific secondary legislation.[114] The *Océano*[115] case concerned a dispute in civil proceedings between buyers and sellers of encyclopaedias. The contract between the parties stipulated that the court having jurisdiction should be determined on the basis of the domicile of the sellers. The national court considered that this clause could constitute an unfair contract term, in breach of Directive 93/13/EC, but under Spanish law it was doubtful whether the national court could decline jurisdiction on its own initiative in proceedings between private parties. The question put to the ECJ was therefore whether Directive 93/13/EC obliged national courts to determine of their own motion whether a contract term was unfair. The ECJ answered this affirmatively, since this constituted the proper means both of achieving the result

110 Paras 36–37.

111 Prechal 2005, 163 who interprets *Eco-Swiss* narrowly on the basis of the facts of the case. The debate has been particularly thorough in the Netherlands; for references to literature see Jans 2005a, 10–12.

112 Case C–168/05 *Mostaza Claro* [2006] ECR I–10421, paras 35–38.

113 See opinion in Joined Cases C–222 to 225 *van der Weerd and Others* [2005] C193/12, paras 28 and 35–37.

114 Although this might raise questions concerning the prohibition on horizontal direct effect in relation to non-transposed directives, see Joined Cases C–240 to 244/98, *Océano* [2000] ECR I–4941, paras 30–32.

115 Joined Cases C–240 to 244/98 *Océano* [2000] ECR I–4941.

sought by the directive (protecting individuals against unfair contract terms) and contributed to achieving its aim (deterring and preventing such terms).[116]

In reaching this conclusion the ECJ also pointed out certain issues which are equally relevant in respect of environmental directives. It noted, for instance, that it was crucial that national courts could raise issues under Directive 93/13/EC of its own motion since consumers are generally in a weaker position than sellers in terms of knowledge, whilst the often limited amounts involved may deter them from seeking expensive legal advice.[117] Furthermore, the ECJ noted that the system of protection laid down by Directive 93/13/EC required the imbalance between the parties to the contract to be levelled out, inter alia, by allowing authorized consumer associations to take action in the general interests of consumers at large. The ECJ inferred from this fact that:

> [i]t is hardly conceivable that, in a system requiring the implementation of specific group actions of a preventive nature intended to put a stop to unfair terms detrimental to consumers' interests, a court hearing a dispute on a specific contract containing an unfair term should not be able to set aside application of the relevant term solely because the consumer has not raised the fact that it is unfair. On the contrary, the court's power to determine of its own motion whether a term is unfair must be regarded as constituting a proper means [...] of achieving the result [of the directive].[118]

This line of reasoning, which was confirmed in *Mostaza Claro*,[119] is equally relevant in respect of environmental directives which have conferred upon environmental associations the task to represent the general interests of members of the public, eg Directives 85/337/EEC, 96/61/EC, and 2004/35/EC.[120]

4.3 *Time limits*

Procedural law contains a variety of time limits which may preclude or limit the effectiveness of Community law. There are always certain time limits within which judicial proceedings must be brought, and there are also time limits for bringing administrative appeal proceedings which may in turn preclude judicial appeal. Time limits may also influence the substance of the proceedings in so far as national law places certain retroactive limitations on the plaintiff's claims.

Whether such rules are incompatible with Community law must be assessed on a case by case basis, having regard to the conditions of the rules

[116] Para 28. [117] Paras 25–26. [118] Para 28.

[119] Case C–168/05 *Mostaza Claro* [2006] ECR I–10421, paras 25–30.

[120] See sections 6.4 and 10.2.

and the circumstances of the case, and no standard answer can be derived from the ECJ's case law.[121] As is well known, the *Emmot*[122] ruling has been interpreted narrowly, arguably on the basis of its particular facts,[123] and the ECJ will examine the legitimacy of time limits ad hoc in light of the principles of equivalence and effectiveness.

Some general observations can still be made, however. First of all, the ECJ will automatically require disapplication of time limits where it may be inferred that the rules are specifically designed to prevent or reduce claims based on Community law.[124] Secondly, time limits which in effect prevent preliminary references to the ECJ are also incompatible with Community law. The ECJ found in *Peterbroeck*[125] that this made the application of Community law excessively difficult, but such rules are also in conflict with the *Simmenthal* doctrine, since the effectiveness of the Article 234 EC procedure is undermined. Thirdly, the ECJ has indicated that time limits which retroactively limit Community claims in such a way as to 'strike at the very essence of the right' conferred by the Community rules must also be held incompatible with the *Rewe* principle of effectiveness.[126]

Outside these situations, the justification for national rules must be assessed in light of the different criteria articulated in *Peterbroeck*, in particular by balancing the need for legal certainty and the effectiveness of Community law. The ECJ indicated in *Peterbroeck* that even a mere 60-day time limit is not objectionable per se, whilst finding that a one-year time limit was acceptable in *Palmisani*.[127] At the other end of the spectrum lies *Cofidis*, in which the ECJ did not accept a two-year time limit barring individuals from invoking Directive 93/13/EC, and even indicated that any time limit would render the application of the rights ensured by the directive excessively difficult.[128] Countering objections to the effect that shorter time limits had been accepted in *Rewe* and *Palmisani*, the ECJ noted that those decisions were merely the results of assessments on a case-by-case basis, which could not be applied 'mechanically in fields other than those in which they were made'.[129]

[121] Opinion in Case C–327/00 *Santex* [2003] ECR I–1877, para 88.

[122] Case 208/90 *Emmot* [1991] ECR I–4269, para 23.

[123] Eg Case C–90/94 *Habr Petroleum* [1997] 4085, para 52.

[124] Eg Case 309/85 *Barra* [1988] ECR 355, paras 18–19; Case 240/87 *Deville* [1988] ECR 3513, para 18; and opinion in Case C–62/00 *Marks & Spencer* [2002] ECR I–6325, para 59.

[125] Case C–312/93 *Peterbroeck* [1995] ECR I–4599, paras 17–21.

[126] Case C–246/96 *Maggorian* [1997] ECR I–7153, para 44; and Case C–78/98 *Preston* [2000] ECR I–3201, para 41.

[127] Case C–261/95 *Palmisani* [1997] ECR I–4025, para 29.

[128] Case C–473/00 *Cofidis* [2002] ECR I–10875, para 36.

[129] Para 37.

Consumer law in many aspects is similar to environmental law, and there are elements in *Cofidis* suggesting that time limits in environmental cases should be subject to a similarly stringent review. Drawing on the *Océano* case, the ECJ argued that the fixing of time limits could jeopardize the protection offered by Directive 93/13/EC, since consumers might be unaware of their rights.[130] This factor is equally relevant in respect of environmental suits, where lack of knowledge might manifest itself in different ways. First, the field of environmental protection has become a highly technical and densely regulated field of law, where even legal experts find it difficult to determine the substance of rights and obligations. Secondly, although environmental pollution or damage may often be easily detected, it can be very difficult and time-consuming to gather data showing the exact extent of damage, the operator responsible, and a causal link.

Article 12(2) and (3) of Directive 2004/35/EC, for instance, stipulates that a request for action by the national authorities against an operator responsible for environmental damage must be accompanied by relevant information and data which demonstrates, in a plausible manner, that damage exists. It is clear under these circumstances that Member States must provide for flexible time limits to allow for the necessary fact-finding for the result and aim of Article 12 to be achieved. Finally, prescription of claims may also have a particularly detrimental impact in the field of environment. As is well known, effects of environmental incidents often manifest themselves years after the event, so-called 'long-tail' damages. Directive 2004/35/EC therefore provides that responsibility for environmental damage only expires 30 years after the damaging event, which may serve as a general guideline to evaluate the compatibility of national rules on prescription of environmental claims outside the field of environmental liability.

4.4 Res judicata

A specific manifestation of temporal restrictions follows from the principle of *res judicata*, which provides that after all rights of appeals against a certain act have been exhausted, that act becomes definitive and may not be challenged again. This is a common legal principle which is recognized in all Member States, although most legal systems afford some possibility to reopen definitive decisions in exceptional cases.[131] The ECJ has in two recent judgments

[130] Paras 32–35.

[131] Case C-224/01 *Köbler* [2003] ECR I-10239, para 48.

nevertheless imposed some limitations on the principle of *res judicata* in order to ensure the precedence and effectiveness of Community law. In *Köbler*[132] the ECJ ruled that the *Francovich* doctrine also applied to erroneous decisions by courts adjudicating at last instance. The ECJ argued that this did not impinge on the principle of *res judicata* since the applicant in a *Francovich*-suit against the state would, if successful, only secure an order against it for reparation of the damage incurred 'but not *necessarily* a declaration invalidating the status of *res judicata* of the judicial decision which was responsible for the damage'.[133] It is noteworthy that the ECJ did not rule out, however, that the decision's force of *res judicata* might come under threat – cf 'not necessarily'. More importantly, the outcome of the ruling in *Köbler* did in fact question the *res judicata* of the national court's decision. Although the Austrian Supreme Court's decision was not overturned, the effect of the ECJ's ruling was nevertheless that the state would have to amend its pension system in certain respects.

The principle of *res judicata* was more directly challenged in *Kuhne*,[134] where the question was whether Community law required an administrative body to reopen a decision that had become final after all judicial remedies had been exhausted. Building on the implicit precedent set in *Köbler*, the ECJ confirmed that Community law did in fact require national authorities to examine their decisions afresh, subject to the following conditions:

1) the authority must have power under national law to reopen that decision
2) the administrative decision must have become final as a result of a judgment rendered by a court ruling at last instance
3) that judgment must have been based on a misinterpretation of Community law, without seeking recourse to the preliminary reference procedure in Article 234 EC
4) a different interpretation has subsequently been adopted by the ECJ, and
5) the persons concerned complained to the administrative body immediately after becoming aware of the ruling of the ECJ.[135]

If these conditions are fulfilled, the ECJ continued, the administrative body must review the final decision in the light of the ECJ's ruling, and determine whether it is required to reopen the final decision, without adversely affecting the interest of third parties.[136] The court has since reaffirmed in *Kapferer* that the first requirement above, competence to reopen a final judicial decision, is unconditional and that Community law does not require national courts to

[132] ibid. For further commentary on the implications of the *Köbler* ruling, see section 11.5 below.
[133] Para 39. [134] Case C–453/00 *Kühne* [2004] ECR I–837. [135] Paras 27–28.
[136] ibid.

disregard such a restriction.[137] But it should be noted that the facts in *Kapferer* were quite different from *Kühne*, and it cannot be excluded that the court may reach a different conclusion where pressing Community interests so require.

In sum, *Kühne* and *Köbler* complement each other in the sense that plaintiffs can attempt to have erroneous final decisions overturned where this would not directly affect third parties, whereas, if this is the case, they may instead seek reparation from the state under the *Francovich* doctrine. Another matter is that the conditions for relief are in both cases very stringent, and only likely to be fulfilled in exceptional circumstances.

4.5 *Legal costs*

The high expenditure involved in legal proceedings, combined with lack of financial incentives, is by many regarded as one of the main bottlenecks for bringing environmental cases – probably as serious as restrictive rules on standing and remedies.[138] A study commissioned by the Commission thus concluded that high costs explained why relative few environmental actions were brought in some Member States with liberal standing rules.[139]

However, the Aarhus Convention requires in Article 9(4) that environmental proceedings are not 'prohibitively expensive'. The same obligation is laid down in Article 10a of Directive 85/337/EEC, Article 15a of Directive 96/61/EC, and Article 10 of the Commission proposal for a directive on access to justice in environmental matters.

The question of costs and the application of the *Rewe* doctrine were at the heart of the *Clean Car Auto* case.[140] The question referred to the ECJ was whether a national rule obliging a successful party to bear its own legal expenses incurred in the context of a preliminary reference under Article 234 EC was incompatible with Community law. The Advocate General argued that only the first limb of the *Rewe* doctrine, the principle of equivalence, was suitable for reviewing the compatibility of national rules on costs, whilst it was in his opinion impossible to assess whether national rules on costs impinged on the second rule of the *Rewe* test, namely whether such a rule made the application of Community law virtually impossible or excessively difficult.[141] The ECJ was of a different opinion and held that the national rules on costs would have to be subject to compatibility with both conditions

137 Case C–234/04 *Kapferer* [2006] ECR I–2585, para 23.

138 de Sadeleer, Roller and Dross 2005, 196.

139 ibid.

140 Case C–472/99 *Clean Car Auto* [2001] ECR I–9687.

141 Opinion, ibid para 28.

laid down in *Rewe*, although in the case at hand it indicated that the national rules were compatible with Community law.[142]

Although wrong in principle, the Advocate General was right in pointing out the practical difficulties in determining when national rules on costs make the application of Community law excessively difficult.[143] The notion 'prohibitively expensive' used in the Aarhus Convention and secondary Community legislation does not offer much guidance either. The reasoning employed in *Océano, Cofidis* and *Mostaza Claro* suggests by analogy that the compatibility of national rules on costs must be assessed on a case-by-case basis, and that rules on costs which may be acceptable in one area of EC law may be assessed differently in another area.[144] Although these cases did not concern the compatibility of rules on legal costs with Community law, the ECJ nevertheless pointed out that legal costs could hamper the enforcement of consumer law, given that the 'lawyers' fees may be higher than the amount at stake'.[145] The compatibility of rules on legal costs should therefore not be assessed in the abstract, but by taking account of the extent to which financial incentives exist to bring private suits in any relevant field of law. This suggests particularly stringent review of rules on costs in the field of public interest litigation, such as environmental law, where there are often no financial incentives at all. Indeed, some scholars have argued that in these types of suits, where the plaintiffs are essentially providing a public service and complementing the efforts of national authorities, the state should compensate the plaintiffs' costs.[146]

The requirements imposed by Community law in relation to legal costs was addressed in *Evans*.[147] This case concerned implementation of Directive 84/5/EEC (motor vehicle insurance), and one of the question posed was whether the UK was required to reimburse legal costs incurred by plaintiffs when applying for compensation from the body responsible for awarding compensation, ie the Motor Insurers' Bureau (MIB). The ECJ found that the directive did not regulate the matter, and therefore examined it in light of the *Rewe* doctrine. It then stated, in view of the less advantageous position victims found themselves vis-à-vis the MIB and the conditions under which they

[142] Paras 29–30.

[143] The compatibility of national rules on legal costs was one of the questions raised in Case C-376/03 *D* [2005] ECR I-5821, but the ECJ found it unnecessary to respond on this specific issue.

[144] Sections 4.2 and 4.3.

[145] Joined Cases C-240 to 244/98 *Océano* [2000] ECR I-4941, para 26; Case C-473/00 *Cofidis* [2002] ECR I-10875, para 34; and Case C-168/05 *Mostaza Claro* [2006] ECR I-10421, paras 28–29.

[146] Buxton 2002, 54.

[147] Case C-63/01 *Evans* [2003] ECR I-14447.

could submit comments, that legal assistance was indeed necessary. The ECJ subsequently ordered the national court to examine whether the principles of equivalence and effectiveness required that the legal costs were reimbursed.[148] Although leaving the matter to the national court, the judgment illustrates that the *Rewe* doctrine may thus require reimbursement of legal costs in cases where the plaintiffs would otherwise not be in a position to enforce the applicable Community rules. To this one should add that the special procedure established in the UK had, according to the ECJ, the advantages of speed and economy of legal costs,[149] whilst the opposite is true for ordinary judicial proceedings.

The precise delimitation of a numerical threshold above which national rules on costs would be incompatible with EC law is clearly something that should be harmonized through secondary legislation. But, in the absence of harmonization, it may nevertheless be questioned whether certain expenses should be deemed incompatible with Community law. There are essentially four categories: court fees, witness and expert fees, lawyers' fees, and, in some countries, the legal fees of the winning party.[150] It is the two last fees which constitute the most significant expenses, and the risk of having to pay the expenses of the other party in particular is liable to have a deterrent effect on environmental actions.[151] Proceedings brought by private persons against large companies may become onerous since they often incur high legal expenses. There is also a risk of misuse, in the sense that the defendant could threaten plaintiffs with setting up a vast legal team and thus incur very high legal costs in order to deter law suits. The fact that plaintiffs will find it difficult to assess beforehand the financial risk of bringing cases is also likely to deter plaintiffs with limited resources. National rules whereby the winning party's costs are compensated by the other party are hence liable to make application of EC environmental law 'excessively difficult' and 'prohibitively expensive'. One solution to this problem would be to make greater use of so-called 'pre-emptive orders', according to which the court at the outset of proceedings informs that there will be no order for the other parties' costs. Such a possibility exists for instance in the UK.[152]

Community requirements concerning costs do not only apply to the cumulative costs of a given case, but may also have to be examined specifically

[148] Paras 77–78. [149] Para 53.

[150] This is the case in the majority of the Member States; see Prieur 1998, 75.

[151] de Sadeleer, Roller and Dross 2005, 32 claim that the reason why so few environmental claims are brought in civil proceedings in the Netherlands is to a large part due to the risk of having to compensate the other party's legal expenses.

[152] See Carnwath 2006, 321.

in respect of the costs involved when seeking a specific remedy. A practically important example in this respect is the obligation to provide cross-guarantees when asking for interim relief.[153] Such guarantees will often involve sums which the average environmental plaintiff cannot afford, and there are several examples where the required deposit was so substantial that even large and wealthy environmental organizations were prevented from obtaining interim relief. This was illustrated in a case before the UK Court of Appeal where Greenpeace was denied an interim stay of operations against British Nuclear Fuels for the operation of the Sellafield nuclear plant.[154] Although Greenpeace sought a stay for only five to six days, the loss per day was stipulated by Sellafield in the range of £250,000, for which Greenpeace was unable to provide guarantees. Needless to say, financing guarantees, even if concerning smaller operations than that mentioned above, is often impossible where a preliminary ruling is required, which would normally require suspension of operations for years.[155] Hence, in the *Lappel Banks* case,[156] the Royal Society for Protection of Birds (RSPB) was unable to provide guarantees for the loss that would result from suspending development works in a vulnerable wetlands area for birds pending a preliminary ruling on whether the project was in breach of Directive 79/409/EEC.[157] The ECJ found in favour of the RSPB in the end,[158] but when the ruling was rendered, Lappel Banks had already been converted into a large parking lot.

The requirement of placing guarantees in order to obtain interim relief will therefore in many cases effectively render access to preliminary rulings from the ECJ nugatory, and thus not only render the application of the Community rules excessively difficult but also undermine the effectiveness of the Article 234 EC procedure. This is in conflict with the *Simmenthal* judgment, and more specifically the right to effective interim relief as provided by the *Factortame* ruling.[159] Cross-guarantees could moreover violate Article 9(4) of the Aarhus Convention since proceedings become 'prohibitively expensive'. In some cases Community law may therefore require that environmental plaintiffs

[153] Interim relief is dealt with in section 9.

[154] *R v Inspectorate of Pollution, ex parte Greenpeace Limited* [1994] 1 WLR 570.

[155] See data in chapter 4, section 4.6.1.

[156] *R v Secretary of State for the Environment, ex parte the Royal Society for the Protection of Birds* [1997] Env LR 430.

[157] The presumption for a requirement of guarantees in Common Law was confirmed in a recent Privy Council Appeal (no 47, 2003) *Belize Alliance of Conservation Non-Governmental Organisations v Department of the Environment and Belize Electricity Company Limited.*

[158] Case C-44/95 *R v Royal Society for the Protection of Birds (Lappel Banks)* [1996] ECR I-3805.

[159] See section 9.

obtain interim relief without having to post a bond, which for instance happened in the 'German Baltic Sea Motorway' case.[160]

On the other hand, allowing for interim relief without any guarantees at all may represent a breach of the right of legal protection and legal certainty for the defendant, principles which are also part of Community law. Since guarantees are usually required in civil suits brought against private operators, a solution could be for environmental plaintiffs to seek an interim injunction ordering the authorities to take action against the alleged offender instead, eg by suspending permits. This was in fact what Greenpeace and RSPB did in the above-mentioned cases, but the national courts held in both cases that what the plaintiffs sought was essentially an injunction against the private party, and therefore upheld the requirements of guarantees. One could argue, however, that strictly speaking there is no need for guarantees under circumstances where authorities are required to intervene and provide the necessary interim measures, since the operator could then, if appropriate, seek damages from the state for loss incurred.[161] This is not as unfair on the state as it might seem at first glance, since interim relief presupposes in most legal systems that the national court has been persuaded that there is a prima facie infringement, urgency, and balance of convenience in favour of the application.[162]

5 Acts susceptible to review

5.1 *Introduction*

The scope of environmental acts subject to review is in most Member States essentially limited to individual decisions, eg individual licenses and planning permissions, or failure to take such decisions.[163] Non-binding acts are generally excluded from review, and there is often no right to contentious appeal in respect of general acts, such as environmental plans and programmes, unless they are equivalent to administrative acts or decisions with the force of law or involving specific obligations.[164] However, challenges to individual decisions

[160] Referred to in Carnwath 2006, 319. [161] Nash 1997, 131.

[162] Section 9, cf chapter 4, section 4.6.2.

[163] Prieur 1998, 11. Furthermore, the meaning given to the terms 'plans and programmes', their legal status and and procedures for their adoption differ among the Member States; see IMPEL Network 2000, 19–20. [164] Prieur 1998, 11.

often provide for judicial review of the legality of underlying general acts, eg environmental regulations, similar to the procedure under Article 241 EC. In some Member States it is also possible to challenge environmental regulations directly, what is sometimes referred to as 'abstract review', whilst in others ie Germany, Finland, Denmark, and the Netherlands, this is not possible.[165]

5.2 *Case law*

The first question is whether Community law requires that non-binding environmental measures may also be challenged. The principle of coherence suggests an affirmative answer on the basis that the ECJ has allowed preliminary references concerning the 'conformity' of non-binding Community acts – given that they are nevertheless capable of producing legal effects.[166] Practically significant non-binding acts in the environmental sphere include national plans and programmes drawn up in preparation for the adoption of Community acts and decisions. One example is the obligation to designate special protection areas (SPAs) under Directive 92/43/EC, from which the Commission draws up a list of sites of Community importance which must subsequently be implemented by the Member States. The drawback of this two-step procedure from a judicial control perspective is that plaintiffs will generally not be allowed under national law to challenge the lawfulness of such preparatory acts, whilst the Commission decision cannot be challenged (even presupposing standing under Article 230 EC) on the basis of an unlawful national measure.

This problem is analogous to that posed by the *Borelli* case.[167] The facts of the case were that Italian authorities had issued an unfavourable opinion to the Commission on an application by Borelli for Community aid under Regulation (EEC) 355/77. The Commission subsequently denied the application, which led Borelli to challenge this decision under Article 230 EC. The ECJ dismissed the claim since it could not rule on the national measure, and the validity of the Commission decision could in any event not be affected by a defect pertaining to the national opinion. Borelli argued subsidiary that this effectively would result in denial of justice, as it was not possible to challenge preparatory acts in national courts.[168] With reference to the principle of judicial control, the ECJ

[165] Ebbesson 2002, 35.

[166] C–322/88 *Grimaldi* [1989] ECR 4407, para 8. See chapter 4, section 4.3.

[167] Case C–97/91 *Borelli* [1992] ECR I–6313.

[168] Para 8.

held that national courts, if necessary after obtaining a preliminary ruling, had to rule on the lawfulness of a preparatory measure on the 'same terms which they review any definitive measure . . . which is capable of affecting third parties and consequently to regard an action brought for that purpose as admissible even if domestic rules of procedure do not provide for this in such a case'.[169] Subject to the condition that the preparatory act is capable of affecting the legal interests of concerned parties, which is discussed in section 6, it follows analogously that national courts may have to review the conformity of preparatory environmental acts against Community law, such as designation of protected areas under Directive 92/43/EC.

As for binding acts, it is clear that national courts must be able to review the compatibility of individual decisions with Community law.[170] The same should apply to omissions to adopt individual decisions required by Community law. Furthermore, national courts must adhere to the dictum employed by the ECJ, according to which it is the content of the acts, not their form, which determine their classification.[171] Hence, individual permits issued in the form of regulations, as happens in some Member States,[172] should be considered individual decisions that are subject to judicial review.

Where a decision is challenged on the basis of the illegality of the underlying national regulation, effective judicial control dictates that national courts must be able to carry out incidental review of the relevant provisions. This follows from an analogy with Article 241 EC, which according to the ECJ expresses 'a general principle of law'.[173] Conversely, the ECJ held in *Unibet* that national courts do not need to accommodate free-standing actions for the examination of whether national provisions are compatible with Community law, provided that effective preliminary review of the relevant provisions can be ensured through challenges of individual decisions or actions for damages, and subject as always to the principle of equivalence.[174] Claims for damages will seldom be a relevant instrument in environmental cases, however, and in some situations there might not be any individual decision to challenge. This could for instance occur where erroneous transposition of an environmental directive has the consequence that national authorities fail to adopt further implementing measures, eg where

169 Para 13.

170 See eg Case 222/86 *Heylens* [1987] ECR 4097, para 14; and Case C–340/89 *Vlassopoulou* [1991] ECR I–357, para 22.

171 See references in chapter 5, Section 2.3.

172 IMPEL Network 2000, 21.

173 Case C–441/05 *Roquette Frères* [2006] OJ C36/25, para 39.

174 Case C–432/05 *Unibet* [2006] OJ C36/23, paras 48–65.

the national regulation erroneously excludes certain operations from permit requirements.[175]

There is also a temporal aspect which in some circumstances militates in favour of accommodating free-standing actions against acts of general scope. Many environmental directives require Member States to draw up plans and programmes for the management of natural resources, which they in turn have to implement in practice. If it is clear from the outset that these plans and programmes are incompatible with the directives, plaintiffs should in my opinion be able to challenge these general acts directly, without having to await adoption of individual decisions implementing these unlawful measures.[176] This proposition gains support from the general obligation resting on national courts to ensure that Community rules take immediate effect.[177] It follows also from an analogy with the ruling in *British American Tobacco*,[178] in which the ECJ allowed for preliminary rulings on the validity of directives in respect of which the deadline for implementation had not yet expired.[179]

5.3 *The Aarhus Convention and implementing legislation*

Article 9(3) of the Aarhus Convention requires Member States to provide for judicial review of acts and omissions by public authorities and private parties. The notion of an act or omission is not further defined, but follows indirectly from the notion of public authorities. This term is defined in Article 2(2) as including state authorities as well as local authorities, and any natural or legal persons performing public administrative duties under national law, or otherwise providing public services.[180] Bodies or institutions acting in a judicial or legislative capacity are excluded, which thus means that judicial and legislative acts fall outside the scope of the Aarhus Convention. This provides for a somewhat paradoxical result, in that the ECJ's case law requires Member States to implement in law provisions *intended to grant rights on individuals* so that they can rely on their rights before national courts. This means that erroneous transposition of such Community provisions falls ostensibly outside the

[175] As illustrated by Case C–129/96 *Inter-Environment* [1997] ECR I–7411, paras 16–20.

[176] A prerequisite would be that the deadline for implementing the directive as regards the drawing up of plans and programmes has expired so that the relevant provisions had direct effect. However, it is conceivable that plaintiffs could also challenge plans and programmes drawn up before this period in time on the basis of the *Inter-Environnement* case; see chapter 2, section 2.2.3.

[177] See, to this effect, Case 13/68 *Salgoil* [1968] ECR 661, para 3; Case 106/77 *Simmenthal* [1978] ECR 629, para 23; and Case C–213/89 *Factortame and Others* [1990] ECR I–2433, para 20.

[178] Case C–491/01 *British American Tobacco* [2002] ECR I–11453, para 40.

[179] See chapter 4, section 4.3.

[180] This includes private subjects; see section 3.4.

scope of judicial review under Aarhus. However, Article 9(3) should probably be understood to the effect that private parties cannot require free-standing actions for review of legislative provisions, whilst still requiring incidental review of such provisions in challenges of individual decisions which derive their illegality from the underlying law.

It follows implicitly from Articles 7 and 9(2) read in conjunction that plans and programmes are not deemed acts made in a legislative capacity. Such acts fall therefore within the scope of Article 9(3), but Member States may also choose to afford judicial review under the more liberal conditions in Article 9(2). The inclusion of plans and programmes suggests furthermore that non-binding acts are subject to judicial review. This proposition gains further support from the fact that acts or omissions by public authorities or *private parties* fall within the remit of Article 9(3). The proposed Directive on Access to Justice in Environmental Matters essentially copies the relevant provisions of the Aarhus Convention as regards the acts that are susceptible to judicial review. However, the notion of public authority appears somewhat more restrictively defined in Article 2(1)(a) of the proposal compared with Article 2(2) of the Aarhus Convention.[181]

6 Standing

6.1 *Introduction*

A study commissioned by the Commission in preparation for the implementation of the third pillar of the Aarhus Convention identified three basic approaches to standing in the Member States.[182] The most liberal model is based on *actio popularis*, whereby public interest actions are in general granted access to justice. *Actio popularis* in its pure form is not recognized in any of the Member States, but some Member States' laws place very lenient conditions for NGOs, which are presumed to have a legal interest.[183] Other countries have developed similarly liberal standing requirements through case law,

[181] The same applies to Regulation 1367/2006 on the application of the Aarhus Convention on Access to Information, Public Participation in Decision-making and Access to Justice in Environmental Matters to Community institutions and bodies (Regulation 1367/2006), see chapter 5, section 3.4.1.

[182] de Sadeeler, Roller, and Dross 2005, 183–87. See also Ebbeson 2002, 24–32.

[183] Eg Portugal, ibid 184.

according to which established environmental organizations are again often presumed to have an adequate legal interest.[184]

The intermediate approach, favoured by most Member States in relation to individuals, requires that the plaintiff has a relevant and sufficiently strong 'interest' in invoking the environmental rules. But there are significant variations in practice to the application of the interest test. In the UK it is essentially used to filter claims by 'meddlesome busybodies' and a similarly lenient interpretation is applied in the Netherlands. In Belgium and France, in contrast, the plaintiff's interests must not only be affected, but they must also be individualized and distinct from those of other citizens.[185]

The third and most restrictive approach reserves standing to cases where breaches of 'subjective rights' are alleged. According to this doctrine, the infringed rule must have been intended to protect the plaintiff's specific interests, as opposed to the public at large. The main proponents of this system are Germany and Italy. Thus, neither an individual nor a NGO has standing to defend general environmental interests, unless specifically authorized in legislation. The exception in German law relates to nature conservation.[186]

6.2 *Case law*

The requirements Community law places on standing rules in the Member States have until recently not been subject to much scrutiny by the ECJ, and locus standi has been described as 'probably the most important aspect of national remedies which remains to be fully considered by the ECJ'.[187] Indeed, the ECJ held in *Verholen* that it is 'in principle for national law to determine an individual's standing and legal interest to bring proceedings', subject to the *Rewe* doctrine and the principle of effective judicial protection.[188] Before examining how those principles may limit national procedural autonomy in this respect, it is noteworthy that *Verholen* only applies in the absence of Community harmonization. Conversely, if Community rules stipulate the entities entitled to bring actions before national courts, the matter is in principle regulated by Community law. Examples in the environmental sector include Article 10a of the Directive 85/337/EEC (EIA), Article 15a of Directive 96/61/EC (IPPC), and Article 13 of Directive 2004/35/EC (Environmental Liability).[189] The ECJ has furthermore held that the

[184] Eg UK, see de Sadeeler, Roller, and Dross 2005, 185–86.
[185] ibid 184–85.
[186] Ebbesson 2002, 30.
[187] Oliver 1998, 54.
[188] Joined Cases C–87, 88 and 89/90 *Verholen and Others* [1991] ECR I–3757, para 24.
[189] See section 10.2.

personal scope of rules on access to justice or administrative appeal must be interpreted broadly, in light of 'the Community requirement for judicial review of any decision of a national authority'.[190]

Furthermore, if Community rules specifically define the beneficiaries of obligations ('directly conferred rights'[191]), it seems clear that these individuals, who in effect are the addressees of the act, must be entitled to enforce those obligations in court.[192] When Community law specifies the persons who enjoy protected interests, it would in my view conflict with the principle of supremacy if national law effectively limited this group through its rules on locus standi. Environmental legislation normally does not contain directly conferred rights of this type, but in recent years individuals have been equipped with procedural rights in relation to access to information and public participation. In these cases Community law thus defines the 'persons concerned', although leaving some discretion to Member States.[193]

In summary, the notion that it is in principle for national law to determine individuals' standing and legal interest to bring proceedings applies only in those situations where the personal scope is not regulated by Community rules, or – as was the case in *Verholen* – where the plaintiff falls outside the personal scope of the Community rules. In the latter situation, Community law may still require that the plaintiff is awarded standing if he or she can demonstrate a 'direct interest' in the fulfilment of the relevant obligations as against the persons falling within its protective scope. *Verholen* indicated that this was the case where a husband suffers the effects of discrimination against his spouse, and the same rationale has granted employers direct interest to bring proceedings on behalf of their employees.[194]

But Community rules seldom clearly define the personal scope, especially in the field of environment. This begs the question to what extent national law may in effect delimit the scope of Community obligations through standing rules. It should be noted from the outset that national standing rules, according to the principle of equivalence, must in any event grant standing for Community suits on similar terms as for claims based on national law. Hence, when the referring national court in *Rewe* (butterboats) asked whether Community law required it to grant standing to plaintiffs seeking to challenge national measures allegedly infringing certain Community regulations, adding

[190] Case C–459/99 *MRAX* [2002] ECR I–6591, para 101.

[191] On the notion of directly and indirectly conferred rights, see Eilmansberger 2004, 1238–43.

[192] To this effect, see Oliver 1998, 55; and Tridimas 1999, 296–97.

[193] Similarly, Prechal 2005, 150.

[194] Case C–345/89 *Stockel* [1991] ECR I–4047; and Case C–158/91 *Levy* [1993] ECR I–4827.

that they probably would have had standing if the suit had been based on national law, the ECJ held that standing had to be granted 'on the same conditions [...] as would apply were it a question of ensuring observance of national law'.[195]

Apart from these situations, it appears from more recent case law that the ECJ will examine whether a plaintiff is affected by an interest protected by Community provisions and, if so, it would seem that national courts are obliged to grant standing. The ECJ thus noted in *Muñoz* that the plaintiff had to be allowed to bring civil proceedings against a competitor for infringements of Regulation (EEC) 1035/72 and Regulation (EC) 220/96.[196] The plaintiff suffered from the fact that a competitor sold incorrectly labelled table grapes in violation of the Community regulations, and the ECJ stipulated that the effectiveness of those rules required that it be possible to enforce the relevant obligations in civil proceedings. The ruling was unconditional on this point, and it is noteworthy that the ECJ refrained from referring to *Verholen* and the principle of procedural autonomy.

The question in *Streekgewest*[197] was essentially whether Article 88(3) EC could be relied upon by a litigant who was subject to tax compromising state aid, but who was not affected by cross-border competition arising from that measure. The ECJ answered this question affirmatively, which essentially concerned the scope of the rule and its direct effect, but interestingly added some remarks concerning the consequences of this finding in relation to the issue of standing. After recalling the point of departure of *Verholen*, the ECJ held that the fact that the plaintiff had been subject to an unlawful tax was a sufficient ground for assessing his interest in bringing proceedings, ie that fact constituted a sufficient interest for bringing proceedings.[198]

The *Transalpine*[199] case concerned the question whether a company which is in a competitive relationship with companies that have received state aid in the form of tax rebates must be granted leave to seek the same rebate in national courts in order to level out the aid. AG Jacobs started his opinion by reciting *Verholen* and noting that the matter of standing was in principle a matter for national courts to determine, especially as regards the assessment whether there was a competitive relationship in this case. Having said that, he

195 Case 33/76 *Rewe* [1976] ECR 1989.
196 Case C–253/00 *Muñoz* [2002] ECR I–7289, para 30.
197 Case C–174/02 *Streekgewest* [2005] ECR I–85.
198 Paras 18–19.
199 Case C–368/04 *Transalpine* [2006] ECR I–9957.

noted that under these circumstances it seemed clear that the undertaking in question must enjoy rights under Community law which the national courts must protect, and that standing therefore had to be granted.[200] The ECJ did not comment on this aspect of the case.

What is striking about these recent cases is that the ECJ no longer leaves it to national courts to assess the compatibility of its standing rules with *Rewe* and the principle of effective judicial protection, but in fact applies those principles to the case at hand, essentially dictating that national courts must grant standing under the circumstances of the case. In fact, the ECJ is not even applying these minimum requirements, but is essentially saying that if the plaintiff is asserting interests protected by Community rules and infringement of those rules has adversely affected him, then national courts have to grant standing to seek redress, irrespective of national rules on locus standi. It is also noteworthy that the ECJ has not required that the infringed Community rules protect the plaintiff's interest specifically, or that he or she has to be affected by certain attributes particular to him or her – as is required under Article 230 EC. Indeed, AG Geelhoed proposed in his opinion in *Muñoz* that Community requirements on standing should be aligned to the direct and individual concern requirements under Article 230 EC,[201] but this was implicitly rejected by the ECJ. If anything, the fact that the rules on standing are so restrictive in direct actions before the ECJ suggests that judicial relief must be available under less stringent terms in national courts in order to ensure a complete system of judicial control.[202]

If we seek to transpose this case law to environmental law suits, national courts should be similarly obliged to grant standing for plaintiffs affected by infringements of environmental directives that seek to protect human health. This proposition gains further support from the ECJ's case law on implementation of environmental directives concerned with the protection of public health, in which it has ruled that Member States must implement the rules in such a way that the persons concerned can ascertain the full extent of their rights and, where appropriate, rely on them before national courts.[203] It is noteworthy that in one of the judgments in which the

[200] Opinion, paras 97–98.

[201] Opinion in Case C–253/00 *Muñoz* [2002] ECR I–7289, paras 68–75. See also comment by Biondi 2003, 1248.

[202] Similarly, Oliver 1998, 56.

[203] Chapter 2, section 2.1.4.1 see eg Case C–361/88 *Commission v Germany* [1990] ECR I–2567, para 16; Case C–59/89 *Commission v Germany* [1991] ECR I–2607, para 19; and Case C–58/89 *Commission v Germany* [1991] ECR I–4983, para 14.

ECJ ruled in this manner it chose to ignore the following concerns by AG Jacobs:

It seems to me, however, that the Commission may go too far in suggesting that the national measures must be such as to confer rights on third parties to challenge inadequate compliance or implementation. It is true that the public at large, as well as ecologists and environmental pressure groups, have a general interest in water quality, and indeed in the respect for Community law. It does not however automatically follow that enforceable rights must be made available to them in the national courts.[204]

Furthermore, it follows implicitly from *Muñoz* and other judgments,[205] that the mere fact that Community rules promote various interests does not prevent a plaintiff having a cause of action for infringements of one of these interests. Hence, the fact that a directive promotes protection of the environment as well as public health does in any event not hinder a plaintiff from invoking his rights in the latter relation.

Conversely, it might follow that the judicial protection doctrine affords Member States ample discretion to determine individuals' standing and legal interests in bringing proceedings against infringements of environmental directives concerned with the protection of genuinely environmental interests, eg Directives 79/409/EEC and 92/43/EC.[206] However, one should be cautious in adopting such reasoning. First of all, it is noteworthy that the tenor of the case law examined above is concerned with ensuring that Community rules take full effect and that the ECJ has noted in this respect that suits brought by individuals in national courts are 'contributing substantially' to ensuring that goal.[207] Secondly, it should be recalled that the principle of judicial control lays down 'the requirement for judicial review of any decision of a national authority'.[208] Thirdly, and more specifically, the ECJ has held in relation to Directive 92/43/EC that proper implementation is necessary, inter alia, in order to allow individuals and environmental organizations to assert their interests in nature conservation before national courts.[209] For all these reasons it seems clear that national courts must in any event consider some plaintiffs to have a legal interest capable of being affected by infringements of

[204] Opinion in Case C–58/89 *Commission v Germany* [1991] ECR I–4983, para 34.

[205] Case C–253/00 *Muñoz* [2002] ECR I–7289, para 29; and Case C–178/94 *Dillenkofer* [1996] ECR I–4845, para 39.

[206] To this effect, see Geddes 1992, 38.

[207] See, in particular, Case C–253/00 *Muñoz* [2002] ECR I–7289, paras 30–31. See also Case C–200/91 *Russell* [1994] ECR I–4389, para 23.

[208] Case C–459/99 *MRAX* [2002] ECR I–6591, para 101. See also Case C–97/91 *Borelli* [1992] ECR I–6313, para 13.

[209] Case C–374/98 *Commission v France* [2000] ECR I–10799, para 54. See comment by Somsen 2002, 1449.

rules protecting ecological interests. This does not mean that Community law recognizes *actio popularis* – which studies have demonstrated in any event is a highly unlikely scenario since environmental *actio* is in fact not very *popularis*[210] – but Member States could, for instance, adopt the model employed in the Netherlands and the UK, where organizations that according to their statutes serve to protect the environment are presumed to have a legal interest.

Finally, it should be pointed out that Community law does not necessitate standing in relation to every infringement of Community rules which adversely affect the plaintiff's interests. *Österreichischer Zuchtverband für Ponys*[211] and *Safalero*[212] both made it clear that Community law does not always require standing to challenge decisions addressed to third parties. Analogous use of these rulings could suggest that Community law does not require that environmental litigants have standing to challenge the lawfulness of permits issued under environmental directives since those decisions are, in this relation, addressed to third parties. However, the ruling in *Österreichischer Zuchtverband für Ponys* can be explained by the obvious fact that standing does not have to be granted where it is clear at the outset that the relevant Community rules do not entitle the plaintiff to the result sought.[213] The reasoning in *Safalero* was that an importer's interest in not having his trade impeded because of a national provision which was contrary to Community law was sufficiently protected where he could obtain incidental review of that provision by challenging a decision addressed to him. For that purpose it was not necessary also to allow him to challenge a decision addressed to a third party on the same grounds. Outside of these particular situations, it is clear that Community law may require environmental plaintiffs to be able to challenge decisions addressed to third parties, eg permits issued to operators in breach of Directive 85/337/EEC or Directive 92/43/EEC.[214]

6.3 *The Aarhus Convention and implementing legislation*

Article 9(3) of the Aarhus Convention provides for standing to 'members of the public', where they meet the criteria, if any, laid down in national law. This notion is defined in Article 2(4) as 'one or more natural persons or legal

[210] Dross 2005, 29.

[211] Case C-216/02 *Zuchtverband für Ponys* [2004] ECR I-10683, para 26.

[212] Case C-13/01 *Safalero* [2003] ECR I-8679, para 56.

[213] See chapter 2, section 2.1.4.

[214] See eg Case C-201/02 *Wells* [2004] ECR I-723; and Case C-127/02 *Waddenzee* [2004] ECR I-7405.

persons, and, in accordance with national legislation or practice, their associations, organizations or groups, all of which must also meet the criteria, if any, laid down in national law. The criteria set in Article 9(3) are, in contrast to Article 9(2) (on standing in matters concerning public participation, see section 6.4 below), very vague and it does not contain any mention of 'wide access to justice' or preferential treatment of NGOs promoting the environment, as Article 9(2) does. This has caused some debate as to whether Article 9(3) basically confers complete discretion on the parties to the convention to lay down the conditions for legal interest in accordance with national law. Several Member States have thus argued that the proposed Directive on Access to Justice in Environmental Matters[215] (the proposed directive) is superfluous as the Aarhus Convention in principle leaves it to national law to determine standing. This interpretation would, however, render Article 9(3) meaningless, and thus conflict with the general principle in public law that international agreements are interpreted in light of their aim and purpose, and thus ensure their effectiveness.[216]

Articles 4 and 5 of the proposed directive implement Article 9(3) of the Aarhus Convention. These provisions are more specific than Article 9(3) of the Aarhus Convention, and upon closer scrutiny it emerges that they essentially reflect the requirements laid down in Article 9(2) of the Aarhus Convention. Article 4 stipulates that members of the public shall have standing where 'they have a sufficient interest or maintain the impairment of a right, where the administrative procedural law requires this as a precondition'. It is still for Member States to determine in accordance with domestic law the specific content of those notions, but the discretion is limited by the requirement that the standing rules comply with the 'objective of granting broad access to justice'. This sets minimum requirements that allow for some judicial scrutiny of national rules on standing, at least in respect of restrictive rules such as the German Schutznorm.[217]

Article 5 provides for specific standing rules concerning environmental organizations. Member States must extend standing to 'qualified entities' in so far that the subject matter of the judicial review falls within the scope of their statutory activities and the specific geographical area of activities of that

[215] COM(2003) 622.

[216] Article 31(1) of the Vienna Convention on the Law of Treaties (1969).

[217] de Sadeleer, Roller and Dross 2005, 167 report that only 0.0148 per cent of all the administrative court cases in Germany are environmental actions brought by NGOs, which presents some indication as to the restrictive impact of standing rules.

entity. The notion of 'qualified entities' is further defined in Article 8. That provision stipulates that an international, national, regional or local association, organization or group must be recognized as a 'qualified entity', subject to four conditions:

a) it must be an independent and non-profit-making legal person, which has the objective to protect the environment
b) it must have an organizational structure which enables it to ensure the adequate pursuit of its statutory objectives
c) it must have been legally constituted a and worked actively for environmental protection, in conformity with its statutes, for a period to be fixed by the Member State in which it is constituted, but not exceeding three years
d) it must have its annual statement of accounts certified by a registered auditor for a period to be fixed by each Member State, in accordance with the provisions set out by virtue of paragraph 1(c).

The procedure for recognition of qualified entities is set out in Article 9, the details of which will not be dealt with further here. In sum, whereas the proposal essentially leaves standing for private persons to be determined by national law, subject to the caveat that domestic law must be consistent with the objective of granting wide access to justice, it more or less exhaustively regulates the conditions for locus standi of environmental organizations. Although the requirements for recognition have been criticized by NGOs for being too strict, the upside is that once an environmental organization has obtained recognition as a qualified entity it may lodge complaints without having to demonstrate a specific interest or impairment of a right in each and every case. The Community therefore places priority on enabling NGOs to enforce EC environmental law, whereas individuals are afforded an ancillary role, to be further determined by Member States.

Another important question is the notion of 'environmental law'. Whereas Article 9(3) of the Aarhus Convention uses the broad notion 'law relating to the environment', Articles 4 and 5 of the proposal allow for challenges of acts and omissions contravening 'environmental law', which at first sight is narrower in scope. Article 2(1)g of the proposal defines environmental law as 'Community legislation and legislation adopted to implement Community legislation which have as their objective the protection or the improvement of the environment, including human health and the protection or the rational use of natural resources', which is followed by a non-exhaustive list of environmental policy areas. This definition is somewhat ambiguous as to whether it suffices that environmental protection is one of several objectives, or whether it must be the predominant goal. In other words, is standing restricted to suits based on Community legislation adopted under Article 175 EC, or can plaintiffs also rely on infringements of quasi-environmental acts adopted under other Treaty provisions, eg Article 95 EC? In light of the Aarhus Convention and in order to ensure coherence with Regulation 1367/2006 on the application of the Aarhus Convention on Access to Information, Public Participation in Decision-making and Access to Justice in Environmental Matters to Community institutions and bodies (Regulation 1367/2006),[218] it must suffice that the relevant Community legislation, irrespective of legal basis, as one of its objectives pursues environmental protection.

6.4 *Standing in matters concerning information and public participation*

Individuals or NGOs which prima facie have a right to information have in all Member States the possibility to challenge any decision refusing access to information,[219] whilst access to justice is normally more limited in respect of public participation. However, in some Member States, eg the Netherlands and Portugal, individuals and in particular NGOs, which have made use of their right to public participation, eg concerning the issuing of permits, thereby gain standing to challenge the legality of those acts in national courts.[220]

Article 9(1) of the Aarhus Convention stipulates that any person who considers his request for information wrongfully refused shall have standing to challenge that decision in national courts. This provision is *in verbatim* implemented by Article 6 of Directive 2003/4/EC on Access to Information.

Article 9(2) provides that the 'public concerned' entitled to public participation in respect of issuing of permits and other projects that may have significant adverse effects on the environment have a right to challenge acts or omissions in this respect, if they can also assert a 'sufficient interest or impairment of a right'. These notions must be defined by domestic law in respect of individuals, albeit with the objective of granting wide access to justice, whereas any NGOs fulfilling the criteria for public participation are automatically presumed to have a sufficient interest or impaired rights. These provisions have been copied in Article 10a of Directive 85/337/EEC and Article 15a of Directive 85/337/EEC. Given the extensive scope of Directives 85/337/EEC and 96/61/EC, environmental organizations should have a right judicially to review a significant proportion of individual decisions

[218] [2006] OJ L264/13; see chapter 5. [219] Ebbesson 2002, 36.
[220] ibid 28; and see de Sadeleer, Roller, and Dross 2005, 184.

in the environmental sphere,[221] which is a significant step towards more effective enforcement of EC environmental law.[222]

Finally, it should be mentioned that Article 9(2) of the Aarhus Convention does not guarantee judicial review of acts and omissions concerning public participation in relation to environmental plans and programmes, but leaves this to the discretion of the parties. It comes therefore as no surprise that the Community opted to leave out provisions on access to justice in Directive 2003/35/EC concerning public participation in respect of the drawing up of certain plans and programmes.[223]

6.5 *Standing in proceedings against private parties*

Most Member States allow some scope for individuals and NGOs to bring civil actions against private parties. However, the conditions for such suits are generally more restrictive compared with suits brought against the public authorities.[224]

Article 9(3) of the Aarhus Convention provides that members of the public shall have standing to challenge acts and omissions by private parties, seemingly on the same terms as in actions brought against public authorities. This is implemented in Article 3 of the proposed Directive on Access to Justice in Environmental Matters[225] which, however, essentially confers complete discretion on Member States to set the requisite criteria for such suits.

But, as will be recalled, the ECJ has already held in *Muñoz*[226] that national courts may have to grant private parties standing in civil proceedings against private entities infringing Community rules. Yet, there are some elements to this case which suggest that it cannot be automatically transposed to environmental cases. First, the fact that the case concerned Community regulations, which by virtue of being directly applicable can be applied horizontally. Nonetheless, as shown in chapter 2, environmental directives that have not

[221] de Sadeleer, Roller, and Dross 2005, 193, report that the most frequent procedural grounds for challenging environmental acts are lacking or insufficient environmental impact assessments and public participation.

[222] Cf section 7.3 on the scope of review.

[223] [2003] OJ L157/17.

[224] IMPEL Network 2000, 162 states that only in some Member States do private parties have a possibility under civil law to bring actions directly against the polluter, whilst in others claims must be made against the authorities with a view to having them enforce the relevant obligations against the private party. It appears in general that the common remedy in horizontal proceedings is compensation, which may not always be a relevant remedy in environmental matters, whilst some countries afford injunctive relief as well, eg UK, Germany, Italy, Sweden and the Netherlands: IMPEL Network 2000, 26. See also de Sadeleer, Roller and Dross 2005, 180–81.

[225] COM(2003) 624.

[226] Case C–253/00 *Muñoz* [2002] ECR I–7289, para 30.

been transposed may through various constructions be applied horizontally. Furthermore, *Marks & Spencer*[227] clarified that plaintiffs may also rely on the direct effect of provisions which have been implemented in law – in relation to which the ban on horizontal direct effect of directives does not apply since any obligations imposed are based on national law.

The second closely related issue is whether the judgment in *Muñoz* should be interpreted restrictively on the basis of the specific nature of the Community regulations at issue. AG Geelhoed argued that the reason why Community regulations had been selected, instead of directives, was that the legislature intended to impose obligations directly on traders not to act in such a way as to affect trade, and the main intention was thus 'not to require the Member States to set up inspectorates'.[228] The AG also drew an analogy with Articles 81 and 82 EC, in respect of which it is established case law that undertakings can sue competitors for non-compliance with those provisions, and argued that a similar cause of action had to be extended to infringements by private parties of Regulations (EEC) 1035/72 and (EC) 2200/96.[229] The ECJ omitted to draw such a parallel and, in contrast to the opinion, the judgment's *ratio decidendi* for requiring national courts to entertain law suits against other private parties was phrased in a very general manner. The main thrust of its reasoning was that national courts had to ensure the effectiveness of Community rules.[230] In this relation it noted that:

> The possibility of bringing such proceedings [against private parties] strengthens the practical working of the Community rules on quality standards. As a supplement to the action of the authorities designated by the Member States to make the checks required by those rules it helps to discourage practices, often difficult to detect, which distort competition. In that context actions brought before the national courts by competing operators are particularly suited to contributing substantially to ensuring fair trading and transparency of markets in the Community.[231]

This reasoning is equally relevant in relation to environmental law.[232] By analogy, it is therefore submitted that environmental plaintiffs may under similar circumstance require standing to bring civil proceedings against undertakings which for instance infringe quality standards laid down in Community rules concerning air, water and soil – subject to the condition that the provisions may be invoked horizontally.

[227] Case C–62/00 *Marks & Spencer* [2002] ECR I–6325, para 31.

[228] Opinion, ibid para 42.

[229] Opinion, ibid paras 58–60.

[230] Opinion, ibid paras 28–30.

[231] ibid para 31.

[232] Biondi 2003a, 1243.

7 Grounds and intensity of review

7.1 *Introduction*

The scope and intensity of review of environmental acts differ significantly among the Member States. In some legal systems, review is often limited to an assessment of the formal legality of disputed decision, whilst courts in other systems also examine the exercise of discretion and the merits of the case, ie the weighing of interests.[233] It is interesting to note that the intensity of review appears to vary according to the conditions for access to justice. In countries with liberal standing rules, eg the Netherlands, UK, and France, courts tend to show restraint, whilst in Member States where access to justice is narrowly construed, eg Germany, there is a tradition of a more fully-fledged review.[234]

7.2 *Case law*

The requirements posed by Community law in terms of judicial review by national courts was at issue in *Upjohn*,[235] where the plaintiff argued that the national court had to conduct a more stringent judicial review of national measures' compatibility with EC law than otherwise was required under national law. The plaintiff argued in particular that the domestic court should not only review whether the authorities had erred in law, but also examine the factual assessment underlying the disputed decision. The ECJ initiated its ruling by drawing a comparison with judicial review of Community acts under Article 230 EC, and noted that Community authorities enjoy a wide measure of discretion where they are called upon to make complex assessments – decisions which therefore were subject to limited judicial review.[236] The Community judicature could not substitute its assessment of the facts for the assessment made by the authority concerned, the ECJ said, but had to restrict itself to examining the accuracy of the findings of fact and law made by the authority concerned, verifying that the action taken by that authority was not vitiated by a manifest error or a misuse of powers, and finally that it did not clearly exceed the bounds of discretion. Reaching its conclusion, the ECJ held that national courts were not obliged to conduct a more extensive review than that carried out by the ECJ in similar cases.

[233] Ebbesson 2002, 34. [234] De Sadeleer, Roller, and Dross 2005, 193.
[235] Case C–120/97 *Upjohn* [1999] ECR I–223. [236] Paras 34–37.

Some commentators have taken the view that the ECJ employed a deferential approach to national law governing judicial review in this case.[237] Others have commented that it follows that 'national differences in the intensity of judicial review and the methods used must be accepted, and are only subject to a *Rewe* test'.[238] More specifically, it has been argued that the minimalist judicial review employed by UK courts under the *Wednesbury* test may thus be compatible with *Rewe*, even though the result is a less intense review than that used by, for instance, German courts under the 'legitimacy test'.[239]

It seems to me, however, that this is stretching the applicability of the *Upjohn* case, and I also interpret its *ratio decidendi* differently. In the first place it should be stressed, as the ECJ did in *Upjohn*, that 'nevertheless, any national procedure for judicial review of decisions of national authorities revoking marketing authorisations must enable the court or tribunal seized of an application for annulment of such a decision effectively to apply the relevant principles and rules of Community law when reviewing its legality'.[240] Hence, any limitation in this respect is clearly not subject to the *Rewe* test.

Secondly, the Community legislation at issue in the case – Directive 65/65/EEC – conferred an exceptional margin of discretion. The AG pointed out that the wording of the directive made it clear that the national authorities alone were competent with regard to licences for medicinal products, which was warranted in light of the fact that these decisions required complex assessments on the basis of 'technical and scientific factors which were capable of rapid evolution'.[241] Furthermore, the assessments were not only objectively, but also subjectively complex in the sense that it required authorities to make 'sensitive choices'.[242] These are matters which the judiciary clearly is not well-suited to review in any depth, and the comments in *Upjohn* must be understood against this background. Indeed, the few cases in which the ECJ has referred to *Upjohn* have essentially concerned Community directives concerning medicinal products.[243]

It is also interesting in this respect to see how the court distinguished the cases in *Menari*.[244] The question was whether the court could only conduct a limited review of a decision by the Commission regarding the labelling of a

[237] De Búrca and Ryall 2002, 159. [238] Jans and Prinssen 2002, 120. [239] ibid.

[240] Case C–120/97 *Upjohn* [1999] ECR I–223, para 36. This point has subsequently been stressed in Joined Cases C–211, 299 and 316 to 318/03 *HLH and Others* [2005] ECR I–5141, para 77.

[241] Para 51. [242] Para 45.

[243] Joined Cases T–74, 76, 83 to 85, 132, 137 and 141/00 *Artegodan and Others* [2002] ECR I–4945, para 201; and Joined Cases C–211, 299 and 316 to 318/03 *HLH and Others* [2005] ECR I–5141, para 77. [244] Case T–179/00 *Menarini* [2002] ECR II–2879.

certain medicinal product. This question turned essentially on a balancing between the commercial interest of the company marketing the product versus the risk of misleading consumers and the usefulness of the information for health education purposes. Albeit not technically complex, the review clearly required a delicate balancing exercise of incommensurable values, and the Commission had followed the expert opinion of the Community's pharmaceutical committee. Against this background one could have expected that the court would fall back on the marginal review indicated in *Upjohn*. However, the court held that the 'assessment of the usefulness of that logo for health education is not of such complexity as to justify a restriction on the scope of judicial review, since, in particular, it does not call for any particular expertise or technical knowledge', went on to conduct a full judicial review and eventually annulled the Commission decision.[245]

Advocates General have similarly stressed that *Upjohn* has a limited scope of applicability,[246] and the ECJ has, to my knowledge, never cited *Upjohn* in an environmental case, but regularly applied more stringent standards.

This brings me to the third noteworthy element of *Upjohn*, namely the implication that the principle of coherence applies to judicial review.[247] In other words, national courts must, as a minimum, apply the same intensity of review as the ECJ has applied to the subject matter or a similar subject matter. This does not only apply to the review which the ECJ has applied to the Community institutions, but must a fortiori apply to the court's review in the context of preliminary references and infringement proceedings.

A significant aspect of Article 234 EC cases is that the court in these cases often, either explicitly or more often implicitly, classifies fact-oriented assessments as matters of law. The principle of coherence requires national courts to classify the matter accordingly, with the consequence that the marginal review in *Upjohn* concerning assessment of facts does not apply. This is important since what are perceived as factually and legally discretionary issues differ among the Member States, and consequently the intensity of review.[248] For instance, UK courts traditionally deemed the assessment of whether a given project fell within the different categories in Annex II of Directive 85/337 as a matter of fact and not law, and thus applied only the marginal *Wednesbury* type of review.[249] But the ECJ's ruling in *Kraaijeveld* implied that such determinations were in fact a matter of law, and the English

245 Paras 44–45.

246 Opinion by AG Maduro in Case 136/03 *Dörr and Ünal* [2005] ECR I–4759, para 47.

247 Similarly, De Búrca and Ryall 2002.

248 Ebbesson 2002, 34.

249 Macrory 2004, 286.

Court of Appeal held accordingly in the *Big Yellow Property*[250] case that such assessments were in principle subject to full judicial review.[251]

Secondly, if one looks at the intensity of review which the ECJ has applied in infringement cases it quickly becomes obvious that it has not been deferential in its approach, but in fact applied a quite stringent review of legality. As will be recalled, the ECJ has for instance been confident in determining whether individual bird habitats should have been designated as special protection areas under the Birds Directive 79/409/EEC[252] as well as finding that specific areas should have been classified as vulnerable zones under 91/767/EEC (nitrates).[253] The principle of coherence, as implied in *Upjohn*, would require national courts to apply a similarly in-depth form of review in such instances. Approached from this perspective, *Upjohn* is by implication a progressive case on judicial review.

7.3 *The Aarhus Convention and implementing legislation*

Article 9(3) of the Aarhus Convention, which as will be recalled is the general clause concerning access to justice in environmental matters, merely provides that the public concerned must have access to ***administrative or judicial procedures*** to challenge acts or omissions allegedly infringing environmental law. It does not, however, stipulate the grounds for review or the requisite intensity of review. Article 9(2) is slightly more detailed as it requires that the persons concerned for the purposes of public participation have a right to challenge the *substantive and procedural legality* of any decision, act or omission subject to the provisions of Article 6, ie the rules providing for public participation in respect of issuing of permits and other projects that may have significant adverse effects on the environment. The crucial question here is what is meant by 'the substantive and procedural legality of any decision, act or omission subject to the provisions of Article 6'. Does it refer only to judicial review of acts or omissions failing to grant the public concerned the right to public participation, or does it (also) grant a right to challenge the validity of the final decision? There are several arguments in favour of the latter interpretation. First, the reference to substantive legality suggests a review of the

[250] [2003] EWCA Civ 140; [2003] Env LR 28.

[251] Albeit not explicitly referring to *Kraaijeveld*, see further comment by Macrory 2004, 286 et seq who has some reservations as to the level of judicial review in practice.

[252] Chapter 2, section 2.2.5. See Case C–355/90 *Commission v Spain* [1993] ECR I–4221, paras 26 et seq; and Case C–374/98 *Commission v France* [2000] ECR I–10779, paras 23–29.

[253] Case C–258/00 *Commission v France* [2002] ECR I–5959, paras 64–70.

legality of the final decision, as infringements concerning strictly procedural guarantees pertaining to public participation, eg right to information, to be heard etc, are procedural errors and not substantive errors. Secondly, the 'acts . . . subject to the provisions in Article 6' are the decisions to issue permits and authorize projects which may have significant adverse effects on the environment. It should therefore be concluded that the scope of judicial review required by Article 9(2) of the Aarhus Convention covers not only infringements of the procedural rights to participation, but also challenges to the substantive legality of the final decision to approve permits or projects which may have a significant adverse effect on the environment. The same interpretation must therefore be given to Article 10a of Directive 85/337/EEC and Article 15a of Directive 96/61/EC which implement that provision.

8 Legal consequences and basic remedies

8.1 *Introduction*

Infringements of substantive environmental provisions in all Member States are sufficient grounds for the act or omission to be declared illegal, but the consequences of procedural defects differ. In some Member States, procedural defects will automatically render the underlying decision illegal, whilst in other Member States such consequences will only arise if the procedural error is 'obvious and must have influenced the decision'.[254] This begs the question whether, and to what extent, Community law dictates the legal consequences of procedural infringements (section 8.2).

Furthermore, in some Member States, eg the UK, a finding of illegality does not necessarily result in the award of remedies against the act, but the national courts have for instance discretion as to quashing an illegal decision.[255] The *forms* of setting aside national measures found to be incompatible with EC environmental law may also vary considerably. Thus, an infringement of Directive 85/337/EEC may in one Member State result in the permit being suspended, the same error may in other Member States result in the permit being revoked, whilst in yet others the permit might be held automatically void (nullity).[256] This raises the question as to what consequences Community law

[254] Ebbesson 2002, 34; de Sadeleer, Roller, and Dross 2005, 193.
[255] Harlow 2002. See also references to case law below.
[256] Cf reports from Germany, the Netherlands, and the UK in Ladeur 2002.

attaches to infringements, and what remedies it requires national courts to make available (sections 8.3–8.4).

8.2 *Legal consequences of procedural infringements*

As seen above, in some Member States procedural defects do not necessarily have the effect of rendering an act or decision invalid, and similar claims have been made in the context of EC law. AG Jacobs opined in *Van Schijndel* that the principle of supremacy only applies to conflicts of substantive law whereas, as regards procedural rules, the primacy of Community law does not require that they should be overridden in all circumstances.[257] Moreover, in *Enichem Base* the ECJ held that failure to notify national measures to the Commission in conflict with Article 3(2) of Directive 75/442/EEC did not warrant the annulment of the national act.[258] On the basis of the judgment in *Enichem Base*, several Member States argued in *CIA Security*[259] that lacking notification under Directive 83/139/EEC could not render the national regulation inapplicable since a) that provision merely created procedural obligations and b) the Directive contained no express provisions relating to any effects attached to non-compliance with those procedural obligations. The ECJ dismissed both arguments. The fact that the breach concerned a procedural obligation was in principle irrelevant, and the ECJ held likewise that no express provisions were necessary for the breach of the procedural obligation to result in the inapplicability of the act in question, since it was clear from the aim and the purpose of Directive 83/189/EEC that the obligation to notify the Commission was 'essential for achieving Community control'.[260] Distinguishing the case from *Enichem Base*, the ECJ emphasized that the obligation to notify under Directive 83/189/EEC was part of the procedure for Community control of draft national regulations, and the entry into force of the national measure was made subject to the Commission's approval or lack of opposition.[261] Finally, as an argument of more general relevance, the ECJ noted that the effectiveness of Community law militated in favour of interpreting the directive to the effect that breach of the obligation to notify constituted a substantial procedural defect such as to render the technical regulations in question inapplicable to individuals.[262]

[257] Opinion in Joined Cases C-430 to 431/93 *Van Schijndel* [1995] ECR I-4705, paras 24–25.

[258] Case C-380/87 *Enichem Base* [1989] ECR 2491, para 24.

[259] Case C-194/94 *CIA Security* [1996] ECR I-2201. [260] Para 48. [261] Paras 49–50.

[262] Para 48.

The following preliminary conclusions can thus be drawn:

a) infringements of procedural obligations laid down in EC law may result in inapplicability of the national act;
b) this will automatically be presumed to be the case if there are express provisions relating to any effects attached to non-compliance with those procedural obligations, but this is not a condition;
c) In the absence of any express provisions, the effects of infringements must be interpreted in the light of the aim and purpose of the obligation and the directive in general.

Most procedural obligations in EC environmental law are not accompanied by any express provisions regulating the effect of non-compliance, and national courts will therefore normally have to seek recourse to the aim and the purpose of the obligation in order to determine whether the infringement requires non-application of the contested act. In the following we shall examine how this works out in relation to some important categories of procedural obligations.

8.2.1 *Notification to the Commission*

The combined effect of *Enichem Base* and *CIA Security* is that lacking notification will render national measures inapplicable where they are subject to Commission approval, eg under Article 95 EC or Directive 98/38/EC,[263] which is the successor of Directive 83/189/EEC. However, in most cases the legality of national measures is not made conditional upon the Commission's approval, and failure to notify will therefore rarely invalidate national acts. There are nonetheless some notification obligations which, although not explicitly subject to Commission approval, suggest that a failure to comply with this duty should render the measure inapplicable because it would otherwise undermine the Commission's judicial control. One example is Article 2(3)(c) of Directive 85/337/EEC, according to which national authorities may exempt certain projects from undergoing an environmental impact assessment, as long as prior to granting consent they inform the Commission of the reasons justifying the exemption. This suggests that the Commission may object to such consent being granted, and it follows therefore that a failure to notify under the circumstances must result in the setting aside of the authorization of the relevant project.[264]

[263] [1998] OJ L204/37. [264] Similarly, Jans 2000, 196.

8.2.2 *Environmental impact assessments*

In some instances, infringements of procedural obligations will lead to infringements of substantive provisions, with the consequence that the national measure must be set aside in accordance with the principle of supremacy. This is illustrated by Article 6(3)–(4) of Directive 92/43/EC, according to which an environmental impact assessment revealing that a project will have significant adverse effects on the environment may only be granted for reasons of overriding public interest and if compensatory measures are taken. If a project has been granted without an environmental impact assessment, and thus without considering whether this is justified by overriding public interest, the failure to carry out an environmental impact assessment will thus also lead to a material infringement of Directive 92/43/EC, and the act is therefore clearly illegal.[265]

The situation is different, however, in respect to the general obligation to conduct environmental impact assessments under Directive 85/337/EEC. The obligations stipulated therein are merely intended to ensure that authorities dispose of proper scientific grounds on which to base their decisions but do not impose substantive restrictions in respect of the subsequent decision-making. In other words, even if an environmental impact assessment demonstrates that a certain project would have significant adverse effects on the environment, Directive 85/337/EEC does not contain any provisions prohibiting authorities from approving the project. Article 2(1) of Directive 85/337/EEC nevertheless requires that an environmental impact assessment is carried out prior to the grant of a development consent in respect of projects which are likely to have significantly adverse effects on the environment, and the ECJ has held that a failure to do so in principle results in the setting aside of that act.[266]

8.2.3 *Plans and programmes*

A common feature of environmental directives is that they often require the Member States to draw up plans and programmes, but the consequences attached to this obligation differ. Some directives, eg Directive 1999/31/EC (Waste Landfills), explicitly state that individual permits may not be issued unless the project is in line with the relevant plans and programmes, whilst others, eg Directive 75/442/EEC (Waste) are silent on the matter. The *Commune*

[265] See, to this effect, Case C–127/02 *Waddenzee* [2004] ECR I–7405, paras 67–68.

[266] See, to this effect, Case C–435/97 *WWF* [1999] ECR I–5613, para 70; and Case C–201/02 *Wells* [2004] ECR I–723, para 65. See also further comment in section 8.3.

de Braine-le Château[267] case concerned a failure by authorities in Belgian Wallonia to draw up waste management plans under Article 7 of Directive 75/442/EEC, and more specifically whether the legality of two permits issued for the operation of waste landfills could be challenged on this ground. The ECJ noted that the drawing up of plans in accordance with Article 7 of Directive 75/442/EEC was essential in order to ensure protection of public health and the environment, eg in order to ensure an adequate waste network and ensuring that waste is disposed at the nearest installations, and that Article 7 accordingly presupposed that individual permits should only be issued when consistent with those plans.[268] However, the ECJ nevertheless held that a failure in this regard did not prevent permits being issued.[269] This conclusion was derived from the fact that the Member States had an additional time limit ('as soon as possible')[270] to draw up plans after the expiry of the deadline for implementing Directive 91/156/EEC, amending Directive 75/442/EEC, which implied that provision for permits to be issued before (and thus without) such plans had been made.[271] This result was moreover called for because it would otherwise lead to a situation where there might be an inadequate number of legally operating disposal sites.[272] Finally, the ECJ conceded that Directive 1999/31/EC explicitly ruled that permits could only be issued on the basis of waste management plans required under Article 7 of Directive 75/442/EEC, but pointed out that the permits at issue had been issued before expiry of the deadline for transposing Directive 1999/31/EC, and was therefore subject to the requirements in Directive 75/442.[273]

The crucial question which this judgment invites is whether the reasoning is of general application or specific to Directive 75/442/EEC. The juxtaposition of Directive 75/442/EEC and Directive 1999/31/EC suggests that permits issued without the requisite plans and programmes will be held illegal in relation to directives which explicitly preclude this (eg Directive 1999/31/EC), but not in relation to directives which do not specifically regulate this issue (Directive 75/442/EEC). However, this argument is not coherent with the reasoning employed earlier in the judgment. The ECJ interpreted Article 7 of Directive 75/442/EEC in such a way that individual authorizations for landfills should in principle only be issued on the basis of previously adopted plans and programmes, but held that permits should nevertheless not be set aside since this would lead to inadequate numbers of waste disposal sites – thus undermining the very environmental objectives

[267] Joined Cases C–53 and 217/02 *Commune de Braine-le Château* [2004] ECR I–3251.
[268] Para 41, first sentence, read in conjunction with para 33. [269] Para 41.
[270] See chapter 2, section 2.2.3. [271] Para 43. [272] Para 44. [273] Para 45.

pursued by Directive 75/442/EEC. If this indeed warrants an exception from the system laid down in Directive 75/442/EEC, it is difficult to see why such overriding considerations should not also apply to Directive 1999/31/EC.

Another matter is that this reasoning is at odds with previous case law. In the *French Waste Incinerator* case, the ECJ explicitly refused the argument proffered by France that closing down nine waste incinerators operating in violation of Directives 89/369/EEC and 89/429/EEC would defeat the objective in those directives owing to resulting lack of capacity to cope with the excess waste volume. The ECJ tersely noted that the French Government had not shown that, if certain plants were taken out of service, it would in practice be impossible to transport municipal waste to neighbouring plants as a temporary arrangement.[274] One could question why the ECJ did not require similar justification for upholding permits issued without the requisite plans and programmes in place, eg by considering whether the waste could have been transported to waste landfills in neighbouring areas or regions which have been regulated in accordance with plans and programmes. This is especially opportune bearing in mind the lack of incentives which would otherwise occur. The ECJ noted in this relation that the Commission could in any event bring proceedings for failure to draw up plans and programmes under Article 226 EC,[275] but this is hardly an effective remedy concerning the temporal aspect of such proceedings.[276]

8.2.4 *Public participation*

It follows from the ECJ's case law that one of the key issues in examining whether infringements of procedural rules should result in illegality of national measures is whether the Community rules are designed to accommodate checks and balances of Member State actions.[277] The rules on public participation are in many ways intended to serve such purposes, eg as concerns the duty to inform the public concerned of planned acts and the duty to state reasons for the acts. Moreover, the ECJ has held in relation to the procedural legality of Community acts that the right to be heard, the right of consultation, and the duty to state reasons are all essential procedural requirements, infringements of which lead to illegality of the acts in question.[278] Furthermore, the fact that Article 10a of Directive 85/337/EEC and 15a of Directive 96/61/EC explicitly stipulate that the public concerned is entitled to

[274] Case C–60/01 *Commission v France* [2002] ECR I–5879, para 40. [275] Para 42.

[276] See chapter 6, section 5.1.

[277] See eg Case C–194/94 *CIA Security* [1996] ECR I–2201, paras 49–50.

[278] See chapter 5, sections 4.4.2 and 4.5.

a review of the *procedural legality* of acts relating to the public participation requirements stipulated in those directives, suggest a fortiori that infringements of such procedural obligations may result in the act being held invalid. These obligations include in particular:

- the obligation to inform the public, provided by Article 6(2)–(3) of Directive 85/337/EEC and paragraphs 1–2 in Annex V to Directive 96/61/EC;
- the obligation to facilitate consultation and allow the public concerned to express opinions, provided by Article 6(4) of Directive 85/337/EEC and paragraph 3 of Annex V of Directive 96/61 EC;
- the obligation to take into account the opinions and submissions from the public concerned, provided by Article 8 of Directive 85/337/EEC and paragraph 4 of Directive 96/61/EC; and
- the duty to state reasons, including if applicable, comments on the submissions received, provided by Article 9 of Directive 85/337/EEC and Article 15(5) of Directive 96/61/EC.

8.3 *Remedies against illegal acts*

It follows from the principle of supremacy, as laid down in *Costa-Enel*, that national law conflicting with EC law must be set aside.[279] The ECJ clarified in *Simmenthal* that this applies regardless of whether the national provisions were adopted prior or subsequent to the applicable Community legislation.[280] This applies similarly to administrative acts, as well as legislative measures.[281] Furthermore, it has been held in *Ciola* that individual administrative decisions must also be set aside if adopted in breach of EC law.[282]

In the *Lück*[283] case, the national court queried whether Community law placed any particular requirements in respect of the forms in which unlawful national law should be disapplied, in particular whether it should be held invalid *ex nunc* or void *ex tunc* from the date the Community rule entered into force. The ECJ essentially held that it was a matter to be determined according to the domestic legal system, and that national courts should apply from among the various procedures available under national law, those which were appropriate for the purpose of protecting individual rights conferred by

[279] Case 6/64 *Costa-Enel* [1964] ECR 585.

[280] Case 106/77 *Simmenthal* [1978] ECR 629, para 21.

[281] Case 158/80 *Rewe* [1981] ECR 1805, para 43; and Case C–224/97 *Ciola* [1999] ECR I–2517, para 31.

[282] Case *Ciola*, ibid para 32.

[283] Case 34/67 *Lück* [1968] ECR 245.

Community law.[284] This was later confirmed in *INCOGE*,[285] in which the ECJ held that the principle of supremacy did not require that national measures adopted in breach of Community law should be presumed to be non-existent with retroactive effect. It sufficed that national law was disregarded in the case at hand. The effect of this ruling is that the setting aside of a national law must not, as a matter of Community law, automatically render invalid, for instance, contracts entered into under that law. Thus, in *Sapod Audic*[286] the ECJ held that a French regulation on waste collection would have to be set aside if the national court could establish a breach of Directive 83/189/EEC, but in respect of the contracts entered into in accordance with this regulation, the ECJ held that:

> It should, however be observed that the question of the conclusions to be drawn in the main proceedings from the inapplicability of the [French regulation] as regards the severity of the sanction under the applicable national law, such as nullity or unenforceability of the contract between Sapod and Eco-Emballages, is a question governed by national law, in particular as regards the rules and principles of contract law which limit or adjust that sanction in order to render its severity proportionate to the particular defect found.[287]

Dougan has pointed out that as a 'matter of policy, it would seem desirable for Community law itself to insist... that the disapplication of unnotified domestic legislation must have some legal effect upon the enforceability also of related contracts'.[288] Thus, he argued, 'national autonomy must be qualified by the principle of effectiveness, at least to the extent that domestic rules should impose some sanction against not only the defective legislation, but also the contracts intended to implement it in practice'.[289] This criticism is clearly called for, since Member States could otherwise use their procedural laws to circumvent the principle of supremacy as, albeit the legislation would have to be set aside, the practical effect of the legislation would continue to exist through the contracts and thus create barriers to trade. The ECJ's seemingly deferential attitude might be explained, however, by the particular facts of the case. Many thousands of contracts had been adopted under the French waste regulation, and it would clearly have far-reaching and immediate detrimental effects – also from a Community perspective – if all of these contracts were to be automatically void.[290]

[284] ibid 251.
[285] Joined Cases C–10 to 22/97 *INCOGE* [1998] ECR I–6307, paras 21 and 26.
[286] Case C–159/00 *Sapod Audic* [2002] ECR I–5031. [287] Para 52.
[288] Dougan 2003, 203. [289] ibid 204. [290] Opinion, para 62.

But the ECJ's ruling in *Wells*[291] raises more serious questions about the unconditional nature of the principle of supremacy. The ECJ noted that national authorities had breached Directive 85/337/EEC by issuing a permit for a mining operation without first conducting an environmental impact assessment. This raised the question as to the legal consequences, as a matter of Community law, of this breach. This question gives rise to a host of different issues – many of which will be discussed in following sections – but the issue relevant for our purposes here concerns the legal consequences of the failure to conduct an environmental impact assessment on permits. In that regard the ECJ held:

> [I]f the working of Conygar Quarry should have been subject to an assessment of its environmental effects . . . the competent authorities are obliged to take all general or particular measures for remedying the failure to carry out such an assessment. In that regard, it is for the national court to determine *whether it is possible under domestic law* for a consent already granted to be revoked or suspended in order to subject the project in question to an assessment of its environmental effects.[292]

The fact that a permit issued in breach of Directive 85/337/EEC should be set aside was already implicit in previous case law. What is novel and remarkable is that the ECJ accepted in principle the legitimacy of domestic restrictions preventing national courts to do so, albeit subject to the *Rewe* doctrine. This suggests that the *Simmenthal* doctrine, according to which 'any provisions of the national legal system [. . .] withholding from the national courts the power [. . .] to set aside national legislative provisions which might prevent Community rules from having full force and effect are incompatible with Community law',[293] has been substituted in favour of the more lenient *Rewe* test. If the discretion conferred in *Wells* concerns the *forms* in which the act is set aside, ie by revoking or suspending the permit, there is no problem, but if it means that Member States have procedural autonomy, subject to *Rewe*, in respect of the question *whether* the permit issued under Directive 85/337/EEC must be set aside, the judgment is much too open-ended and deferential.

On the other hand, since *Wells* implicitly raises questions concerning principles of legal certainty and national courts' competence, one could ask whether this matter is governed by the more deferential test laid down in

[291] Case C-201/02 *Wells* [2004] ECR I-723.
[292] Paras 68–69 (emphasis added).
[293] See section 2.2.2.

Kühne.[294] However, one has to bear in mind the context in which that ruling was made. The question was whether a decision by an administrative organ, which had become final after being upheld by a national court ruling, was obliged to reopen that decision in light of subsequent case law from the ECJ. Such an obligation would, as pointed out by the referring court, 'give rise to administrative chaos', and there was therefore little wonder that the ECJ held that a duty to reopen the decision presupposed inter alia that there was a possibility to do so under national law. The question in *Wells*, in contrast, was whether a national court was obliged to set aside an administrative decision in breach of the legislation existing at the time of that decision. It is, in my opinion, clear that *Kühne* does not govern these types of situations. The result would otherwise be that the domestic law restricting the national court's competence to set aside the administrative decision in *Wells* would not even be subject to the *Rewe* test.

It seems to me, as I have stated before,[295] that the *Simmenthal* principle of effectiveness requires disapplication of remedial rules that are clear obstacles to the application of Community obligations. *Rewe*, on the other hand, governs incidental restrictions, eg time limits prescribing the period in which illegal acts must be challenged and rules specifying the forms in which they must be set aside.[296] If, for the sake of argument, the domestic procedural law applicable in *Wells* would in general preclude that permits issued without prior environmental impact assessment are revoked or suspended,[297] the national court should be required to disapply this national law on the basis of *Simmenthal*. And even if *Rewe* were to apply to this issue, it seems clear that the phenomenon of national rules that hinder national courts from setting aside decisions taken in breach of Directive 85/337/EEC 'strikes at the very essence of rights' derived from this directive as well as rendering its application excessively difficult.[298]

[294] Case C–453/00 *Kühne* [2004] ECR I–837. Professor Jans has voiced such thoughts in discussions.

[295] Sections 2.1 and 2.2.2.

[296] See the ECJ's usage of the two principles in Case C–453/99 *Courage* [2001] ECR I–6297, paras 25–26, cf 29–31. See also opinion in Case C–453/00 *Kühne* [2004] ECR I–837, paras 70–72.

[297] Harwood 2004, 276 reports interestingly that in the UK the Secretary of State has discretion to revoke planning permissions, but this is seldom done. The national courts have held, taking into account legal certainty, that there is only such a duty where the decision is grossly wrong. However, the legal certainty argument was, as rightly pointed out by Harwood, rejected in *Wells*. He concludes that UK courts will thus have to amend their practices in this regard following *Wells*.

[298] See, by analogy, Case C–246/96 *Maggorian* [1997] ECR I–7153, para 44.

On the other hand, if the national court enjoys discretion under national law to set aside a decision infringing Community rules, the principle of loyal co-operation in Article 10 EC requires it do so in order to ensure the effectiveness of the Community law.[299] The reasoning in the English *Berkeley* case is interesting to note in this respect. The Court of Appeal stated that even if a planning decision allowing for the construction of a football stadium in Fulham should have been subject to an environmental impact assessment under Directive 85/337/EEC, it would as a matter of discretion refuse to quash that decision. The House of Lords noted on appeal that 'to do so [refuse to quash] would seem to conflict with the duty of the Court under Article 10 EC to ensure fulfilment of the United Kingdom's obligations under the Treaty', and went on to set aside the planning decision.[300]

8.4 *Remedies against illegal failures to act*

The ECJ has held on several occasions that Article 249 EC, read in conjunction with Article 10 EC, requires national authorities, including national courts, to take all general or particular measures for remedying the failure to carry out obligations flowing from environmental rules.[301] If authorities have taken a decision refusing to act which is incompatible with binding EC environmental law, national courts are obliged to set aside that act on the same terms as other unlawful decisions. If authorities have failed to take a position altogether, the proper remedy is that national courts either issue a declaration stating that there has been an unlawful failure to fulfil a binding obligation under EC law, or provide an injunction ordering the authorities to take the necessary measures.

Hence, the obligation on national courts to provide a remedy against failure to act is relatively clear, but the more complex issue is what form this should take, eg declaration of unlawful failure to act, or an injunction ordering the respondent to act. The basic differences between the two remedies is that an injunction is a coercive remedy, which also regularly specifies the substance of the action to be taken, whilst a declaration is not coercive and

[299] See, by analogy, the reasoning employed in relation to the duty on national courts to raise Community law of their own motion, cf chapter 2, section 4. See also the duty on national courts to allow for judicial review of acts which have become final, if they – among other conditions – have discretion to do so under national law, cf section 4.4.

[300] See also Jans and Prinssen 2002, 120–2.

[301] Eg Case C–127/02 *Waddenzee* [2004] ECR I–7405, para 65; and Case C–201/02 *Wells* [2004] ECR I–723, para 65.

normally does not stipulate concretely the measures to be taken as a consequence. Injunctions can be mandatory as well as prohibitory, and may be directed at private parties as well public authorities. The majority of Member States confer competence on courts to issue injunctions against the authorities, although this remedy is curtailed in some countries (Belgium and Sweden).[302] In some countries (France, Greece, Italy, and Portugal) injunctions are in principle prohibited.[303]

It follows from analogous use of *Factortame*, which concerned interim relief,[304] read in conjunction with the *Simmenthal* principle of effectiveness to which the ECJ referred in that judgment, that final injunctions must in principle also be available in national courts. *Factortame* suggests furthermore that injunctions may be required not only against national authorities but also against the legislature.[305] *Muñoz* further indicates that injunctions must in principle also be available against private parties,[306] and always subject to the condition that the Community provisions can be enforced horizontally. It is noteworthy that in none of these cases did the ECJ examine whether the infringements were particularly serious, and there seems therefore little justification for the views proffered by some academics[307] to the effect that injunctions must only be made available subject to the conditions in *Francovich*.[308]

Article 9(4) of the Aarhus Convention provides in addition that Member States must provide 'adequate and effective remedies, including injunctive relief as appropriate', although the proposed directive on access to justice does not contain any reference to injunctions. The right to this remedy may nevertheless be derived from Article 10 which states that proceedings must be 'adequate and effective'.

Nevertheless, the fact that national courts must in some cases allow for injunctive relief does not require that they do so in all cases. The justification

302 Prieur 1998, 66–67. 303 ibid.

304 Case C–213/89 *Factortame and Others* [1990] ECR I–2433, paras 20–21. See section 9 on interim relief.

305 The Dutch Supreme Court came to a different conclusion in the well-known *Waterpakt* case; see commentary by Besselink 2004. Dutch procedural law not only restricts, but prohibits injunctions against the legislature. It follows from the above that the *Waterpakt* case was, in my view, wrongly decided.

306 Case C–253/00 *Muñoz* [2002] ECR I–7289, para 32. Although the court referred more generally to the right to bring civil proceedings, what Muñoz sought, and had been denied in the Court of Appeal, was an injunction against the other party, cf para 2. This specific right would appear to form part of the right to bring civil proceedings, as confirmed by the court.

307 Jans 2000, 214; and Prechal and Hancher 2002, 108.

308 Joined Cases C–6 and 9/90 *Francovich and Others* [1991] ECR I–5357; see section 11.

for *Factortame* was that national courts must provide an effective remedy.[309] The question is therefore in what cases declaratory relief fulfils this criterion and when injunctions are necessary. In order to answer this question, is it necessary to examine more closely the advantages of injunctions over declarations.

The coercive aspect of injunctions is mostly relevant in the context of actions brought against private parties, and to a lesser extent against public authorities, which is also why injunctions were originally seen as a private law instrument. Public authorities are likely to respect a declaratory judgment, and injunctions can in any event not be enforced against the state.[310] Although injunctions may be practical against local and regional authorities, against private parties the coercive dimension of injunctions may be crucial. This is particularly the case in environmental disputes, where damage may not be remedied by compensation.

More important for the purpose of enforcement against national authorities is that injunctions normally prescribe the substance of the obligation placed on the defendant.[311] In some instances this may follow directly from a declaration of unlawfulness, eg if a decision refusing access to information under Directive 2003/4/EC is declared unlawful on substantive terms, the authorities will usually have no choice but to provide access to that information. But in other cases the consequences of a declaration are not so obvious. Take for example a situation where a decision refusing access to information is challenged because of failure to state reasons. A declaration of unlawfulness may under such circumstances not necessarily result in a new decision allowing access, but a new refusal properly reasoned. If a national court can ascertain that a plaintiff fulfils the conditions for access to information under Directive 2003/4/EC, the proper remedy should be that an injunction is granted obliging authorities to release the information.

There are also temporal dimensions that favour injunctions. A declaration of unlawfulness will typically result in the case being returned to the authorities for reconsideration. The case will go through the administrative machinery all over again, and administrative backlog will often result in a considerable lapse of time before a new decision is issued which, if negative, may have to be challenged in court again. In cases where time is of the

[309] Case C–213/89 *Factortame and Others* [1990] ECR I–2433, paras 20–21. See also section 2.2.3.

[310] In the UK one talks therefore about declaratory injunctions when issued against the state, Cane 2004.

[311] In the *Waterpakt* case the plaintiffs thus sought a court order requiring the Dutch legislature to enacts laws in respect of certain directly effective obligations in the Nitrates Directive.

essence, eg failure to provide for public participation under Directive 85/337/EEC or Directive 96/61/EC in relation to pending authorizations, a declaration may be insufficient to ensure effective enforcement of EC environmental law. In such circumstances, with the caveat that the Community rule in question is sufficiently precise and the national court has the facts necessary to substitute the assessment of the authorities with its own, it would appear that it should grant an injunction that obliges the authorities to fulfil the obligations immediately.

As this brief analysis illustrates, whether injunctions should be available depends on the circumstances of the case, and the justification for granting injunctions may differ depending on whether the addressee is a public authority or a private party. National courts therefore have a margin of discretion in this matter, but where an injunction is the only effective remedy – as illustrated by some of the examples above – they should be obliged, by virtue of Article 10 EC, to grant this remedy.

9 Interim relief

9.1 *Introduction*

An application for judicial review will in most Member States not have automatic suspensive effect,[312] and the plaintiff may therefore have to seek a suspensory injunction with the aim of upholding the status quo pending the trial. If the action concerns a failure to act and there is a risk of irreversible damage pending proceedings, interim relief may also be granted in the form of positive interim injunctions. Studies have shown that interim relief in environmental matters is in principle available in all the (old) Member States, but that the conditions vary considerably.[313] Article 9(4) of the Aarhus Convention provides that Member States must provide 'adequate and effective remedies, including injunctive relief as appropriate'. The notion of 'injunctive relief' should be understood as covering both interim and final injunctions. This is reflected in Articles 4 and 5 of the proposal for a directive on access to justice, which provides that interested parties and qualified entities must have access to interim relief.

[312] The exceptions are Germany and Finland, see Prieur 1998, 67; and IMPEL Network 2000, 26.
[313] Ebbesson 2002, 33–34.

9.2 *Case law*

The ECJ held in *Salgoil*[314] that national courts are obliged to protect the interests of those persons who might be affected by an infringement of Community law, and must do so 'directly and immediately'. In *Simmenthal* the ECJ held that any domestic restrictions to the effectiveness of the Article 234 EC procedure, 'even if such an impediment to the full effectiveness of Community law were only temporary' had to be set aside.[315] The logical corollary of those rulings was pronounced in *Factortame*,[316] where the ECJ held that any national rule preventing interim relief pending a preliminary ruling from the ECJ had to be disapplied.[317] This conclusion could also have been based on the principle of a complete system of procedures and remedies, since the ECJ does not have the power to order interim relief in preliminary rulings.[318]

Because the ECJ's ruling in *Factortame* was negatively phrased, there has been much academic discussion whether it also obliged Member States to make interim relief available in circumstances where this remedy is not provided for in national law.[319] Some have answered this in the affirmative since there existed no possibility of interim relief against the Crown in the UK, yet the House of Lords interpreted the ECJ's ruling so as to provide such a remedy.[320] This is a largely academic discussion, in my view, and it does not matter whether one takes the position that *Factortame* requires the creation of new remedies, or merely disapplication of rules restricting the scope of existing ones. All Member States have interim relief in one form or another, and they would thus in any event have to disapply any restrictions in order to ensure an effective remedy.[321] Indeed, the ruling in *Unibet* affirmed that the principle of effective judicial protection requires national courts to be able to grant interim relief where this is necessary to ensure the effectiveness of a ruling on the compatibility of national acts with Community law.[322] The ECJ added that even where it is uncertain, at that stage, whether the main action is admissible under national law the courts must nonetheless be able to grant interim relief.

[314] Case 13/68 *Salgoil* [1968] ECR 661, para 3.

[315] Case 106/77 *Simmenthal* [1978] ECR 629, para 13.

[316] Case C–213/89 *Factortame and Others* [1990] ECR I–2433, paras 20–21.

[317] See commentary by Papadias 1994.

[318] Case C–186/01 R, *Dory v Germany* [2001] ECR I–7823, para 6.

[319] Toth 1990.

[320] Arnull 1997. Indeed, the UK submitted that a ruling requiring interim relief against the Crown would amount to an obligation to create a new remedy, which would conflict with the ECJ's ruling in Case 158/80 *Rewe II* [1981] ECR 1805, para 44 in which it held that the Member States were not required to create new remedies.

[321] Similarly, Oliver 1992, 16–17.

[322] Case C–432/05 *Unibet* [2006] OJ C36/23, paras 72 and 76.

The general phrasing in *Factortame* suggests that interim relief must be available against private parties as well as the state.[323] This interpretation gains indirect support from the *Wells* ruling, in which the ECJ indicated that national authorities should suspend a permit against a private operator pending an environmental impact assessment of the project.[324] Although the proceedings in *Wells* were brought against the authorities, the practical effect of the case was that the plaintiff obtained interim relief against a third party, ie the operator. It seems to me that plaintiffs should on similar terms be allowed to bring civil proceedings directly against operators, and obtain suspension of unlawful activities.

The ECJ did not formulate any conditions for interim relief in *Factortame*, despite the House of Lords explicitly asking for guidance on this matter. It would appear that the ECJ implicitly left it for domestic legal systems to provide more detailed rules, subject as always to the *Rewe* doctrine.[325] But in *Zuckerfabrik* and *Atlanta* the ECJ construed a right to interim relief pending challenges to the validity of Community regulations, and specified the conditions for such interim relief.[326] There has been some uncertainty whether these conditions only apply to interim relief where there is a challenge to a Community measure, or whether they also apply, either directly or by analogy, if a plaintiff is seeking interim relief against national actions or omissions without challenging the underlying Community law.[327] This question is of great practical importance since the *Zuckerfabrik* conditions for interim relief, derived from Article 243 EC, are more stringent than normally required in domestic legal systems.

Some academics cite the following passage to argue that the *Zuckerfabrik* conditions apply directly to the *Factortame* situation:[328]

> The interim legal protection which Community law ensures for individuals before national courts must remain the same, irrespective of whether they contest the compatibility of national legal provisions with Community law or the validity of secondary Community law, in view of the fact that the dispute in both cases is based on Community law itself.[329]

[323] ibid.

[324] The level of procedural autonomy enjoyed in this respect is discussed in section 8.3.

[325] Which was the answer proffered by AG Tesauro.

[326] Joined Cases 143/88 and C–92/89 *Zuckerfabrik* [1991] ECR I–415, para 20; and Case C–465/93 *Atlanta* [1995] ECR I–3761, para 28.

[327] See eg Prechal 2005, 169 who leaves the question open.

[328] Steiner and Woods 2000, 402; and de la Sierra 2004, 54.

[329] Joined Cases 143/88 and C–92/89 *Zuckerfabrik* [1991] ECR I–415; para 20, repeated in C–465/93 *Atlanta* [1995] ECR I–3761, para 24.

The question remains, however, whether the ECJ is thereby saying that the conditions of interim relief – which it proceeded to lay down in the next paragraphs – must be the same, or whether the statement is restricted to saying that interim relief, as a remedy, must be available in both situations, without suggesting that they should be subject to the same conditions.

Other academics argue that the conditions laid down in *Zuckerfabrik* should apply by analogy to the *Factortame* situation.[330] This interpretation finds some support in the passage in *Zuckerfabrik* where the ECJ gives the following justification for laying down uniform Community conditions:

> As regards the other conditions concerning the suspension of enforcement of administrative measures, it must be observed that the rules of procedure of the courts are determined by national law and that those conditions differ according to the national law governing them, which may jeopardize the uniform application of Community law.[331]

Although the principle of uniformity is similarly applicable to the *Factortame* situation, it is also clear that the need for uniformity is much greater in respect of national measures suspending a Community regulation than interim relief against national measures allegedly in breach of Community law. This difference is clearly reflected in the different language the ECJ used in the two cases. The ECJ held in *Factortame* that interim relief was required in order to ensure the effectiveness of Community law,[332] in contrast to *Zuckerfabrik* and *Atlanta*, where the emphasis was on preventing interim relief being granted against Community acts in such a way as to undermine the effectiveness of Community law.[333] Oliver has thus commented that:

> [t]o preclude a national court from suspending a national measure because such relief would be unavailable before the Court of Justice in similar circumstances would scarcely serve the interests of the Community and would, it is respectfully suggested, constitute an unwarranted interference by the Community in national law.[334]

For these reasons the better view is that the conditions in *Zuckerfabrik* do not apply to the *Factortame* situation.[335] This has recently been confirmed by the

[330] Van Gerven 1995, 688.

[331] Joined Cases 143/88 and C–92/89 *Zuckerfabrik* [1991] ECR I–415, para 27; and Case C–465/93 *Atlanta* [1995] ECR I–3761, para 39.

[332] Case C–213/89 *Factortame and Others* [1990] ECR I–2433, paras 21–22.

[333] Joined Cases 143/88 and C–92/89 *Zuckerfabrik* [1991] ECR I–415, paras 25 and 31; and Case C–465/93 *Atlanta* [1995] ECR I–3761, paras 43–44.

[334] Oliver 1992, 17.

[335] The conditions for interim relief against Community acts are dealt with in chapter 4, section 4.6.2.

Unibet ruling.[336] The ECJ noted that the case concerned an application for interim relief which did not seek to suspend the effects of a national provision adopted in accordance with a Community regulation where the legality of that regulation was challenged, but the effects of national legislation where the compatibility of that legislation with Community law was disputed. In such a case, the conditions for interim relief were governed by domestic law, subject to the principles of equivalence and effectiveness.

10 Reparation on the basis of direct effect

10.1 *Introduction*

Reparation for environmental damage is often perceived as one of the lacunae in EC environmental law. Commentators have tended to analyse this issue from the perspective of state liability, and most have dismissed its relevance on the basis of lacking individual rights and relevant heads of damage (section 11). What has been forgotten is that reparation may often be secured simply by relying on the direct effect of environmental provisions. This is fairly obvious in respect of Directive 2004/35/EC and other environmental directives that contain specific provisions on remediation (section 10.2). Perhaps more important for practical purposes is that reparation may be ensured by requiring specific performance of obligations of result in general (section 10.3). Some of these do not lend themselves to 'retroactive' direct effect,[337] however, which begs the question whether and to what extent plaintiffs may nevertheless require national authorities to undo harm caused on the basis of Article 10 EC (section 10.4). To the extent that there is such a possibility, this in turn raises the issue of how this relief and its conditions relate to state liability under the *Francovich* doctrine (section 10.5). The final issue discussed in this section concerns the conditions under which plaintiffs may seek reparation from private parties (section 10.6).

Before starting this analysis, the limitations which follow from the prohibition directly to impose obligations on private parties should be borne in mind.[338] In this respect, it should be recalled that it follows from the *Wells* case

[336] Case C-432/05 *Unibet* [2006] OJ C36/23, paras 79–82.
[337] See Case C-150/99 *Stockholm Lindöpark* [2001] ECR I-493, para 35.
[338] Chapter 2, section 2.3.

that 'mere adverse repercussions', as opposed to imposition of direct obligations, are not prohibited in so-called triangular relationships (which is particularly relevant under section 10.3).[339] Furthermore, often damage is caused by improper application or enforcement of environmental directives implemented in the national law. In these situations the prohibition on horizontal direct effect does not apply, since any obligations imposed are based on national law. Another matter, as illustrated by *Marks & Spencer*,[340] is that the obligation to take all necessary measures to fulfil these obligations still flows from the direct effect of the underlying Community provisions, which we will turn to below.

10.2 *Directive 2004/35/EC and other liability legislation*

The adoption of Directive 2004/35/EC on the Prevention and Remedying of Environmental Damage[341] (the Environmental Liability Directive)[342] marked the end of a 12-year long struggle to put in place a Community-wide regime pursuant to which the polluter has to pay for environmental damage.[343] This is not the place for an in-depth analysis of this directive,[344] and for our purposes it suffices to identify its main elements. The environmental liability directive essentially obliges national authorities to ensure that preventive and reparatory measures are taken by operators that have infringed environmental directives listed in Annex III and thereby caused environmental damage or a risk of damage. Private parties are not entitled to bring claims directly against operators, but Articles 12 and 13 confer rights on individuals concerned and NGOs to request the authorities to take action against the operator responsible and, if necessary, judicial review before national courts. It follows from Articles 5(4) and 6(3) that authorities are not obliged to take preventive or remedial measures if the operator fails to take the requisite measures to prevent or remediate environmental damage, cannot be identified, or is not required to bear the costs under the directive.

[339] Chapter 2, section 2.3.3.

[340] Case C–62/00 *Marks & Spencer* [2002] ECR I–6325, para 31.

[341] [2004] OJ L143/56.

[342] The notion of the 'Environmental Liability Directive' is used for the sake of simplicity, notwithstanding the fact that it might be more proper to view it as an administrative remediation system.

[343] The Commission issued a Green Paper as early as 1993 (COM(93) 47). However, one might say that the proposed directive is a continuation of the Commission's first initiative in 1976 to include a provision on liability in the proposal for a hazardous waste directive. In the end, this clause was left out when the directive was adopted in 1978; see Krämer 2002a.

[344] Eg Bergkamp 2005; Faure 2005; and Wennerås 2005.

However, authorities may under certain circumstances still be required to take such measures themselves. First of all, several of the directives listed in Annex III of Directive 2004/35/EC contain obligations requiring authorities to take compensatory measures. Thus, Article 4(4) of Directive 79/409/EEC and Article 6(2) of Directive 92/43/EC require Member States to take appropriate steps to avoid pollution or deterioration of habitats or any disturbances affecting birds or species; Article 6(4) of Directive 92/43/EC obliges authorities 'to take compensatory measures' where a project has been permitted which will adversely affect the integrity of a special protection area; and under Article 4(6) litra d of Directive 2000/60/EC, Member States must ensure that 'all practicable measures are taken with the aim of restoring the body of water to its status prior [to an unforeseen accident]'.

10.3 *Specific performance*

For the purposes discussed here, environmental damage may be defined as the discrepancy between a factual situation and required standards stipulated in environmental directives. It is immaterial in this respect whether this discrepancy has always existed, eg because of improper application and enforcement of obligations, or owing to an accident that has led to a deterioration of the environment. Plaintiffs may in any event invoke the relevant obligations and require them to be fulfilled. The general conditions for direct effect were dealt with in chapter 2, so that this analysis is restricted to an examination of the 'reparative direct effect' of three distinct categories of obligations. The requisite remedies which must be available in national law for these purposes, eg declarations or injunctions, have been discussed above,[345] and need not be further dealt with here.

The first category concerns those environmental directives which lay down unconditional and sufficiently precise obligations of result, eg quality limit values in air, soil, or water. If these values refer to specific localities, individuals may ask for remediation measures to be taken in order to ensure fulfilment of quality values. For instance, if there has been water pollution in an area designated under Directive 76/160/EEC, plaintiffs may require necessary measures to be taken in order to achieve the limit values set in accordance with Article 3 of the directive.[346]

Under the second category of directives, Member States must take the necessary measures to ensure that certain objectives formulated in general

[345] Section 8.4.

[346] See, by implication, Case C–92/96 *Commission v Spain* [1998] ECR I–505.

and unquantifiable terms are attained, whilst leaving discretion in respect of the nature of the actual measures to be taken. Although such provisions thus confer a margin of discretion, it may nevertheless be possible to identify the minimum content of the obligation to be fulfilled. In *San Rocco*, the ECJ held that Italy had infringed Article 4 of Directive 75/442/EEC by failing to stop illegal fly-tipping of waste that endangered human health and the environment.[347] Although the obligation in Article 4 – to prevent the risk of endangering human health and the environment – afforded Member States a margin of discretion, the consequence of the judgment was nevertheless that Italy was required to take the necessary remediation measures to ensure that the contaminated area no longer endangered human health or the environment. Private parties should similarly be able to rely on Article 4 of Directive 75/442/EEC with a view to obtaining a declaration or injunction ordering national authorities to take such measures.[348]

The third and final relevant category includes environmental directives which lay down technical means for achieving substantive aims, without articulating concrete binding values.[349] The most important example is Directive 96/61/EC, under which national authorities are free to substitute emissions limits with 'equivalent parameters or technical measures'.[350] Other examples include Directive 89/369/EEC on the Prevention of Air Pollution from New Municipal Waste Incineration Plants and Directive 89/429/EEC on the Reduction of Air Pollution from Existing Municipal Waste Incineration Plants. These directives regulate the conditions under which waste must be incinerated, eg as concerns temperature, level of oxygen and pressure, with a view to fulfilling certain carbon dioxide emissions limits, which are not framed in legally binding fashion. If national authorities fail to ensure compliance with these criteria, private parties can seek a declaration or injunctions against the national authorities ordering them to ensure that the plants concerned are equipped with the necessary technology promptly, if necessary revoking the permits in the meantime. However, there are no provisions which can be invoked in order to address excess air pollution that is a consequence of the infringements.[351]

Thus, in respect of environmental directives which only provide means requirements, substantive reparation may not be obtained by requiring positive

[347] See chapter 2, section 2.2.5.
[348] See also Case C–1/03 *Van de Walle* [2004] ECR I–7613.
[349] Similar distinction is used by Bergkamp 2001, 242–43.
[350] Chapter 2, section 2.2.6. See also Wenneras 2005b, 175 et seq.
[351] See, by implication, Case C–60/01 *Commission v France* [2002] ECR I–5879, para 20.

performance of the obligations. This gives rise to the follow-up question whether there are other grounds for seeking reparation on the basis of direct effect. This issue is dealt with in the next section.

10.4 *Nullify unlawful consequences*

The principle that the Member States shall nullify the unlawful effects stemming from infringements of Community law was already articulated in 1960 in the *Humblet* case.[352] Member States must thus take all measures necessary to undo the effects of either a failure to act or an unlawful action under Community law. This obligation stems from Article 249 EC read in conjunction with Article 10 EC, according to which Member States must ensure that Community law is applied from the time it enters into force or the deadline for its implementation has expired.[353] It would undermine the binding effect of those obligations and the uniform application of Community law if Member States are not required retroactively to apply those obligations where they have failed to do so, or failed to do so correctly.[354]

In the environmental sphere, this obligation was implicit in a series of cases where the ECJ held that authorities have to set aside any law or national measure adopted in breach of Directive 85/337/EEC, and take all general or specific measures necessary to ensure that an environmental impact assessment is carried out where the authorities have failed to do so.[355] But the principle of nullifying unlawful effect was not explicitly voiced in the environmental sphere until the *Wells* ruling, in which the ECJ held that Member States have to make good any harm caused by the failure to carry out an environmental impact assessment.[356]

This means that, when national authorities have infringed 'means requirements', as contained in Directives 85/337/EEC, 96/61/EC, 89/369/EEC, and 89/429/EEC, to mention but a few, they are obliged to undo the adverse environmental effects that have ensued as a consequence. Excess emissions to air, water and soil may of course not be undone, but national authorities can take future measures to compensate for past behaviour. In the *French*

[352] Case 6/60 *Humblet* [1960] ECR 559. For more recent judgments, see eg Case C–212/04 *Adelener and Others* [2006] ECR I–6057, para 102; and Case C–180/04 *Vassalo* [2006] ECR I–7251, para 38.

[353] Case C–201/02 *Wells* [2004] ECR I–723, paras 64–65; opinion in Case C–299/01 *Commission v Luxembourg* [2002] ECR I–5899, para 23 with references cited.

[354] See analysis in opinion in Case C–453/00 *Kühne* [2004] ECR I–837, paras 65–72.

[355] Case C–435/97 *WWF* [1999] ECR I–5613, para 70; Case C–287/98 *Linster* [2000] ECR I–6717, para 33; Case C–201/02 *Wells* [2004] ECR I–723, para 65.

[356] Case C–201/02 *Wells*, ibid, para 66.

Waste Incinerator[357] case some nine plants operated in breach of Directives 89/369/EEC and 89/429/EEC, and excess pollution had resulted as a consequence. In order to make good the harm caused (in the form of air pollution), national authorities could take compensatory measures *ex nunc* by restricting operating hours or obliging operators to fulfil more stringent incineration conditions for a period appropriate to offset the consequences of the breach.

10.5 *Nullify unlawful consequences v state liability*

There are close links between the principle that unlawful consequences should be nullified, and the principle of state liability, and it is therefore necessary to clarify their relationship. When the ECJ laid down the principle of state liability in *Francovich*, it based this on, inter alia, Article 10 EC and the obligation to nullify the unlawful consequences of a breach of Community law. Conversely, when the ECJ in *Wells* required national authorities to make good any harm caused, it referred to the principle that the Member States should nullify unlawful consequences as laid down in *Humblet* and *Francovich*. This begs the question whether the obligation to nullify unlawful consequences of a breach of Community law is in fact commensurate with state liability, so that the *Francovich* conditions also apply?

It seems to me that the proper view is that the obligation to nullify unlawful consequences applies both to mere infringements and the *Francovich* situation where a serious breach has occurred. The point is that Member States enjoy different degrees of procedural autonomy in respect of the two situations. In relation to mere infringements plaintiffs must rely on procedures and remedies available under domestic law and Member States are entitled to set restrictions on such claims, subject to the *Rewe* doctrine. Whereas this is to some extent also true for claims based on the *Francovich* doctrine, the ECJ has reviewed national restrictions to such actions more stringently. Thus, the ECJ has accepted that expiry of a time limit precludes plaintiffs from requiring restitution of illegal levies,[358] or that plaintiffs could not obtain interest on reimbursed social security payments,[359] and directed such plaintiffs to seek state liability instead.

It may appear contradictory that Community law should allow Member States to restrict the obligation retroactively to fulfil their obligations in this way, while at the same time leaving plaintiffs free to bring claims under the

[357] Case C–60/01 *Commission v France* [2002] ECR I–5879.
[358] Case C–261/95 *Palmisani* [1997] ECR I–4025, paras 28–29.
[359] Case C–66/95 *Sutton* [1997] ECR I–2163, paras 23–27.

Francovich doctrine instead. However, this paradox must be appreciated against the background that claims may only be brought under *Francovich* for serious infringements of Community law, and this is what warrants different standards of relief. As the Advocate General held in *Fantask*:

> The existence of a wholly independent claim for damages, subject to longer time-limits than the comparatively short ones prescribed for restitution and entitlement claims in many Member States, is consistent with the different nature of the claim. Its basis is not merely the unjust enrichment of the State resulting from simple error in the routine application of technical legislation but a serious violation of individual rights, calling for a reappraisal of the balance between such rights and the collective interest in a measure of legal certainty for the State.[360]

Hence, the *Wells* ruling should be understood as conferring a twofold avenue of relief for plaintiffs with corresponding duties for national authorities. First, national authorities must take all necessary measures available under national law to make good the harm caused by infringements of EC environmental legislation. Secondly, if national law curtails the necessary remedies in ways compatible with *Rewe*, plaintiffs may instead seek remediation on the basis of *Francovich*, but then be subject to more stringent conditions.

Another concern voiced by some is that the ECJ has increasingly applied a deferential attitude when reviewing the compatibility with the *Rewe* doctrine of national rules hindering the obligation to nullify unlawful consequences of infringements of Community provisions, and simply relied on the *Francovich* doctrine so as to guarantee judicial sanctions.[361]

10.6 *Reparation by private parties*

For the purposes discussed here, as was noted above (section 10.1), it is presupposed that Community provisions may be invoked against individuals – eg on the basis of consistent interpretation or because the obligations have been implemented in national law. The next question is to what extent environmental obligations may be invoked against individuals for purposes of reparation, and to what extent Community law requires national courts to extend remedies for private parties to enforce these obligations horizontally.

The first issue is fairly straightforward – the obligation must lend itself to 'reparative' direct effect as outlined above in section 10.3, and must be addressed substantively to individuals.[362] Many of the directives discussed above fulfil these

[360] Case C–188/95 *Fantask* [1997] ECR I–6783, para 83. [361] Dougan 2000, 116–26.
[362] See also Prechal 2005, 95.

conditions. Article 8(1) of Directive 75/442/EEC, for instance, requires 'any holder of waste' duly to dispose of it in accordance with the provisions of the directive. If Directive 75/442 is implemented in national law, private plaintiffs may, on the basis of Article 8(1) read in conjunction with Article 4(1), for instance require Texaco to remediate soil contamination following a leak from one of its petrol stations – as the authorities did in *Van de Walle*.[363] It is noteworthy that this does not necessarily require plaintiffs to rely on national liability regimes, as in *Van de Walle*, but they may simply seek an injunction ordering operators to fulfil the obligation laid down in the said provisions.

Conversely, if reparation cannot be ensured by requiring specific performance, Community law may under certain circumstances require national courts to allow plaintiffs to seek reparation from a private party who has infringed Community law. Support for this proposition flows from the *Courage* ruling.[364] That case concerned an agreement which infringed Article 81 EC, and the question was whether one of the parties could sue the other for damages. The national court refused to grant compensation since English law denied a person the right to rely on his own illegal action to obtain damages. The matter was referred to the ECJ, which essentially said that the effectiveness of Community law and Article 81 EC in particular required that plaintiffs could seek compensation for harm suffered.[365] The ruling has recently been confirmed in *Manfredi*.[366]

It seems to me that *Courage* and *Manfredi* imply analogously that national laws may not bar the possibility of claiming reparation for damage caused by infringements by private parties of EC environmental legislation that has been implemented in national law. Although some commentators have adopted a narrow interpretation of the substantive scope of *Courage*,[367] there are in my view no reasons why a similar logic could not be applied generally to infringements of Community law,[368] including EC environmental law.[369]

[363] Case C–1/03 *Van de Walle* [2004] ECR I–7613.

[364] Case C–453/99 *Courage* [2001] ECR I–6297.

[365] Paras 25–31. The court added that some certain restrictions could be justified in order to prevent unjust enrichment.

[366] Joined Cases C–295 to 298/04 *Manfredi* [2006] ECR I–6619 para 60.

[367] Biondi 2003, 48 argued that it is restricted to infringements of EC competition law, whereas van Gerven 2004, 272 argues that the ruling may be extended to cover more generally infringements of economic freedom provisions in so far as the rules have horizontal direct effect.

[368] Similarly, Drake 2006, 858–61. She makes a resvervation for directives, however, since they are not capable of horizontal direct effect. But, as demonstrated above in this section and section 6.1, directives may still have horizontal direct effect if they are implemented in law (*Marks & Spencer* by implication) or horizontal effect by virtue of the principle of consistent interpretation.

[369] See section 2.4.

Another matter is that national procedural law may place restrictions on such claims, which begs the question whether for instance national law may exclude environmental damage as a relevant head of damage. It follows from the principle of equivalence, as recognized in *Manfredi*, that national courts must at the very least award 'particular damages' pursuant to Community actions on the same terms as claims based on domestic law.[370] Hence, if national law for instance allows for an award of reparation *in natura* for environmental damage caused by infringements of domestic provisions, the same remedy must be available for infringements of EC environmental law.

Some might argue, however, that the conditions under which private parties may be held responsible for environmental damage have been exhaustively harmonized following the adoption of Directive 2004/35/EC, which does not provide a possibility for individuals and NGOs to bring actions directly against operators. However, it seems more reasonable to adopt the view that the conditions under which private parties may seek remediation against other private parties falls outside the scope of Directive 2004/35/EC, and that the *Courage* and *Manfredi* rulings therefore still regulate the minimum requirements placed by Community law in this regard. Furthermore, Article 3(2) of Directive 2004/35/EC provides that the directive applies without prejudice to more stringent Community legislation, and it cannot therefore in any event prevent private parties from seeking reparation from private parties on the basis of infringement of specific directives, eg Directive 75/442/EEC.

11 State liability

11.1 *Introduction*

The first hints of state liability doctrine in Community law appeared in the above-mentioned 1960 *Humblet* case, in which the ECJ derived from Article 86 of the ECSC Treaty, which is analogous to Article 10 EC, the obligation on Member States to nullify unlawful consequences of a breach of Community law.[371] Later, in *Russo*, the ECJ held without any specific justification that 'if damage has been caused through an infringement of Community law the state is liable to the injured party of the consequences in the context of the provisions of national liability of the state'.[372] But it was not until *Francovich*

[370] Joined Cases C–295 to 298/04 *Manfredi* [2006] ECR I–6619 para 93.

[371] Case 6/60 *Humblet* [1960] ECR 559.

[372] Case 60/75 *Russo* [1976] ECR 45.

that the ECJ stipulated the constitutive conditions for state liability and held that the principle of state liability was inherent in the Treaty.[373]

The principle of state liability applies 'whichever is the authority of the Member State whose act or omission was responsible for the breach', and includes local as well as federal authorities,[374] the legislature,[375] and – as was recently clarified – the judiciary.[376] This section will try to avoid repeating the wealth of academic discourse produced on this topic, and instead consider its application specifically to infringements of EC environmental law.[377]

The fundamental question is whether the *Francovich* doctrine is applicable to infringements of EC environmental law. This question is probably best approached by examining the first condition – grant of rights – in conjunction with the notion of relevant damage (section 11.2). Thereafter follows an analysis of the notion of 'sufficiently serious breach' (section 11.3), and the requirement of causation (section 11.4). After having mapped the general conditions applicable to state liability, it becomes necessary to examine the recent *Köbler*[378] case in more detail with a view to answering two distinct questions: do the conditions for state liability for infringements committed by the judiciary differ in practice from those applicable to administrative authorities and the legislature (section 11.5.1) and, more generally, what impact will *Köbler* have for the purposes of environmental enforcement (section 11.5.2).

11.2 *Rights and damage*

The original phrasing of the conditions in *Francovich* was, in addition to the requirement of a causal link between the infringement and the damage, first, that the 'result prescribed by the directive should entail the grant of rights to individuals' and, secondly, that it should be possible to identify the content of those rights on the basis of the relevant Community rules.[379] The ECJ has since subsumed the two latter requirements under one condition – 'the rule of law infringed must be intended to confer rights on individuals'.[380] This formulation has caused some commentators to argue that the state liability

[373] Joined Cases C–6 and 9/90 *Francovich and Others* [1991] ECR I–5357, para 35.

[374] C–302/97 *Konle* [1999] ECR I–3099, paras 62–63; and Case C–424/97 *Haim* [2000] ECR I–5123, paras 30–32.

[375] Joined Cases C–46 and 48/93 *Brasserie du Pêcheur* [1996] ECR I–1029, paras 34–36.

[376] Case C–224/01 *Köbler* [2003] ECR I–1023, paras 32–50.

[377] See, in this respect, Somsen 1996.

[378] Case C–224/01 *Köbler* [2003] ECR I–10239.

[379] Joined Cases C–6 and 9/90 *Francovich and Others* [1991] ECR I–5357, para 40.

[380] Case C–190/94 *Dillenkofer* [1996] ECR I–4845, paras 21–23. See also Case C–222/02 *Peter Paul* [2004] ECR I–9425, discussed further below.

doctrine is of limited value for environmental purposes.[381] There have indeed been cases, in particular *Dillenkofer*,[382] where the ECJ seemingly examined whether there was a legislative intent to confer specific rights on individuals. However, as regards the ruling in *Dillenkofer*, closer scrutiny shows that the ECJ's examination of the legislative intent of Directive 90/314/EEC was made in order to rebuke submissions from Germany and the UK to the effect that the directive's objective was to promote competition and not the protection of consumers.[383] This was necessary in order to address the question whether plaintiffs could hold the state responsible for infringements of a rule that protected an interest different from the one they were claming reparation for. The judgment does therefore not address the question whether, in case of directives which only protect one branch of interests, eg environmental protection, the ECJ will in addition look for a legislative intent to confer specific rights on the plaintiffs.[384] But even in the alternative, a significant proportion of environmental directives still qualify on the basis of their link to protection of public health, which the ECJ has held is sufficient reason to state a legislative intent to confer rights.[385] Therefore, at the very least, the requirement of legislative intent to confer rights is not a particularly stringent one.[386]

In order to gain better understanding of exactly what the ECJ meant with the notion of 'rights' in *Francovich*, it is necessary to examine *Brasserie*, in which the ECJ elaborated the reasoning behind the principle of state liability and defined its conditions in more detail. For purposes of clarity, recourse will also be had to the opinion of AG Tesauro, which the ECJ followed closely.[387] As regards the first condition, AG Tesauro commented that 'having

[381] Eg Zuleeg 1992, 31; Shockweiler 1993, 44 (both references from Prechal and Hancher 2002, 103); Barav 1997, 367–68; and van Gerven 1998, 445. For a presentation of the different schools of thought on state liability in the field of environment, see Wennerås 2004, 330.

[382] Case C–190/94 *Dillenkofer* [1996] ECR I–4845. [383] ibid para 38.

[384] For a different view, see the ruling in *Bowden v South West Water and Another* [1998] 3 CMLR 330. The English High Court, applying *Dillenkofer*, rejected a claim of state liability based on the breach of three Community directives for the protection of the environment on the basis that they protected public interests, and could as such not give rise to reparation. The Appeal Court accepted the High Court's understanding of *Dillenkofer*, but had some reservations to its application to the case at hand; see [1999] 3 CMLR 180.

[385] See Opinion of AG Jacobs in Case C–237/90 *Commission v Germany* [1992] ECR I–5973, para 15; and references in chapter 2, section 2.1.4.2.

[386] Similarly, Lenaerts and Corthaut 2006, 313.

[387] The seminal importance of AG Tesauro's opinions (in addition to *Brasserie*, he delivered on the same day opinions in Joined Cases C–392/93 *British Telecommunications and Others* [1996] ECR I–1631and Case C–190/94 *Dillenkofer* [1996] ECR I–4845) on the construction of the state liability doctrine has also been emphasized by Oliver 1997, 641.

regard to the relevant case law, it must be considered that the ECJ intended by those words [grant of rights] to refer generally to all individual legal positions protected by Community law; hence – by definition – this condition is always met in the case of provisions having direct effect'.[388] Echoing the opinion, the ECJ held that state liability was warranted:

> [a]ll the more so in the event of infringement of a right directly conferred by a Community provision upon which individuals are entitled to rely before the national courts. In that event, the right to reparation is the necessary corollary of the direct effect of the Community provisions whose breach caused the damage sustained. In this case it undisputed that the Community provisions at issue [. . .] have direct effect in the sense that they confer on individuals rights upon which they are entitled to rely directly before the national courts.[389]

Hence, infringements of Community provisions that are directly effective satisfy the first condition for state liability, and the right referred to must thus be understood as a procedural right to invoke directly effective provisions before national courts.[390] Put differently, 'any rule having direct effect is a protective rule' for the purposes of state liability.[391] This covers both infringements of provisions that are directly effective in the narrow *Becker*-sense, as well as *Kraaijeveld*-type provisions which can be made operational in national courts – as was demonstrated in *Francovich*.[392]

This proposition gains support also from the *raison d'être* for the state liability doctrine. When introducing this principle in *Francovich*, the ECJ was not only concerned with protecting rights of individuals, but relied heavily on the need to ensure the *effet utile* of Community law.[393] This may have been what *Murgatroyd* was referring to when saying that the 'tenor of the [*Francovich*] judgment' suggested that the ECJ may allow class action suits brought against a Member State in relation to environmental damage caused by failure to implement a directive.[394] Furthermore, the ECJ stressed in *Brasserie* that 'the full effectiveness of Community law would be impaired if individuals were unable to obtain redress when their rights were infringed by a breach of Community law'.[395] Therefore, protection of individual rights is a means of achieving the aim of full effectiveness of Community law,

388 Para 56. 389 Paras 22–23.
390 Similarly, Ward 2000b, 145. Contrast Prechal 2005, 283. 391 Waelbroek 1997, 328.
392 Jans 2000, 211. 393 Caranta 1995, 705; and Jacobs 2001, 131.
394 Murgatroyd 1993, 14–15.
395 Joined Cases C-46 and 48/93 *Brasserie du Pêcheur* [1996] ECR I-1029, para 20.

sometimes called 'functional subjectivisation'.[396] The opinion in *Brasserie* is noteworthy in this respect:

'[W]hat was contemplated [in *Francovich*]... was the means made available in order to reinforce the effectiveness of Community provisions through the effectiveness of judicial supervision of the legal interests created by those provisions and likewise in order not to leave the Member States' failure to fulfil obligations without – inter alia, tangible – consequences. Consequently, it is precisely in the light of those objectives that the position of the individual has been used and given its proper importance'.[397]

The interpretation that *Francovich* applies in principle to any infringements of binding Community provisions that can be made operational by national courts was also indicated in *Konle*, in which the ECJ ruled that Member States must ensure 'reparation for damage caused... by *non-compliance* with Community law'.[398] But most important for our purposes is *Wells* which concerned infringements of Directive 85/337/EEC. Apart from the procedural provisions relating to information and public participation, which were not specifically invoked by Mrs Wells, Directive 85/337/EEC clearly does not confer subjective rights in the traditional sense.[399] One scholar has in fact used this very piece of legislation as an example of Community law that does not grant rights for the purposes of state liability.[400] But without even examining the issue of protective scope, the ECJ ruled as follows:

Under the principle of cooperation in good faith laid down in Article 10 EC the Member States are required to nullify the unlawful consequences of a breach of Community law (see, in particular, Case 6/60 *Humblet* [1960] ECR 559, at 569, and Joined Cases C–6 and 9/90 *Francovich and Others* [1991] ECR I–5357, paragraph 36) [...] The Member State is likewise required to make good any harm caused by the failure to carry out an environmental impact assessment.[401]

This confirms our position, ie that the justification for state liability is not to be found exclusively in protection of individuals rights, but – on the basis of

[396] Ruffert 1997, 316. [397] Para 17.

[398] C–302/97 *Konle* [1999] ECR I–3099, para 62 (emphasis added).

[399] Cf Opinion by AG Elmer in Case C–72/95 *Kraaijeveld* [1996] ECR I–5403, para 70.

[400] Dougan 2005, 240.

[401] Paras 64 and 66. Jans, Lange, Prechal, and Widdershoven 2006, chapter 8 (forthcoming) assert that this statement was an obiter dictum. Leaving aside the different weight which should be accredited an obiter dictum as opposed a ratio decidendi, I would in any event disagree that this statement should properly be deemed obiter. The question from the referring court concerned 'the scope of the obligation to remedy the failure to carry out an assessment of the environmental effects of the project in question'. In light of this question, I fail to see how the ECJ's answer to the effect that the Member State must make good any harm could be deemed an obiter dictum, even though the ECJ had not been informed of what harm might have ensued from the infringement.

the principle of co-operation in Article 10 EC – in ensuring the binding effect of EC law, so that in turn the results of Community obligations are achieved. It is therefore submitted that infringements of environmental provisions that can be invoked by individuals and which thus confer rights on them provide sufficient reason to fulfil the first condition for state liability.

One might question, however, whether *Peter Paul*[402] marks a shift of opinion. Some scholars[403] have deduced from this judgment that state liability presupposes that the Community rule which has been infringed must specifically aim to protect the rights of individuals, and that the ECJ as such adopted more or less the same approach as the House of Lords did in the *Three Rivers* case.[404] I am of a different opinion. As will be recalled,[405] the first question in *Peter Paul* was whether supervisory obligations concerning credit institutions laid down in Directives 77/780/EEC,[406] 89/299/EEC,[407] 89/646/EEC,[408] and 94/19/EC[409] precluded a national rule which barred compensation for infringements of supervisory obligations carried out in the public interest. The second question was whether infringements of these obligations in any event could lead to compensation based on *Francovich* liability. As for the first question, the ECJ admittedly echoes the *Three Rivers* judgment when it first observes that 'Directives 77/780/EEC, 89/299/EEC and 89/646/EEC do not contain any express rule granting [...] rights to depositors'.[410] However, unlike the House of Lords, it then emphasized that Directive 94/19 introduced a protection regime which was meant to provide a guarantee where unavailability of deposits resulted from defective supervision under the older directives.[411] The directives could therefore not confer rights on depositors to compensation over and above the harmonized right to compensation in Directive 94/19/EC, which the plaintiffs had already obtained. On the subsequent issue of *Francovich* liability, the ECJ answered in the following manner:

> [I]t is clear from the answers given to the first two questions that Directives 94/19, 77/80, 89/299 and 89/646 do not confer rights on depositors in the event that their deposits are unavailable as a result of defective supervision on the part of the

402 Case C–222/02 *Peter Paul* [2004] ECR I–9425.
403 Jans, Lange, Prechal, and Widdershoven 2006, chapter 8 (forthcoming).
404 House of Lords, *Three Rivers District Council v Bank of England* [2000] 2 WLR 1220–76.
405 Chapter 2, section 2.1.5.
406 [1977] OJ L322/30.
407 [1989] OJ L239/33 as amended by Directive 92/16/EEC [1992] OJ L75/48.
408 [1989] OJ L386/1 as amended by Directive 95/26/EC [1995] OJ L168/7.
409 [1994] OJ L135/15 as amended by Directive 2005/1/EC [2005] OJ L79/9.
410 Para 41.
411 Paras 45–46.

competent national authorities, *if the compensation of depositors prescribed by Directive 94/19 is ensured*.[412]

Hence, the reason why the conditions for state liability was not deemed fulfilled in *Peter Paul* was due to the fact that the right to – and the level of – compensation had been harmonized by Directive 94/19/EC. The ruling does therefore not alter the conclusions based on the general case law examined above.

As for the requirement that the content of the right – or the obligation rather[413] – must be identifiable on the basis of the Community rules, it has been argued that the discretion inherent in many environmental directives often preclude fulfilment of this condition.[414] However, as was made clear in *Francovich* and confirmed by subsequent case law, discretion does not mean that a minimum content cannot be identified.[415] In fact, the judgment in *Wells* raises the question whether this condition must necessarily be fulfilled in all cases – the requisite level of compensation could not be inferred from the content of the provisions in Directive 85/337/EEC.[416] Furthermore, inherent to the obligation to nullify unlawful consequences, of which *Francovich* is a specific expression, is that Member States may have to take compensatory measures whose substance are not stipulated in the Community rules.

This leads us to the issue whether environmental damage is a relevant head of damage under *Francovich*, or whether it is restricted to economic loss. The cases that have been before the ECJ until now have concerned traditional economic damage, and the issue has therefore not been resolved.[417] Furthermore, the ECJ has held that it is in principle for the Member States to determine the relevant heads of damage. Yet, it may be argued that this tenet of the case law has also been altered by *Wells*. The operative part of the judgment is not too remarkable: the ECJ essentially held that Mrs Wells could seek compensation for harm suffered. But the ratio decidendi is formulated in a manner suggesting that not only economic loss is a relevant head of damage. Indeed, the ECJ ruled that national authorities were required 'to make good *any harm* caused by the failure to carry out an environmental impact assessment'.[418] Although it is not clear from the judgment exactly what harm had been caused in this

412 Para 50 (emphasis added).

413 See Opinion of AG van Gerven in Case 131/88 *Commission v Germany* [1991] ECR I–825, para 7.

414 Prechal and Hancher 2002, 102.

415 Joined Cases C–6 and 9/90 *Francovich and Others* [1991] ECR I–5357, paras 18–20; Case C–190/94 *Dillenkofer* [1996] ECR I–4845, para 45.

416 Case C–201/02 *Wells* [2004] ECR I–723.

417 Jans 2000, 214.

418 Case C–201/02 *Wells* [2004] ECR I–723, para 66.

specific case, on a literal interpretation of the ratio decidendi – 'to make good any harm' – it seems that national authorities can also be required to provide reparation for environmental harm, eg in the form of remediation.

It seems to me that such a general obligation to remedy any damage was already present in *Brasserie*, in which the ECJ required that reparation must be 'commensurate with the loss or damage sustained'.[419] Since damage to ecological resources owed to the public at large cannot be repaired by pecuniary compensation, it seems that restoration is the only form of reparation which is commensurate with the damage sustained. Dougan has on the basis of the rulings in *Maso and Bonifaci*,[420] given the following comment:

> Francovich does not create a right specifically to damages against the Member State for its breach of Community law, but has instead introduced a general right to reparation in whatever form the Member State finds it most convenient to provide [...] Francovich would [thus] become a cause of action but not necessarily a form of relief.[421]

Although he arrives at this conclusion from the perspective of subsidiarity, the implicit corollary of Dougan's reasoning is that *Francovich* is not restricted to economic compensation.

Such an interpretation significantly improves the effectiveness of EC law, and ensures that the state liability doctrine has a deterrent effect on infringements of EC environmental law. It is also consistent with earlier signs in the case law, indicating that the ECJ views compensation as a sanction rather than a remedy.[422] It should be recalled that the ECJ held in *Von Colson*: 'It follows that where a Member State chooses to *penalize the breach ... by the award of compensation*, that compensation must in any event be adequate in relation to the damage sustained'.[423] The recent ruling in *Vassallo* similarly refers to compensation as a means to 'punish' infringements of Community law.[424] Although these judgments did not concern *Francovich* liability, the rationale must be the same, if not more so, in respect of serious breaches of Community

[419] Joined Cases C–46 and 48/93 *Brasserie du Pêcheur* [1996] ECR I–1029, para 82.

[420] Joined Cases C–94 and 95/95 *Bonifaci and Others* [1997] ECR I–3969; and Case C–373/95 *Maso v INPS* [1997] ECR I–4051.

[421] Dougan 2000a, 109–110.

[422] Similarly, Case C–177/88 *Decker* [1990] ECR I–3941, para 23; and Case C–297/91 *Marshall II* [1993] ECR I–4367, para 23. Van Gerven 2000, 530 criticizes the ECJ for 'incorrectly' equalling compensation with 'sanctions'. It seems a dubious proposition to say that the ECJ has an incorrect understanding of the purpose of compensation, what van Gerven apparently overlooks is that compensation under EC law is an autonomous concept, which aim and purpose may validly differ from that given to the concept in the (private law of the) Member States.

[423] Case 14/83 *Von Colson* [1984] ECR 1891, paras 22–23.

[424] Case C–180/04 *Vassallo* [2006] ECR I–7251, para 38 read in conjunction with para 40.

law by national authorities. The same pragmatic viewpoint has influenced the ECJ's construction of *Francovich* liability, the primary purpose of which was, according to AG Tesauro, to ensure that infringements of Community law should entail 'tangible consequences' for Member States.[425]

The ECJ has held that it is for the domestic legal system of each Member State to determine whether punitive damages may be awarded, subject to the principle of equivalence and effectiveness. However, the ruling in *Brasserie* is ambiguous in this regard since the ECJ held that 'an award of exemplary damages pursuant to a claim or an action founded on Community law *cannot be ruled out* if such damages could be awarded pursuant to a similar claim or action founded on domestic law', whilst in the next paragraph stating that it 'must be possible' to award exemplary damages under such circumstances.[426] The recent ruling ruling in *Manfredi* fortunately clarified that the principle of equivalence indeed dictates that punitive damages must be available to actions based on Community law, if such damages may be awarded in similar suits based on domestic law.[427]

Manfredi concerned liability for mere infringements (by private parties), however. In the context of *Francovich* liability, one could argue that exemplary awards should be available regardless of whether national law provided for such damages. The case law on sanctions for infringements of Community law (section 12) suggests a fortiori that sufficiently serious breaches committed by national authorities could qualify for an order of exemplary damages. Where the sufficiently serious breach involves lack of compliance with previous judgments by the ECJ,[428] exemplary damages could be justified by analogy with Article 228 EC.[429] The problem which arises, however, is to whom punitive damages should be paid in matters concerning public interest. It would seem necessary that the infringed provisions conferred rights on specific individuals in order for punitive damages to be collected.

11.3 *Sufficiently serious breach*

It may be purposeful, as a point of departure, to distinguish between two different types of infringements. First, a failure on the part of a Member State to take any measure to achieve the result required within the expiry of the

[425] Opinion in Joined Cases C–46 and 48/93 *Brasserie du Pêcheur* [1996] ECR I–1029, para 17.

[426] Judgment, ibid para 89 cf para 90.

[427] Joined Cases C–295 to Case 298/04 *Manfredi* [2006] ECR I–6619 para 93.

[428] See below and Joined Cases C–46 and 48/93 *Brasserie du Pêcheur* [1996] ECR I–1029, para 79.

[429] Chapter 6, section 4.

deadline for implementation constitutes a serious breach per se.[430] This is of particular relevance in EC environmental law, the sector of Community law in which the Member States most often fail to transpose Community legislation in time.[431] The second situation is where a Member State has taken implementing measures, but insufficiently or incorrectly. In such circumstances the seriousness of the breach must be examined taking into account, in particular:

— the clarity and precision of the rule breached;[432]
— the degree of discretion left by that rule to the national or Community authorities;
— whether the infringement and the damage caused was intentional or accidental;
— whether any error of law was excusable or inexcusable; and
— whether the position taken by a Community institution may have contributed towards the omission.[433]

The *Francovich* criteria are exhaustive and Member States cannot, for instance, make reparation conditional upon fault, although 'certain objective and subjective factors connected with the concept of fault may well be relevant for the purpose of determining whether or not a given breach of Community law is serious'.[434]

A breach of Community law will in any event be considered sufficiently serious if it has persisted despite a judgment from the ECJ establishing the infringement, or where it may be clearly deduced from earlier case law that the conduct in question constituted an infringement.[435] In such cases the infringement and the damage may be seen as intentional and inexcusable, at least from the time the relevant judgment was rendered.[436]

430 See Case C–5/94 *Hedley Lomas* [1996] ECR I–2553, para 28.

431 Commission report on implementation and enforcement (2003).

432 See eg Case C–392/93 *British Telecommunications and Others* [1996] ECR I–1631, para 43; and Case C–319/96 *Brinkman* [1998] ECR I–5255, para 32.

433 See eg Case C–392/93 *British Telecommunications and Others* [1996] ECR I–1631, para 44; Joined Cases C–283, 291, and 292/94 *Denkavit* [1996] ECR I–5063, para 51; and Case C–319/96 *Brinkman* [1998] ECR I–5255, para 31.

434 Joined Cases C–46 and 48/93 *Brasserie du Pêcheur* [1996] ECR I–1029, para 79. Proof of misfeasance in public office, for instance, is not a legitimate condition; see para 73.

435 ibid para 57; cf Case C–470/04 *N* [2006] ECR I–7409, para 66. For a deferential approach, see Case C–224/01 *Köbler* [2003] ECR I–10239 below.

436 An interesting question in this respect is whether the Member States in such a situation are only responsible for damage that occurred after the relevant judgment was rendered, or from the time the infringement occurred. Although preliminary rulings have retroactive effect, since the

The possibility of incurring state liability for failing to comply with judgments by the ECJ may prove very important in environmental cases, especially as deterrence. It is striking that three of the currently five cases in which Member States have failed to comply with judgments of the ECJ and been fined under Article 228(2) EC have been related to environmental protection.[437] State liability actions brought under the *Francovich* doctrine should thus complement the sanctions available under Article 228(2) EC.

Apart from these situations, the assessment of a sufficiently serious breach will in most cases revolve around the precision of the Community rules and the discretion conferred on the authorities. In its case law under Article 288(2) EC, the ECJ has laid down very restrictive conditions for liability whenever the Community institutions enjoy a wide margin of discretion. Consequently, the Community cannot incur liability unless the institution concerned has 'manifestly and gravely disregarded the limits on the exercise of its powers'.[438] The ECJ has justified its restrictive approach with reference to the fact that exercise of the legislative functions must not be hindered by the prospect of actions for damages whenever the general interest of the Community requires legislative measures to be adopted that may adversely affect individual interests. The ECJ held in *Brasserie* that the same applied under the *Francovich* doctrine whenever a Member State acts in a field where it enjoys wide discretion comparable with that of the Community institutions in implementing Community policies.[439]

The premise for analogous application of the ECJ's case law under Article 288(2) EC thus rests on whether the legislative functions of national authorities are 'comparable' to those of the Community institutions, which for several reasons will rarely be the case. First of all, it is questionable whether the risk of incurring state liability may hinder Member States from taking the necessary legislative measures required under Community law. Whereas the Community legislature may be deterred from drafting particular legislation due to risk of liability under Article 288(2) EC, Member States essentially have

infringements only became 'sufficiently serious' from the point in time when the ECJ rendered its ruling, it would appear that plaintiffs may only seek reparation for damage that has occurred after the date of the ruling.

[437] See chapter 6, section 4. One of the three cases referred to, Case C–304/02 *Commission v France* [2005] ECR I–6263 concerned the Community fisheries policy, but the issue in the case was protection of fish stocks and I therefore count this as an environmental case.

[438] Joined Cases 83/76, 94/76, 4/77, 15/77, and 40/77 *HNL and Others v Council and Commission* [1978] ECR 1209, paras 5–6.

[439] Joined Cases C–46 and 48/93 *Brasserie du Pêcheur* [1996] ECR I–1029, para 47; and Case C–392/93 *British Telecom* [1996] ECR I–1631, para 40.

no choice but to implement such legislation, or risk infringement proceedings under Article 226 EC. Secondly, although Member States may have a certain margin of discretion in implementing Community law, that margin of discretion will rarely be 'comparable' with that enjoyed by the Community institutions when drafting secondary legislation. Environmental directives often confer on Member States discretion as to the requisite measures to be adopted, but they regularly contain obligations to achieve a particular result which, as emphasized in *Brasserie*, 'reduce its margin of discretion, sometimes to a considerable degree'.[440] Furthermore, it follows from *Hedley Lomas* that where a Member State has reduced or no discretion, the mere infringement of Community law may be sufficient to establish the existence of a sufficiently serious breach.[441] This is clearly the case where there have been infringements of environmental directives stipulating unconditional and precise obligations of result in the form of limit values in air, soil, or water.

The situation is different in respect of directives containing environmental objectives formulated in general and unquantifiable terms. Yet, the threshold for establishing an infringement in these situations is set to so high that this is tantamount to a 'sufficiently serious breach'. A failure to achieve an environmental objective for a 'protracted period of time', as in *San Rocco* and *Pera Galini*,[442] must imply that authorities have manifestly and gravely disregarded the limits on the exercise of its powers. The same goes for cases requiring complex assessments, in respect of which the national authorities may only be held responsible if they have made a 'manifest error' or 'clearly exceeded the bounds of discretion'.[443]

11.4 *Causation*

It has been argued that the perhaps most onerous hurdle for effective application of the *Francovich* doctrine in environmental proceedings, apart from the concept of rights and relevant damage discussed above, is the requirement of causation.[444] The ECJ refrained initially from providing any guidance on the conditions pertaining to causality, instead leaving this to national law subject to the *Rewe* doctrine.[445] More recent case law has seen the ECJ specifying certain conditions.

[440] ibid para 46. [441] Case C–5/94 *Hedley Lomas* [1996] ECR I–2553, para 28.
[442] See references and comment in chapter 2, section 2.2.5.
[443] Case C–120/97 *Upjohn* [1999] ECR I–223, paras 34–35. But see analysis in section 7(2).
[444] Scott 1998, 161; Jans 2000, 213; and Ward 2000b, 147.
[445] See criticism by eg van Gerven 2000, 512.

The *Andersson* ruling confirmed that state liability may only arise following events occurring after expiry of the deadline for implementation of Community directives.[446] The ECJ held furthermore in *Brinkman* that where the authorities have failed to implement a directive in law, there is no causal link between that omission and any loss when the authorities give immediate effect to the relevant provisions of the directive.[447] The Danish authorities had applied the relevant provisions erroneously, but the consequence of the ECJ's reasoning was that that infringement did not automatically constitute a sufficiently serious breach according to the *Dillenkofer* rationale. It had instead to be assessed according to the *Brasserie* criteria, and the ECJ eventually found that the infringement was excusable, and thus not sufficiently serious.[448]

The ECJ also made it clear in *Rechberger* that once a causal link has been established between an infringement and the damage sustained a Member State cannot be exempted from liability due to 'imprudent conduct by third parties' or the 'occurrence of exceptional and unforeseeable events'.[449] However, it is not clear whether this finding holds general applicability in light of the fact that the legislation in question – Directive 90/314/EEC – was specifically meant to offer protection against exceptional or unforeseeable events.[450] It should also be added that a causal link may a fortiori be precluded where the effects of the national measures are 'too uncertain and indirect', making it impossible to establish an infringement in the first place.[451]

Another matter is whether the causal link between the infringement and the damage sustained is wholly or partially broken where the injured party could have mitigated the loss. The ECJ held in *Brasserie* that national courts can for these purposes indeed examine if the person concerned has shown reasonable diligence in avoiding or limiting loss, and whether he has availed himself of all legal remedies available to him.[452] This issue may have limited relevance for ecological damage where there typically is not a single injured party, but it is the public at large that suffers damage. However, the question may be asked whether, for example, a NGO which has failed to rely on directly effective provisions against national authorities in order to prevent

[446] Case C–321/97 *Andersson* [1999] ECR I–3551, paras 44–45. But this absolute statement may perhaps have to be modified in light of the *Inter-Environnement Wallone* ruling; see chapter 2, section 2.2.3.

[447] See Case C–319/96 *Brinkman* [1998] ECR I–5255, para 29.

[448] See criticism by Tridimas 2001, 306–307.

[449] Case C–140/97 *Rechberger* [1999] ECR I–3499, para 75.

[450] Para 74.

[451] See Case C–379/92 *Peralta* [1994] ECR I–3453, para 24; and Case C–67/97 *Bluhme* [1998] ECR I–8033, para 22.

[452] Joined Cases C–46 and 48/93 *Brasserie du Pêcheur* [1996] ECR I–1029, para 84.

damage may be precluded from subsequently requiring reparation on the basis of the state liability doctrine. Following the ruling in *Metallgesellschaft* this question must be answered negatively.[453] The ECJ ruled explicitly in that case that the failure to rely on the direct effect of the relevant provisions did not preclude bringing a subsequent state liability suit. Some have criticized this ruling and emphasized certain facts particular to the case,[454] as well as pointing out that in the subsequent ruling in *Stockholm Lindöpark*[455] the ECJ noted that a suit for damages did not seem necessary since the plaintiffs could have relied on the direct effect of the relevant provisions. However, if anything the ruling in *Stockholm Lindöpark* would appear implicitly to confirm *Metallgesellschaft*. Despite the fact that the plaintiffs could have relied on direct effect, as noted by the ECJ, it continued to examine at length whether the national authorities had committed a sufficiently serious breach which could render the Member State liable for damages, and answered that question affirmatively. It appears consequently that a failure to rely on the direct effect of the relevant provisions does not preclude a state liability suit.

A more pressing question is whether infringements of procedural obligations, as opposed to substantive obligations, can give rise to a causal link with damage caused. This is a particularly important question in the environmental sphere, in which the Community has increasingly relied on harmonizing procedural aspects of environmental protection, eg by requiring environmental impact assessments, and access to information and public participation for the public concerned etc.[456] These obligations are intended to ensure proper procedures in terms of environmental governance and decision-making, but they are usually not accompanied by substantive obligations to act in a particular manner. In other words if, for instance, an environmental impact assessment demonstrates that a particular project may have significant adverse effects on the environment, or public participation reveals broad opposition to a project, Directive 85/337/EEC still leaves Member States in principle free to approve the project. It thereby becomes difficult to demonstrate that a failure to carry out an environmental impact assessment, or make allowance for public participation, has caused damage. It is therefore all the more surprising that the ECJ in *Wells* nevertheless held that a failure to carry out an environmental impact assessment under Directive 85/337/EEC obliged Member

453 Joined Cases C–397 and 410/98 *Metallgesellschaft and Others* [2001] ECR I–1727, paras 98 et seq.

454 Jans, Lange, Prechal, and Widdershoven 2006, chapter 8 (forthcoming).

455 Case C–150/99 *Stockholm Lindöpark* [2001] ECR I–493, para 35.

456 See references to legislation in section 3.2.

States to make good any harm caused. One should probably apply some caution in deriving any firm conclusions from the *Wells* ruling, however, bearing in mind that the ECJ did not explicitly deal with the issue of causation.

11.5 *Acts and omissions by the judiciary*

11.5.1 *Conditions*

That the ECJ would rule in *Köbler*[457] that decisions by national judiciaries are subject to the *Francovich* doctrine was expected.[458] The real question was whether the ECJ would modify the conditions in some way. Austria and intervening Member States, perhaps not surprisingly, all claimed that there should be more restrictive conditions due to the distinct nature of the judiciary. From the outset, the ECJ dismissed this invitation to construe different conditions.[459] However, the ECJ conceded in relation to the second condition for state liability – 'sufficiently serious breach' – that regard should be had to the specific nature of the judicial function, and to the legitimate requirements of legal certainty. Only in exceptional cases, where a court has manifestly infringed the applicable law, could the state incur liability.[460] However, evaluation of this condition should nonetheless be conducted according to the traditional criteria mentioned in *Brasserie*.[461]

A failure to refer questions to the ECJ under Article 234(3) EC does not necessarily constitute a sufficiently serious breach. Only decisions made in manifest breach of the ECJ's case law automatically fulfil this condition.[462] This appears to refer to cases that are *acte éclairé.* Paradoxically, however, if the issue is *acte éclairé* a national court is not obliged or even supposed to refer a question to the ECJ in the first place,[463] and the issue becomes nugatory. Conversely, in the cases where the national court should have referred a question to the ECJ, ie questions that are neither *acte clair* nor *acte éclairé*, it follows that an erroneous decision by the supreme court cannot constitute a 'manifest breach of the ECJ's case law' and consequently not a 'sufficiently serious

[457] Case C–224/01 *Köbler* [2003] ECR I–10239. See also Case C–129/00 *Commission v Italy* [2003] ECR I–14637.

[458] For an analysis of this case and its impact for the purposes of enforcement of EC environmental law, see Wennerås 2004. For a critical acount, see Wattel 2004.

[459] Para 52.

[460] Para 53.

[461] Para 55.

[462] The Netherlands argued that wrongful decisions as such should not warrant liability, only breaches of the obligation to refer questions under Article 234 EC; see para 18.

[463] Chapter 4, section 2.2. See Case 283/81 *CILFIT and Others* [1982] ECR 3415, paras 14 and 16: the national ECJ is not obliged to refer questions to the ECJ if the point of law at issue was clear from the case law of the ECJ or left no room for reasonable doubt.

breach'. In practice, however, it is likely that an intentional or manifestly negligent failure to refer, ie when a supreme court must understand that the question is not *acte clair*, warrants state liability, even though the decision taken by that court is not strictly in manifest breach of the ECJ's case law.

When considering actual application of the state liability doctrine pursuant to the *Köbler* case it appears that, whereas the conditions might formally be the same irrespective of what authority has committed the breach, in practice the conditions differ. The Austrian court made not just one error, but committed several mistakes, the cumulated effect of which one would have expected to have cleared the threshold of 'sufficiently serious breach' with some margin.[464] Departing from the opinion,[465] the ECJ nevertheless concluded that the mistakes of the Austrian Supreme Court were not manifest in nature and thus not sufficiently serious to incur state liability.[466]

It was perhaps to be expected that the ECJ would shy away from holding a supreme court liable in the same case as it introduced the principle of state liability for decisions of the judiciary. Even so, the ECJ's conclusion indicates that supreme courts are judged according to lenient standards, less strict than those pertaining to the administration and the legislature. The ECJ was generous in finding that the question was not obvious, and also inconsistent with its earlier case law.[467] It appears, furthermore, that the ECJ put considerable emphasis on the fact that the national court apparently acted in good faith when it withdrew the request for a preliminary reference. Thus, the overall impression is that the ECJ intends to use the state liability regime restrictively as against national courts of last instance, limiting its application to instances of intentional or manifestly negligent failure to apply Community law or to request preliminary references under Article 234(3) EC.

But this conclusion should perhaps be qualified in light of the particular circumstances of this case, namely the involvement of the ECJ's registrar. The Austrian court withdrew its request for a preliminary reference – and thereby got into trouble – following a suggestion from the registrar of the

[464] First, it significantly misread the ECJ's earlier ruling in *Schöning* on two accounts (paras 81 and 116). Secondly, the Austrian supreme court was not – under any view of the case law – entitled to consider the matter *acte clair*, and should therefore have upheld its request for a preliminary ruling (para 118).

[465] Opinion, para 174.

[466] Paras 122–23.

[467] It refrained from pointing out that the national court had in the first place erroneously construed – on a misreading of the *Schöning* case – the Austrian scheme as a loyalty bonus, a system which, moreover, the ECJ earlier in the judgment concluded entailed an obstacle that 'clearly cannot be justified in the light of such an objective [loyalty bonus]' (para 83).

ECJ to reconsider whether it was still necessary to seek guidance from the ECJ in light of the ruling in *Schöning*.[468]

The ECJ has since affirmed in *Traghetti* that national law may not impose stricter requirements for liability than what already follows from the condition that the infringement by the court of last instance must be manifest.[469] More specifically, the court ruled that national law may not preclude liability on the general grounds that the error committed concerns interpretation of law or assessment of facts. This was hardly surprising since, as noted by the ECJ, these activities form the very essence of judicial functions.[470] The ECJ also dismissed the legality of a national rule reserving state liability solely to cases of intentional fault and serious misconduct by the judiciary, which the ECJ had previously made clear in *Brasserie* in relation to infringements by the legislature.[471]

11.5.2 *Added value*

What impact will the *Köbler* doctrine have, and in what kind of cases is it likely to make a difference? Most cases where national courts are faced with questions of Community law concern domestic measures that are allegedly in conflict with EC law. If a court fails to request a preliminary ruling and erroneously upholds an unlawful domestic act, the authority responsible for that act – be it the administration or the legislature – may still be liable for breach of Community law. Individuals could therefore in any event hold Member States responsible for infringements committed by the latter authorities under the *Francovich/Brasserie* doctrine. Furthermore, since it is more difficult to establish a sufficiently serious breach committed by the judiciary than the legislature or administrative authorities, it would seem that *Köbler* is prima facie a less attractive prospect for plaintiffs.

On the other hand, errors that the legislature or administration might commit when implementing Community law are different – and therefore assessed differently – from failures of national courts to judicially review and repair such errors. An example is provided by the *British Telecom* case.[472] When implementation of Community legislation is particularly complex, national authorities are granted a certain margin of discretion that will bar state liability if implementation ultimately proves faulty, but not manifestly so.[473] If a court of last instance under such circumstances is subsequently

468 Paras 110–115. 469 Case C-173/03 *Traghetti* [2006] ECR I-5177 para 44.

470 Paras 34 and 38. 471 See section 11.3.

472 Case C-392/93 *British Telecommunications and Others* [1996] ECR I-1631.

473 ibid paras 43–45.

asked to rule on the issue and concludes that the national authorities have acted correctly without asking for guidance from the ECJ, that court faces a greater risk of incurring liability. Individuals may under certain circumstances would therefore be better off suing a Member State for erroneous decisions committed by the judiciary rather than for failures committed by national authorities. This is surely the case if a national court finds that the point of law is not *acte clair*, yet refrains from requesting a preliminary ruling. Such an omission may only be excused – as in *Köbler* – if it was due to a misinterpretation of the complexity of the matter.

The significance of *Köbler* resides perhaps not so much in enforcing the obligation to refer questions under Article 234(3) EC or boosting the principle of supremacy, but in giving national courts of last instance a strong incentive to honour the obligation in Article 10 EC to ensure that Community law takes full effect. This includes interpreting national law consistent with Community law,[474] raising issues of their own motion,[475] and actively reviewing national law on procedures and remedies in light of the *Rewe* doctrine, the *Simmenthal* principle of effectiveness and the principle of effective judicial protection and control.[476] A more vigilant enforcement of these duties would contribute significantly to the effectiveness of Community law, and especially environmental law. If, for instance the German Administrative Supreme Court (the *Bundesverwaltungsgericht*) is asked to adjudicate whether its *Schutznorm* concerning standing rules makes the application of Community environmental law excessively difficult,[477] or the House of Lords is queried whether a requirement to place often exorbitant guarantees in order to obtain an interlocutory injunction in environmental cases conflicts with the right to an effective remedy,[478] failing to review these issues and request a preliminary reference from the ECJ would be at their peril.

In such cases, individuals and environmental NGOs could in principle ask for reparation from the Member State. But more important than the possibility of obtaining reparation, which is seen as difficult for various reasons, is that cases are no longer lost simply because supreme courts refuse to refer questions to the ECJ. By way of asking for state liability for failure to refer questions to the ECJ, individuals have a possibility of obtaining an incidental

[474] See chapter 2, section 4.4.

[475] This applies primarily when domestic law allows national courts to raise issues of their own motion, but national courts are under certain circumstances also obliged to raise issues ex officio regardless of restrictions in national law; see chapter II, section 5and this chapter, section 3.5.4, respectively.

[476] See sections 2.2.1–2.

[477] See section 3.1.2.

[478] See section 6.2.2.

review of the underlying substantive issue. The importance of this was illustrated in *Köbler*: although the Supreme Court was in the end considered not to have committed a sufficiently serious breach, the ECJ nevertheless held that the Austrian remuneration system was unlawful, and the end of the matter was thus that these rules had to be disapplied.[479]

12 Sanctions

As for sanctions for infringements of Community law, the ECJ has consistently held that:

> It should be observed that where Community legislation does not specifically provide any penalty for an infringement or refers for that purpose to national laws, regulations and administrative provisions, Article 5 of the Treaty [Article 10 EC] requires the Member States to take all measures necessary to guarantee the application and effectiveness of Community law. For that purpose, whilst the choice of penalties remains within their discretion, they must ensure in particular that infringements of Community law are penalized under conditions, both procedural and substantive, which are analogous to those applicable to infringements of national law of a similar nature and importance and which, in any event, make the penalty effective, proportionate and dissuasive.[480]

Furthermore, national authorities must proceed with the same diligence with respect to infringements of Community law as they bring to bear vis-à-vis national laws.[481] Prechal has reported that since the mid-1990s Community legislation often included a standard clause incorporating these requirements, or even specific clauses obliging Member States to provide certain sanctions.[482] As a rule, however, the nature of the sanctions is left to the discretion of Member States, which in the case of criminal sanctions followed from the Community's perceived lack of competence in this field.[483]

[479] Para 125.

[480] See, with regard to Community regulations, Case 68/88 *Commission v Greece* [1989] ECR 2965, paras 23 and 24, and in Case C–7/90 *Vandevenne and Others* [1991] ECR I–4371, para 11; Case C–36/94 *Siesse v Director da Alfândega de Alcântara* [1995] ECR I–3573, para 20. As for directives, see eg Case C–382/92 *Commission v UK* [1994] ECR I–2435 para 55 and Joined Cases C–58 and 75/95 *Galloti and Others* [1996] ECR I–4345, para 14.

[481] Case 68/88 *Commission v Greece* ibid para 25.

[482] Prechal 2005, 88.

[483] Case 203/80 *Casati* [1981] ECR 2595, para 27; and Case C–226/97 *Lemmens* [1998] ECR I–3711, para 19.

However, in 2003 the Council adopted Framework Decision 2003/80 on the basis of Articles 29 EC, 31(e) EC and 34(2)(b) EC.[484] The decision requires Member States to impose criminal sanctions on certain listed types of infringements of EC environmental legislation. The legality of the framework decision was subsequently challenged before the ECJ by the Commission, with the support of the Parliament, on the grounds that it should have been based on Article 175 EC.[485]

The background to this dispute was that the Commission had put forward a proposal for a Directive on the Protection of the Environment through Criminal Law,[486] which had gone through a first reading before the EP, after which the Council decided instead to support the proposal for the framework decision submitted by Denmark. The ECJ noted that Article 47 EC provided that acts which fell within the scope of Title VI of the Treaty of the EU must not encroach upon the powers conferred by the EC Treaty on the Community. Hence, the legality of the framework decision turned on whether harmonization of criminal law in the field of the environment could have been adopted under Article 175 EC. Although noting that criminal law in principle fell outside the remit of Community competence, the ECJ added the following important remark:

> However, the last-mentioned finding does not prevent the Community legislature, when the application of effective, proportionate and dissuasive criminal penalties by the competent national authorities is an essential measure for combating serious environmental offences, from taking measures which relate to the criminal law of the Member States which it considers necessary in order to ensure that the rules which it lays down on environmental protection are fully effective.[487]

Having thus established incidental Community competence in criminal matters under Article 175 EC, it followed that the framework decision had to be annulled.[488] One may now expect that the proposed directive will resurface, but it remains to be seen how co-operative the Council will be in the legislative process, and it is likely that it will in any event seek to introduce amendments to bring it in line with the framework decision. Krämer is more sceptical – in his view it is unlikely that there will for the foreseeable future be legislation providing for criminal provisions for the whole area of environmental law. He argues that any legislative activity is more likely to be reserved

484 [2003] OJ L29/55.
485 Case C–176/03 *Commission v Council* [2005] ECR I–7879.
486 [2001] OJ C180/E 238.
487 Case C–176/03 *Commission v Council* [2005] ECR I–7879, para 48.
488 See also the similar Case C–440/05 *Commission v Council*, pending.

to specific, high-profile areas, such as ship-source pollution, illegal trade in timber, endangered species, waste, and ozone-depleting substances.[489]

13 Conclusion

The frequent reference to individual rights in the context of the ECJ's case law on procedures and remedies may explain why the significant impact of this jurisprudence on enforcement of EC environmental law has been overlooked, disputed, and underestimated. But the ECJ is foremost a guardian of the full effectiveness of Community law, and in this respect all sectors of EC law are equal. It has therefore used the notion of rights, not as a means of narrowing the applicability of its judicial protection and control doctrines to specific areas of law, but to justify what could otherwise be perceived as highly intrusive inroads into national procedural law. The autonomous Community notion of rights has accordingly been given a very broad interpretation, which embraces both plaintiffs' right to enforce Community interests, and their own individual interests. The ECJ's usage of rights may therefore be described as 'pragmatic'[490] or 'functional',[491] although these terms fail to do justice to the positive spillover effects on public interest litigation in fields like the environment. In the words of one scholar, 'EC law may have given rise to a new notion of "rights", the observance of which, as a matter of Community law, may require national remedies even where these do not exist for similar national "rights" '.[492]

Indeed, the findings in this chapter indicate that the ECJ's judicial protection principles apply in full to environmental law suits, which will require Member States to adapt their procedures and remedies in many aspects. Furthermore, the specific characteristics of environmental litigation demand a particularly critical treatment of procedural rules that are inherently capable of limiting effective enforcement of EC environmental law in particular. Perhaps the most important finding is that the state may incur liability for environmental damage, including ecological damage, under the *Francovich* doctrine, although it was noted that reparation can regularly be obtained more easily through the direct effect doctrine. The deterrent effect of EC environmental law is, moreover, ensured by the obligation for national

[489] Krämer 2006a, 287–88. [490] Jacobs 2004, 308.
[491] Ruffert 1997, 316. [492] Somsen 2000, 332.

authorities to provide adequate sanctions – which is especially likely to induce compliance once the EC adopts harmonizing measures on criminal sanctions for infringements of environmental law.

The corollary of these findings is that the Aarhus Convention, and secondary legislation implementing it, has limited added value in relation to access to justice in national courts. Article 9(2) of the Aarhus Convention and the implementation in Articles 10a and 15a of Directive 85/337/EEC may have strengthened the Community requirements concerning judicial review of acts subject to public participation, but the general provisions on access to justice – Article 9(3) of Aarhus and, if adopted, the proposed directive on access to justice in environmental matters – hardly make a dent in Member States' national laws. Contrary to forecasts that the Aarhus Convention should be a 'critical instrument in sharpening the effectiveness of environmental rights based on both national and EC law',[493] it seems that the requirements concerning access to justice rarely go beyond the procedural and remedial guarantees already flowing from the ECJ's case law, and in some respects fall short of these guarantees.

This is not so surprising given that the Aarhus Convention was negotiated at inter-governmental level by Member States and others who to varying degrees were preoccupied with safeguarding national procedural autonomy through inclusions of vague terms and open-ended goals. Such concerns have clearly not been afforded similar weight by the ECJ in its stride towards ensuring full effectiveness of Community law, including environmental law.

[493] See eg De Búrca and Ryan 2000, 150 albeit they take a reservation as concerns future developments in ECJ jurisprudence.

4

Preliminary references

1 Introduction

This chapter concerns the interplay between national courts and the ECJ through the preliminary reference procedure of Article 234 EC. In accordance with this provision, national courts may refer questions to the ECJ concerning the interpretation or validity of Community acts. There are significant differences between the two actions, however.

Preliminary references on the interpretation of Community acts, in particular environmental law, are often brought in the context of actions against national authorities for lacking or incorrect implementation.[1] Article 234 EC therefore complements the infringement procedure of Article 226 EC in some respects. Preliminary references on the validity of Community acts, on the other hand, complement the Article 230 EC procedure. In the first situation, procedural and remedial rules are mostly governed by national law, whilst in the second case, when EC acts are challenged, Community law regulates the rules on procedures and remedies to a larger extent. After a brief introduction of the features which the two procedures have in common (section 2), I shall therefore treat issues of interpretation (section 3) and the review of validity (section 4) in separate sections. Sanctions are dealt with in section 5, which is followed by conclusions (section 6).

The preliminary reference procedure has of yet been applied modestly in environmental cases. Of the approximately 225 preliminary rulings the ECJ issues annually, less than 5 per cent concern EC environmental law,[2] and many of these are driven by commercial rather than environmental interests.[3]

[1] Implementation here is understood in the broad sense as to include transposition, application, and enforcement; see Opinion in Case 494/01 *Commission v Ireland* [2005] ECR I–3331, paras 23–29.

[2] Krämer 2004, 134.

[3] Somsen 2000, 326–27.

Between 1995 and 2003 there have been on average six preliminary rulings concerning environmental law each year.[4] An explanation for these low numbers can be found in the features of environmental law that were discussed in chapter 3, eg lacking standing, high legal costs and the general lack of financial incentives to bring environmental cases. At the same time, the data can partly be explained by structural and institutional deficits inherent in the Article 234 EC procedure. This chapter will therefore attempt to assess the system of preliminary references with a view to determining its effectiveness for the purposes of environmental law suits.

2 General conditions

2.1 *Competence*

It should be noted from the outset that plaintiffs cannot refer questions to the ECJ themselves, but must persuade national courts to do so. It is also for national courts to articulate questions to be referred, and parties cannot alter the wording of those questions,[5] or add questions in proceedings before the ECJ.[6] As poignantly put by Lord Denning, 'The European Court would not listen to any party who went moaning to them'.[7]

Article 234 EC confers the right to request preliminary rulings on 'any court or tribunal of a Member State'. Administrative organs and national parliaments can therefore not ask for preliminary rulings. The term 'court or tribunal' is an autonomous concept of EC law, and need not coincide with those existing in domestic legal orders. Apart from the ordinary courts of the Member States, special courts may also qualify under Article 234 EC. It is therefore not relevant whether the organ is formally operating as a court in the domestic legal order. What matters is whether it factually functions as one. Relevant factors include whether the court is independent, whether it is a permanent body, whether it is supported by the public authorities of the Member State, whether it is taking decisions in accordance with law, whether the procedure is contradictory, whether parties are obliged to refer disputes

[4] Krämer 2004, 128.

[5] Case C-297/94 *Bruyère and Others* [1996] ECR I-1551, para 19; and Case C-466/00 *Kaba* [2003] ECR I-2219, para 40.

[6] See eg Case C-261/95 *Palmisani* [1997] ECR I-4025 para 31; and Case C-500/04 *Proxxon* [2006] ECR I-1545, paras 16–18.

[7] Reference in Lenaerts and Arts 1999, 29.

to the organ in question, whether decisions have the force of *res judicata*, and whether rulings are enforceable.[8] However, not all these factors need to be fulfilled in order for a body to be regarded a court for the purposes of Article 234.

Administrative appeal boards will generally not qualify under these conditions for want of independence and impartiality.[9] However, some doubts may occur in respect of quasi judicial appeal bodies. In Denmark, for instance, the majority of environmental litigation occurs before highly specialized environmental appeals boards, which among its members rank officials from the Supreme Court.[10] However, although functionally independent, the panels are formally part of the administration, which is responsible for their funding.[11] It would therefore seem that they are not independent review bodies for the purposes of Article 234 EC.[12]

Organs which are also normally not considered courts or tribunals in the context of Article 234 EC are arbitral tribunals established by contract between private parties,[13] but this, of course, holds in any event limited relevance for purposes of environmental litigation.

2.2 *Obligations*

Article 234(3) EC places an obligation on national courts 'against whose decision there is no judicial remedy' to refer any questions concerning interpretation or the validity of Community acts. Before examining the courts and tribunals falling inside this definition, it should be noted that a lower court is also obliged to refer questions to the ECJ where it has doubts about the validity of Community acts, irrespective of whether this has been raised by the parties or advanced ex officio.[14] This flows from the fact that the ECJ is exclusively competent to render rulings on the validity of Community measures.[15] The ECJ reaffirmed recently in *Gaston Schul* its exclusive competence in this regard, and rejected that a court of last instance could render rulings on the validity of the provisions of a regulation, even where the ECJ

[8] See eg Case C–61/65 *Vaassen* [1966] ECR 272; Case C–416/96 *Nour Eddline El-Yassini* [1999] ECR I–1209, para 17; and Case C–259/04 *Emanuel* [2006] ECR I–3089, para 19.

[9] See eg the system of administrative appeal to the Planning Inspectorate in the UK, as described in de Sadeleer, Roller, and Dross 2005, 139.

[10] ibid 23–25.

[11] ibid.

[12] See, by implication, Case C–53/03 *Syfait* [2005] ECR I–4609.

[13] Case C–126/97 *Eco Swiss* [1999] ECR I–3055, para 34; and Case C–125/04 *Denuit* [2005] ECR I–923, paras 14–16.

[14] Case C–344/04 *International Air Transport Association* [2006] ECR I–403, paras 29–30.

[15] Case C–314/85 *Foto-Frost v Hauptzollamt Luebeck-Ost* [1987] ECR 4199, para 20.

had already declared analogous provisions of another comparable regulation invalid.[16] It also clarified that *CILFIT*, discussed below, cannot be applied analogously to matters concerning the validity of Community acts.[17]

The bodies formally designed as courts of last instance in the Member States clearly fall within the scope of Article 234(3) EC, be it a general supreme court, as the House of Lords in the UK, or a court of last instance in a particular sector, eg la Cour de Cassation and le Conseil d'Etat in France. The question is whether lower courts which deliver judgments which may not be appealed also fall under Article 234(3) EC.[18] A literal interpretation of the Treaty supports this view, and that has been confirmed by the ECJ in the *Costa Enel* case, where the lowest branch of the Italian judiciary, acting as a court of last instance due to the small pecuniary interest involved, was held to fall under the obligation in Article 234(3) EC to refer the matter to the ECJ.[19] The same must apply to specialized tribunals which act as courts of last instance, eg the Swedish Superior Environmental Court (Miljööverdomstolen).[20] On the other hand, the fact that an appeal is dependent on being held admissible, subject to the discretion of the national court of last instance, does not render the lower court's decision deprived of a remedy for the purposes of Article 234(3) EC.[21]

Although the text of Article 234(3) EC suggests that 'any question' of Community law would have to be referred by a court of last instance, the ECJ has allowed for certain exceptions. It first clarified in *Da Costa* that there is no obligation to refer when a question is materially identical with a question that has already been subject to a preliminary ruling in a similar case.[22] The ruling in *CILFIT*, went further and stipulated more generally the conditions under which a court of last instance could omit to request preliminary rulings:

1) if the question is irrelevant; or
2) when the Community provision has already been interpreted by the ECJ, irrespective of the proceedings which led to those proceedings, even though the questions at issue are not strictly identical (*acte éclairé*); or

[16] Case C–461/03 *Gaston Schul* [2006] ECR I–10513, para 25. [17] Para 19.

[18] This issue has often be discussed under the headings of the 'abstract theory' v the 'concrete theory', ie whether the formal position of the court was the determining factor or whether the decisive factor was whether in concrete cases it acted as a court of last instance.

[19] Case C–6/64 *Costa Enel* [1964] ECR 592.

[20] Ebbesson 2002, 443, with the caveat that some decisions can be further appealed to the Swedish Supreme Court. [21] Case C–99/00 *Lyckeskog* [2002] ECR I–4839, para 16.

[22] Joined Cases C–28 to 30/62 *Da Costa* [1963] ECR 31.

3) when the correct application of Community law is so obvious as to leave no scope for any reasonable doubt[23] (*acte clair*). In this respect, the national court must in particular be convinced that the matter is equally obvious to the courts of the other Member States and to the ECJ.[24]

The conditions in *CILFIT* have been much criticized for being too strict and thereby encroaching on the discretion of the national courts of last instance,[25] whilst, consequently, overloading the ECJ. However, the ECJ has not been willing to amend the criteria in *CILFIT* and they remain applicable[26] – although calls for a change have reoccurred in the wake of *Köbler*.[27] That case affirmed, as will be recalled, that infringements of the duty to refer preliminary questions in breach of Article 234(3) EC may result in state liability under the *Francovich* doctrine.[28] It is noteworthy in this respect that Spanish, Portuguese, Greek, and Irish courts have not (as at 2004) referred one environmental case for a preliminary ruling.[29]

2.3 *Admissibility*

The point of departure is that where a question submitted by a national court concerns the interpretation of Community law, the ECJ is, in principle, bound to give a ruling.[30] However, it may reject the application, or require clarification from the national court, where it is manifest that the question referred is not related to Community law.[31] The same applies to questions which are phrased in such a general manner that the ECJ finds itself unable to provide an answer.[32] Finally, but importantly, hypothetical questions will be held inadmissible as a genuine dispute must underlie the reference. The ECJ originally applied this norm stringently, most notably in the two *Foglia* cases.[33] However, following massive academic criticism of the ECJ acting as an

[23] Case C–283/81 *CILFIT* [1982] ECR 3415, para 21; see also paras 13–16.

[24] See Case C–495/03 *Intermodal* [2005] ECR I–8151, para 39.

[25] Bebr 1983, 466 et seq; Rasmussen 1984, 342; and Mancini/Keeling 1991, 4.

[26] See eg the unsuccessful attempt by AG Jacobs in Case C–338/95 *Wiener* [1997] ECR I–6495, para 64. For a good overview of the discussions concerning *CILFIT*, see opinion of AG Stix-Hackl in Case C–495/03 *Intermodal* [2005] ECR I–8151, paras 76–106.

[27] Wattel 2004, 179.

[28] Chapter 3, section 11.5.

[29] Krämer 2004, 134.

[30] See eg C–167/01 *Inspire Art* [2003] ECR I–10155, para 43; and Case 144/04 *Mangold* [2005] ECR I–9981, para 35.

[31] See eg Case C–105/79 *Hayange* [1979] ECR 2257; Case C–95/96 *URSSAF* [1996] ECR I–12, paras 1–7.

[32] See eg Case C–14/86 *Pretore de Salo* [1987] ECR 2545, para 16.

[33] Case 104/79 *Foglia v Novello* [1980] ECR 745; and Case 244/89 *Foglia v Novello II* [1981] ECR 3045.

arbitrator of the relevance of national courts' questions, the ECJ has retreated from this policy and since reiterated in several cases that it is in principle for national courts to determine the relevance of their questions and whether or not they are hypothetical.[34] Hence, the ECJ now suffices to say:

> A reference by a national court can be rejected only if it appears that the procedure laid down by Article 177 of the Treaty [now 234 EC] has been misused and a ruling from the Court elicited by means of a contrived dispute, or it is obvious that Community law cannot apply, either directly or indirectly, to the circumstances of the case referred to the Court.[35]

Between 1991 and 2000, only 27 preliminary references have been rejected by the ECJ of Justice, ie approximately 1 per cent.[36]

2.4 *Ex officio*

The system of cooperation laid down in Article 234 EC provides that the ECJ plays a passive role in the proceedings in that it is for national courts to determine the relevant questions and for the ECJ to respond to the issues submitted to it. It is now settled case law that it is for the national court alone to assess the relevance of its questions in the context of preliminary references.[37] The ECJ has held, on the other hand, that Article 234 EC is an instrument of judicial cooperation, by means of which it provides national courts with the points of interpretation of Community law which may be helpful to them in assessing the effects of a provision of national law at issue in the disputes before them.[38] The ECJ may to this end reformulate the national court's questions, which it did for instance with great effect in *Kraaijeveld*.[39] This could be contrasted with the strict adherence to the national court's question in *Comitato* concerning Article 4 of Directive 75/442/EEC, which prevented a broader review of discretion as occurred later in *San Rocco* (albeit in infringement proceedings).[40] Furthermore, the ECJ may also find it necessary to

[34] Case C–415/93 *Bosman* [1995] ECR I–4921, paras 63–67.

[35] Case C–130/97 *Giloy v Hauptzollamt Frankfurt am Main-Ost* [1997] ECR I–4291, para 22; and Case C–1/99 *Kofisa* [2000] ECR I–207, para 22.

[36] Edward 2000, 122.

[37] Joined Cases C–515, 519 to 524 and 526/99 to 540/99 *Reisch and Others* [2002] ECR I–2157, para 25; and Case C–300/01 *Salzmann* [2003] ECR I–4899, para 30.

[38] Case C–254/98 *TK-Heimdienst* [1998] ECR I–151, para 12, and Joined Cases C–515, 519 to 524 and 526/99 to 540/99 *Reisch and Others* [2002] ECR I–2157, para 22; and C–300/01 *Salzmann* [2003] ECR I–4899, para 28.

[39] See eg Case C–72/95 *Kraaijeveld* [1996] ECR I–5403; and Case C–127/02 *Waddenzee* [2004] ECR I–7405, discussed in chapter 3, sections 2.1.3 and 2.2.2.

[40] See also Prechal and Hancher 2002, 98–99.

consider provisions of Community law which the national court has not referred to in its question,[41] and it even has a duty to do so where this is required in order for the national court to decide the pending case correctly.[42]

The main rule is that the ECJ will not examine the validity of an EC act on its own initiative in a case where the national court has referred questions concerning its interpretation.[43] But it has on occasion construed questions from national courts on the interpretation of Community law as concerning validity of Community acts.[44] Furthermore, the ECJ did exceptionally examine the validity of a Community measure ex officio in the *Internationale* case, ruling that 'failure to provide the necessary publicity [concerning the act] can be considered by the ECJ of its own motion'.[45] It has been inferred from this case that the ECJ may thus raise questions concerning the validity of an EC act for reasons of public policy, as well as in instances of manifest substantive infringements of (superior) EC law.[46] On the other hand, it seems that the ECJ does not have any obligation to raise such issues on its own initiative, which creates certain incoherence as compared with national courts in this respect.[47]

3 Interpretation

3.1 *Introduction*

Through the preliminary reference procedure in Article 234 EC national courts may seek guidance from the ECJ on the substantive meaning of EC environmental law. The ECJ interprets the relevant provisions, whilst leaving the national court to apply the interpreted rule to the facts of the case. In practice, however, the ECJ increasingly shapes its rulings in such a manner so as indirectly, or directly in some cases, to rule on the legality of national measures or the lawfulness of failures to take certain measures. The preliminary reference procedure has therefore gradually acquired some of the characteristics of the infringement procedure under Article 226 EC. This has

41 Case C–45/06 *Campina*, nyr, para 31.

42 Case C–304/00 *Shawson and Gagg & Sons* [2002] ECR I–10737, paras 57–58; Case C–439/01 *Kvasnicku* [2003] ECR I–745, para 22.

43 See eg Case C–185/73 *König* [1974] ECR 617, para 7; and Case 28/76 *Milac* [1976] ECR I–1653.

44 Case C–16/65 *Schwarze* [1965] ECR I–877.

45 Joined Cases 73 and 74/63 *Internationale* [1964] ECR 1 at 14.

46 Schermers and Waelbroek 2001, 497.

47 See chapter 2, section 4; and chapter 3, section 4.2.

been criticized by some on the basis that the preliminary reference procedure is less comprehensive than the infringement procedure of Article 226 EC.[48] The ECJ is usually less well informed about the facts of the case and Member States have fewer procedural rights under the Article 234 EC procedure compared with the extensive rights of negotiation and submissions guaranteed under Article 226 EC.

Although this criticism certainly has a sound theoretical basis, the ECJ's more activist use of the preliminary reference procedure is to some extent a logical corollary of the introduction of direct effect. As will be recalled, the direct effect of the Community legal order was inter alia justified for the purpose of employing the vigilance of individuals seeking to protect their rights as a complementary form of supervision to the Commission's mandate under Article 226 EC.[49] It is also noteworthy in this respect that the Articles 234 and 226 EC procedures are not mutually exclusive; the fact that an infringement proceeding has been initiated does not prevent the ECJ from issuing a preliminary ruling on the same matter.[50] Conversely, the fact that the Commission discontinues infringement proceedings against a Member State has no effect on the possibility of obtaining a preliminary reference concerning the same subject matter, or the obligation of a court of last instance of that Member State to refer a question.[51]

It should be added that the Article 234 EC procedure is of course not only used for purposes of challenging the legality of national measures, but national courts will often seek guidance from the ECJ for the purpose of interpreting national law consistently with Community legislation. This is perhaps especially relevant in a densely regulated and complex area such as EC environmental law.

3.2 *Acts susceptible to interpretation*

The acts susceptible to interpretation are enumerated in Article 234(1) EC. National courts can ask for preliminary rulings concerning the interpretation of the Treaty, acts of the Community institutions and the European Central Bank (ECB), and the statutes of bodies established by an act of Council – where provided by those acts. It is noteworthy that the Treaty referred to is the EC Treaty, and the second and third pillars of the EU Treaty consequently fall

[48] See eg Schermers and Waelbroek 2001, 649.

[49] Chapter 2, section 2.1.2.

[50] See eg Case C–221/89 *Factortame* [1991] ECR I–3905, cf Case C–246/89 *Commission v UK* [1991] ECR I–4585.

[51] Case C–393/98 *Gomes* [2001] ECR I–01327, para 19.

outside the ambit of Article 234 EC.[52] Article 46 EU does, however, confer jurisdiction to give preliminary references on certain specifically listed issues, cf Article 35 EU.[53] This would be particularly relevant in relation to Community measures concerning criminal and judicial cooperation in environmental matters, but following the recent ruling in *Commission v Council*[54] such acts shall in principle be adopted under Article 175 EC and the matter has become moot.[55]

The notion of 'acts of the institutions' include all binding legislative and administrative acts, eg environmental regulations, directives and decisions. Moreover, it follows from the fact that the ECJ ranks among the Community institutions that its judgments fall within the scope of Article 234 EC, and it has on several occasions accepted questions concerning the interpretation of its case law.[56] Acts of the institutions also include international agreements to which the Community is party.[57] But mixed agreements, ie where competence is shared between the Community and Member States and both are parties to an international agreement, may raise complex problems of jurisdiction concerning provisions relating exclusively to the relationship between the Member States and third parties. The ECJ has until now dodged this issue by construing the relevant provisions as also concerning the Community's powers.[58] In fact, the ECJ has even found that it has jurisdiction to interpret international agreements which only the Member States ratified, but in doing so was deemed to have 'acted in the interest and on behalf of the Community'.[59]

Acts of the institutions have also been held to include non-binding acts, eg resolutions, opinions, and recommendations.[60] Courts may thus seek interpretation of environmental action programmes, for instance.[61]

The notion of Community institutions has, moreover, been interpreted broadly so as to cover any 'Community institution or agency', which has

[52] See Article 46 of the Treaty of the European Union, which notably lists certain exceptions.

[53] See eg Case C–105/03 *Puppino* [2005] ECR I–5285.

[54] Case C–176/03 *Commission v Council* [2005] ECR I–7879.

[55] Albeit see pending Case C–440/05 *Commission v Parliament and Council.*

[56] See eg Case C–13/67 *Becher* [1968] ECR 197; and Joined Cases C–46 and 48/93 *Brasserie du Pêcheur* [1996] ECR I–1029.

[57] Case C–181/73 *Haegeman* [1974] ECR 449, paras 3–5.

[58] See eg Joined Cases C–300 and 392/98 *Dior* [2000] ECR I–11307, para 33.

[59] Case C–439/01 *Kvasnicka* [2003] ECR I–745, paras 23–24.

[60] Case 9/73 *Schlüter* [1973] ECR 1135, para 40; Case 113/75 *Frecassetti* [1976] ECR 983, paras 8–9; Case C–322/88 *Grimaldi* [1989] ECR 4407, paras 7–9; and Case C–188/91 *Shell* [1993] ECR I–363.

[61] For an overview of soft law instruments in EC environmental law, see Somsen 1998.

taken part in the adoption of the act.[62] Some scholars have taken this to mean that this covers virtually 'any Community body', in addition to the institutions mentioned in Article 7 EC.[63] This is of course practically important as regards acts adopted by Community bodies acting under delegated powers.[64]

National courts may naturally refer questions on the interpretation of environmental principles in so far as they are codified in the Treaty, eg Articles 3, 6, and 174 EC, and in secondary legislation, but the ECJ has also accepted jurisdiction in relation to general principles of EC law which have not been codified.[65]

3.3 *Consequences*

Article 234 EC gives the ECJ jurisdiction to provide preliminary rulings on the interpretation of Community law, whilst the application of that interpretation to the facts of the case rest with national courts. The ECJ will therefore normally not apply the interpreted rule to the facts of the domestic dispute,[66] or provide a ruling on the validity of national law:

> Although in proceedings brought under Article 177 [now 234 EC] of the Treaty, it is not for the ECJ to rule on the compatibility of national rules with provisions of Community law, the ECJ is competent to give a ruling on the interpretation of Community law in order to enable the national court to assess the compatibility of those rules with the Community provisions.[67]

But there is a fine line between interpretation and application, and the more detailed the ECJ ruling on the interpretation of the Community rule, the less there is left for the national court to decide.[68] The ECJ often refers to 'the need to afford a helpful interpretation of Community law',[69] or the necessity to 'provide the national court with the factors of interpretation depending on national law which might be useful to it in evaluating the effects of such

[62] See, by implication, Case 152/83 *Demouche* [1987] ECR 3833, paras 15–21.

[63] Lenaerts and Arts 1999, 120.

[64] Schermers and Waelbroeck 2001, 295, claim that this must apply to powers which have been 'regularly delegated', but it seems difficult to understand why the same should not apply generally, including powers which have been delegated on an 'ad hoc' basis.

[65] See eg Case C–260/89 *ERT* [1991] ECR I–2925, para 42; and Case C–177/94 *Perfili* [1996] I–161, para 20.

[66] See eg Joined Cases C–134 and 135/91 *Kerafina* [1992] ECR I–5699; and Joined Cases C–260 to 263/00 *LohmanandMedi Bayreuth* [2002] ECR I–10045, para 26.

[67] See Case C–130/93 *Lamaire* [1994] ECR I–3215, para 10.

[68] See eg Case C–291/03 *My Travel* [2005] ECR I–8477, paras 43–45. See also Somsen 2000, 323–24.

[69] Case C–244/78 *French Dairy* [1979] ECR 2663.

[a] provision'.[70] The ECJ's answer may then be phrased so as more or less to dictate its opinion on the legality of the national measures. In the recent *Waddenzee* case, for instance, the ECJ clearly indicated that permitting cockle fishing in Waddenzee was in breach of Article 6(3) of Directive 93/42/EC, although formally leaving this to be determined by the national authorities.[71] The *Radlberger* case similarly left little doubt that the ECJ considered certain provisions in German waste legislation to be in breach of Article 28 EC.[72] Furthermore, it does exceptionally occur that the ECJ finds the facts provided sufficient to give a final ruling, and thus provide a judgment directly on the compatibility of the contested national measures with Community law. This has happened in particular in the context of preliminary rulings on the interpretation of the *Francovich* doctrine, where the court has provided answers concerning the question whether a disputed national measure represented a 'sufficiently serious breach'.[73]

Interpretations of Community law are binding on the national court that referred the questions and the parties to the proceedings. Although the EC does not formally have a strict principle of precedent,[74] the ECJ has clearly implied in *CILFIT* that other national courts should take its rulings into consideration and apply the interpreted rule accordingly on similar cases.[75] It has for instance held that the Article 234 EC procedure 'makes it possible to ensure a uniform interpretation of the Treaty and is capable of bringing about its identical application'.[76] Thus, when the ECJ receives a question on which it has delivered an interpretation before, it frequently sends the national court a copy of the relevant judgment and asks whether the preliminary reference is still needed,[77] or even simply issues a reasoned order referring to its previous ruling.[78] Finally, and importantly, if a court of last instance fails to apply settled case law of the ECJ, the state may be held liable under the *Köbler*

[70] See eg Case C–66/77 *Kuyken* [1977] ECR 2311, para 10.

[71] Case C–127/02 *Waddenzee* [2004] ECR I–7405. As a consequence of the ECJ's ruling, all cockle fishing in Waddenzee was temporarily put on a hold pending further inquiry into the legality of the permits.

[72] Case C–309/02 *Radlberger* [2004] ECR I–11763, para 83.

[73] Case C–392/93 *British Telecom* [1996] ECR I–1631, paras 41–45; Case C–319/96 *Brinkman* [1998] ECR I–5255, para 26; and Case C–224/01 *Köbler* [2003] ECR I–10239, paras 101 and 124.

[74] See analyis by Arnull 2000, 528–33.

[75] See section 2.2 above.

[76] Case C–28/67 *Molkerei-Zentrale* [1968] ECR 143.

[77] But Case C–224/01 *Köbler* [2003] ECR I–10239 illustrates that the ECJ, or its registrar rather, should be careful doing this when it is not clear whether the issues are identical.

[78] See Article 104(3) of the Rules of Procedure, according to which the ECJ can issue a reasoned order inter alia where 'the question is identical to a question on which the ECJ has already ruled'.

doctrine.[79] Preliminary rulings on interpretation of EC law do therefore for practical purposes function as precedents.

National courts are in turn obliged by virtue of Article 10 EC to take all necessary measures in order to comply with the ECJ's preliminary ruling, eg by consistent interpretation or, if this is not possible, setting aside a conflicting national measure.[80] Furthermore, the court must also ensure that national authorities nullify the consequences of unlawful breaches and make good any harm thus caused, as emphasized in *Wells*.[81]

In line with most legal traditions, the ECJ's interpretation of the law has retroactive effect. It is settled case law that preliminary rulings on the interpretation of Community law under Article 234 EC clarify and define how that rule of law should have been understood and applied from its entry into force, which courts must apply accordingly even to legal relationships existing prior to the judgment.[82] National courts cannot restrict the retroactivity of the ECJ's judgment, but the ECJ consistently adds the caveat 'provided that in other respects the conditions enabling an action relating to the application of that rule to be brought before the courts having jurisdiction, are satisfied'. This refers to the general procedural autonomy of the Member States, eg in respect of setting time limits for bringing proceedings and the principle of *res judicata*.[83] The retroactivity of the judgment may therefore be limited in practice,[84] although such national rules must comply with Community minimum requirements.

Owing to the *quasi erga omnes* effects noted above, retroactive effect of preliminary rulings could have far-reaching consequences and seriously impede legal certainty. The ECJ has therefore on occasion limited its ruling only to take effect *ex nunc*.[85] However, this has been reserved to exceptional cases,[86] as illustrated by the ECJ's decision not to limit the temporal effects of its judgment in *Sapod Audic*, the consequences of which threatened to render invalid thousands of waste collection contracts entered into under legislation implementing Directive 75/442/EEC.[87] Furthermore, the ECJ will not limit

[79] Chapter 3, section 11.5. [80] Chapter 3, section 8.3. [81] Chapter 3, section 10.4.

[82] See eg Case C–415/93 *Bosman* [1995] ECR I–4921, para 141; and Case C–402/03 *Bilka* [2006] ECR I–199, para 50.

[83] See eg Case C–159/00 *Sapod Audic* [2002] ECR I–5031, para 52; and Chapter 3, sections 4.3–4.

[84] Lenaerts and Arts 1999, 134.

[85] Eg Joined Cases C–367 to 77/93 *Roders* [1995] ECR I–2229, para 43.

[86] Case C–372/98 *Cooke* [2000] ECR I–8683, para 42; and Case C–402/03 *Bilka* [2006] ECR I–199, para 51. Two essential criteria must be fulfilled before such a limitation can be imposed, namely that those concerned should have acted in good faith and that there should be a risk of serious difficulties.

[87] See chapter 3, section 8.3.

the temporal effects of a judgment in respect of the parties to the case, but only in relation to parties which have not yet brought any action in national courts. This is not a serious impediment to the effectiveness of preliminary rulings on environmental rules protecting public interests, since the authorities will be bound to take all the necessary measures to fulfil the judgment *ex tunc* in respect of the plaintiff, thereby protecting the interests of the public at large.

4 Judicial review

4.1 *Introduction*

The EC Treaty has established a dual-track for the review of validity of EC acts. Plaintiffs may either seek preliminary rulings from national courts under Article 234 EC, or bring direct actions before the ECJ under Articles 230 and 241 EC. The ECJ has consistently emphasized that these are two mechanisms in the same system,[88] and that together they form a complete system of procedures and remedies.[89]

However, as we shall see in chapter 5, the conditions for bringing direct actions before the ECJ are very stringent, in particular as concerns locus standi, and the only currently viable path for private parties to challenge the validity of Community acts in practice is to seek preliminary references in national courts. This raises the question whether Article 234 EC is capable of forming a complete system of procedures and remedies more or less in isolation, and we will therefore assess any gaps and deficiencies in this respect. However, the recently adopted Regulation 1367/2006 on the application of the Aarhus Convention on Access to Information, Public Participation in Decision-making and Access to Justice in Environmental Matters to Community Institutions and Bodies (Regulation 1367/2006) may to some extent remedy the situation and clear the way for environmental challenges directly before the ECJ.[90] We will therefore take Regulation 1367/2006 into account in assessing the interplay between Articles 230 and 234 EC.

[88] Case C–112/83 *Produits de Mais* [1985] ECR 719; para 17; Joined Cases C–143/88 and C–92/89 *Zuckerfabrik* [1991] ECR I–415, para 18.

[89] Case C–112/83 *Produits de Mais* [1985] ECR 719, para 23; Case 314/85 *Foto-Frost* [1987] ECR 4199, para 16; Case C–50/00 *UPA* [2002] ECR I–6677, para 40.

[90] [2006] OJ L264/13; see chapter 5.

4.2 *Time limits*

The fact that the Articles 230 and 234 EC procedures are complementary does not mean that plaintiffs are completely free to choose between the two. The ECJ held in *Deggendorf* that a national court is not entitled to seek a preliminary reference on the validity of a Community act which a plaintiff could have challenged directly under Article 230 EC but failed to do so within the applicable time limits, ie within two months following the publication of the measure, its notification to the plaintiff, or in the absence thereof, the day it came to the knowledge of the plaintiff.[91] This conclusion was warranted in order to prevent circumventions of the time limits in Article 230 EC and ensure legal certainty. However, as was indicated in *Deggendorf* and clarified in subsequent case law, it must have been 'obvious'[92] or 'undoubtedly'[93] clear that the plaintiff would have had standing to challenge the measure under Article 230 EC in order to preclude a challenge in the national courts, ie the measure must have been addressed to the plaintiff or clearly of 'individual and direct concern'.

This issue has been moot for environmental purposes, since plaintiffs will practically never have standing under Article 230 EC. However, it may become relevant again, following the adoption of Regulation 1367/2006 which will have the effect of granting standing to certain NGOs. The question is whether a NGO that fails to bring proceedings under Article 230 EC under the auspices of Regulation 1367/2006 is subsequently precluded from challenging the relevant act through national courts. For an answer to this question, it is necessary briefly to present the system of the regulation.[94] A NGO may request internal review of certain environmental acts, and the responsible Community institution will in turn address the outcome of that review to the NGO, which can then bring proceedings to challenge the internal review decision before the ECJ. The NGO will thus only have standing to challenge the internal review decision, and *Deggendorf* does therefore not stand in the way of a preliminary reference on the contested act subject to internal review.

Another matter which will probably have to be dealt with by the ECJ is whether the *Deggendorf* formula can be applied analogously to the situation where a qualified entity does not ask for an internal review, and thereby

[91] Case C-188/92 *TWD Textilwerke Deggendorf v Germany* [1994] ECR I-833, para 17.

[92] Case C-241/95 *Accrington Beef* [1996] ECR I-6699, para 15.

[93] Case C-239/99 *Nachi* [2001] ECR I-1197, para 30.

[94] For a full account, see chapter 5, sections 3–4.

foregoes the possibility of obtaining a decision addressed to it that could be challenged under Article 230 EC.

Although this argument is perhaps in line with the *raison d'être* of *Deggendorf*, there are reasons why it should not be accepted, as it would subject qualified entities to a much stricter duty to react than intended in the *Deggendorf* jurisprudence. That case law concerns persons who are addressed by a decision or are directly and individually concerned by a Community act. Under such circumstances it is perhaps not unreasonable to require that they react within a short time limit. However, Regulation 1367/2006 sets up a mechanism under which some NGOs have the possibility of requesting internal review of acts which are neither addressed to them, nor of direct and individual concern. Under such circumstances it is unreasonable if a failure to respond within the six-week time limit in Regulation 1367/2006 would preclude a later challenge in national courts.[95] Add to this that the six-week time limit in the regulation places NGOs at a further disadvantage compared with the general two-month limit in Article 230 EC. All in all, it seems clear that the *Deggendorf* formula should not apply analogously in this situation.

4.3 *Reviewable acts*

The scope of Community acts susceptible to review of validity is essentially the same as in respect of interpretation and it may in this respect be referred to section 3.2 above. Hence, the validity of any binding acts adopted by the Community institutions may be reviewed, including acts adopted by Community bodies acting under delegated powers. The same applies to the validity of international agreements, with the caveat already articulated in relation to mixed agreements.

Some largely self-explanatory differences remain. National courts may not ask for preliminary references on the validity of the EC Treaty, and the same goes for judgments of the ECJ.[96] The latter is no longer as obvious as it used to be, since the ECJ has recently held that the principle of *res judicata* does not prevent challenges to judgments of courts of last instance in the Member States, which introduces an element of double standards.[97]

There were also some doubts whether non-binding acts could be subject to review, but the ECJ answered this affirmatively in *Grimaldi*.[98] It pointed out that Article 234 EC, unlike Article 230 EC, referred to any acts adopted by

[95] Chapter 5, section 3.3.
[96] Case C–69/85 *Wunsche* [1986] ECR 947.
[97] See chapter 3, section 4.4.
[98] C–322/88 *Grimaldi* [1989] ECR 4407.

the Community institutions and did not contain any reservations as concerns recommendations and opinions. Furthermore, the ECJ noted that even non-binding acts were liable to produce legal effects, since national courts are obliged to take such measures into consideration when interpreting national provisions intended to implement them, or where they are designed to supplement binding Community provisions.[99] This suggests that preliminary references may be sought on the conformity of environmental policy documents, eg environmental action programmes, in so far as they have influenced national laws or supplement binding Community acts.[100]

The scope of review under Article 234 EC is broader than under Article 230 EC, as we shall see in chapter 5, and the preliminary reference procedure thus complements direct actions in important respects. There is one significant lacuna, however. The ECJ held prejudicially in *T Port*[101] that national courts may not seek preliminary references on a failure to act by the Community institutions. It noted that the wording of Article 234 EC merely referred to acts by the Community institutions and included 'no provision for a reference for a preliminary ruling by which a national court asks the Court of Justice to rule that an institution has failed to act'.[102]

This is a surprisingly formalistic interpretation from a court with a proven affinity for teleological interpretation in matters concerning judicial control in particular.[103] It is also quite ironical that the ECJ in the same judgment interpreted the conditions for bringing proceedings under Article 232 EC liberally so as to harmonize its standing requirements with those under Article 230 EC, arguing that these provisions 'merely prescribe one and the same method of recourse' and that 'the possibility for individuals to assert their rights should not depend upon whether the institution concerned has acted or failed to act'.[104]

By its rigid interpretation of Article 234 EC, it has of course created exactly such arbitrariness in relation to preliminary references, which for practical purposes would be the only way for private plaintiffs to challenge the legality of a failure to act by Community institutions in environmental matters.[105]

[99] Para 18.

[100] The fact that the ECJ held in Case C–142/95 *Rovigo* [1996] ECR I–6669, para 32 that the 5th environmental action programme did not contain any rules of a mandatory nature obliging the Commission to consult third parties does not detract from this conclusion; action programmes may still have other quasi legal effects as outlined in the *Grimaldi* case above.

[101] Case C–68/95 *T Port & Co* [1996] ECR I–6065. [102] ibid para 53.

[103] See also the dichotomy noted by AG Jacobs in his opinion in Case C–50/00P *UPA* [2002] ECR I–6677, paras 68–70. [104] Para 59.

[105] Peers 1998, 154.

National courts could in principle attempt to circumvent the obstacle posed by *T Port* by asking for interpretations of the Community provisions allegedly obliging the Community institutions to act, but such questions would appear of hypothetical interest and thus inadmissible. Regulation 1367/2006 on the application of the Aarhus Convention on Access to Information, Public Participation in Decision-making and Access to Justice in Environmental Matters to Community Institutions and Bodies (Regulation 1367/2006),[106] will provide some plaintiffs the possibility of challenging a failure to act before the ECJ – thus representing an exceptional example of direct actions complementing lacunae in the Article 234 EC procedure, and not the other way around – but this is not adequate to ensure a complete system of judicial control since individuals are excluded and the substantive scope is very narrowly drawn.[107]

On a slightly more positive note, a failure to act may in some cases render an existing Community act unlawful and thus be challengeable under Article 234 EC. The consequence of a failure by the Commission to carry out the common obligation to adapt environmental directives in light of scientific and technical progress is that the relevant directives may eventually fail to provide a high level of protection as required by Article 174 EC,[108] and thus become susceptible to challenge.

In most instances challenges to EC acts through the Article 234 EC procedure represent an intermediate step in a challenge of national implementing acts. In some situations, however, there may be a need to seek declarations on the validity of Community acts in the absence of implementing measures. This is particularly the case for directly applicable Community measures, eg regulations, where there may not be any implementing measures to challenge, and the question then arises whether such measures may be challenged 'directly' through the preliminary reference procedure. The ECJ accepted such a referral in *Omega Air* concerning the validity of a Community regulation, and it also presupposed such a possibility in *UPA*.[109]

A more difficult question, and more important for environmental purposes, is whether the same is possible in relation to Community acts which are not directly applicable, eg directives. At first glance there may seem to be no need for direct challenges of such measures, since the plaintiffs could challenge the legality of the national measures transposing the directive, and ask a national court to refer a question on the validity of the underlying

[106] [2006] OJ L264/13. [107] Chapter 5, sections 3.2 and 3.4. [108] Section 4.44.
[109] See also comments in Lang 2003 and Lang 2004.

directive. However, this has the obvious drawback that plaintiffs must await the adoption of national transposition measures, for which Member States often are granted several years, with further delays if the national authorities fail to implement the directive in time. This undermines the temporal effectiveness of EC law as well as legal certainty.

The ECJ was therefore asked in *Imperial Tobacco*[110] to consider whether a preliminary reference on the validity of Directive 98/43/EC could be sought even though the directive had not yet been implemented in the UK. The ECJ unfortunately did not have to comment on the admissibility of the action, since it had on the same day annulled the directive in another case. AG Fennelly did thoroughly examine the issue, however, and held that the question was admissible, since there was a concrete threat to the interests of the parties, and the question was not hypothetical since the Member States clearly would have to implement the directive.[111]

The question has now been resolved in *British American Tobacco*, in which the ECJ allowed a preliminary reference on the validity of a directive prior to expiry of the deadline for implementation.[112] The general applicability of the ruling could be limited, however, by the ECJ's emphasis of the fact that an invalid directive precluded the adoption of transposition measures according to English law, and that the plaintiffs therefore had a genuine interest.[113] However, this would amount to allowing the judicial control provided by the preliminary reference procedure to depend on national law (the effects of invalid Community acts in the national legal order[114]), which the ECJ has explicitly ruled out in the context of direct actions.[115] Since the ECJ has consistently held that the Articles 230 and 234 EC are two mechanisms in the same system, it follows that the review of legality of directives may be sought irrespective of the precise legal consequences stipulated in national law.

Importantly, the implicit corollary of these developments is that national courts must allow plaintiffs standing to seek declarations directly on the validity of Community acts of general application, even if such causes of action are not normally possible in relation to national acts of this nature.[116] This has been confirmed in *UPA*, in which the ECJ held that national courts must 'as far as possible' entertain such actions in relation to directly applicable acts,[117]

[110] Case C–74/99 *Imperial Tobacco Ltd and Others* [2000] ECR I–8599.

[111] Opinion of AG Fennelly in Case C–74/99 *Imperial Tobacco Ltd and Others* [2000] ECR I–8599, paras 29–30.

[112] Case 491/01 *British American Tobacco* [2002] ECR I–11453.

[113] Para 37.

[114] On the effects of invalid directives in national law, see Vandamme 2005.

[115] Case C–50/00 P *UPA* [2002] ECR I–6677.

[116] See chapter 3, section 5.1–2.

[117] Case C–50/00 P *UPA* [2002] ECR I–6677, paras 41–42.

which must apply similarly in relation to directives for which the deadline for implementation has not yet expired. In fact, since national restrictions in this regard would undermine the effectiveness of the Article 234 EC procedure, as now construed by the ECJ, and conflict with the obligation for Member States to ensure that Community law takes immediate effect, it seems that rules preventing national courts from making preliminary references in these situations must be set aside.[118]

4.4 *Grounds of review*

4.4.1 *Introduction*

The ECJ reviews the validity of Community acts in the context of preliminary references, as opposed to the prima facie broader review of illegality conducted under Article 230 EC. Germany submitted thus in the *Internationale* case that the grounds for review of validity of Community acts under Article 234 EC should be narrower than in actions for annulment under Article 230 EC, and that mere review of the formal validity would suffice in the former situation.[119] This was dismissed by AG Roemer and, although not explicitly dealing with the issue, the ECJ did not adhere to such a distinction either. In the subsequent *International Fruit* case it was held, taking into account the broad formulation of Article 234 EC, that the ECJ's jurisdiction to conduct judicial review of EC acts extended to 'all grounds capable of invalidating those measures'.[120]

It follows, also taking into consideration the principle of coherence, that the grounds for review under Article 234 EC are the same as those listed in Article 230(2) EC, ie 1) lack of competence, 2) infringement of an essential procedural requirement, 3) infringement of the Treaty or any rule of law relating to its application, and 4) misuse of powers.[121] For this reason and in order to avoid repetition in chapter 5 (direct actions), the following analysis incorporates case law developed under Articles 230 and 241 EC, in addition to Article 234 EC, in order to present a full picture of how the ECJ has

[118] Cf Case 106/77 *Simmenthal* [1978] ECR 629, read in conjunction with Case 13/68 *Salgoil* [1968] ECR 453 and C-213/89 *Factortame and Others* [1990] ECR I–2433.

[119] See the submission of Germany in Joined Cases C–73 and 74/63 *Internationale* [1964] ECR 1.

[120] See Joined Cases C–21 to 24/72 *International Fruit* [1972] ECR 1226, paras 4–6. Schermers and Waelbroek 2001, 498 have submitted that this might be considered differently, however, if the ECJ increasingly applies direct challenges brought under Article 234 EC, as I argued in favour of in the section above.

[121] Similarly, Schermers and Waelbroek 2001, 498; and Hartley 2003, 412.

applied the grounds of review in practice. This structure also is most purposeful in light of the fact that the preliminary reference procedure is currently by far the most accessible way for individuals and environmental organizations to seek judicial review of Community acts.

As for the specific grounds of review examined below, it should be added that misuse of powers will normally presuppose an infringement of one of the other grounds of review, and will therefore not be treated separately.

4.4.2 *Essential procedural requirements*

The most significant procedural issues for individuals and NGOs are the right to be heard and for their views to be taken into account, as well as the duty on the Community institutions to state reasons for their acts. The two first grounds of review may be quickly dispensed with since there are currently no rights of public participation in relation to Community acts in the field of the environment. The Aarhus Convention requires such procedural guarantees, but Regulation 1367/2006 falls short of the mark in most respects, as will be discussed further in chapter 5.[122] The only ground for review in this relation would be infringements of Article 9 of the regulation, which requires public participation in relation to environmental plans and programmes.

As for statements of reasons required by Article 253 EC, the ECJ has consistently held that they must be appropriate to the act at issue and disclose in a clear and unequivocal fashion the reasoning followed by the relevant institution(s) in such a way as to enable persons to ascertain the reasons for the measure, and to enable the ECJ to exercise its power of review.[123] The requisite statements of reasons are thus relative to the act in question, and it appears that the ECJ has placed relatively lenient conditions as concerns acts of general application, eg regulations and directives. With regard to such acts, it suffices that the preamble indicates the general situation which led to their adoption and the general objectives which they are intended to achieve.[124]

These minimum requirements are necessary in order to accommodate subsequent review of issues pertaining to competence and choice of legal basis (see below). Decisions taken by the Commission in the exercise of its implementing powers, on the other hand, are generally subject to more

[122] Chapter 5, section 2.3 (at the end of the section).

[123] Case C–159/01 *Netherlands v Commission* [2004] ECR I–4461, para 65; Case C–445/00 *Austria v Council* [2003] ECR I–8549, para 49; and Case C–304/01 *Spain v Commission* [2004] ECR I–7655, para 50.

[124] Eg Case C–342/03 *Spain v Council* [2005] ECR I–1975, para 55.

stringent conditions. Such decisions must mention the factual and legal matters which provided the legal basis for the measure, and the considerations which led to its adoption, although it is not necessary to deal with all the issues of fact and law raised during the administrative procedure.[125] The ECJ has thus held that Commission decisions taken under Article 95(5) EC, for instance, must contain a sufficient and relevant indication of the factors taken into consideration when determining whether the conditions for the grant of derogation are met.[126]

4.4.3 *Competence*

The Community does not have unrestricted competence to act, but may only do so in fields in which the Member States have conferred powers to the Community. This is not a serious limitation in respect of adoption of environmental acts, however, since Articles 174 EC and 175 EC grant general competence for the Community to act within this field. Even if an act might be held to fall outside the scope of Article 174 EC, the doctrine of implied powers[127] and Article 308 EC[128] make it possible to justify practically any act *ratio materiae* in so far that it is necessary to ensure the achievement of the Community's (environmental) objectives.

But the recent controversy in *Commission v Council* surrounding the adoption of legislation for the protection of the environment through criminal law illustrates that it might occasionally be difficult to determine under which EU pillar an act should be adopted.[129] Yet again, the ECJ's resolution of this legal battle between the Council and the Commission clarified that even in areas which are ancillary to environmental protection and where the Community strictly does not have competence under the first pillar, it may still act if this is necessary to ensure the full effectiveness of environmental rules:[130]

> However, the last-mentioned finding [that the Community did in principle not have competence in criminal matters] does not prevent the Community legislature, when the application of effective, proportionate and dissuasive criminal penalties by

[125] Eg Case T–290/94 *Kaysersberg v Commission* [1997] ECR II–2137, para 150.

[126] Eg Case T–366/03 and T–235/04 *Austria v Commission* [2005] ECR II–4005, para 53.

[127] According to the broad version of this theory, whenever the EC Treaty confers a task on a Community institution it follows by implication that the necessary powers to achieve this aim must also be deemed conferred; see eg Joined Cases 281, 283–285/85 *Germany v Commission* [1987] ECR 3203.

[128] Eg Case C–209/97 *Commission v Council* [1999] ECR I–8067.

[129] Case C–176/03 *Commission v Council* [2005] ECR I–7879. See comment in chapter 3, section 12.

[130] ibid para 48.

the competent national authorities is an essential measure for combating serious environmental offences, from taking measures which relate to the criminal law of the Member States which it considers necessary in order to ensure that the rules which it lays down on environmental protection are fully effective.[131]

The specific choice of legal basis under the EC treaty (the first pillar) may still cause concern, raising not only questions about substantive competence but also personal competence. In trade-related environmental matters the choice of Article 100a (Article 95 EC) or Article 130s (Article 175 EC) as legal basis was, prior to the Treaty of Amsterdam, an important battleground for inter-institutional power struggles, particularly as the decision-making procedure differed under the two procedures.[132] Since the co-decision procedure applies to both Articles 95 and 175 EC, the issue has become less relevant. However, the issue is still important in other grey areas where the decision-making procedures differ, eg the delimitation between Article 37 (agriculture) and 175 EC.[133] The choice of legal basis may also have significant consequences as regards Member States' possibilities to apply more stringent environmental standards, in view of differences between Articles 95(4)–(6) and 176 EC.

In order to determine the correct legal basis, the ECJ will examine the aim and substance of a measure with a view to determining the predominant objective of the measure, eg environment or trade.[134] If the Community act promotes dual objectives 'without one being secondary and indirect in relation to the other', it should be adopted on a dual legal basis,[135] unless the procedures are incompatible or liable to undermine the rights of Parliament.[136]

One would think that this should apply mutatis mutandis where the 'procedures' for Member State derogations differ so that Articles 95 and 175 EC, for instance, could never serve as a dual legal basis, but the ECJ's recent rulings in the *Dangerous Chemicals* cases has cast some doubts in this respect.[137] The ECJ in those cases annulled Council Decision 2003/106/EC[138] and Regulation

[131] Para 48. See also Case C–440/05 *Commission v Council*, pending.

[132] See eg Case C–300/89 *Commission v Council* [1991] ECR I–2867; Case C–155/91 *Commission v Council* [1993] ECR I–939; and Case C–187/93 *Parliament v Council* [1994] ECR I–2857.

[133] Joined Cases C–164 and 165/97 *Parliament v Council* [1999] ECR I–1139.

[134] See eg Case C–281/01 *Commission v Council* [2002] ECR I–12049, para 35.

[135] Case C–336/00 *Huber* [2002] ECR I–7699, para 31; Case C–281/01 *Commission v Council* [2002] ECR I–12049, para 35; and Case C–211/01 *Commission v Council* [2003] ECR I–8913, para 40.

[136] Case C–300/89 *Commission v Council (Titanium Dioxide)* [1991] ECR I–2867.

[137] Case C–178/03 *Commission v Parliament and Council* [2006] ECR I–107; and Case C–94/03 *Commission v Parliament and Council* [2006] ECR I–1.

[138] [2003] OJ L63/27.

(EC) 304/2003[139] because those measures had been adopted under Article 175 EC, whereas the ECJ found that Articles 133 and 175 EC should have served as a dual legal basis. Leaving aside whether the ECJ applied the centre of gravity test correctly – in my view these are predominantly environmental acts – the choice of dual-basis is incompatible with the different conditions for derogations by Member States under Articles 134 and 176 EC, a matter which was not addressed by the ECJ.

A different type of restriction stems from the principle of subsidiarity, articulated in Article 5(2) EC. Since Member States and the Community share competence in the field of the environment, the Community must only act 'if and insofar as the objectives of the proposed action cannot be sufficiently achieved by the Member States, and can therefore, by reason of scale or effects of the proposed action, be better achieved by the Community'. The Community has often justified action in relation to the subsidiarity principle because of the need for uniformity and ensuring a level playing field, but these factors do not appear very relevant in relation to environmental acts that are not of direct concern to the internal market or competition.

One might therefore expect the principle of subsidiarity to constitute a potent ground for review in the environmental sphere. Directive 2004/35/EC on environmental liability, for instance, has been criticized by several scholars for impinging on the principle of subsidiarity in so far as it also regulates damage that does not have cross-frontier elements.[140] In fact, however, the principle of subsidiarity has had virtually no impact as a ground of review, and the ECJ has as yet not annulled any Community measure for breach of this principle.[141] Some argue that it may nevertheless have a certain potential as a procedural ground of review, eg as regards statements of reasons.[142]

Closely linked to the principle of subsidiarity is the principle of proportionality, laid down in Article 5(3) EC. According to settled case law, in order to establish whether a Community measure complies with the principle of proportionality, it must be ascertained whether the means which it employs are suitable for the purpose of attaining the desired objective and whether they are limited to what is necessary for that purpose.[143] The principle of

139 [2003] OJ L63/1.

140 Faure 2005, 5; and Bergkamp 2005, 102.

141 Tridimas 2005, 121.

142 ibid.

143 Case C–284/95 *Safety Hi-Tech* [1998] ECR I–4301, para 57; Case C–210/03 *Swedish Match* [2004] ECR I–11893, para 47; Joined Cases C–453/03, 11, 12, and 194/04 *ABNA and Others* [2005] ECR I–10423, para 68.

proportionality has for instance been invoked in a challenge to the legality of Directive 91/676/EEC on the grounds that it restricted use of farming land without requiring evidence that that source was solely responsible for pollution of water by nitrates,[144] and was successfully invoked by producers of animal feeding stuff in the recent *ABNA* case concerning labelling requirements under Directive 2002/2/EC.[145]

It might appear that the principles of subsidiary and proportionality are largely irrelevant for purposes of actions by environmental NGOs, since they seemingly only place negative limitations on the Community's competence to protect the environment. However, acts that have a negative environmental impact may likewise be challenged for lack of competence with reference to these principles. Plaintiffs should in principle be able to challenge the legality of a Community measure adopted under Article 175 EC on the grounds of subsidiarity if the act in question is not conducive to offering better environmental protection than that which already exists in some Member States. One might instinctively retort that such actions would not serve any environmental purpose: Community legislation may still offer a higher level of protection than in Member States with a poor track record, and more progressive Member States can in any event apply more stringent measures under Article 176 EC. However, this argument does not apply to instances of a total harmonization measure, which makes it more difficult for the progressive Member States to maintain their standards of protection in the absence of Community legislation.[146]

It is also possible to envisage a Community measure being challenged on the basis of the principle of proportionality if it is not suitable for the purpose of attaining its environmental objectives. For example, a decision granting financial assistance to a project under Regulation 1655/2000 (LIFE)[147] could be contested on this ground if it were to materialize that the project has adverse effects on the environment outweighing the environmental benefits which justified the grant. As noted by Krämer, the environmental nature of projects which receive funding for environment purposes is not always clear.[148]

The ECJ has occasionally, although in the context of reviewing the legality of national measures, examined whether acts were proportional *strictu senso*,

[144] Case C-293/97 *Standley* [1999] ECR I-2603.

[145] Joined Cases C-453/03, 11, 12, and 194/04 *ABNA and Others* [2005] ECR I-10423, paras 83–85.

[146] See analysis in Jans 2000, 119–120; and Pagh 2006.

[147] [2004] OJ L308/1.

[148] Krämer 2006, 571.

ie by weighing competing interests.[149] If this is indeed a legitimate element of the proportionality test, it should in principle be equally applicable to acts by Community institutions, although the intensity of review may differ according to the discretion enjoyed. It cannot be excluded, therefore, that the ECJ may find a Community measure disproportionate which promotes one Community interest at the manifest detriment of another, equally important interest, eg internal market over environment. This conclusion is supported by Article 6 EC, which requires the Community to integrate environmental requirements in the implementation of all its policies and activities listed in Article 3 EC, and more specifically the obligation in Article 95 EC to ensure a high level of environmental protection. These issues are discussed in more detail below.

The legality of acts by the Community institutions may also be challenged on the grounds that they fail to apply the proportionality principle correctly when assessing the compatibility of national measures with Community law, eg as concerns national measures notified under Article 95 EC or Directive 98/38/EC.[150] Another matter is that the ECJ will only review whether the Community institution has committed a manifest error of assessment – it will not substitute the Commission's assessment with its own in this regard.[151]

Tertiary acts implementing basic directives or regulations may often be challenged on the grounds of lack of competence. The most fundamental ground for review in this respect stems from the fact that such acts, which are administrative in nature, must not modify the scope of the obligations laid down in the basic regulation without following the legislative procedure pertaining to the latter act.[152] For instance, the ECJ has annulled a Council directive intended to implement Directive 94/43/EC on plant protection products, since it effectively lowered the degree of environmental protection for groundwater under the latter directive without consulting the Parliament.[153] Similar types of challenges may be brought against Commission implementing

[149] See Case 302/86 *Commission v Denmark (Danish Bottles)* [1988] ECR, paras 20–21; and Case C–169/91 *Stoke-on-Trent (Sunday Trading)* [1992] ECR–6635, para 15. See also by implication Case C–379/98 *Preussen Elektra* [2001] ECR I–2099, paras 73–77. For a thorough analysis on the principle of proportionality, see Jans 2000a. See also the balancing act conducted in the context of interim relief, section 4.6.2.

[150] [1998] OJ L204/37.

[151] See eg Case C–3/00 *Denmark v Commission* [2003] ECR I–2643, para 125. For a critical comment, see Wennerås 2003, 176–77.

[152] See eg Case C–22/86 *Vreugdenhil and Others* [1989] ECR 2049; and Case C–303/94 *Parliament v Council* [1996] ECR I–2943.

[153] Case C–303/94 *Parliament v Council* [1996] ECR I–2943.

measures on the basis that an erroneous comitology procedure has been followed.[154]

4.4.4 *The Treaty or rules relating to its application*

The notion 'acts relating to its [the Treaty's] application' encompasses all Community rules not found in the Treaty, eg principles of Community law, secondary legislation, decisions, as well as commitments flowing from international law.[155] It also includes non-binding Community measures relating to the application of the Treaty, eg Decision 1999/468/EC on the procedures for the exercise of implementing powers conferred on the Commission (the second comitology decision).[156] We will focus on review of Community measures on the basis of the environmental provisions laid down in the Treaty, bearing in mind that these requirements are often codified and given a more precise content in secondary legislation.

Article 174 EC articulates objectives, principles and requirements that govern the Community's environmental policy. Article 174(1) EC provides that this policy contributes inter alia to preservation, protection, and improvement of the quality of the environment, including rational utilization of natural resources, and protection of human health. Article 174(2) EC stipulates that the Community must aim at a high level of environmental protection. Policy is guided by the principles of precaution, prevention, the polluter pays, and that damage should as priority be rectified at source. Finally, Article 174(3) EC requires that in the elaboration of environmental policy account should be taken of, inter alia, available scientific and technical data, cost/benefit analyses, and regional differences concerning environmental conditions and socio-economic development.

Our question is whether these objectives, principles, and requirements may serve as grounds for review of Community acts. Initially, this appears difficult, since Article 174 EC refers consistently to 'environmental policy', implying that it cannot be invoked to challenge individual Community measures implementing that policy.[157] It was therefore surprising that the ECJ in *Safety Hi-Tech* found that Article 174 EC laid down objectives, principles, and criteria which the 'Community legislature must respect in *implementing*

[154] See, by implication, Case C–378/00 *Commission v Parliament and Council (LIFE)* [2003] ECR I–937; and C–122/04 *Commission v Parliament and Council (Forest Focus)* [2006] ECR I–2001.

[155] Case 21–24/72 *Fruit Company* [1972] ECR 1226, paras 5–6.

[156] Case C–378/00 *Commission v Parliament and Council (LIFE)* [2003] ECR I–937; and Case C–122/04 *Commission v Parliament and Council (Forest Focus)* [2006] ECR I–2001.

[157] Krämer 1996, 113.

environmental policy',[158] and proceeded to examine whether Regulation (EC) 3093/94 on ozone depleting substances was adopted in breach of Article 174 EC. The ECJ has since applied Article 174 EC in various cases for purposes of judicial review of Community environmental legislation, which should apply mutatis mutandis to administrative provisions and decisions. But the ECJ has at the same time made it clear that it will only engage in marginal judicial review under Article 174 EC:

> [I]n view of the need to strike a balance between certain of the objectives and principles mentioned in Article 130r [Article 174 EC] and of the complexity of the implementation of those criteria, review by the Court must necessarily be limited to the question whether the Council, by adopting the Regulation, committed a manifest error of appraisal regarding the conditions for the application of Article 130r [Article 174 EC].[159]

Furthermore, since the provisions in Article 174 EC are not all unconditional and vary as to their precision, it is likely that the intensity of review will differ depending on the specific elements which are invoked.

The objectives in Article 174(1) EC are so open-ended that hardly any Community measure should normally fall short of their minimum content. The ECJ has indeed noted that they merely define the general objectives of the Community, and the decision as to what action is to be taken rests with the Community institutions.[160] Still, as seen above, the objectives are important for the purpose of ascertaining if Community acts have been adopted on the correct legal basis.

The principles in Article 174(2) EC are also vague and sometimes conditional. Some authors have thus typified them as guidelines rather than binding environmental rules.[161] The principle of a high level of protection, also found in Article 95(3) EC, is difficult to review, if only in view of the caveat 'shall aim at'. The ECJ nevertheless held in *Safety Hi-Tech* that Community legislation could be reviewed in the light of this principle,[162] which presupposes that Article 174(2) EC provides for a legal duty to ensure a high level of protection.[163] The level of protection need not be the highest level technically

[158] Case C–284/95 *Safety Hi-Tech* [1998] ECR I–4301, para 36 and 38 (emphasis added).

[159] Para 39.

[160] Case C–379/92 *Peralta* [1994] ECR I–3453, para 57; and Case C–284/95 *Safety Hi-Tech* [1998] ECR I–4301, para 43.

[161] Krämer 2003, 13.

[162] Case C–284/95 *Safety Hi-Tech* [1998] ECR I–4301.

[163] This has been recognized by former Advocate General Jacobs, although he asserts that the standard of environmental protection set at Community or national level is likely to be high and thus unlikely to be subject to judicial scrutiny unless patently inadequate; see Jacobs 2006, 198. Although I agree in principle, I would respectfully question the presupposition that environmental standards

possible, however, since the Member States are authorized under Article 176 EC to pursue higher levels of protection than the Community.[164] This line of reasoning suggests *a contrario* that acts adopted under Article 95 EC should be subject to more stringent judicial review as to the obligation to ensure high levels of environmental protection since the Member States have more restricted possibilities to maintain or introduce more stringent provisions under this provision.[165]

If the Community act in question lays down more stringent standards than in international obligations, it seems that the ECJ will readily find the condition of a high level of protection fulfilled.[166] This has rightly been criticized, as applicable standards in international environmental law by no means automatically secure high levels of protection,[167] leaving aside the Community's ambition to be world leader in terms of environmental protection.

Closely related is the precautionary principle, which the ECJ has held is 'one of the foundations of the high level of protection pursued by Community policy on the environment'.[168] The essence of this principle is that, where there is scientific uncertainty as to the existence or extent of risks to human health or environment, the Community institutions may take protective measures without having to wait until the reality and seriousness of those risks become fully apparent.[169] Such a risk exists if it cannot be excluded on the basis of objective information that adverse effects on the environment may incur.[170] Most cases in which there has been an alleged breach of the precautionary principle have been brought by plaintiffs adversely affected by the Community's actions, and they have argued that there was insufficient evidence of risk or insufficient analyses of those risks. The ECJ therefore has tended to emphasize the competence of Community institutions to take protective measures.[171] However, the precautionary principle does not only have an 'enabling function'.[172] A mandatory element is implied in Article 174(2) EC,

are generally high. This is in any event something the ECJ must first verify, and adapt its intensity of review accordingly.

164 Para 49.

165 For analysis of Article 95 EC, see Sevenster 2000 and de Sadeleer 2003.

166 Para 48.

167 Epiney 2006, 28.

168 Case C–127/02 *Waddenzee* [2004] ECR I–7405, para 44.

169 See eg Case C–180/96 *UK v Commission* [1998] ECR I–2265, para 114; Case T–13/99 *Pfizer* [2002] ECR II–3305, para 139.

170 See, by analogy, Case C–180/96 *UK v Commission* [1998] ECR I–2265, paras 50, 105, and 107; and Case C–127/02 *Waddenzee* [2004] ECR I–7405, para 44.

171 See eg Case C–180/96 *UK v Commission* [1998] ECR I–2265, para 114; CaseT–13/99 *Pfizer* [2002] ECR II–3305, para 139.

172 See Winter 2003, 5.

which states that Community policy 'shall be based' on this principle. Furthermore, the principle of precaution is accompanied by the principle that 'preventive action should be taken'. The binding nature of the precautionary principle was recently illustrated in the *Waddenzee* case, in relation to Member States. In this case, the ECJ interpreted Article 6(3) of Directive 93/42/EC in light of the precautionary principle to the effect that national authorities could only authorize projects under that provision where no reasonable scientific doubt remained as to the absence of adverse effects on the environment.[173]

The precautionary principle might seem most useful as a ground to review a failure to act,[174] but it can also be invoked as a ground to challenge acts. The latter is in particular relevant in instances where the Commission has authorized a hazardous substance with reference to the fact that there is no conclusive scientific evidence as to its adverse environmental impact.[175]

As for the 'polluter pays' principle, various Community measures are based on this principle, and the ECJ has in many instances interpreted Community legislation in light of this requirement. The *Standley*[176] case revealed that the ECJ is prepared to review the legality of Community measures on the basis of the polluter pays principle. The plaintiffs in that case argued that Directive 91/676/EEC should be held invalid because it placed a disproportionate responsibility for nitrate pollution on farmers (by disregarding other sources of pollution). The more interesting issue from an environmental perspective, which has not yet been clarified, is whether a Community act may be annulled for failing to attribute responsibility for pollution to any party. Directive 2004/35/EC, for instance, could be challenged on this basis since it allows for a permit defence exonerating operators responsible for environmental damage that acted in compliance with an authorization whilst, at the same time, it fails to assign subsidiary responsibility to national authorities to remedy damage caused as a result of evidently improper permitting.[177]

The final principle mentioned in Article 174(2) EC provides that damage must as a priority be rectified at source. The Community's waste legislation,

[173] Case C–127/0 *Waddenzee* [2004] ECR I–74052, paras 58–59. See also Case C–236/01 *Monsanto Agricoltura Italia and Others* [2003] ECR I–8105, paras 106 and 113.

[174] In these situations judicial review may only be ensured by bringing direct actions under Article 232 EC, cf section 4.3 and chapter 5.

[175] See Case C–14/06 *Parliament v Commission* pending, commented upon in chapter 5, section 4.5.

[176] Case C–293/97 *Standley* [1999] ECR I–2603, paras 51–52.

[177] See criticism in Wennerås 2005a, 175.

for instance, is based on this principle.[178] It is again uncertain to what extent this principle may be effective as a ground for review, in particular since it does not unconditionally require that damage be rectified at source, but merely as a 'priority'.[179] The limits of discretion may be exceeded if a Community act fails to take this principle into account altogether, and provides unlimited discretion on Member States or individuals to rectify damage at other places. Directive 2004/35 on environmental liability may again serve by way of illustration. Point 1.3.2 of Annex II confers *carte blanche* to provide remediation for environmental damage at other but similar locations to the place where the damage occurred, if this is possible at a lower cost.[180]

The last example brings us to the criteria to be taken into account according to Article 174(3) EC, inter alia that the Community institutions must take into account the potential benefits and costs of action or omission. Some scholars have argued that this puts the other principles on a 'more realistic footing'.[181] For instance, it would not be necessary to provide for rectification at source if it is cost-efficient to do otherwise. However, close reading of the wording of Article 174(3) EC reveals that the Community institution may only take cost-benefit considerations into account in deciding whether or not to act. Once the Community institution has determined that it is necessary to act, it cannot excuse inadequate action, eg by failing to provide a high level of protection, on the basis of cost-benefit considerations. This conclusion is also supported by the system in Article 174 EC, which indicates that the principles in paragraph 2 are *lex superior* to the requirements in paragraph 3.

The most important requirement in Article 174(3) EC for the purposes of judicial review is that the Community institution shall take into account 'available scientific and technical data' in preparation of Community acts. The Community institutions do not enjoy any margin of discretion in this respect, in contrast to the other principles and criteria examined. Any decision based on inadequate scientific and technical information will automatically result in its annulment.[182] Conversely, lacking information may result in the Community institutions being unaware of environmental risks, which could allow for direct actions under Article 232 EC for failure to act.[183] Moreover,

[178] Case C–2/90 *Commission v Belgium (Wallonia Waste)*[1992] ECR I–4431; and Case C–422/92 *Commission v Germany* [1995] ECR I–1097.

[179] See brief treatment in Case C–293/97 *Standley* [1999] ECR I–2603, para 53.

[180] See criticism in Wennerås 2005, 266–67.

[181] Winter 2003, 3.

[182] Case C–3/00 *Denmark v Commission* [2003] ECR I–2643, paras 109–115; and Joined Cases T–74, 76, 83 to 85, 132, 137, and 141/00 *Artegodan and Others* [2002] ECR I–4945, paras 210–11 and 220–21.

[183] Chapter 5.

the notion of 'available' data indicates that the Community institutions must continue to upgrade their data. Community institutions must also base their assessment of national measures on available scientific and technical data. Hence, the ECJ has annulled a Commission decision refusing Denmark to maintain more stringent standards than Directive 95/2/EC on the use of food additives, because the Commission failed to take sufficient account of an opinion by the Scientific Committee on Food, which criticized the standards in the Community legislation.[184]

Environmental principles are also found elsewhere in the EC Treaty,[185] the most important for our purposes being the principle of integration laid down by Article 6 EC. This principle obliges Community institutions to integrate environmental requirements into the definition and implementation of other Community policies. In theory, this is a far-reaching obligation as it means that all the principles and criteria of Article 174 EC impact on all Community policies listed in Article 3 EC. Community policy in the field of agriculture and fisheries, for instance, should be based on the precautionary principle and be compatible with the principle of a high level of environmental protection.[186] Furthermore, the reference to 'implementation' in Article 6 means that specific Community measures may be reviewed against the principle of integration, although the ECJ has not yet been faced with this issue.[187]

Most of the objectives, principles, and requirements examined above confer a significant margin of discretion on the Community institution, and the ECJ is therefore likely to conduct a marginal review only. However, there is a symbiotic relationship between many of these environmental requirements, and infringements of one of them may consequently lead to infringements of another. This is illustrated by the pending *Paraquat* case[188] concerning a challenge of Commission Directive 2003/112/EC amending Directive 91/414/EEC concerning plant protection products. Sweden has submitted that:

> [By authorizing paraquat] the Commission failed to apply the principle of precaution when assessing and dealing with the risk posed by paraquat both to human and to

[184] Case C-3/00 *Denmark v Commission* [2003] ECR I-2643. See also comment by Wennerås 2003, 169.

[185] Winter 2003, 3 identifies 10 principles.

[186] See, by implication, Case C-180/96 *UK v Commission* [1998] ECR I-2265, paras 99–100; and Krämer 2003, 20. Another matter, which has been asserted by Krämer 2006, 560–62, is that there are no horizontal structures at the Community level which can effectively put the integration principle into practice.

[187] But infringement of the principle of integration is one of the pleas put forward in the pending Case T-229/04 *Sweden v Commission* [2004] OJ C106/24.

[188] Case T-229/04 *Sweden v Commission* [2004] OJ C106/24. See also the similar Case T-5/06 *Denmark v Commission*, pending.

animal health. Its failure to apply the principle of caution has in turn made it impossible to ensure the high level of protection required by the EC Treaty [. . .]. In disregarding the need for a high level of protection, the Commission must also be considered not to have fulfilled the requirements of environmental protection and the principle of integration laid down in the EC Treaty.[189]

The cumulative effect of these environmental requirements may therefore limit the Community institution's discretion to a significant degree.

4.5 *Consequences*

In preliminary rulings, the ECJ does not annul the act – as it does under Article 230 EC – but declares it invalid.[190] This is binding on the referring national court and parties to the proceedings, but does not formally have any direct legal effects on other parties in similar cases. In other words, the act is not nullified but remains effective as an invalid act.[191] However, the ECJ has held that a preliminary ruling of invalidity is sufficient reason for other national courts to regard the relevant act invalid and to refuse to apply it, which means that a declaration of invalidity in a preliminary ruling for practical purposes has similar *erga omnes* effects as an annulment under Article 230 EC.[192]

The ECJ's preliminary rulings on the validity of EC acts have retroactive effect, similar to acts that are nullified under Article 230 EC.[193] Furthermore, in order to ensure the 'necessary consistency' between the two procedures and to safeguard the principle of legal certainty, the ECJ has applied Articles 231(2) and 233 EC analogously to preliminary references and in some cases specified the temporal effects of its ruling. Hence, the ECJ has occasionally declared a Community act only to be invalid *ex nunc*,[194] or even stipulated that national authorities must continue to apply the invalid Community act, or certain aspects therein, until new measures have been adopted.[195]

A ruling of invalidity under Article 234 EC automatically obliges the Community institution(s) concerned to take the necessary measures to remedy

[189] ibid.

[190] See eg Joined Cases C–453/03, C–11, 12, and 194/04 *ABNA and Others* [2005] ECR I–10423.

[191] Case C–16/65 *Schwartze* [1965] ECR 886; see also the opinion for an instructive comment on the different consequences between declaring an act void rather than annulling it.

[192] Case C–66/80 *International Chemical Corporation* [1981] ECR 1191.

[193] Case C–228/92 *Roquette Frères* [1994] ECR I–1445, para 17.

[194] Supra no 184–185, para 22.

[195] Case C–445/00 *Austria v Council* [2003] ECR I–8549, paras 104 and 106.

the situation.[196] The ECJ has stated that they 'are to take the measures that are required in order to comply with the judgment containing the ruling in the same way as they are, under Article 176 of the Treaty [now 233 EC] in the case of a judgment annulling a measure or declaring that the failure of a Community institution to act is unlawful'.[197] It added more specifically that where the Commission has the necessary powers to take measures remedying the illegality found by the ECJ in a preliminary ruling, its obligation to act follows also from its general supervisory obligation laid down in Treaty Article 155 [now Article 211 EC].[198]

Although plaintiffs may not seek damages from the Community institutions under Article 234 EC[199] – as they can under Article 288(2) EC – the ECJ has held that Article 233 EC requires Community institutions to 'restore the situation prevailing prior to the occurrence of the facts found unlawful by the Court'.[200] Since the ECJ has held that Article 233 EC applies analogously to the Article 234 EC procedure, it must follow that the Community institutions are under the same obligation to nullify the consequences of acts that are found unlawful in preliminary judgments. It should be recalled that this principle has been interpreted as requiring national authorities to make good any harm caused, including environmental damage,[201] and the principle of coherence therefore requires that the same apply mutatis mutandis to the Community institutions.

National authorities are of course similarly required by the principle of loyal cooperation of Article 10 EC to take all necessary measures to comply with the judgment. They may no longer apply the invalid act, and must take the necessary measures to remedy unlawful effects stemming from the invalid act.[202] The ECJ may also instruct the necessary measures to be taken by the national authorities pending new acts adopted by the offending institution.[203] Apart

[196] Joined Cases C–117/76 and C–16/77 *Ruckdeschel* [1977] ECR 1753; Joined Cases C–124/76 and C–20/77 *Moulins* [1977] ECR 1795; Case C–145/79 *Roquette* [1980] ECR 2917, para 51; Case C–300/86 *MERA* [1988] ECR 3443, para 22.

[197] Case T–220/97 *Ecroyd* [1999] ECR II–1677, para 49. See also chapter 5, section 4.5.

[198] ibid, para 50. See also Case C–804/79 *Commission v United Kingdom* [1981] ECR 1045, para 30.

[199] See chapter 5, section 6.

[200] Joined Cases T–17/90, T–28/91 and T–17/92 *Alloisio and Others v Commission* [1993] ECR II–841, para 79. See also Wyatt and Dashwood 2000, 280.

[201] Chapter 3, section 10.4.

[202] Case 23/75 *Rey Soda* [1975] ECR 1279, para 75; Case C–199/86 *BALM* [1988] ECR 1169, paras 12–19; and Case C–127/94 *Ecroyd* [1996] ECR I–2731, para 58. See also chapter 3, section 10.4–5.

[203] Case C–300/86 *MERA* [1988] ECR 3443, para 24; Case C–264/82 *Timex* [1985] ECR 849, para 32.

from this, the legal consequences of the invalid acts are governed by national law,[204] subject to the general minimum requirements of Community law.[205]

4.6 *Interim relief*

4.6.1 *Introduction*

The duration of preliminary references in environmental cases has become increasingly lengthy as the ECJ's workload has increased. The average length of preliminary references, ie the time from the national court's reference until the ECJ delivers its ruling, was 18 months for the period 1992–1994.[206] This number increased to 26 months by 2003, with some cases taking as long as 39 months.[207] This amounts to a significant disincentive for plaintiffs to bring cases, and it may also be difficult to persuade national courts to request preliminary references under such circumstances. Furthermore, in urgent matters where there is a risk of irreversible damage, which is of course a particularly important issue in environmental cases where compensation may not offset damage, the duration of the preliminary reference procedure may defeat the purpose of the action altogether.[208]

National courts may admittedly ask for an accelerated procedure, in accordance with Article 104a of the court's Rules of Procedure, and the president of the ECJ may then immediately set a date for a hearing, shorten the time period for observations and require the parties to restrict their arguments to the essential points.[209] However, this is only applicable in matters of exceptional urgency and subject to the ECJ's discretion. Furthermore, the grant of such an application does not necessarily render superfluous the need for interim relief nor will it entail a presumption that interim relief will be issued, if required by the plaintiffs.[210]

In the absence of this exceptional cause of action, the effectiveness of the preliminary reference procedure therefore rests on the availability of interim relief. However, under Article 234 EC the ECJ is not empowered to grant interim relief pending a preliminary ruling on the validity of Community acts.[211] In order to ensure judicial protection and coherence in the system, the

[204] See eg Case C–23/75 *Rey Soda* [1975] ECR 1279; and Case 199/86 *BALM* [1988] ECR 1169.

[205] See chapter 3, sections 8 and 10. For an overview of the effect of invalid directives in national legal orders, see Vandamme 2005.

[206] Krämer 2004, 131.

[207] ibid.

[208] See eg the *Lappel Banks* case discussed in chapter 3, section 4.5.

[209] For a review of the practice, see Barbier da La Serre 2006.

[210] See, by analogy Joined Cases T–195, and 207/01 *Gibraltar v Commission* [2001] ECR I–3915, para 94.

[211] Case C–186/01 R *Dory v Germany* [2001] ECR I–7823, para 6.

ECJ therefore held in *Zuckerfabrik*[212] that national courts are competent under Community law to order interim relief pending preliminary rulings challenging the validity of a Community regulation. Furthermore, the ECJ confirmed in *Atlanta*[213] that national courts are also empowered to order positive interim relief, ie 'settling or regulating the disputed legal position or relationships for theirs [the plaintiffs'] benefit'. The ECJ has since clarified that interim relief is not only available in respect of regulations, but any act adopted by the Community institutions, including directives and decisions.[214]

On the other hand, the ECJ held in *T Port* that national courts are not competent to order interim relief against a failure to act by a Community institution.[215] This followed *a fortiori* from its finding, as critically discussed above, that preliminary references cannot be obtained on the legality of a failure to act by a Community institution.[216]

The ECJ proclaimed in *Zuckerfabrik* that the jurisdiction for national courts to grant interim relief corresponded to the ECJ's jurisdiction to grant interim relief under Articles 242 and 243 EC, and they could therefore grant interim relief 'only on the same conditions as [. . .] the Court'.[217] Although this may instinctively seem persuasive from the perspective of uniformity and coherence in the legal system, it does raise problems in relation to the principle of a complete system of remedies and procedures. To harmonize completely the conditions for interim relief under Articles 242 and 243 EC, rules which are inherently restrictive, with those applicable in the context of the 234 EC procedure jeopardizes its complementary nature. However, the ECJ said in the paragraph preceding the statement that the conditions must be the same, that interim relief 'whilst it is governed by national procedural law, in particular as regards the making and the application, must in all the Member States be subject, at the very least, to conditions which are uniform so far as the granting of such relief is concerned'.[218] Hence, complete harmonization of interim relief on the national and Community level was in any event not intended.

Before we turn to the specific substance of the relevant conditions, it may be helpful first briefly to consider the situations in which interim relief is practical, and in which form.

212 Joined Cases 143/88 and C–92/89 *Zuckerfabrik* [1991] ECR I–415, para 21.

213 Case C–465/93 *Atlanta* [1995] ECR I–3761, para 30.

214 See Joined Cases C–453/03, C–11, 12, and 194/04 *ABNA and Others* [2005] ECR I–10423, para 103.

215 Case C–68/95 *T Port & Co* [1996] ECR I–6065, para 53. See section 4.3 and Alberts-Lorentz 1998.

216 Section 4.3.

217 Joined Cases 143/88 and C–92/89 *Zuckerfabrik* [1991] ECR I–415, para 27; and Case C–465/93 *Atlanta* [1995] ECR I–3761, para 39.

218 Para 26.

Interim relief is likely to be a relevant remedy foremost in situations where the validity of an EC decision is challenged, eg for purposes of suspending a national permit issued in accordance with a Commission decision approving the marketing of a hazardous product,[219] or for obtaining a temporary ban against the issuing of permits of the relevant product. Interim relief against enforcement of general acts may be less practical. It would normally not make much sense to seek suspension of the enforcement of a directive because it fails to adhere to the environmental principles in Article 174 EC or because it has been adopted on the wrong legal basis, as it is presumably better to have meagre protection than nothing.[220] Indeed, it is for these reasons that the ECJ often states that invalid acts remain effective until the responsible Community institution has taken the necessary measures to correct it.[221] In addition, national courts cannot normally grant positive interim relief in these situations as this would usurp the discretion enjoyed by the Community institutions.

Interim relief against general acts can nevertheless be practical if the alleged illegality only pertains to individual provisions. If, for instance, Directive 2004/35/EC on environmental liability is challenged on the basis that Article 8(4) litra a and b violates the polluter pays and precautionary principles by allowing for so called permit and state of the art defences,[222] the national court could suspend the enforcement of the said provisions and continue to apply the directive thus corrected.

4.6.2 *Conditions*

The first condition is that the factual and legal circumstances of the case must lead the national court to entertain 'serious doubts' about the contested measures.[223] A relevant factor in this context is the degree of discretion of the Community institutions when adopting the relevant act.[224] The ECJ has emphasized that 'only *the possibility* of a finding of invalidity . . . can justify the granting of suspensory measures',[225] but this is in fact a more lenient condition than 'serious doubt'. It makes it clear that there is no need to demonstrate

[219] For illustration, see Case T–94/04 *European Environmental Bureau v Commission* [2005] ECR II–4919.

[220] See, by analogy, Case T–37/04 R *The Autonomous Region of the Azores v Council* [2004] ECR II–2153, paras 128–30.

[221] Section 4.5 and Case C–445/00 *Austria v Council* [2003] ECR I–8549, paras 104 and 106.

[222] See criticism in Wennerås 2005, 262–63 and 2005a.

[223] Joined Cases 143/88 and C–92/89 *Zuckerfabrik* [1991] ECR I–415, para 23.

[224] Case C–465/93 *Atlanta* [1995] ECR I–3761, para 37.

[225] ibid para 35 (emphasis added).

likelihood that the measure will be held invalid, but it suffices that there is a reasonable chance that the act may be overturned.[226] This appears sound since a higher threshold would risk pre-empting the ECJ's judicial review and thus disturb the proper procedure of cooperation between the national court and the ECJ. This is in particular important in challenges to Community acts based on failure to achieve the requisite environmental standards required in Article 174 EC, eg a high level of protection, where it would be difficult to come up with the necessary facts and scientific evidence to indicate unequivocally that the measure falls short of these standards within the relatively short time before an interim hearing takes place.

As interim relief can only be granted for the period until a ruling on the validity has been rendered, the national court must refer the question of validity to the ECJ – if that has not already happened – before granting interim relief.[227] The corollary of this requirement is that national authorities may not grant interim relief, as has now been confirmed in *ABNA*.[228]

The second condition is that there must be urgency, ie that the application of the Community act is 'likely to result in irreversible damage to the applicant which could not be made good if the Community act were to be declared invalid'.[229] The ECJ has in its case law under Articles 242 and 243 EC held that this does not require absolute certainty that harm is imminent, but it suffices that it should be foreseeable with a sufficient degree of probability. This is nonetheless a very stringent requirement – especially in the environmental sphere where it may often be almost impossible to prove a likelihood that a risk will result in damage. This is illustrated by *Azores v Council*,[230] in which the plaintiff sought partial suspension of Regulation 1954/2003/EC[231] because of the threat its liberalization of the fisheries policy posed to the aquatic habitat and fish species in the waters outside the Azores. The CFI first required the plaintiff to prove that damage would 'certainly and imminently ensue due to the contested regulation'.[232] Secondly, although the plaintiffs

[226] Similarly, Bebr 1996, 801–802. Cf the UK's submission that it should be 'highly probable' that the Community act would be held void by the ECJ before the national court could grant interim relief, referred to (and rebutted) in the opinion of AG Elmer in Case C–465/93 *Atlanta* [1995] ECR I–3761, para 18.

[227] Joined Cases 143/88 and C–92/89 *Zuckerfabrik* [1991] ECR I–415, para 24; Case C–465/93 *Atlanta* [1995] ECR I–3761, para 36. This is of course nothing but the logical corollary of Case C–314/85 *Foto-Frost* [1987] ECR 4199, according to which only the ECJ may rule on the validity of EC acts.

[228] Joined Cases C–453/03, C–11, 12, and 194/04 *ABNA and Others* [2005] ECR I–10423.

[229] Joined Cases 143/88 and C–92/89 *Zuckerfabrik* [1991] ECR I–415, para 41.

[230] Case T–37/04 R *The Autonomous Region of the Azores v Council* [2004] ECR II–2153.

[231] [2003] OJ L289/1. [232] Para 153.

submitted scientific reports from inter alia the Community's own expert organ which affirmed that certain deep-sea fish species were at risk, the CFI essentially dismissed these studies since they 'raise[d] significant uncertainty' and 'd[id] not prevent evidence proving that the contested regulation [. . .] would lead to depletion of fishing stock'.[233]

It is highly questionable, in my view, whether requiring such a high level of proof, in particular bearing in mind the fact that only irreversible damage is relevant, is consonant with the precautionary principle. As will be recalled, this principle provides that Community institutions may take protective measures without having to wait until the reality and seriousness of the risks become fully apparent,[234] and that such risk is presumed to exist if it cannot be excluded on the basis of objective information that adverse effects on the environment may incur.[235] The Community courts as well as national courts are obliged to apply the precautionary principle, and it is therefore submitted that applications for interim relief in environmental cases cannot be refused for want of proof that damage will incur when objective information reveals a risk that irreversible damage may occur.[236]

As for the requirement that the damage must be irreversible, the court has held that this condition is not fulfilled if it may be rectified through financial compensation.[237] This aspect is however not likely to cause problems in relation to environmental damage which rarely may be offset by compensation. Indeed, the court has on several occasions affirmed that environmental harm is in principle irreversible since it normally cannot be eliminated retroactively,[238] whilst it would be 'extremely difficult, if not impossible, to compensate adequately' for such harm.[239]

The third condition is perhaps the most onerous and complex to apply in practice, namely that the interest of the Community must be taken into account.[240] The ECJ held more specifically that national courts must ascertain

[233] Paras 178–80.

[234] See eg Case C–180/96 *UK v Commission* [1998] ECR I–2265, para 114; Case T–13/99 *Pfizer* [2002] ECR II–3305, para 139.

[235] See, by analogy, Case C–180/96 *UK v Commission* [1998] ECR I–2265, paras 50, 105 and 107; and Case C–127/02 *Waddenzee* [2004] ECR I–7405, para 44.

[236] Ebbesson 2002, 25 notes in comparison that many Member States allow the public to act only when there is a risk to the environment, in line with the precautionary principle.

[237] Case C–465/93 *Atlanta* [1995] ECR I–3761, para 41.

[238] Case C–320/03 R *Commission v Austria* [2003] ECR I–11665, para 92.

[239] Case C–445/00 R *Austria v Council* [2001] ECR–1461, para 106.

[240] This is reminiscent of the 'balance of convenience test' applied by UK courts when assessing claims for interim relief; see Sharpston 1997.

whether the Community measure would be 'deprived of all effectiveness if not immediately implemented'.[241] This requirement was in fact not particularly stringent since it contained the qualifier 'all effectiveness', but that was before this notion was further clarified in *Atlanta*:

> In that respect the national court must take account of the damage which the interim measure may cause the legal regime established by that regulation for the Community as a whole. It must consider, on the one hand, the cumulative effect which would arise if a large number of courts were also to adopt interim measures for similar reasons and, on the other, those special features of the applicant's situation which distinguish him from the other operators concerned.[242]

It has been questioned whether national courts must assess only the likelihood that other courts in the Member State are liable to grant interim relief, or generally national courts throughout the Community territory.[243] Given that the *raison d'être* for the examination is to assess the risk interim relief poses to the effectiveness of the Community measure in general, it would appear that national courts would have to assess the effects not only on the national territory but on the Community in general. Another matter is that this appears very difficult to determine in practice.

More important for our purposes is the requirement to take into account 'those special features of the applicant's situation which distinguish him from the other operators'. Is this a manifestation of the *Plaumann* criteria, ie that only individual interests are relevant, or is the point that if the applicant has specific features that distinguish him from others, there is little risk that a large number of courts would grant interim relief for 'similar reasons'?[244] Since the examination of this element occurs in the context of assessing the risk that there will be an avalanche of interim relief actions undermining the effectiveness of the EC measure, and not in the context of damages, it would appear that the latter alternative is intended.

However, later in the judgment, concerning the obligation of national courts' duty to respect earlier decisions by the ECJ, it gave obiter dicta which could be understood as implying that only individual interests are relevant.[245]

[241] Para 31. [242] Case C–465/93 *Atlanta* [1995] ECR I–3761, para 44.

[243] Bebr 1996, 803.

[244] Bebr 1996, 803, notes that 'neither the criteria for such a distinction nor its purpose is quite clear. It may suggest that interim legal protection is rather exceptional, intended to protect a special situation of the plaintiff only'.

[245] See Case C–465/93 *Atlanta* [1995] ECR I–3761, para 47, which seems to indicate that it is for the Member States to protect general interests and the national courts may seemingly only order interim relief for individual interests.

Indeed, in its case law under Articles 242 and 243 EC the ECJ has held that applications for interim relief could only be furthered for the protection of the plaintiff's own individual interests, not for the protection of third parties or general interests.[246] In my view, however, this case law should not be applied analogously in the context of interim relief in national courts. The ECJ's case law under Articles 242 and 243 EC requiring the protection of individual interests which are distinguishable from that of other operators, is the corollary of the standing doctrine under Article 230(4) EC. The ECJ has consistently emphasized that the Treaty provides a complete system of judicial control whereby individuals may seek to challenge Community acts under Articles 230 and 241 EC or, if this is not possible, seek preliminary references under Article 234 EC.[247] It would be inconsistent with this aim, and liable to undermine the complementary effect of the Article 234 EC procedure, if *Plaumann* criteria were in effect smuggled into the Article 234 EC procedure in respect of interim relief.

It is interesting to see, however, that a local environmental organization was deemed to have a 'direct and certain interest' for the purposes of intervening in the aforementioned *Azores v Council*[248] case. The applications of Seas at Risk, the largest Federation of European NGOs, and WWF failed, however, since their interests in environmental protection was deemed 'too wide and general to be significantly affected' by the outcome of the case.[249] This argumentation is peculiar in regard to Seas at Risk, which is a NGO specializing in fisheries protection, whilst the order ironically implies that WWF will never have a sufficient interest in any specific case since its 'aim and activities cover large geographical areas'.[250]

Although the 'balancing of risk/interests' has been generally perceived as a significant bottleneck for interim relief, there are reasons to believe that this will not be such a limitation in environmental cases. The strict obligation to take into account the Community interest, as laid down in *Atlanta*, must be interpreted in light of the specific circumstances of that case, ie a regulation setting up a common market of agricultural products (bananas). This area of Community law and the choice of a regulation signify that uniform application is crucial. These concerns are not as acute in the environmental sector, which serves to explain why most legislation is exercised through directives. Furthermore, the court has

[246] Case T–13/99 R *Pfizer* [1999] ECR II–1961, para 136.

[247] See references and comment in section 4.1.

[248] Case T–37/04 R *The Autonomous Region of the Azores v Council* [2004] ECR II–2153, paras 63–65.

[249] ibid para 69.

[250] Para 70.

recently held that interests linked to environmental protection must as a rule prevail over economic considerations.[251]

The ECJ added in *Atlanta* that 'if the grant of interim relief represents a financial risk for the Community, the national court must also be in a position to require the applicant to provide adequate guarantees, such as the deposit of money or other security'.[252] Hence, in contrast to what has been argued in respect of interim relief against purely domestic measures (the *Factortame* situation),[253] the ECJ seems to presuppose that financial guarantees are not only allowed, but prima facie required when seeking interim relief against a Community act. It would appear, however, that the Community will rarely be directly at financial risk in environmental cases, except perhaps for environmental acts which have a direct influence on the internal market, eg waste and product regulations.[254]

It is also noteworthy that the ECJ did not explicitly oblige national courts to require guarantees, but only to be in a 'position' to do so, which suggests that national courts have some discretion when assessing the need for such guarantees and the extent of those.[255] Indeed, Article 86(2) of the ECJ's rules of procedure governing the Article 243 EC procedure stipulates that interim relief 'may' be made conditional on security, the amount and nature of which shall be fixed 'in the light of the circumstances'. It should be recalled in this context that Article 9(4) of the Aarhus Convention requires that interim relief be available and not prohibitively expensive.[256]

5 Sanctions

As much as proof of the pudding lies in the eating, the effectiveness of the Article 234 EC procedure rests in the measures taken by national courts and authorities in order to comply with the judgments. It is interesting to note that Member States have a poor track record in this respect as concerns

[251] Case C–320/03 R *Commission v Austria* [2003] ECR I–11665, para 58. See commentary by Schrauwen 2005, 855–58.

[252] Joined Cases 143/88 and C–92/89 *Zuckerfabrik* [1991] ECR I–415, para 32; Case C–465/93 *Atlanta* [1995] ECR I–3761, para 45.

[253] Chapter 3, section 4.5.

[254] On the other hand, if the Community's interest is at risk it is questionable whether any plaintiff could provide sufficient security in any event; see Hardcastle 1994, 98 – although he refers specifically to regulations.

[255] Similarly, Apter 2003.

[256] See chapter 3, section 4.5.

compliance with Article 226 EC judgments,[257] and one might expect that compliance with Article 234 EC judgments are not necessarily much better – at least as concerns administrative authorities (in contrast to the national courts).[258]

Whereas Article 228(2) EC provides for the possibility of hefty lump sums and penalty payments in order to induce compliance with Article 226 EC judgments,[259] Article 234 EC does not contain any provisions concerning sanctions for lacking compliance with preliminary rulings. However, plaintiffs may hold Member States liable if national courts fail to comply with a preliminary ruling, or where national authorities fail to carry out the national court's ruling in accordance with the preliminary ruling.[260] But there is still some uncertainty as to the application of the state liability doctrine in environmental matters, and it does in any event not entail punitive damages.[261] Preliminary rulings therefore lack the deterrent effect of Article 228(2) EC, which undermines the effectiveness of the Article 234 EC procedure in terms of accommodating supervision of Member States' application of EC environmental law by private parties compared with the supervision entrusted to the Commission's under Articles 226 and 228.

6 Conclusion

Article 234 EC has been broadly construed by the ECJ, and it will entertain practically any request for interpretation of a Community act, including non-binding acts, unless the questions are clearly hypothetical. The same holds true for judicial review of Community acts, the legality of which may now also be challenged 'directly' without any national implementing measures in place and before the expiry of the deadline for implementation.

[257] Between 1997 and 2001, there were annually approximately 30 environmental judgments with which the Member States had failed to comply by the end of the year. In 2002 that number rose by nearly 100 per cent to 58 judgments not complied with at the end of the year; see Krämer 2004, 129.

[258] Somsen 2000, 357–59 suggests that national courts' compliance rates with preliminary judgments are generally good, but there is a divergence to be noted between referring courts and the precedent compliance required by other courts. He also indicates different practices depending on the national legal system in the latter relation; precedent-bound courts such as the House of Lords have generally been more compliant than their French and German counterparts.

[259] See chapter 6, section 4.

[260] See chapter 3, section 11.

[261] Chapter 3, section 11.2.

There remains one lacuna, however, which concerns the fact that preliminary rulings may not be sought on the legality of a failure to act by the Community institutions. This is a relatively significant drawback, since in the field of the environment it may be as important, if not more so, to challenge omissions of Community intervention as the legality of existing acts. The Commission in particular has a responsibility to act in response to a wide range of developments, new scientific evidence, new risk-scenarios etc, and it is clearly very serious if individuals and NGOs cannot obtain judicial review of omissions by the Commission in this regard. It also calls into question the assertion of a complete system of procedures and remedies since environmental plaintiffs will not have standing to lodge a challenge under Article 232 EC either. This will change with Regulation 1367/2006, but this is only a partial remedy as both the personal and substantive scope are more restricted than Article 234 EC.

A more general problem with the Article 234 EC procedure for private enforcement purposes is that plaintiffs do not have a right to refer questions to the ECJ. Whether a question should be referred and how it should be phrased remains within the ambit of national courts' discretion. Furthermore, only courts of last instance are obliged to refer questions on the interpretation of Community law, which weakens the temporal effectiveness of the Article 234 EC procedure. Although *CILFIT* provides a low threshold for the obligation of courts of last instance to refer questions to the ECJ, there are few sanctions applicable when they fail to do so. *Köbler* liability is one possibility, but the conditions are likely to be applied stringently in practice, in particular as concerns 'sufficiently serious breach' and causation.

One reason why national courts may be tempted not to refer questions to the ECJ is the significant time during which proceedings will have to be suspended, coupled with very stringent conditions for interim relief, at least as far as challenges to Community acts are concerned. In environmental cases this may often undermine the very purpose of the legal action. Since a solution to the temporal delays inherent in the Article 234 EC procedure arguably requires institutional reform, it is paramount that the ECJ addresses the lack of effective interim relief. Instead of focusing so much on the possible short-term detrimental effects interim relief may have for the Community, it should be aware of the long-term risk to the *acquis communautaire* posed by national courts increasingly refraining from referring questions to the ECJ.

The final deficit that should be mentioned concerns the lack of sanctions for failure by the national authorities to comply with preliminary rulings. Article 234 EC does not contain punitive sanctions analogous to Article 228 EC.

The importance of this deficit should not be underestimated, especially taking into account the extremely poor implementation record under Article 226 EC. The Commission can of course initiate infringement proceedings for failure to implement Article 234 EC rulings in a timely and adequate manner, but that is hardly an effective remedy (or a deterrent) since that would require another two rounds before the ECJ (first an Article 226 EC case, and then Article 228 EC proceedings). It is therefore submitted that the ECJ should reconsider whether punitive sanctions should not only be allowed under the state liability doctrine but also required to form part of that remedy. But that would in turn raise new problems in relation to the entities which could collect such damages in environmental cases where the infringements have affected the public at large.

5

Judicial review before Community courts

1 Introduction

This chapter examines possibilities for individuals and NGOs to challenge the legality of environmental acts and omissions by Community institutions and bodies in direct actions before Community courts. As is well known, the ECJ has interpreted the standing rules under Articles 230 and 232 EC very restrictively and there is currently little judicial relief for environmental plaintiffs available at the Community level.

This is set to change, however, following the Community's ratification of the Aarhus Convention[1] and the subsequent adoption of Regulation 1367/2006 on the application of the Aarhus Convention on Access to Information, Public Participation in Decision-making and Access to Justice in Environmental Matters to Community Institutions and Bodies (Regulation 1367/2006 or the regulation).[2] Regulation 1367/2006 will require the Community institutions and bodies to adapt their rules of procedure, and Articles 13 and 14 thereof provide that it will apply from 28 June 2007.

The Aarhus Convention and Regulation 1367/2006 cannot, of course, alter the standing rules expressed in the Treaty provisions. However, they have the potential indirectly to liberalize application of those rules in two respects: first, by virtue of granting the public concerned participation rights in Community decision-making, which could in turn make them 'individually concerned' for the purposes of standing under Articles 230 and 232 EC and, secondly, by conferring on the public concerned rights to request Community institutions to conduct an internal review of the legality of their acts and omissions, the outcome of which is addressed to them and can subsequently be challenged before Community courts.

[1] See chapter 3, section 3.1. [2] [2006] OJ L264/13.

We will deal with these issues as follows. The next section (section 2) examines the ECJ's interpretation of the standing rules in Articles 230 and 232 EC, which is the framework in which the Aarhus Convention and Regulation 1367/2006 must work. This section will more specifically address whether public participation rights may have spillover effects in terms of standing and, if so, to what extent Regulation 1367/2006 guarantees public participation rights at the Community level. An analysis then follows of the right to internal review under Regulation 1367/2006 (section 3), and the possibility of judicial review of the outcome of the internal review procedure (section 4). This is followed by an examination of possible flanking remedies in the context of the regulation, ie interim relief (section 5) and Community liability (section 6). The chapter rounds off, as usual, with conclusions (section 7).

2 Direct and individual concern

2.1 *Introduction*

There are two scenarios in which individuals may challenge Community decisions under Article 230(4) EC – either by virtue of the decision being addressed to them, or because they are directly and individually concerned by a Community act. The condition under Article 232(3) EC appears more stringent, as it only provides for standing where a Community institution has failed to address a decision to a natural or legal person. However, the ECJ has taken the view that Articles 230 and 232 EC prescribe one and the same method of recourse, and has therefore aligned the two procedures so that direct and individual concern is also sufficient condition for standing under the latter.[3] We will therefore examine the ECJ's interpretation of the standing rules under Articles 230 and 232 EC in tandem.

2.2 *Decision addressed to the plaintiff*

This ground for standing has been important in competition law, where the Commission regularly addresses decisions directly to private undertakings. In the field of environment, however, decisions – to the extent that such acts are used – are very rarely addressed to private parties, but to Member States.

[3] See eg Case C–15/70 *Chevalley* [1970] ECR 975, para 6; and Case C–68/95 *T Port* [1996] ECR I–6065, para 59.

Decisions to provide financial support under the various Community funds, listing and classification of substances under the environmental directives concerning hazardous substances, and decisions allowing for the marketing of GMOs under Directive 2001/18/EC, to name but a few examples, are all addressed to Member States. There is one important exception, however, as concerns access to information. Regulation (EC) 1049/2001[4] on access to documents allows plaintiffs to request environmental information, and the relevant Community institution is accordingly obliged to release the information or give a written reply stating the reasons why the request is rejected. The ECJ has consistently held under Regulation (EC) 1049/2001, as well as under its predecessor Decision 94/90/EC, that a reply refusing access to information constitutes a decision for the purposes of Article 230(4) EC, which by virtue of being addressed to private parties grants standing under that provision.[5] This is, we shall see, the model under which Regulation 1367/2006 seeks to grant NGOs access to judicial review before Community courts (section 4). It should be added that Article 3 of Regulation 1367/2006 extends the scope of Regulation (EC) 1049/2001 to cover information held by Community bodies as well as the institutions in order to align it with the Aarhus Convention.

2.3 *Community acts of direct and individual concern*

It should be made clear from the outset that decisions are not the only acts that may be of direct and individual concern to plaintiffs for the purposes of Articles 230 and 232 EC. The ECJ has clarified that the classification of an act as a decision depends on its substance and not its form.[6] This is reflected in the wording of Article 230(4) EC, which provides that a decision in the form of a regulation may be challenged if it is of direct and individual concern to the plaintiff. The ECJ traditionally approached this issue by examining whether the act is of a normative or administrative nature, or of general or individual application.[7] In more recent case law, however, it has held that genuinely legislative acts may be also be of direct and individual concern to

[4] [2001] OJ L145/43.

[5] See Case T–124/96 *Interporc v Commission* [1998] ECR II–231, para 48; Case T–174/95 *Svenska Journalistförbundet v Council* [1998] ECR II–2289, paras 64–68; Case T–194/94 *Guardian Newspaper* [1995] ECR II–2765, para 39; and Case T–76/02 *Messina* [2003] ECR I–3203, para 10.

[6] See eg C–147/96 *Netherlands v Commission* [2000] ECR I–4723, para 27; and Case T–84/01 *Association contre l'heure d'été v Parliament and Council* [2002] ECR II–99, para 23.

[7] Eg Case T–298/94 *Roquette* [1996] ECR II–1153, paras 38–40, with references cited.

the plaintiff, and thus subject to judicial review.[8] The ECJ has accepted that directives may in principle also be subject to judicial review, although it has never actually allowed for such a challenge.[9] With these clarifications in place, it is necessary to examine the personal criteria for standing.

The notion of direct and individual concern appears quite vague and flexible on a literal reading, but the ECJ has nevertheless opted for an extremely narrow interpretation of Article 230(4) EC. The least problematic interpretation concerns direct concern. The ECJ has held that this implies that the act must:

> directly affect the legal situation of the individual and leave no discretion to the addressees of that measure who are entrusted with the task of implementing it, such implementation being purely automatic and resulting from Community rules without the application of other intermediate rules[10]

The latter part of this definition is reminiscent of the requirements for direct effect, albeit more stringent.[11] The point is that a non-addressee may only be directly concerned by an act where the addressee does not have any discretion in terms of implementing the decision or altering its content. This is a serious limitation, since most Community acts in the environmental sphere require implementing measures and confer often significant degrees of discretion on Member States for this purpose.[12]

The most important restriction still follows from the notion of individual concern. In the seminal *Plaumann* judgment the ECJ held that:

> for natural and legal persons to be regarded as individually concerned by a measure not addressed to them, it must affect their position by reason of certain attributes peculiar to them, or by reason of a factual situation which differentiates them from all other persons and distinguishes them individually in the same way as the addressee.[13]

This is a very strict test, and the fact that a measure has had adverse affects on plaintiffs is not sufficient reason to grant standing. In practice, only plaintiffs

[8] Eg Case C-451/98 *Antillean Rice Mills v Council* [2001] ECR I-8949, para 46; and Case T-43/98 *Emesa Sugar v Council* [2001] ECR II-3519, para 47.

[9] Eg Case T-321/02 *Vannieuwenhuyze-Morin v Parliament and Council* [2003] II-1997, para 21 and cited references.

[10] See eg Case C-386/96 P *Dreyfus v Commission* [1998] ECR I-2309, para 43; Joined Cases T-198/95, T-171/96, T-230/97, T-174/98, and T-255/99 *Comafrica and Dole Fresh Fruit Europe v Commission* [2001] ECR II-1975, para 96; and Case T-177/01 *Jego-Quere* [2002] ECR II-2365, para 26.

[11] Schermers and Waelbroek 2001, 455.

[12] See chapter 2, section 2.2.

[13] Case C-25/62 *Plaumann v Commission* [1963] ECR 95. See also Case C-231/82 *Spijker v Commission* [1983] ECR 2559; and Case C-97/85 *Deutsche Lebensmittelwerke and Others v Commission* [1987] ECR 2265.

who belong to a closed group of individuals may be deemed individually concerned, something which is rarely the case, particularly in environmental cases. However, the rulings in *Codorniu*[14] and *Extramet*[15] signalled a more liberal interpretation than *Plaumann*, according to which particularly adverse effects could be sufficient reason to give rise to individual concern.[16] These judgments were rendered shortly before the setting up of the Court of First Instance (CFI), and some saw these judgments as an attempt by the ECJ to launch a more liberal legacy on standing.[17] The CFI was not swayed by these cases, however, and interpreted these rulings narrowly in light of their particular underlying factual circumstances, hence returning to the *Plaumann* orthodoxy.[18]

The *Greenpeace* judgments[19] – the CFI judgment and the ECJ judgment on appeal – are the leading environmental cases on standing, and illustrate how *Plaumann* effectively excludes plaintiffs' access to justice under Article 230(4) EC. The case concerned construction of two power stations on the Spanish Canary Islands, a project which had received financial assistance from the Commission under the auspices of the European Regional Development Fund (ERDF). Several individuals living on the Canary Islands, including local residents, fishermen, and farmers, brought proceedings under Article 230(4) EC challenging the Commission's decision to grant support on the grounds that the project had not been subject to an environmental impact assessment under Directive 85/337 and was thus unlawful. Although the CFI accepted that some of these plaintiffs were adversely affected by the construction, eg because of nuisance or due to the economic loss suffered by farmers and fishermen, none of the plaintiffs was deemed individually concerned since they were all affected 'in the same manner as any other local resident, fisherman, farmer or tourist who was, or might be in the future, in the same situation'.[20]

The next question was whether Greenpeace, which was also a plaintiff in the case, could be granted standing on the basis that it represented the general interests of local residents on the Canary Islands. It is a fairly common

[14] Case C–309/89 *Codorniu v Council* [1994] ECR I–1853, paras 21–22.

[15] Case C–358/89 *Extramet Industrie v Council* [1991] ECR I–2501, para 17.

[16] For an extensive analysis, see Arnull 2001.

[17] Wyatt and Dashwood 2000, 237–38.

[18] Eg Case T–99/94 *Asocarne v Council* [1994] ECR II–871, paras 20–21; upheld on appeal in Case C–10/95 P *Asocarne v Council* [1995] ECR I–4149, para 43. See also opinion in Case C–321/95 *Greenpeace and Others v Commission* [1998] ECR I–1651, para 27.

[19] Case T–585/93 *Greenpeace and Others v Commission* [1995] ECR II–2205; and (on appeal) Case C–321/95 *Greenpeace and Others v Commission* [1998] ECR I–1651.

[20] Case T–585/93 ibid, paras 54–55.

occurrence in many domestic legal systems that organizations representing the cumulative public interest may be granted standing, although its members would not individually have standing,[21] and the prospect of success therefore appeared promising when seen through the lens of national law. Under Community law and Article 230(4) EC more specifically this is different, however, and referring to settled case law the ECJ noted that 'an association formed for the protection of the collective interests of a category of persons could not be considered to be directly and individually concerned [...] by a measure affecting the general interests of that category'.[22] Since the local residents Greenpeace represented were deemed not individually concerned, it followed that Greenpeace could not be considered individually concerned either.[23]

Greenpeace submitted also that the 'individual concern' test had been developed with economic activities in mind, and should not be applied in the same fashion in environmental cases. The CFI dismissed this argument as well, commenting that, although the individual concern test had predominantly been applied in cases revolving around economic interests, it 'nevertheless remains applicable whatever the nature, economic or otherwise, of those of the applicants' interests which are affected'.[24]

Greenpeace subsequently appealed the case to the ECJ, which essentially upheld the CFI's judgment on all points.[25] One issue sparked a debate, however. Greenpeace argued that the CFI's approach to individual concern created a 'legal vacuum in ensuring compliance with Community environmental legislation, since in this area the interests are, by their very nature, common and shared, and the rights relating to those interests are liable to be held by a potentially large number of individuals so that there could never be a closed class of applicants satisfying the criteria adopted by the Court of First Instance'.[26] Furthermore, Greenpeace held that this legal vacuum could not be filled by the preliminary reference procedure in this case, since it was not possible to challenge the Commission's decision in national courts.

The ECJ quickly dismissed the invitation to change the interpretation of individual concern, but added with reference to the judicial protection argument that the plaintiffs had in fact lodged proceedings in national courts

[21] Chapter 3, section 6.1. [22] Paras 59–60.

[23] Para 60. See also eg Case C–117/86 *UFADE v Council and Commission* [1986] ECR 3255, para 12; and Joined Cases T–447, T–448, and 449/93 *AITEC and Others v Commission* [1995] ECR II–1971, para 58 and 59. [24] Paras 50–52.

[25] Case C–321/95 P *Greenpeace and Others v Commission* [1998] ECR I–1651, paras 27–31.

[26] Paras 18–19.

against the failure of Spanish authorities to conduct an environmental impact assessment under Directive 85/337/EEC.[27] However, the national proceedings only concerned the legality of the administrative authorities' approval of the projects in breach of Directive 85/337/EEC, not the legality of the Commission's decision to fund these projects in the absence of environmental impact assessments. The ECJ conceded this, but held that both actions were based on the same rights afforded to individuals by Directive 85/337/EEC, so that those rights were fully protected by national courts which could if necessary refer a preliminary ruling to the ECJ.[28]

Some commentators read this obiter dictum as suggesting that, if conversely there would be no judicial relief at national level, the ECJ might still consider changing its interpretation of Article 230(4) EC in order to ensure a complete system of remedies, as they did in *Les Verts*.[29] Although this line of reasoning was taken up in the opinion in *UPA*[30] and the CFI in *Jego-Quere*,[31] the ECJ effectively ended this discussion with the *UPA* judgment (and by overturning the CFI on appeal in the *Jego-Quere* judgment).[32]

The *UPA* case has been commented upon before, and it therefore suffices to recall the basic facts of that case. The plaintiffs were Spanish agricultural producers who wanted to challenge a Community regulation which changed the rules on subsidies. Since the regulation did not require implementing measures and there were no national measures which could form the basis for a challenge in national courts, the plaintiffs were in effect barred from obtaining a preliminary ruling by the ECJ on the validity of the Community act. They argued therefore that the ECJ had to allow for a direct challenge under Article 230 EC and to this end amend the test of individual concern in order to ensure effective judicial protection. The ECJ dismissed this for two reasons.

The first argument relied upon by the ECJ was that it could not devise a standing test under Article 230(4) EC that was dependent on national standing rules.[33] This would require the ECJ to interpret national procedural law before determining standing under Article 230(4), which it is not competent

[27] Paras 32–33.

[28] This is strictly not correct since Directive 85/337/EEC, regardless of the outcome of the environmental impact assessment, would not have required the national authorities to stop the project, whilst a decision finding the Commission funding illegal, and thus requiring withdrawal of the financial grant, would most likely have had this consequence. As tersely noted by Williams 2002, 275: 'Money speaks pretty directly.' See also critique by AG Cosmas in the case, paras 72–74.

[29] Case 294/83 *Les Verts* [1986] ECR 1339, paras 23–25.

[30] Case C-50/00 P *UPA* [2002] ECR I-6677.

[31] Case T-177/01 *Jego-Quere v Commission* [2002] ECR I-5137.

[32] Case C-263/02 P *Commission v Jego Quere* [2004] ECR I-3425.

[33] Para 43.

to do. Secondly, and more fundamentally, it held that the judiciary was not competent to change the wording of Article 230(4) EC, and that a widening of the scope of standing could only be realized by way of a Treaty amendment.[34] This has been widely criticized for being overly formalistic, since the ECJ has applied teleological interpretations of Article 230 EC in other respects,[35] and also since the strict standing rules in Article 230(4) EC are not so much due to its wording, as the strict interpretation the ECJ gave it in *Plaumann*.[36] However, the judgment should be read in light of the fact that the ECJ in 1995 suggested that the Member States should change the wording in Article 230(4) EC in the context of the inter-governmental conference so as to ensure more liberal standing rules,[37] an invitation that was not followed in the Nice Treaty. Against this background, it would have been very bold if the ECJ was to ignore this signal from the Member States, and take it upon itself to liberalize Article 230(4) EC.[38] The ECJ thus concluded that the criteria of direct and individual concern had to be fulfilled even if the end result was that the plaintiffs were stripped of judicial protection at both national and Community levels. This has since been confirmed for environmental purposes in two recent orders in *European Environmental Bureau and Others* (the *EEB* cases).[39]

It may seem like the court's invitation to the Member States in *UPA* has to some extent been incorporated in Article III–365 of the Treaty Establishing a Constitution for Europe, which provides for standing against 'regulatory acts which is of direct concern to [the individual] and does not require implementing measures'. But the notion of 'regulatory act' is not to be found in Article I–33, which causes further confusion by giving new definitions to Community acts, whilst the conditions of 'direct concern' and 'does not require implementing measures' are overlapping. Indeed, the text was the result of a compromise between two factions of the working group,[40] which leaves the text between two stools. Anyhow, it appears that Article III–365 represents only a modest widening of the standing requirements for direct actions for (some) directly applicable Community acts that may not be challenged in national courts, ie the *UPA* situation. As such it will not add much

[34] Para 44.

[35] See references in opinion of AG Jacobs in Case C–50/00 P *UPA* [2002] ECR I–6677, paras 67–70.

[36] Arnull 2002, 509–510; and Craig 2003, 505.

[37] Report of the ECJ of Justice on Certain Aspects of the Application of the Treaty on European Union, Luxembourg, May 1995.

[38] Similarly, Hartley 2003, 370.

[39] Case T–94/04 *EEB and Stichting Natuur en Milieu* [2005] ECR II–4919, para 64; and Joined Cases T–236 and T–241 *EEB and Others* [2005] ECR II–4945, para 68.

[40] Craig 2003, 507–508.

to the field of environmental law, if ratified, since the overwhelming majority of Community acts require implementing measures.[41]

Leaving aside the Constitutional Treaty, there are still some circumstances which may grant individuals or NGOs standing under the *Plaumann* formula. First, 'the fact that, by virtue of specific provisions, the [Community institution] is under a duty to take account of the consequences for the situation of certain individuals of a measure which it envisages adopting may be such as to distinguish those persons individually'.[42] Secondly, individual concern may also be derived from specific procedural rights granted to plaintiffs, eg rights to participate in decision-making and to be heard.[43] However, it does not suffice for plaintiffs to have been de facto involved in decision-making – plaintiffs may only be deemed individually concerned on such grounds if the applicable Community legislation grants them procedural guarantees.[44] Hence, the fact that the plaintiffs in *Greenpeace* had been in contact with the Commission did not render them individually concerned as 'the correspondence which took place between Greenpeace and the Commission and its subsequent meeting with members of the Commission's staff were for purposes of information only, since the Commission was under no duty either to consult or to hear the applicants in the context of the implementation of Decision'.[45] Furthermore, the *EEB* cases clarified that it does not suffice that the plaintiff in general terms has been awarded special consultative status with the Commission or other Community institutions, as long as the applicable Community legislation does not provide for any procedural guarantees as regards the specific decision-making which is challenged.[46]

[41] Jans 2005, 485.

[42] Eg Case C–11/82 *Piraiki-Patraiki v Commission* [1985] ECR 207, paras 21 and 28; Case C–152/88 *Sofrimport v Commission* [1990] ECR I–2477, para 11; Case C–390/95 P *Antillean Rice Mills and Others v Commission* [1999] ECR I–769, paras 25–30; Joined Cases T–480 and 483/93 *Antillean Rice Mills and Others v Commission* [1995] ECR II–2305, para 67; Case T–47/00 *Rica Foods v Commission* [2002] ECR II–113, para 41; and Case T–177/01 *Jego-Quere* [2002] ECR II–2365, para 32.

[43] See eg Joined Cases C–67, 38, and 70/85 *Van der Kooy and Others v Commission* [1988] ECR 219; Case C–313/90 *CIRFS and Others v Commission* [1993] ECR I–1125, paras 29–30; Case T–585/93 *Greenpeace and Others v Commission* [1995] ECR II–2205, paras 56 and 63; Joined Cases T–38 to 50/99 *Sociedade Agrícola dos Arinhos and Others v Commission* [2001] ECR II–585, para 48; and Case T–13/99 *Pfizer v Council* [1999] ECR I–1961, para 101. Once the plaintiff enjoys such procedural rights he or she will be deemed individually concerned regardless of whether the plaintiff has actually exercised these rights or not; see eg Joined Cases T–528, 542 to 543, and 546/93 *Métropole Télévision and Others* [1996] ECR II–649, para 62 and cited references.

[44] See eg Case T–47/00 *Rica Foods v Commission* [2002] ECR II–113, para 55; and Case T–177/01 *Jego-Quere* [2002] ECR II–2365, para 35.

[45] Case T–585/93 *Greenpeace and Others v Commission* [1995] ECR II–2205, para 63.

[46] Case T–94/04 *EEB and Stichting Natuur en Milieu* [2005] ECR II–4919, para 62.

Since there is currently no Community legislation providing for such procedural guarantees in environmental matters, the issue may appear moot. However, this was set to change with the Community's ratification of the Aarhus Convention, which provides for mandatory rules on public participation in decisions on specific activities (Article 6) and plans and programmes (Article 7), as well as non-binding rules on public participation in policies relating to the environment (Article 7 *in fine*) and preparation of executive regulations (Article 8). For our purposes it is the procedural rights in respect of decision-making laid down in Article 6 which are most relevant, since plans and programmes, as non-binding measures, are in any event not subject to judicial review, whilst the other public participation provisions are non-mandatory.[47]

However, Regulation 1367/2006 merely implements Article 7 of the Aarhus Convention (cf Article 9 in Regulation 1367/2006) and does not provide for any public participation in decision-making as required by Article 6 of the Aarhus Convention. Recourse may in this respect be had to the Commission's proposal for the regulation and its explanatory memorandum, which discusses this vital issue in some detail. In order to comment on the Commission's reasoning it is necessary briefly to outline the two situations in which public participation is required under Article 6 of the Aarhus Convention.

First, Article 6(1) litra a requires public participation in respect of decisions to permit certain activities listed in Annex 1, which covers a wide range of activities, inter alia, in the energy sector, production and processing of metals, mineral industry, chemicals industry, waste management and different sorts of heavy industry. The Commission explanatory memorandum explains that this provision was not relevant for the purposes of the regulation, since decisions to authorize the listed activities are not taken at Community level but by Member States.[48]

Secondly, Article 6(1) litra b of the Aarhus Convention provides that public participation shall be provided also in respect of decisions on proposed activities not listed in Annex 1 that may have a significant effect on the environment. The Commission considered whether this might require public participation in respect of its decisions to list (ie approve) specific substances under the various directives on marketing of products containing dangerous substances, but decided against it since also the 'administrative decisions on the authorisation of chemicals, pesticides and biocides are, as a rule, taken at the level of Member States'.[49]

[47] See, by implication, Case C–142/95 P *Rovigo* [1996] ECR I–6669, paras 32–33 on the non-binding nature of environmental actions programmes.

[48] COM(2003) 622, 13.

[49] ibid.

In other words, it seems that the Commission referred to the general procedure in most of these directives where it authorizes dangerous substances, whilst it is still for Member States to authorize products containing these substances. However, this distinction is not necessarily relevant under Article 6(1) litra b. Whilst Article 6(1) litra a refers to decisions 'whether to permit' the proposed activities – which on a narrow reading could refer to the actual permitting of products on the national level – Article 6(1) litra b refers to 'decisions... which may have a significant effect on the environment'. This broader phrasing would in my opinion cover Commission decisions listing dangerous substances, in particular bearing in mind that Member States regularly have limited discretion not to approve, in turn, products containing these substances. This is, of course, also the reason why Member States recently have begun to challenge such Commission decisions.[50]

It seems therefore that Regulation 1367/2006 might be in breach of Article 6 of the Aarhus Convention by failing to provide for public participation in such decision-making. Another matter is that, even if the regulation would have provided for procedural guarantees for concerned individuals and NGOs and thus rendered them individually concerned for the purposes of Article 230(4) EC, they might still have found it difficult to fulfil the condition of 'direct concern'. Although Commission decisions pertaining to the listing of substances, as mentioned, often confer limited discretion on Member States not to approve products containing these substances, implementation of Commission decisions can probably not be described as 'being purely automatic and resulting from Community rules without the application of other intermediate rules'.[51]

A type of Community act which may require public participation under Article 6 of the Aarhus Convention and has 'automatic effect', however, is a Commission decision providing for financial support for activities listed in Annex 1 and other projects that may have a significant effect on the environment. This could for instance concern financing under the ERDF Regulation on the construction of power stations that threaten the environment which, as will be recalled, was the situation in the *Greenpeace* case.

However, public participation in this respect was also left out of Regulation 1367/2006, since 'the Aarhus Convention [ie Article 6] does not *explicitly* require public participation in financial decision-making'.[52] This is a very

[50] Case T–229/04 *Sweden v Commission* [2004] OJ C106/24; and Case T–5/06 *Denmark v Commission*, pending.

[51] See eg Case T–177/01 *Jego-Quere* [2002] ECR II–2365, para 26, discussed above.

[52] COM(2003) 622, 13.

peculiar argument since Article 6(1), in particular litra b, of the Aarhus Convention is drafted broadly precisely to cover a wide range of decisions which may have adverse effects on the environment. It seems that the Commission was aware of its dubious reasoning, and as a subsidiary argument advanced that the Community had left out public participation in financial decision-making at the national level as well, and it would thus 'create different approaches' if the regulation provided for public participation in this respect at the Community level. This reasoning is of course completely irrelevant for the purposes of compatibility with the Aarhus Convention – two wrongs rarely make a right – and it seems to me that by failing completely to provide for public participation in decision-making at the Community level, Regulation 1367/2006 is incompatible with Article 6 of the Aarhus Convention.

This is bad enough as it is, but it also means that individuals and environmental organizations are deprived of procedural rights which could have granted them standing for the purposes of actions under Articles 230 and 232 EC. Furthermore, the consequence of the Community's view that Article 6 does not apply to decision-making at the EC level also had the effect that Regulation 1367/2006 does not implement Article 9(2) of the Aarhus Convention, which requires privileged standing rights to challenge the procedural and substantive legality of decisions falling under Article 6 of the convention. Regulation 1367/2006 instead only implements Article 9(3) of the Aarhus Convention, which stipulates less stringent requirements than Article 9(2). This issue is dealt with in the section below.

3 Internal review

3.1 *Introduction*

Article 9(3) of the Aarhus Convention requires, as will be recalled from chapter 3,[53] that 'members of the public have access to administrative or judicial procedures to challenge acts and omissions by private and public authorities which contravene provisions of its national law relating to the environment'. Regulation 1367/2006 implements Article 9(3) in two stages. Article 10 of Regulation 1367/2006 provides a right for certain members of the public to request Community institutions to conduct an internal review of their acts

[53] Chapter 3, section 6.3.

and omissions, whilst Article 11 allows for judicial review of the outcome of that procedure before Community courts.

The preliminary internal review procedure was introduced as a means of ensuring access to judicial review.[54] For lack of individual concern to challenge Community acts directly under Article 230(4) EC, it was necessary to construe a procedure so that certain members of the public could petition the Community institutions, and by virtue of being the addressee of the internal review decision secure standing under Article 230(4) EC (or Article 232 EC in the event of a failure to provide for an internal review decision).

In this section we will examine the internal review procedure, and in the next section (section 4) assess to what extent Regulation 1367/2006 in fact guarantees access to judicial review. When assessing the compatibility of Regulation 1367/2006 with Article 9(3) of the Aarhus Convention, it should be borne in mind that any restrictions in the internal review procedure limits access to judicial review accordingly. However, there is also the possibility of obtaining preliminary rulings on the validity of Community acts under Article 234 EC,[55] which makes it somewhat difficult to assess to what extent gaps in Regulation 1367/2006 actually violate the Aarhus Convention.

Below, we will therefore articulate shortcomings in Regulation 1367/2006 that prima facie violate the Aarhus Convention, whilst chapter 7 contains final conclusions as to whether Regulation 1367/2006 and the preliminary procedure in tandem constitute a complete system compliant with the Aarhus Convention.[56]

3.2 *Personal scope*

Article 10 of Regulation 1367/2006 confers a right on NGOs to request internal review that meets the criteria set out in Article 11. Individuals are left out. They were also excluded in the Commission's original proposal, but the EP amended the proposals in its first reading so as to include individuals with a sufficient interest or claiming the impairment of a right.[57] This did not find favour with the Council, however, and the EP did not attempt to reintroduce individuals in its second reading. Although Article 9(3) of the Aarhus Convention confers discretion on parties to the convention to set the criteria under which members of the public have access to administrative and judicial review, including criteria favouring NGOs, it seems that the Community

[54] COM(2003) 622, 13. [55] Chapter 4, section 4. [56] Chapter 7, section 4.
[57] [2004] OJ C123E/612.

has exceeded its margin of discretion by completely excluding individuals. According to Article 2(4) of the Aarhus Convention, members of the public are natural persons as well as legal persons, including NGOs, and the Community can thus not exclude altogether one of the major classes of the 'public'. The situation invites comparison with case law under Directive 85/337/EEC, in which the ECJ on various occasions held that Member States enjoy discretion to lay down criteria for the selection of projects subject to environmental impact assessment according to Annex II, but that they would exceed this margin of discretion if these criteria excluded classes of projects in their entirety.[58]

Article 11 contains four cumulative requirements that must be met by NGOs. First, the NGO must be an independent, non-profit legal person according to a Member State's national law or practice. The reference to national law or practice is probably only relevant in respect of the status as a legal person, whilst the notions of independence and non-profit making are likely to be interpreted as autonomous Community law notions. In particular, the requirement of independence may prove a thorny issue in practice, and require auditing of NGO funding. The notion of non-profit making could also lead to problems. For instance, should this criterion be examined on the basis of the statutes of an organization, or in light of the question whether it de facto turns a profit?

The second criterion is that the NGO has the 'primary stated objective to promote environmental protection in the context of environmental law'. This indicates that NGOs need not be exclusively concerned with environmental protection, as long as that is its primary *raison d'être*. It is also noteworthy that the objective of environmental protection must be 'stated', ie it must figure in the statutes of the environmental organization.

Thirdly, the NGO must have 'existed longer than two years and is actively pursuing' the objective of environmental protection. The use of present form suggests that the NGO must not necessarily have been actively pursing that objective during the whole of that past period, as long as it does so when the question arises. Furthermore, Regulation 1367/2006 no longer requires that the NGO is active at the Community level, as was originally proposed by the Commission.[59]

Finally, the subject matter of the internal review must concern an issue which is covered by the NGO's objectives and activities. This could imply a

[58] Eg Case C–133/94 *Commission v Belgium* [1996] ECR I–2623, para 42; and Case C–72/95 *Kraaijeveld* [1996] ECR I–5403, paras 51–53. See also chapter 2, section 2.2.

[59] 'Statement of the Council's reasons' [2005] OJ C264E/25.

requirement of a certain degree of specialization.[60] A decision affecting birds, for instance, in that view could only be challenged by NGOs that have as their specific objective the protection of bird life, eg the UK Royal Society for the Protection of Birds (RSPB), whilst excluding organizations which deal with protection of the environment at large, eg Greenpeace. However, this interpretation would render Article 11(1) litra b meaningless, which merely requires the primary objective of the NGO to be environmental protection. Article 11(1) litra d should therefore be understood as merely excluding specialized organizations from requesting internal review of issues which clearly fall outside their remit. Thus, the RSPB cannot request internal review of environmental acts that do not concern the protection of birds, but general organizations, such as Greenpeace, can challenge decisions concerning specific issues, including bird protection.

Regulation 1367/2006 does not say anything about how the authorization of NGOs will function in practice. Will authorization occur on a case-by-case basis, or through prior approval? Will the Community institution to which the request for internal review is addressed be responsible for determining whether the NGO should be recognised, or the Commission? Article 11(2) indicates that these issues will be decided by the Commission through the adoption of guidelines, but it seems quite unsatisfactory to allow such important issues to be dealt with at a later stage. Another question is whether it is satisfactory from a democratic perspective to delegate the crucial task of elaborating the criteria and operation of the authorization procedure of Article 11(1) to the Commission, which thus to a significant extent determines the NGOs which may request internal review. This is especially dubious considering that the large majority of acts subject to review are likely to be Commission decisions.[61]

However, Article 11 of Regulation 1367/2006 is directly applicable as of 28 June 2007, cf Article 14, and NGOs can then lodge requests for internal review even in the absence of such guidelines, leaving the relevant Community institution obliged to determine whether the conditions of Articles 10 and 11 are fulfilled and, if so, to respond to the request.

3.3 *Time limits*

Article 10(1) provides that a request for internal review must be made in writing within six weeks after the contested act was adopted, notified, or published,

[60] See, by analogy, Case T–37/04 R *The Autonomous Region of the Azores v Council* [2004] ECR II–2153, paras 63–71, discussed in chapter 4, section 4.6.2.

[61] See section 3.2.2 below.

whichever is the latest. The same applies to omissions to act, where the time limit refers to the point in time when the act 'was required'. This notion seems to refer to the moment when the act should have been adopted, which places request for internal review of omissions to act at a temporal disadvantage compared with complaints against existing acts. In so far as the omission concerns failure to adopt an act that must be published, the start of the time limit should be when the Community institution was obliged to act, corrected for the additional time which publication usually takes.

The six-week time limit is in any event very short, and is in fact tighter than the time limit laid down in Article 230(5) EC, which contains more lenient conditions both in respect of the start of the deadline, and its duration. Hence, Article 230(5) refers to the date of publication of a measure, or its notification to the plaintiff or, in the absence thereof, *the day on which it came to the knowledge* of the plaintiff. Secondly, it provides for a two-month time limit. It is difficult to understand the justification for a stricter regime in Regulation 1367/2006. Perhaps more importantly, it is questionable whether the six-week time limit in Regulation 1367/2006 complies with Article 9(4) of the Aarhus Convention, which requires 'adequate and effective remedies'.

But the Commission's proposal for a regulation as well as the Council's Common Position stipulated in fact a mere four-week deadline, and it was not before the conciliation process that the Parliament managed to improve this aspect of the regulation. This has been a long struggle for the Parliament, which attempted to extend the deadline for requesting internal review to 12 weeks in its first reading, and then promoted an eight-week time limit in the second reading.[62] The Commission did not accept this on the grounds that it would undermine legal certainty and slow down procedures.[63] However, if the Commission was referring to the fact that the two-stage procedure of internal review and judicial review procedure will slow down procedures, it is essentially blaming its own system, and the Community cannot remedy this by fixing a prohibitively short time limit for internal review.

3.4 *Substantive scope*

The subject matter for internal review is, according to Article 10(1) of Regulation 1367/2006, 'an administrative act adopted under environmental law, or an alleged administrative omission [to adopt such an act]'. Article 2(1) litra g of Regulation 1367/2006 defines an administrative act as 'any measure

[62] [2004] OJ C 123E/612 (first reading); and P6_TA-PROV(2006)0016, nyr in OJ (second reading).

[63] COM(2006) 81 final.

of individual scope under environmental law, taken by a Community institution or body, and having legally binding and external effect'. Article 2(1) litra h provides the same as regards omissions. This definition is multifaceted, and for purposes of analysis needs to be broken down in separate parts.

3.4.1 *Community institution or body*

Article 2(1) litra c defines a Community institution or body as 'any public institution, body, office or agency established by, or on the basis of, the Treaty except when it acts in a judicial or legislative capacity'. This is a broad definition – significantly broader than that under Article 230(4) EC[64] – since it not only encompasses the Community institutions listed in Article 7(1) EC, but any public body set up on the basis of the Treaty through secondary legislation or decision, eg the European Environmental Agency. However, it is still more narrowly phrased than its counterpart – Article 2(2) of the Aarhus Convention – which also includes natural and legal persons performing public administrative functions (litra b) or providing public functions under the control of a public authority (litra c). This would seem to include private entities performing public administrative functions. Since paragraph 7 of the preamble to Regulation 1367/2006 states that it seeks to define the Community institutions and bodies in the 'same broad manner' as the Aarhus Convention, Article 2(1) litra c of Regulation 1367/2006 must therefore be interpreted so as to include also private entities performing public functions under environmental law.

The fact that public authorities are excluded when acting in a legislative or judicial function is unproblematic in relation to the Aarhus Convention, which in Article 2(2) makes the same exception. What is more questionable, however, is the fact that Article 2(2) of Regulation 1367/2006 adds that that exception shall apply similarly to acts and omissions by a Community institution or body acting 'as an administrative review body'. This includes decisions taken under Articles 81, 82, 86, and 87 EC (competition and state aid), Articles 226 EC and 228 EC (infringement proceedings), Article 195 EC (ombudsman proceedings), and Article 280 EC (European Anti-Fraud Office proceedings). Jans has criticized in particular the exception concerning Commission decision-making under the competition rules, and rightly queried whether it is correct to say that it is acting in an administrative review capacity in these cases.[65] However, it is dubious to exclude administrative

[64] ibid. [65] Jans 2006, 480.

review decisions in any event, since Article 2(2) of the Aarhus Convention explicitly only refers to judicial decisions. The Commission's decisions in the context of the prejudicial stage of the Article 226 EC procedure, for instance, may perhaps be described as a form of administrative review, but they are clearly not judicial.[66] It is also noteworthy in this respect that the guidelines to the Aarhus Convention explain that judicial acts should be excluded due to the fundamentally different nature of such decision-making 'where tribunals must apply the law impartially and professionally without regard to public opinion'.[67] This description clearly does not fit with the Commission's actions under the competition rules, or the administrative phase of infringements proceedings, under which the ECJ has deferred reviewing certain parts of the Commission's discretion – in particular whether or not to act – owing to the political nature of these decisions.[68] But this causes new problems in relation to the requirement discussed in the section below.

3.4.2 *Legally binding and external effects*

The acts subject to internal review must have 'legally binding and external effects'. This excludes decisions takes under Article 226 EC, which the ECJ has found to be administrative preliminary acts which are non-binding.[69] The same goes for other preparatory acts, eg environmental action programmes[70] and plans drawn up under the auspices of such programmes.

It is noteworthy that Article 9(3) of the Aarhus Convention does not contain the condition that the acts must be legally binding to be amenable to administrative or judicial review. This restriction also runs counter to the ECJ's case law under Article 234 EC, in which it has accepted judicial review of non-binding Community acts since they may nevertheless have legal effects which 'the national courts are bound to take . . . into consideration in order to decide disputes submitted to them, in particular where they cast light on the interpretation of national measures adopted in order to implement them or where they are designed to supplement binding Community

[66] Chapter 6, section 6.4. See eg Case 48/65 *Luetticke and Others v Commission* [1966] ECR 19 at 27; Case C–247/87 *Star Fruit* [1989] ECR 291, para 37; and Case T–126/95 *Dumez v Commission* [1995] ECR II–2863, para 44.

[67] 'The Aarhus Convention, An Implementation Guide' United Nations Publication (2000) 34.

[68] Eg Case C–422/92 *Commission v Germany* [1995] ECR I–2189, para 18.

[69] Case 48/65 *Luetticke and Others v Commission* [1966] ECR 19 at 27; Case C–247/87 *Star Fruit* [1989] ECR 291, para 12; and Case T–126/95 *Dumez v Commission* [1995] ECR II–2863, para 44.

[70] See, to this effect, Case C–142/95 P *Rovigo v Commission* [1996] ECR I–6669, paras 32–34.

provisions'.[71] However, the approach chosen in Regulation 1367/2006 is logical considering that non-binding acts in any event fall outside the scope of review under Article 230(4) EC.[72]

The condition of external effect will primarily exclude acts which only have relevance for the internal workings of Community institutions,[73] procedures governing the relationship between different Community institutions, or specific Community practice.[74] However, under certain circumstances, such rules may have legal effects for third parties, and thus be subject to review.[75]

3.4.3 *Administrative act taken under environmental law*

The administrative act must have been taken 'under environmental law', which is defined in Article 2(1) litra f as 'Community legislation, which irrespective of its legal base, contributes to the pursuit of the objectives of Community policy on the environment according to the Treaty establishing the European Community: preserving, protecting and improving the quality of the environment, protecting human health, the prudent and rational utilisation of natural resources, and promoting measures at international level to deal with regional or worldwide environmental problems'.

This is a broad definition of environmental law and notably shows, in contrast to the Commission proposal,[76] that it is the objective and not the legal basis which determines whether the legislative act should properly be considered as part of 'environmental law'. This means that not only measures adopted under Article 175 EC are included, but also acts adopted under other provisions in the EC Treaty to the extent that they pursue environmental objectives, eg acts adopted under Articles 95 (internal market), 37 (agriculture and fisheries), 71 (transport), 152 (public health), and 153 EC (consumer protection). This broad definition of environmental law is merely a logical consequence of the integration principle of Article 6 EC, according to which environmental protection shall be taken into account when drafting legislation and policy in other areas of EC law.[77]

[71] Case C–322/88 *Grimaldi* [1989] ECR 4407, para 18. See also chapter 3, section 4.4.

[72] See eg Case C–301/03 *Italy v Commission* [2005] ECR I–10217.

[73] See eg Case C–314/91 *Weber v Parliament* [1993] ECR I–1093, para 10; Case C–69/89 *Nakajima v Council* [1991] ECR I–2069, para 49; and Case T–17/00 *Willi Rothley v Parliament* [2002] ECR II–579, paras 53–54.

[74] Case C–159/96 *Portugal v Commission* [1998] ECR I–7379.

[75] Case T–17/00 *Willi Rothley v Parliament* [2002] ECR II–579, paras 55–56.

[76] COM(2003) 622.

[77] See chapter 4, section 4.4.4. For a thorough analysis of the principle of integration, see Dhondt 2003.

3.4.4 *Measure of individual scope*

It already follows from the abovementioned criteria that the substantive scope of Regulation 1367/2006 is rather narrow and is confined to legally binding administrative acts adopted under environmental law. However, Article 2(1) of Regulation 1367/2006 further restricts the scope of acts subject to internal review by adding that the administrative measure must be of 'individual scope'. It follows from case law that a Community measure which 'applies to situations determined objectively and has legal effects with regard to categories of persons viewed generally and in the abstract' is deemed of general scope and would thus fall outside Regulation 1367/2006.[78] The requirement of individual scope would thus exclude, inter alia, the drawing up of implementing rules by the Commission in accordance with Article 202 EC, which are acts of general application, and only encompass 'the application of rules to specific cases by means of acts of individual application'.[79] A significant proportion of Commission and Council decisions would not qualify under these terms, eg Commission (or Council) authorizations under the various environmental directives on hazardous substances, as well as Commission decisions on notified national regulations under Article 95(6) EC and Directive 98/38/EC.[80] In fact, bearing in mind that Regulation 1367/2006 has excluded Commission decisions taken under competition and state aid rules, it would seem that Regulation 1367/2006 would essentially be limited to internal review of Commission decisions on financial assistance to individual projects. But even such decisions may fall foul of Regulation 1367/2006. In the *Rovigo*[81] case, the ECJ held for instance that a Commission decision to grant financial assistance to various national actions for the protection of the habitats and nature was of general scope. This even applied to the part of the decision which concerned a specific project – the Italian Po delta programme – since the decision as a whole was of 'general scope which applies to situations determined objectively and has legal effects with regard to categories of persons viewed generally and in the abstract'.[82] Hence, if the notion of 'individual scope' in Regulation 1367/2006 is interpreted strictly, it would in fact appear that hardly any Community acts are subject to internal review.

There are various reasons why this interpretation should be refuted, however. First of all, Article 9(3) of the Aarhus Convention is not limited to acts of

[78] Case T–117/94 *Rovigo and Others v Commission* [1995] ECR II–455, para 24.
[79] Case C–16/88 *Commission v Council* [1989] ECR 291, para 11.
[80] [1998] OJ L204/37.
[81] Case T–117/94 *Rovigo and Others v Commission* [1995] ECR II–455.
[82] Para 24.

individual scope, but requires review of any administrative 'acts and omissions [...] which contravene [...] law relating to the environment'.[83] It follows from settled case law that Community measures must as far as possible be interpreted in conformity with international agreements, in particular in such a case as this where the provisions are intended specifically to give effect to an international agreement concluded by the Community.[84] Secondly, the notion of individual scope as outlined above has traditionally been closely linked to the issue of individual concern and the application of the *Plaumann* doctrine in relation to standing.[85] Since the internal review procedure has been devised inter alia in order to make this condition unnecessary under Article 230 EC,[86] it would conflict with the aim and the system of Regulation 1367/2006 if an equivalent barrier in the form of 'individual scope' was introduced. These concerns inform an alternative reading of Regulation 1367/2006, namely that the notion of individual scope is merely designed to distinguish administrative acts from legislative acts. This interpretation gains support from a close reading of the wording of Article 2(1) litra g of Regulation 1367/2006, which provides that an ' "administrative act" means any measure of individual scope', which is not strictly the same as 'administrative act of individual scope'. The insertion of the words 'individual scope' may therefore simply have been a reference to the ECJ's case law which sometimes employs this as a criterion for separating legislative acts from administrative acts.[87]

This interpretation of Regulation 1367/2006 is in conformity with Article 9(3) of the Aarhus Convention and results in some Community acts being subject to internal review. Although Commission decisions granting financial assistance to certain projects may be found to be of general scope (which is debatable, one may equally well argue that such decisions listing the projects subject to financial assistance should be regarded as a 'conglomeration of individual decisions'),[88] it is nonetheless clear that they are not legislative

[83] Indeed, this was how Regulation 1367/2006 was originally drafted by the Commission, cf COM(2003) 622, and it was only after the Council's first reading that the words 'of individual scope' were added.

[84] Chapter 2, section 3.2. Case C–61/94 *Commission v Germany* [1996] ECR I–3989, para 52; and Case C–341/95 *Safety-Hitech* [1998] ECR I–4355, para 20.

[85] Eg Joined Cases 16 and 17/62 *Producteurs de Fruits v Council* [1962] ECR 478 at 479.

[86] Section 4.2 and COM(2003) 622, 16.

[87] Eg Case T–298/94 *Roquette* [1996] ECR II–1153, paras 36 and 42 with cited references; and Case T–43/98 *Emesa Sugar v Council* [2001] ECR II–3519, para 46.

[88] By analogy Joined Cases 41 to 44/70 *International Fruit* [1971] ECR 411, para 21.

acts. The same goes for Commission decisions which reject notified national measures, eg under Article 95(6) EC[89] and Directive 98/38/EC.[90]

Whether implementing measures by Commission or Council, in accordance with Article 202 EC, are legislative or administrative acts is more difficult to determine. Although it may be difficult to draw a formal distinction between legislation and implementing measures in so far as they may be adopted in identical form,[91] it is nevertheless clear that the Community maintains a substantive distinction between the two:

> Both the legislative scheme of the Treaty, reflected in particular by the last indent of Article 155 [Article 211 EC], and the consistent practice of the Community institutions establish a distinction, according to legal concepts recognised in all the Member States, between the measures directly based on the Treaty itself and derived law intended to ensure their implementation.[92]

In order to be a legislative act, it must have been adopted under a legislative procedure, which separates implementing acts from legislative acts.[93] This is why, on the one hand, a delegation of implementing powers requires the institution charged with a legislative task to determine the general objectives of the policy to be carried out as well as supervising the exercise of discretion,[94] whilst, on the other hand, the implementing measure must not modify the scope of the obligations laid down in the basic regulation without following the legislative procedure pertaining to the latter act.[95] The fact that implementing measures, even if of general scope, are to be distinguished from legislation is also implied by Article 207(3) EC, which provides that the Council must define in which cases it should be regarded as acting in its legislative capacity with a view to allowing greater public access to documents. Hence, it is submitted, the drawing up of implementing acts by the Commission or Council in light of technical and scientific progress, eg amendments of directives to add or remove listed substances, amounts to administrative acts[96] subject to internal review.

[89] Case C–3/00 *Commission v Denmark* [2003] ECR I–2643, paras 39–40.

[90] [1998] OJ L204/37.

[91] Article I–33 of the Constitution, if ratified, would provide a formal distinction.

[92] Case C–25/70 *Köster* [1970] ECR 1170, para 6.

[93] See, by implication, Case C–25/70 *Köster* [1970] ECR 1170; Case 23/75 *Rey Soda* [1975] ECR 1300; and Case C–3/00 *Commission v Denmark* [2003] ECR I–2643, paras 39–40.

[94] ibid.

[95] See eg Case C–22/86 *Vreugdenhil and Others* [1989] ECR 2049 and Case C–303/94 *Parliament v Council* [1996] ECR I–2943.

[96] Similarly Ward 2004, 48 and 54 who views these as executive acts, as opposed to normative acts.

Summing up this section, there are two possible interpretations of Regulation 1367/2006 as concerns acts subject to internal review. According to a narrow interpretation, only administrative acts which are of individual scope fall within its ambit. This would effectively exclude practically all Community acts, perhaps with the exception of decisions granting financial assistance to a particular project. However, if Regulation 1367/2006 is interpreted in conformity with the Aarhus Convention, it militates in favour of the conclusion that acts that by nature are administrative, even if not of an individual scope, are subject to internal review. This interpretation will be presupposed for the purposes of the subsequent sections, and also because Regulation 1367/2006 would otherwise hardly be of any practical consequence.

3.5 *Grounds and nature of review*

Regulation 1367/2006 does not stipulate the grounds for internal review which the relevant Community institutions must conduct for their own acts. However, it follows implicitly from Article 10(1) that it is the plaintiff who must state the grounds for review, and the Community institutions must respond accordingly. The question is therefore which grounds for review the plaintiffs are entitled to request. Article 9(3) of the Aarhus Convention confers a right on the public to challenge acts which contravene 'provisions [...] relating to the environment'. Since environmental provisions contain substantive as well as procedural requirements, it follows that Regulation 1367/2006 confers a right on NGOs to contest a decision on both substantive and procedural grounds. This conclusion is supported by the ECJ's case law under the analogous system in Regulation (EC) 1049/2001 according to which the Community institutions are required to conduct internal review of decisions to refuse access to documents on both procedural and substantive grounds.[97]

In accordance with Article 10(2) of Regulation 1367/2006, the Community institution must consider any such request unless clearly unsubstantiated, and state its reasons in a written reply as soon as possible, and within 12 weeks at the latest. This must be understood as obliging the Community body either to approve the complaint and indicate what actions are to be taken, or to state the reasons why the complaint has been rejected.

If, in reconsidering the contested act, the Community institution becomes aware of infringements which would have rendered the act or omission illegal

[97] By implication, eg Case T-187/03 *Scippacercola v Commission* [2005] ECR II-1429; and Joined Cases T-110, 150 and 405/03 *Sison v Council* [2005] ECR II-1429, paras 15-16.

in Article 230 EC or Article 232 EC proceedings, it would seem that the Community institution is under a duty to take all the necessary measures to nullify the unlawful consequences of its breach. This follows from analogous use of Article 233 EC. It is also noteworthy that point 19 of the preamble stipulates that the purpose of the internal review procedure is to provide the Community institution an opportunity to 'reconsider' the contested act, which implies that it must draw the necessary consequences from any infringements revealed in doing so. In case of procedural infringements, it may suffice to adopt a new act fulfilling the requisite procedural rules, whilst substantive infringements may require the Community institution to amend the act or withdraw it altogether.

Article 10(3) extends the deadline to state reasons to 18 weeks where the Community institution is unable, despite due diligence, to act within the deadline prescribed in Article 10(2). It is difficult to see why such an extensive time limit is called for when in comparison the Community institutions under Article 232 EC have a maximum of two months to define their position. This is also worrisome in light of the fact that there is no possibility of obtaining interim relief in this period. But it is noteworthy that the NGOs are in these circumstances entitled to information stating why an extended time period is required, as well as an indication of when the review will take place. If the Community institution fails to comply with this obligation, the NGO can initiate judicial proceedings after expiry of the 12-week deadline stipulated in Article 10(2).

4 Judicial review

4.1 *Introduction*

Article 12 of Regulation 1367/2006 provides that a NGO may institute proceedings before the ECJ in accordance with the relevant provisions of the Treaty (ie Articles 230 and 232 EC) subsequent to the internal review procedure. It should be noted that the subject matter for the judicial review is the written reply, or failure to reply, under the internal review procedure – not the contested act or omission that was originally challenged in the internal review procedure (the original act or omission). Since the conditions for judicial review under Articles 230 and 232 EC are in most respects identical, I will consider them in tandem. In order to prevent repetitions and to make the text more readable, I will focus on challenges to the written reply under Article

230 EC, and only refer to challenges of omissions to reply under Article 232 EC where it differs from the conditions under Article 230 EC.

4.2 *Standing*

The primary purpose of the internal review procedure, as laid down in the Commission proposal, was to ensure NGOs standing under Article 230(4) EC by way of an internal review decision addressed to them, thus making the requirement of individual and direct concern superfluous.[98] But whilst the Commission proposal required the Community institution to issue a 'decision' addressed to the NGO following the internal review, the Council changed the wording of Article 10 of Regulation 1367/2006 to a 'written reply'. This caused an outcry among several NGOs, including the European Environmental Bureau, which protested that the change of wording was designed to exclude them from standing under Article 230(4) EC, which reserves standing to 'decisions' addressed to the plaintiff.[99]

This criticism is misguided for several reasons. First, it follows from settled case law that it is the substance of an act, not its form, which determines its classification,[100] and the change of wording could therefore in any event not have material consequences for the purposes of standing. Secondly, the reason for the Council amendment was apparently to align the text of Regulation 1367/2006 with Articles 7 and 8 of Regulation (EC) 1049/2001 on access to information, which employs the notion of 'written reply' in response to requests to documents. It follows from the case law under Regulation (EC) 1049/2001 – as well as its predecessors, Decisions 93/731/EC and 94/90/EC – that the ECJ has understood a written reply to constitute a decision addressed to the plaintiff for the purposes of Article 230(4) EC, which is capable of granting standing to challenge that decision.[101] This will apply similarly in respect of a written

[98] COM(2003) 622, 16.

[99] EEB briefing to the EP Environmental Committee, available at <http://www.eeb.org/publication/general.htm>.

[100] See eg C–147/96 *Netherlands v Commission* [2000] ECR I–4723, para 27; and Case T–84/01 *Association contre l'heure d'été v Parliament and Council* [2002] ECR II–99, para 23.

[101] See Case T–124/96 *Interporc v Commission* [1998] ECR II–231, para 48; Case T–174/95 *Svenska Journalistförbundet v Council* [1998] ECR II–2289, paras 64–68; Case T–194/94 *Guardian Newspaper* [1995] ECR II–2765, para 39; and Case T–76/02 *Messina* [2003] ECR I–3203, para 10. The ECJ has similarly held that that a letter from the Commission which gives a negative reply to a request from a third party to take action against alleged state aid in accordance with the procedure under Article 88(2), 'constitutes a decision rejecting the complaint to the Commission . . . [which] has definitive legal effects as far as the plaintiff is concerned'; see eg Joined Cases C–166 and 220/86 *Irish Cement* [1988] ECR 6473, para 11.

reply under Regulation 1367/2006 or a failure to issue a written reply. Support for this conclusion may, moreover, be derived from point 19 of the preamble to Regulation 1367/2006, which states that the internal review procedure is appropriate in order to 'ensure adequate and effective remedies, *including those before the Court of Justice*'.

The next requirement for standing is that the written reply is addressed by one of the Community institutions listed in Article 230(1), eg the Parliament, Council or the Commission. The problem which occurs in this respect is that Regulation 1367/2006 also includes Community agencies and bodies, and it is therefore conceivable that an internal review decision taken by an entity other than the Community institutions listed under Article 230 EC may consequently not be subject to judicial review.

This is not very likely to cause problems in practice, however. The ECJ has first of all not interpreted the personal scope of Article 230 EC very restrictively, and reviewed decisions by bodies not listed in that provision.[102] Furthermore, acts by Community bodies acting under delegated powers and subject to supervision by a Community institution will normally be accredited to the latter, and thus subject to judicial review.[103] The different comitology committees, for instance, are seen as emanations of the Commission.[104]

4.3 *Time limits*

It follows from Article 230(5) EC that NGOs must challenge the written reply within two-months of its notification. As for failure to act proceedings, Article 232(2) EC provides that plaintiffs must first call upon the Community institution to act. If it has failed to do so after expiry of a two-month time limit, the plaintiff may bring proceedings within a further two months. After a NGO has called upon a Community institution to act within the context of the internal review procedure, it would seem superfluous that this should have to be repeated under Article 232(2) EC. Indeed, the ECJ held in the *ENU* case that where a plaintiff has called upon an institution to act under a

[102] Case C–294/83 *Les Verts* [1986] ECR 1339, para 25; and Case C–370/89 *SCEEM* [1992] ECR I–6211, paras 15–16.

[103] Joined Cases T–369/94 and T–85/95 *International Film and Others* [1998] ECR II–357, paras 52–53. See also Joined Cases 32 and 33/58 *SNUPAT* [1959] ECR 136 at 137–38.

[104] See eg Case T–188/97 *Rothmans* [1999] ECR II–2463, para 62 (in the context of access to information). For an example where legal action against such a scientific committee was held manifestly inadmissible; see eg order in Case T–149/96 *Coldiretti* [1998] ECR II–3841. See also Vos 1999, 27–28 and St Clair Bradley 1999, 88 et seq.

specific provision of the Euratom Treaty it was not necessary to do so again for the purposes of Article 148 of the Euratom Treaty – which is identical to Article 232 EC.[105] This should also apply in the context of judicial review of failure to act under Regulation 1367/2006.

It should be added that if the Community institution acts after expiry of the applicable time limit but before proceedings before the ECJ have been initiated, an action under Article 232 EC will no longer be possible. This is due to the fact that the obligation in Article 233 EC cannot be triggered anymore, and the proceedings thus are without purpose.[106] If not satisfied with the reply, plaintiffs must seek annulment of that decision under Article 230(4) EC in such cases.

4.4 *Grounds of review*

4.4.1 *Introduction*

The grounds for review listed in Article 230(2) EC are 1) lack of competence, 2) infringement of an essential procedural requirement, 3) infringement of the Treaty or any rule of law relating to its application, and 4) misuse of powers. Judicial review by the ECJ in the context of actions brought under Regulation 1367/2006 may for purposes of clarity be divided into three levels.

4.4.2 *First level – error in procedure*

The first line of challenge is that the Community institution has infringed the procedural requirements stipulated in Article 10 of Regulation 1367/2006. Failure adequately to state reasons in response to the grounds of review set out by NGOs is likely to become the most important ground for review. The precise content of this duty is not defined in Article 10. However, it follows from settled case law that the obligation to state reasons implies that 'the reasoning of the Community authority which adopted the contested measure must be shown clearly and unequivocally so as to enable the persons concerned to ascertain the reasons for the measure in order to protect their rights and the Community judicature to exercise its power of review'.[107] Moreover, if the Community institution rejects the request for internal review on the basis that it is 'clearly unsubstantiated', it would seem that it has to state reasons why this is so.[108]

[105] Case C–107/91 *ENU* [1993] ECR I–6, para 21.

[106] See eg Case C–377/87 *EP v Council* [1988] ECR 4017, para 10; Joined Cases C–15 and 108/91 *Buckl and Others* [1992] ECR I–6061, paras 13–18; and Case T–39/97 *T Port* [1997] ECR II–2125, para 25.

[107] Eg Case T–124/96 *Interporc v Commission* [1998] ECR II–231, para 53.

[108] See, by analogy, Case C–360/92 P *Sytraval* [1995] ECR I–23, para 64.

4.4.3 *Second and third levels – error in law*

The second level of review revolves around a substantive examination of the statements of reasons with a view to assessing whether they are vitiated by any error of law. If so, this will affect the legality of the act that was challenged in the internal review procedure (the original act), and thus ensure an indirect judicial review of that act – which of course is the main purpose of NGOs' actions. These errors can pertain to any of the grounds of review listed in Article 230(4) EC set out above and may concern procedural as well as substantive issues.

NGOs could thus argue that the statement of reasons reflects a misinterpretation of the procedural requirements pertaining to the decision-making *under the original act*. This would typically concern the right to be heard and the corresponding duty of authorities to take into account their views, as well as a statement of reasons (under the original act).[109] The first two requirements have little relevance for our purposes, however, since Regulation 1367/2006 does not provide for rights of public participation in respect of acts subject to review, as noted in section 2.3. Errors in law concerning statements of reasons in relation to the original act, on the other hand, will usually be rectified by the statements of reasons in the internal review (cf Section 4.4.2). However, if the Community institution in its written reply states reasons why it is of the opinion that the original act was sufficiently reasoned but in doing so reveals a misinterpretation of the requirements in this regard, the written reply may thus be vitiated by an error of law.[110] More importantly, NGOs could submit that the statement of reasons reveals an error in law as concerns substantive issues pertaining to competence or the interpretation of the Treaty and rules relating to its application in the decision-making concerning the original act. The nature of these grounds of review has been dealt with at length in chapter 4, and will therefore not be repeated here.[111]

The third level of review, which is arguably applicable, consists of an incidental judicial review, in accordance with Article 241 EC, of an act of general application underlying the original act that was subject to internal review.[112] This would for instance be required if a NGO challenges the legality of a Commission decision authorizing a hazardous substance on the basis that the

[109] For an exhaustive presentation of the different 'essential procedural requirements' in EC law, see Schermers and Waelbroek 2001, 376–91.

[110] See, by implication, Joined Cases T–110, 150, and 405/03 *Sison v Council* [2005] ECR II–1429, paras 15–16.

[111] Chapter 4, sections 4.4.2–3.

[112] Although Article 241 EC refers to regulations, it should be understood as including any acts of general application, herein directives – see Case T–125/96 *Boehringer* [1999] ECR II–4342, para 57.

underlying directive is illegal. One could argue, however, that in this situation the directive is strictly not underlying the act subject to judicial review (the internal review decision), and it could thereby be doubtful whether Article 241 EC is applicable. However, since the legality of the directive may nevertheless be relevant for purposes of reviewing whether the statements of reasons in the internal review decision are vitiated by any error of law, it seems to me that Article 241 EC should apply – if necessary by analogy – to this situation.

4.5 *Consequences*

If the ECJ finds that the internal review decision is in breach of the grounds listed in Article 230 EC, the decision will be declared void in accordance with Article 231 EC, whilst an omission to issue a written reply will result in a declaration of a failure to act under Article 232 EC. The responsible Community institution is either way required to take the necessary measures to comply with the judgment, in accordance with Article 233(1) EC. In order to comply with the judgment and to implement it fully, the institution is required to have regard not only to the operative part of the judgment, but also to the grounds which led to the judgment and constitute its essential basis. It is those grounds which indicate the specific reasons which underlie the finding of illegality contained in the operative part, and which the institution must take into account when replacing the annulled measure.[113]

Hence, if the error is of a procedural nature, eg a failure to state sufficient reasons in the reply to a NGO, it may suffice for the Community institution to issue a new written reply with a more complete statement of reasons.[114] Conversely, if the ECJ has found that the written reply is vitiated by an error of law which reflects back on the legality of the original decision, the Community institution will have to reconsider the original decision, and, if appropriate, amend or withdraw it altogether. This may be illustrated by the pending *deca-BDE* case[115] where the Parliament has challenged Commission Decision 2005/717/EC exempting a particular substance from the prohibition in Directive 2002/95/EC.[116] One of the issues in that case is whether the statement of reasons reveals a misinterpretation of the precautionary principle, in

[113] Joined Cases C–97, 99, 193, and 215/86 *Asteris* [1988] ECR 2181.

[114] See eg Case C–331/88 *Fedesa* [1990] ECR I–4023, para 34; opinion of Advocate General Mischo in Case C–331/88 *Fedesa* [1990] ECR I–4042, para 57; Case 8/66 *Cimenteries and Others v Commission* [1967] ECR 93, para 47.

[115] Case C–14/06 *Parliament v Commission* [2006] OJ C86/11.

[116] [2003] OJ L37/19.

so far as the Commission has justified its decision by lack of conclusive evidence about risks. If the ECJ would find that this indeed is the case, it would seem that the Commission would have little choice but to withdraw the authorization. This would apply mutatis mutandis to a similar type of challenge brought in the context of Regulation 1367/2006. Furthermore, although the ECJ cannot issue an injunction against the Community institution specifying the content of the measures which should be taken, it has on occasion 'by way of illustration' indicated the possibilities open to the Community institution to the effect that little discretion remained.[117]

The above applies mutatis mutandis to an act of general application which the ECJ has found inapplicable under its incidental review under Article 241 EC.[118]

5 Interim relief

The lodging of proceedings before the ECJ does not have automatic suspensory effect However, plaintiffs may seek suspension of contested acts under Article 242 EC. Although Regulation 1367/2006 does not refer to interim relief, a NGO that has received a written reply (or failure to receive such within the requisite time limits) will thereby have standing to seek interim relief, subject to the conditions of prima facie illegality, urgency, and balancing of interests. The ECJ has held that these requirements correspond to the conditions under which national courts may grant interim relief against Community acts, and we may therefore refer to the analysis in chapter 4.[119]

Instead we shall focus on a particular problem to which applications for interim relief under Regulation 1367/2006 will give rise. The wording of Article 242 EC provides for suspension of the 'contested act', whilst Article 83 of the Rules of Procedure of the Court of Justice provides that an application for suspension of Community measure is 'admissible only if the applicant is challenging that measure in proceedings before the ECJ'. It would

[117] See eg Case T–84/91 *Meskens v Parliament* [1992] ECR II–2335, para 79; upheld on appeal in Case C–412/92 P *Parliament v Meskens* [1994] ECR I–3757, para 30.

[118] Joined Cases 75 and 117/82 *Razzouk v Commission* [1984] ECR 1509, para 19. See also opinion of AG Lagrange in Joined Cases C–14, 16–17, 20, 24, 26–27/60, and 1/61 *Meroni* [1961] ECR 161; and opinion of AG Roemer in Joined Cases C–9 and 12/60 *Vloebergs* [1961] ECR 197.

[119] Chapter 4, section 4.6 – albeit note some reservations as to whether these conditions in practice are strictly identical.

therefore appear that it is only the written reply to the request for internal review under Regulation 1367/2006 which can be suspended, which of course serves no purpose, and is in fact not even possible since it does not alter the applicant's legal position.[120] What is needed for effective interim relief is suspension of the original decision, which *prima facie* appears to fall outside the scope of Article 242 EC.

However, Article 242 EC has not been interpreted restrictively and the ECJ has for instance allowed for interim suspension of an act which was not the subject matter of review, but the consequence of the act challenged.[121] It is therefore possible to argue that the notion 'contested act' should be interpreted broadly so as to include the incidental review of the original decision, and thus in principle allow for its suspension under Article 242 EC, as otherwise there would be a risk of a lacuna in the judicial protection of plaintiffs.[122]

An alternative route would be for plaintiffs to seek an interim injunction against the Community institution under Article 243 EC – the wording of which is not limited to suspension of the contested act, but allows for any necessary interim measures. If so, the ECJ may also order the Community institution to communicate to the national authorities not to apply the original decision of the Community institution, eg not permit marketing of products containing a substance for which Community authorization has been suspended.[123]

But even if the ECJ would accept the reasoning outlined above, and in principle accept that the original decision may be suspended, it will be very difficult to persuade it to do so in practice. The main problem is that a suspension of the original decision would essentially prejudge the judicial review and also be tantamount to performing the act requested under the internal review. However, in case of significant urgency it cannot be ruled out that the ECJ will nevertheless allow for such an application. The *Paraquat* case referred to earlier,[124] for instance, might have qualified for interim relief on the basis that the substance poses significant risks, even fatal risks, to human health. Decisions on deliberate release of GMOs into the environment under Directive 2001/18/EC provide another example, since any damage might be irreversible.

[120] Lenaerts and Arts 1999, 287.

[121] See eg Case C–18/65 R *Gutman v Commission* [1996] ECR 135.

[122] See eg Case C–399/95 R *Germany v Commission* [1996] ECR I–2441; and Case C–393/96 R *Antonissen* [1997] ECR I–441.

[123] See, by analogy, Case 88/76 R *Ditterich v Commission* [1976] ECR 1586; and Case 160/84 R *Kavallas* [1984] ECR 3217.

[124] Case T–229/04 *Sweden v Commission* [2004] OJ C106/24. See chapter 4, section 4.4.4.

6 Community liability

A judgment under Article 230(4) EC (or Article 232 EC) which in effect requires the Community institution to take a new internal review decision and possibly also repeal or amend the original decision will not offset any environment damage that has occurred. This raises the question whether plaintiffs in these situations can seek reparation under Article 288(2) EC.

It should be noted from the outset that the ECJ has aligned the conditions for Community liability with those elaborated in respect of state liability, so that the *Brasserie* conditions of the grant of rights, sufficiently serious breach and causation are sufficient conditions for Article 288(2) EC actions.[125] Since these conditions have been examined at length in chapter 3,[126] we can confine ourselves to analysing specific application of these requirements in respect of suits brought in the context of Regulation 1367/2006.

6.1 *Grant of rights*

Article 10 EC of Regulation 1367/2006 confers a right to internal review of Community acts on certain NGOs. These NGOs may therefore in principle seek reparation for any relevant damage caused by sufficiently serious infringements that have occurred under the internal review procedure, eg failure to conduct an internal review, or a manifestly flawed internal review decision.[127] The same should apply mutatis mutandis in relation to failures to take the necessary measures under Article 233 EC to comply with a judgment annulling an internal review decision, or declaring a failure to conduct an internal review. This conclusion follows from the fact that the duty to comply with such a judgment is the corollary of the duty to provide an internal review decision under Regulation 1367/2006, and since the latter entails rights for NGOs concerned, the former must similarly confer such rights. A different conclusion would jeopardize the procedural rights granted under Regulation 1367/2006.

As for the notion of relevant damage, it was indicated in chapter 3 that state liability entails an obligation to make good any harmed caused, including

[125] Case C–352/98 P *Bergaderm and Goupil v Commission* [2000] ECR I–5291, para 42; Case T–43/98 *Emesa Sugar v Council* [2001] ECR II–3519, para 59; Case C–312/00 P *Camar and Tico v Commission and Council* [2002] ECR I–11355, paras 52–56; and Case C–234/02 *Médiateur Européen v Lamberts* [2004] ECR I–2803.

[126] Chapter 3, section 11.

[127] See, by implication, Case T–415/03 *San Pedro* [2005] ECR II–4355, para 68 on the merger of the condition of 'rights' for the purposes of Community and state liability.

environmental damage.[128] It follows that the same applies under Article 288(2) EC in respect of harm caused by the Community institutions. This may seem at odds with existing case law under Article 288(2) EC (although no environmental cases have ever been adjudicated upon). However, it should be borne in mind that it was only recently that the ECJ accepted the coherence between the two procedures. It has since amended restrictive aspects of its old case law in order to align it with more progressive features of the state liability doctrine. For example, it has held that it is no longer important for satisfaction of the first condition of Community liability that the rule of law infringed constitutes a higher-ranking rule of law,[129] whilst the decisive test for determining whether there has been a sufficiently serious infringement no longer resides in the individual nature of the act in question, but the discretion enjoyed by the institution.[130] It is therefore submitted that a similar development may occur in respect of relevant heads of damage.

6.2 *Causation*

The condition of a causal link between the infringement and the damage is likely to be the most significant bottleneck for the purposes of Regulation 1367/2006. Any damage caused is likely to be linked to the original act, eg the authorization of an environmentally hazardous substance or grant of financial aid to a project in breach of EC environmental law, and it might therefore at first seem difficult to see how subsequent infringements connected with the internal review procedure have any bearing on the damage caused.

However, there are two ways in which such infringements may have contributed to the damage. The first is a failure to take the necessary measures to amend or withdraw the original act under the internal review procedure. As seen above, the Community institution is obliged under Regulation 1367/2006 to 'reconsider' that act, and if that process reveals, or should have revealed, procedural or substantive errors rendering the act illegal, it must follow that the Community institution has a duty to take all the necessary measures to ensure compliance with the applicable Community rules. Any damage which ensues from this point in time is causally linked to this infringement. The second ground for liability stems from a failure to take all the measures necessary to comply with a judgment annulling the internal

[128] Chapter 3, section 11.2. [129] Case T–415/03 *San Pedro* [2005] ECR II–4355, para 85.

[130] Case C–352/98 P *Bergaderm and Goupil v Commission* [2000] ECR I–5291, para 46; and Case C–312/00 P *Camar and Tico v Commission and Council* [2002] ECR I–11355, paras 55.

review decision. This may in the same fashion require the Community institution to act in respect of the original decision, thus incurring liability for damage caused as a consequence of a failure to do so.

However, the Community institution is of course only responsible for damage caused *ex post* the relevant infringement – hence either from the time it should have acted under the internal review procedure, or from the 'reasonable time' it should have taken the necessary measures to comply with the judgment annulling the internal review decision. One might argue that a judgment annulling an internal review decision presupposes an infringement of the duty to take the necessary measure already under the internal review procedure, so that this would always be the starting point for damage caused. Yet, this argument fails in so far as the former does not necessarily presuppose a 'sufficiently serious' infringement in the latter situation – which brings us to the next and final condition for Community liability.

6.3 *Sufficiently serious breach*

Whether there is a sufficiently serious breach revolves around the margin of discretion afforded to the authorities concerned under the applicable Community rules, and the question is whether the authorities have manifestly and gravely disregarded the limits of their discretion.[131]

It follows from case law in the context of state liability that a complete failure to implement a directive before expiry of the deadline is a sufficiently serious breach per se, since Member States enjoy no discretion in this respect.[132] This should apply analogously to failures by the Community institutions to conduct an internal review within the applicable time limits in Regulation 1367/2006,[133] as well as breaches of Article 233 EC for failing to take any measures to comply with a judgment annulling an internal review decision. Another matter is that Article 233 EC does not stipulate clear time limits in this respect, and the question is whether the Community institution has acted within 'reasonable time'.

The issue is more complex where the Community institution has conducted an internal review in time, but has failed to identify the illegality of the contested act or not taken adequate measures to correct it. Whether there is a sufficiently serious breach in this respect must be assessed by taking into

[131] See eg Case C–472/00 P *Commission v Fresh Marine* [2003] ECR I–7541, para 26; C–234/02 P *Ombudsman v Lamberts* [2004] ECR I–2803, para 49.

[132] See references in chapter 3, section 11.3.

[133] See, by implication, Case T–344/00 *CEVA-Santé* [2003] ECR II–229, paras 99–103.

account 'the clarity and precision of the rule breached, the measure of discretion left by that rule to [...] the Community authorities, whether the infringement and the damage caused was intentional or involuntary, whether any error of law was excusable or inexcusable'.[134] Hence, if it was *acte clair* that the original decision infringed one of the grounds of review in Article 230(2), it would seem that a failure to take all necessary measures to correct the breach under the internal review procedure represents a sufficiently serious breach.

7 Conclusion

The ECJ's narrow construction of direct and individual concern under Articles 230(4) and 232 EC has for practical purposes shut the door for private enforcement in direct actions at Community level. This was set to change with the Community's ratification of the Aarhus Convention, but Regulation 1367/2006 which is intended to implement that convention falls short of the mark in several respects.

First of all, it fails to grant the public concerned rights of participation in Community decision-making, and thereby also strips parties concerned of procedural rights which would have rendered them individually concerned for the purposes of Article 230 and 232 EC actions. The erroneous view that the Community does not conduct decision-making for the purposes of Article 6 of the Aarhus Convention has in turn also translated in a failure to implement Article 9(2) of the Aarhus Convention, which requires privileged rights of access to justice for the entities that had public participation rights under Article 6.

Regulation 1367/2006 has therefore merely sought to implement Article 9(3) of the Aarhus Convention, which lays down more relaxed requirements concerning access to justice. Even so, it appears that Regulation 1367/2006 fails to implement that provision correctly in so far as it excludes individuals from its scope. Furthermore, the tight time limits for requesting internal review would seem to conflict with the requirement of adequate and effective remedies in Article 9(4).

The most important issue still concerns the substantive scope of Regulation 1367/2006. It is not entirely clear whether it should be interpreted as allowing

[134] See eg Case C–392/93 *British Telecommunications and Others* [1996] ECR I–1631, para 43 and further references in chapter 3, section 11.3.

for internal review only of administrative acts of individual scope, or whether the notion of individual scope is merely meant to signify that legislative acts fall outside the scope of Regulation 1367/2006. If the first interpretation is adopted, Regulation 1367/2006 will hardly have any *effet utile* whatsoever, since practically all Community acts will fall outside of its scope for review. Should the ECJ favour the second interpretation, bearing in mind that it is obliged to interpret Regulation 1367/2006 in conformity with the Aarhus Convention, Regulation 1367/2006 will – despite its shortcomings – signify an important breakthrough for private enforcement of environmental law in relation to the Community institutions.

NGOs concerned will be able to request internal review of administrative acts and omissions by Community institutions and bodies, the outcome of which may subsequently be challenged before the ECJ under Article 230 EC or Article 232 EC. By way of judicial review of the statement of reasons in the internal review decision, the ECJ will also be able to conduct incidental review of the original decision, as well as legislative acts of general application underlying that act.

In order to comply with a judgment annulling the internal review decision, the relevant Community institution may therefore have to amend or withdraw the original decision – which of course is the main purpose of actions brought by NGOs. Failure to do so may in turn allow NGOs to seek reparation for any damage that has ensued, in accordance with Article 288(2) EC.

6

Enforcement by the Commission

1 Introduction

The Commission plays a significant role in enforcing EC environmental law. Roughly one-fourth of all cases under investigation for non-compliance with Community law in 2005 concerned the environment,[1] whilst more than one-third of all Article 226 EC proceedings brought in 2004 and 2005 were environmental cases.[2] Furthermore, three of the five judgments handed down under Article 228 EC concerned environmental protection.[3] The role of the Commission is also significant compared with enforcement by individuals. In the period 2004–2006, there were 85 infringement proceedings under Article 226 EC, compared with only 16 preliminary referrals.[4] Furthermore, a significant proportion of preliminary references in environmental cases are motivated by interests other than protection of the environment.[5] It therefore seems safe to conclude that the Commission's position as the guardian of the Treaty is particularly important in this sphere of Community law.

Yet, the mere number of cases brought by the Commission does not necessarily prove that this line of enforcement is correspondingly effective. On the contrary, the repetitive nature of infringement proceedings implies that it is

[1] Seventh Annual Survey on the Implementation and Enforcement of Community Environmental Law (SEC(2006) 1143) 5.

[2] Krämer 2006b, 408–409. The figures were similar in 2003; see Fifth Annual Survey on the implementation and enforcement of Community environmental law 2003 (SEC(2004) 1025) 6.

[3] See section 4. I consider the judgment in Case C–304/02 *Commission v France* [2005] ECR I–6263 as related to environmental protection although it formally concerned the Community's fisheries policy.

[4] Krämer 2006b, 409.

[5] Somsen 2000, 327. Of the mere 46 preliminary referrals that had been made until the mid 1990s, more than half related to the internal market and the waste sector, whilst most of the remaining cases (24) revolved around criminal proceedings, ie individuals invoking EC environmental law as a defence.

not effective, and that it lacks deterrent effect. This hypothesis is examined over the next sections, starting off with an introduction to the Commission's monitoring powers and the anatomy of infringement proceedings (section 2). We then analyse the effectiveness of Article 226 EC proceedings in light of new developments in the case law (section 3) and the recent invigoration of Article 228 EC (section 4). Since the infringement proceeding in part is of a political nature, account will also be had of administrative and political factors that influence its operation in practice (section 5). It is also necessary to assess the rights of private parties in infringement proceedings, because a large proportion of the Commission's actions are instigated after complaints by individuals (section 6). This is followed by a comparison of the Commission's vigilance to ensure compliance with environmental law by Community institutions and its policy vis-à-vis Member States (section 7). Finally, some general observations on the complementary role of private enforcement are articulated (section 8).

2 Article 226 EC

2.1 *Introduction*

The implementation of EC environmental law can be divided into essentially two stages – the transposition phase and the operational phase.[6] The transposition phase may be further divided into a normative and organizational part. The normative phase involves transposing the EC measure into national law in a sufficiently precise manner (unless it is a regulation). The organizational phase concerns the setting up of the 'legal and administrative framework for the proper application and enforcement of the transposing legislation' (eg designating proper authorities, facilitating monitoring and enforcement mechanisms, ensuring legal remedies and laying down effective sanctions for infringements).[7] The operational phase is the actual and continuous process in which national authorities employ their organizational apparatus to apply and enforce Community norms as transposed into national law.

The Commission may bring infringement proceedings against Member States for failures that have occurred in any of these stages of the implementation process. However, in practice the Commission encounters more

[6] Opinion of AG Geelhoed in Case C–494/01 *Commission v Ireland* [2005] ECR I–3331, para 24.
[7] ibid para 25.

difficulties in some of these different stages than in others. This is largely due to the fact that the Commission enjoys different degrees of access to information. Although Member States must provide full information about the normative transposition of environmental directives, there is limited information about the organizational phase, and even less about the operational phase. This is one of the reasons why there are many infringement cases that concern issues of formal implementation, and relatively few cases about insufficient application or enforcement of EC environmental law.[8] In order to understand the Commission's enforcement practice, it is therefore important first to examine how the Commission obtains its information.

2.2 *Monitoring*

Member States must communicate national measures implementing directives to the Commission before the deadline for implementation. This information concerns the transposition phase, ie the normative and organizational measures necessary for the formal implementation of directives. Since the mid-1970s most directives also contain provisions requiring Member States to report to the Commission, every three years, on their application and experience gained.[9] This information serves a dual purpose. It provides feedback which the Commission may use to amend or otherwise strengthen the provisions, and indicates whether Member States are properly applying the directive.[10] But these reports are often furnished too late, and regularly lack detail.[11] Because national reports frequently differ in form and substance, it is difficult for the Commission to gain comparative insights regarding practical application in Member States.[12] For instance, in respect of the very important Directive 96/61/EC on Integrated Pollution Prevention and Control,[13] the Commission conceded that it had been impossible to draw up a report on its application for these reasons.[14]

[8] Hattan 2003, 23 reports that the Commission's policy in environmental matters also tends to focus on communication omission and non-conformity cases rather than non-application cases.

[9] Krämer 2003, 378.

[10] See eg the purpose statement in the Commission's Communication on the Road to Sustainable Development (COM(2003) 354) 4.

[11] Krämer 2003, 379–80.

[12] Somsen 2003, 419. Some suggestions for reform have been provided by Macrory 2005, 388–90.

[13] [1996] OJ L257/26.

[14] 'The reason is not that Member States have not made a real effort, but rather that they all use very different ways of expressing limits, which they are perfectly allowed to do, since the [IPPC] Directive does not require harmonization of these diverse practices'; see Communication from the Commission, 'On the Road to a Sustainable Development' COM(2003) 354, 23.

Directive 91/692/EEC on Standardizing and Rationalizing Reports on the Implementation of Certain Directives Relating to the Environment[15] was adopted in an attempt to address these problems. It restructured the reports so that Member States had to communicate on the application of directives on a sector by sector basis, eg air, waste, or water, instead of reporting on individual directives. Perhaps more importantly, the directive also drew up standardized questionnaires with the aim of achieving uniform reports.

However, Directive 91/692/EEC has had limited success, mainly because few directives have been fully aligned with its reporting system.[16] Furthermore, whilst the national reports may contain adequate information about formal and administrative implementation, for obvious reasons they rarely communicate shortcomings pertaining to monitoring, enforcement, or sanctions in individual cases.[17] Such reports therefore at most indicate that there may be flawed or insufficient practices which may motivate the Commission to seek further information.

This brings us to a fundamental problem in the Commission's role as environmental guardian of the Treaty. Unlike other areas of EC law, eg competition, veterinary, customs, regional, and fisheries policy, in environmental matters the Commission does not possess investigative powers that extend to Member States' territory. The European Parliament proposed that the European Environmental Agency should be given such competences, but it quickly became clear that the Council, ie the Member States, was vehemently opposed to such an idea, and the issue was put to sleep by an agreement to reconsider the question within two years, which never happened.[18]

The Commission may ask the Member State to allow for inspections, but this lies completely within the discretion of the Member State in question and such requests are not likely to be honoured in cases where infringements may be discovered.[19] However, when the Commission initiates a formal investigation of a Member State with a view to determining whether infringements of EC environmental law have occurred, national authorities are bound by the principle of loyal cooperation in Article 10 EC, which requires them to provide all necessary data to the Commission.[20] If they fail to do so, the

15 [1991] OJ L377/48. 16 Krämer 2003, 379. 17 ibid 380.

18 See Article 20 of Regulation 1210/90 [1990] OJ L120/1.

19 One exception is Case C–103/00 *Commission v Greece (the Greek Turtles case)* [2002] ECR I–1147, para 8.

20 See generally Case C–33/90 *Commission v Italy* [1991] ECR I–5987, para 18; and specifically concerning information Case C–192/84 *Commission v Greece* [1985] ECR 3967, para 19; and Case C–82/03 *Commission v Italy* [2004] ECR I–6035, para 15.

Commission can bring infringement proceedings, either separately or in parallel with the substantive issue, for infringement of Article 10 EC.[21]

The Commission nevertheless largely depends on information furnished by individuals, NGOs and – exceptionally – environmental agencies or administrations in the Member States, usually in the form of complaints.[22] The number of complaints in 2005 was 279, which represents a drop compared with previous years.[23] Some cases are initiated following questions from MEPs, but the Commission is then usually left to seek out the relevant information itself.

In sum, the information stream in the environmental sector is best developed in respect of formal implementation, ie normative measures, and to a lesser extent organizational structures, and is insufficient in respect of practical application, ie information about application and enforcement in individual cases.[24]

This fact is reflected by the Commission's figures of open infringement cases. In 2003 there were 88 open cases concerning non-communication of national implementation measures – which the Commission automatically opens once the deadline for implementation has expired – and 118 cases concerning non-conformity with national measures. In contrast, only 95 cases related to wrongful application of EC environmental law.[25] Hence, about two-thirds of all infringement cases concerned formal implementation. This number is in fact even higher, considering that a majority of cases which the Commission has dubbed 'horizontal bad-application' cases concerned failures to designate special protection areas, draw up environmental management plans, or draw up lists of sites for protection of habitats and species. These infringements could be classified as wrongful implementation rather than practical application in the narrow sense, ie application, enforcement, and impositions of sanctions in individual cases.[26] However, the corresponding numbers for 2005 suggest that the Commission has started to focus more on wrongful application. The number of non-communication and non-conformity cases was respectively 124 and 98, whereas open bad-application cases had risen to 279.[27]

[21] See eg Case 494/01 *Commission v Ireland* [2005] ECR I–3331, paras 195–98.

[22] See also section 5 below.

[23] Seventh Annual Survey on the Implementation and Enforcement of Community Environmental Law (SEC (2006) 1143) 11; cf Fifth Annual Survey on the Implementation and Enforcement of Community Environmental Law 2003 (SEC(2004) 1025), 6.

[24] Somsen 2003, 423–24.

[25] Fifth Annual Survey on the Implementation and Enforcement of Community Environmental Law 2003 (SEC (2004) 1025) 35.

[26] ibid 36.

[27] Seventh Annual Survey on the Implementation and Enforcement of Community Environmental Law (SEC(2006) 1143) 66–68.

2.3 *Prejudicial stage*

The prejudicial part of the Article 226 EC procedure consists of an informal and a formal stage. During the first stage the Commission conducts investigations, either *ex officio* or following private complaints, and considers whether there is a prima facie infringement. It will normally require further information from Member States.

If it finds that there is a breach of EC environmental law, it will initiate the formal stage by issuing a letter of formal notice to a Member State. The notice contains a description of the factual and legal basis for the alleged infringement, and invites the Member State to submit observations. If the Member State disputes the Commission's accounts of facts and/or law or otherwise fails to persuade the Commission that there is no breach of Community law, the Commission will normally issue a reasoned opinion, which is a more detailed account of the factual and legal basis for the alleged breach.

The pre-litigation phase thus serves three objectives: to place the Member State concerned in a position to rectify infringements, to enable the Member State to exercise its rights of defence and, finally, to define the subject matter of the dispute in relation to proceedings before the ECJ.[28]

2.4 *Judicial Stage*

2.4.1 *Procedural requirements*

If the Member State fails to comply with the reasoned opinion, the Commission may resort to the judicial stage of the infringement procedure. But the Commission cannot bring proceedings before the time limit for implementing the reasoned opinion has expired. The case may be inadmissible if the time limits provided in the formal notice and/or the reasoned opinion are unreasonably short.[29] What is reasonable in this respect depends on the factual circumstances of the case. The Commission usually allows for a two-month deadline,[30] but the ECJ has held that shorter time limits may be acceptable where there is urgency to remedy the breach, or where the Member State concerned has been aware of the Commission's position well in advance. In a case against Belgium, the ECJ thus accepted in principle that time limits of eight and 15 days to comply with a letter of formal notice and a reasoned opinion, respectively, could be justified, although the case was in

[28] Case C–326/01 *Commission v Ireland* [2002] ECR I–11433, paras 16–18.

[29] See eg Case 293/85 *Commission v Belgium* [1988] ECR 305.

[30] Krämer 2003, 387.

the end found to be inadmissible because the alleged urgency had in effect been caused by the Commission's failure to take expedient action.[31]

There are, on the other hand, in principle no preclusive time limits after which the Commission is barred from bringing proceedings.[32] Thus, in one case against Germany, the Commission brought proceedings more than six years after national legislation had been published, and notably also after the Community policy had changed in the same direction, but the ECJ nevertheless held that it was for the Commission 'to decide, in its discretion, on what date it may be appropriate to bring an action and it is not for the Court to review the exercise of that discretion'.[33] However, where the Commission initiates proceedings years after the expiry of a reasoned opinion and the Member State has taken new measures in the interim, the ECJ has advised that it should instead issue a new reasoned opinion.[34] The court has also indicated that an application may be held inadmissible under such circumstances.[35]

As mentioned, the reasoned opinion is intended, inter alia, to delimit the subject matter of the judicial review and to ensure Member States' right to defend itself, and the Commission can therefore not bring new pleas either in law or fact.[36] This applies to facts that existed before expiry of the deadline for compliance with the reasoned opinion, and a fortiori to facts stemming after this deadline.[37] Hence, the Commission may not bring new complaints concerning infringements that were not mentioned in the reasoned opinion, or new facts concerning pleas which were submitted in the reasoned opinion. But these restrictions may be difficult to apply in practice, and there is certain room for elaboration of the submissions as long as this is done within the scope of the subject matter of the proceedings.[38]

It is often emphasized that the Commission can invoke any binding provisions of EC environmental law regardless whether they are directly effective.[39]

[31] ibid paras 15–18.

[32] See eg Case C–96/89 *Commission v Netherlands* [1991] ECR I–2461, para 15; Case C–317/92 *Commission v Germany* [1994] ECR I–2093, para 4; and Case C–207/97 *Commission v Belgium* [1999] ECR I–275, para 27.

[33] Case C–422/92 *Commission v Germany* [1995] ECR I–1097, para 18.

[34] See, to this effect, Case C–177/03 *Commission v France* [2004] ECR I–1167, para 21.

[35] ibid para 22 by implication. See also the in-depth opinion by AG Mengozzi in Case C–523/04 *Commission v the Netherlands* (pending).

[36] Eg Case C–287/00 *Commission v Germany* [2002] ECR I–5811, para 19; and Case C–350/02 *Commission v Netherlands* [2004] ECR I–6213, paras 20–21.

[37] Eg Case C–446/01 *Commission v Spain* [2003] ECR I–6053, para 15. But note exceptions to this rule discussed in section 3.3.

[38] See, by analogy, Case C–177/04 *Commission v France* [2006] ECR I–2461, paras 37–38.

[39] Eg Case C–431/92 *Commission v Germany* [1995] ECR I–2189, para 26.

But with the watering down of the notion of direct effect, it may be wondered if there remain any differences for practical purposes with actions brought in national courts. Perhaps most important is that the Commission, as the guardian of the Treaty, is not required to demonstrate any specific interest in bringing proceedings:[40]

> Article 169 [Article 226 EC] is not intended to protect the Commission's own rights. The Commission's function, in the general interest of the Community, is to ensure that the Member States give effect to the Treaty and the provisions adopted by the institutions there under and to obtain a declaration of any failure to fulfil the obligations deriving there from with a view to bringing it to an end.[41]

2.4.2 *Subject matter*

The relevant time period for assessing whether a Member State has infringed Community environmental law in the context of the Article 226 EC procedure is the expiry of the deadline for taking the necessary measures to comply with the reasoned opinion.[42] Even if a Member State has failed to comply with a directive for several years, it will escape judgment under Article 226 EC if it complied with the reasoned opinion within the relevant deadline. Conversely, a Member State will be condemned even if it has fulfilled the obligation before the judgment is issued, but after the expiry of the time limit in the reasoned opinion.[43]

The burden of proof resides with the Commission, and it may not invoke any presumption for infringements. However, it appears from more recent case law that although the burden of proof initially rests with the Commission, it might shift to Member States once a prima facie case has been demonstrated. Thus, in *San Rocco* the ECJ held that that once the Commission had shown 'sufficient evidence' that waste had been discharged in the water course in the San Rocco valley, 'it [was] for the Italian Republic to challenge in substance and in detail the data produced by the Commission and to show that the conditions laid down in Article 2(1)(b)(iv) of [Directive 75/442[44]] were

[40] Cf chapter 3, section 6.

[41] Case C–167/73 *Commission v France* [1974] ECR 359, para 15; Case C–422/92 *Commission v Germany* [1995] ECR I–1097, para 16; and Case C–431/92 *Commission v Germany* [1995] ECR I–2189, para 21.

[42] Eg Case C–494/01 *Commission v Ireland* [2005] ECR I–3331, para 26.

[43] This is owing to the fact that a declaration of failure to act under Article 226 EC may be instrumental in relation to subsequent state liability actions against the Member State; see eg Case C–287/87 *Commission v Greece* [1990] ECR I–125.

[44] [1975] OJ L194/39, and [1991] OJ L78/32.

met in the present case'.[45] In other words, the burden of proof is then reversed and placed on the Member State.

Although this view may seem somewhat strict, it is justified by the fact that the Commission does not have investigative powers on the territory of Member States, and it follows from the obligation of genuine cooperation under Article 10 EC that it is 'primarily for the Member State to conduct the necessary on-the-spot investigations'.[46] If the national authorities nevertheless fail to provide evidence which refutes the facts presented by the Commission, the ECJ will adduce that the latter's claim is well-founded.

2.4.3 *Grounds of review*

Although the Commission may not introduce grounds for review not mentioned in the reasoned opinion, the ECJ is not limited to a mere judicial review of the reasoned opinion, but examines the case as a whole independently.[47] The ECJ has full jurisdiction to review the Commission's evaluation of the situation, and it may even substitute the Commission's evaluation with its own.[48]

2.4.4 *Consequences*

Under Article 226 EC the ECJ limits itself to declaring that a Member State has failed to fulfil an obligation under EC environmental law – it can neither set aside illegal national measures, nor stipulate the measures which shall be taken. However, the general obligation to take the necessary measures to comply with a judgment by the ECJ, as codified in Article 228(1) EC, of course applies. This duty applies both *ex nunc* and *ex tunc*, since Member States are also under an obligation to nullify the consequences of their unlawful measures.[49]

For the purposes of subsequent Article 228 EC proceedings, it might nevertheless be preferable that the Commission's reasoned opinion – in addition to claiming that the Member State had failed to implement and/or apply the relevant Community rules – explicitly submits that it has omitted to take the necessary measures to nullify the consequences of the breach so that the ECJ can rule also on this matter. The Commission has adopted such an approach in respect of state aid by seeking a declaration on failure to provide restitution of unlawful aid, in addition to a declaration stating that the state aid is illegal.[50]

[45] Case C–365/97 *Commission v Italy* [1999] ECR I–7773, para 86. [46] ibid para 85.
[47] Hartley 2003, 315–16. [48] ibid. [49] Chapter 3, sections 8 and 10.
[50] Hartley 2003, 323.

In the first case, *Commission v Germany*, the Member State objected to the legality of such a claim, but the ECJ countered as follows:

> Since the aim of the Treaty is to achieve the practical elimination of infringements and the consequences thereof, past and future, it is a matter for the Community authorities whose task it is to ensure that the requirements of the Treaty are observed to determine the extent to which the obligation of the Member State may be specified in the reasoned opinions or decisions delivered under Article 226 EC and 88(2) respectively and applications addressed to the Court.[51]

It is noteworthy that the ECJ consciously phrased its judgment in a general fashion, which suggests that it applies to Article 226 EC proceedings in general, and not only to those concerning state aid.[52]

Hence, in *San Rocco*,[53] for instance, the Commission could have sought a ruling by the ECJ declaring a failure to fulfil Article 4 of Directive 75/442 (Waste) by not adequately stopping fly-tipping of waste, as well as a failure to clean up the San Rocco valley area of the accumulated waste. After Italy failed to respect the ruling, Article 228 EC proceedings could then be initiated on both counts. However, the Commission has as yet not embraced the ECJ's invitation to specify remedial measures in Article 226 EC proceedings outside state aid law. In light of the Commission's new and more aggressive use of Article 226 EC proceedings in environmental matters, however, this could soon change.[54]

2.4.5 *Interim relief*

The Commission does not have any powers to prescribe interim measures, but must like all other plaintiffs seek relief from the ECJ under Articles 242 and 243 EC. The conditions for interim relief have been dealt with elsewhere, and need not be repeated here.[55] Suffice it to point out the specific features of the Article 226 EC procedure which may influence the relevance and application of those conditions.

The fact that the Commission must seek interim measures from the ECJ according to the ordinary procedure in Articles 242 and 243 EC poses a significant problem, since interim relief is thereby not available during the obligatory prejudicial stage of the infringement proceedings. Bearing in mind that this part of the infringement procedure takes on average 26 months,[56] it is

[51] Case C–70/72 *Commission v Germany* [1973] ECR 813, para 13.
[52] Hartley 2003, 324.
[53] Case C–365/97 *Commission v Italy* [1999] ECR I–7773.
[54] Section 3.
[55] Chapter 4, section 4.6 and chapter 5, section 5.
[56] Krämer 2004, 131.

clear that the infringement procedure is ill-suited to deal with urgent environmental hazards.

To make things worse, the ECJ has, somewhat ironically, reasoned that since interim measures are not available during this whole period it may be presumed that there is no urgency once the case has reached the judicial stage. Hence, in the *Leybucht* case the ECJ pointed out that the Commission:

> submitted its application after the regional government's project was well under way, through conclusion of the necessary contracts and the start of construction work. It did not apply for interim measures until a large part of the work had already been completed. In effect, the Commission is requesting the ECJ to stop work which has already been partially completed.[57]

Following this line of argument, the Commission will regularly face an uphill struggle in demonstrating urgency, since interim relief applications will typically only be submitted after the hazardous activities or failures to act are 'well under way'.[58]

The other conditions are less likely to cause problems in the context of infringement proceedings. The exhaustive prejudicial phase means that the Commission will rarely encounter any problems in demonstrating a prima facie case – the Commission has a very high success rate in respect of cases brought before the ECJ under Article 226 EC[59] – and it can also be anticipated that the Commission can put forward the Community's interest more forcefully than individuals under similar circumstances in the context of the 'balance of convenience' test.

However, it is nonetheless clear that interim relief will rarely be available to the Commission. But this does not justify that the Commission has only once (*Leybucht*) requested interim relief for the purposes of environmental protection bearing in mind that it brought 239 environmental infringement cases in the period between 1976 and 2003.[60] In contrast, the Commission brought three applications for interim relief (two asking for it to be prolonged) in the recent *Tyrol Motorway*[61] case where free movement of goods suffered from environmentally justified restrictions of heavy traffic.

[57] Case 57/89 R *Commission v Germany* [1989] ECR 2849, para 17.

[58] Similarly Krämer 2003, 393. [59] Krämer 2004, 133. [60] Krämer 2004, 128.

[61] Case C–320/03 R *Commission v Austria* [2003] ECR I–7929; Case C–320/03 R *Commission v Austria* [2003] ECR I–11665; and Case C–320/03 R *Commission v Austria* [2004] ECR I–3593.

3 General and persistent (GAP) infringements

3.1 *Introduction*

The Commission's traditional approach under Article 226 EC in respect of failures to apply EC environmental directives (as opposed to lacking or flawed transposition) has been to bring infringements proceedings in respect of isolated incidents, eg the failure to apply the Directive 75/442 in respect of individual waste sites.[62] This piecemeal approach is obviously very time-consuming, and also carries the risk that Article 226 EC judgments merely oblige Member States to take action in respect of a specific site, and new proceedings will have to be initiated from scratch if there are similar infringements at other locations. The effectiveness of Article 228 EC is in turn similarly undermined. In light of these enforcement deficits, the Commission recently unveiled a new approach in *Commission v Ireland*[63] (Irish Waste), which gained favour with the ECJ and is likely to invigorate Article 226 EC and consequently also Article 228 EC.[64]

Between 1997 and 2000, the Commission received several individual complaints concerning alleged illegal waste disposals in Ireland. The complaints, which mainly concerned waste operators working without permits and the existence of illegal waste sites, encompassed 18 waste incidents geographically spread over the Irish territory. The Commission subsequently lumped 12 of these complaints together in one case, and brought proceedings under Article 226 EC against Ireland for failure to apply and enforce Articles 4, 5, 8, 9, 10, 13, and 14 of the Waste Directive. In addition to requesting the ECJ to establish infringements in respect of each of the different incidents, the Commission asked the ECJ to declare that Ireland had, in a 'general and persistent' manner, infringed the Waste Directive. The ECJ complied. After finding that each of the 12 complaints was well-founded, the ECJ declared a general and persistent breach of all aforementioned provisions of the Waste Directive.[65]

It is the possibility of extrapolating a 'general and persistent' breach (hereinafter a GAP infringement or GAP case) on the basis of what prima facie appear isolated infringements that is the novel feature of this case, and which warrants further analysis and comment. Indeed, commentators and notably

[62] Eg Case C–45/91 *Commission v Greece* [1991] ECR I–2509; Case C–365/97 *Commission v Italy* [1999] ECR I–7773; and Case C–420/02 *Commission v Greece* [2005] ECR I–11175.

[63] Case C–494/01 *Commission v Ireland* [2005] ECR I–3331.

[64] See also Wennerås 2006.

[65] Paras 139, 152, 171, 185, and 193.

the ECJ's information service instantly recognized the ground-breaking nature of the judgment, and pointed out that this was the first time the ECJ had been susceptible to a finding of a general and persistent unlawful practice on the basis of individual infringements.[66]

Some precedents exist, however, albeit by analogy. The ECJ held in *San Rocco*, as will be recalled, that even though it could not be directly inferred from the fact that a situation was incompatible with the objectives of Article 4 of the Waste Directive that a Member State had not taken the requisite measures, where that situation persisted over a protracted period of time that might be an indication that the discretion had been exceeded.[67] The Commission has also brought proceedings in cases concerning absence or inadequacy of waste management plans 'based on the assumption that an illegal dump may provide evidence of an unsatisfied need for adequate waste management'.[68]

Irish Waste employs similar reasoning, but on a general level: where there are many infringements of the Waste Directive which have persisted over a protracted period of time, it may be deduced that a Member State has failed more generally to apply the relevant provisions of the directive. The fisheries cases against France, which are dealt with more fully below, also offer parallels to the GAP reasoning employed in this case.[69] Hence, *Irish Waste* is the outcome of an evolution, but it nevertheless is the first time that the ECJ devised a practical legal framework for future GAP cases. Below, we will examine the substantive and procedural conditions (sections 3.2–3.3), added value (section 3.4), and further development of the GAP doctrine (section 3.5).

3.2 *Substantive conditions*

In his opinion in *Irish Waste*, AG Geelhoed held that account should be taken of three dimensions in order to determine whether a Member State was guilty of a 'general and structural' infringement of Community law: a dimension of scale, a dimension of time, and a dimension of seriousness.[70]

[66] See Press Release 37/2005 available at <http://curia.eu.int/en/actu/communiques/cp05/aff/cp050037en.pdf>, and J Noonan 'Environmental Objections and Appeals – What Access to Justice?', Third Annual Seminar on Law and the Environment (2005) University College Cork.

[67] Case C–365/97 *Commission v Italy* [1999] ECR I–7773, para 68.

[68] See Fifth Annual Survey on the Implementation and Enforcement of Community Environmental Law 2003 (SEC (2004) 1025) 19 and eg Case C–446/01 *Commission v Spain* [2003] ECR I–6053. Furthermore, in the field of nature and bird protection the Commission has brought cases submitting that the Member State had failed on a general basis to designate sufficient amounts of SPAs under Council Directive 79/409/EEC on the conservation of wild birds; see eg Case C–240/00 *Commission v Finland* [2003] ECR I–2187; and Case C–378/01 *Commission v Italy* [2003] ECR I–2857.

[69] See sections 2.3.1 and 3.

[70] Opinion, para 43.

The first condition, the dimension of scale, related to the number of established infringements.[71] Whereas isolated cases may suffice to demonstrate an infringement, for the purpose of finding a general and structural infringement there had to be a more general practice of non-compliance which was likely to persist.[72] A relevant factor in this respect was that the infringements were not restricted to a particular locality.

The dimension of time pertained to the duration of the infringements of the relevant Community obligations. The AG pointed out that whether a practice has become persistent depends on the subject matter, and has to be examined on a case-by-case basis.[73] The threshold is set quite high, however, and the relevant criterion is whether it is manifestly clear that the non-compliance has become persistent. In the case of Ireland, it was not necessary to fix more precise criteria in this respect, since the failure to put in place a fully operational licence system had existed for some 24 years.[74]

Finally, the dimension of seriousness concerns the discrepancy between the actual situation existing in a Member State, and the result required by Community law. A general and structural infringement is liable to have adverse effects on the specific interests protected by the relevant provisions, as well as the objective promoted by a directive.[75] However, in the opinion of the AG, it did not suffice that the general and structural infringement posed an immediate and likely risk of such adverse effects occurring (and which could thus have been presumed), but the Commission is seemingly required to prove that damage had actually occurred.

The ECJ did not articulate explicit conditions for the establishment of a general and structural infringement, but appeared to emphasize essentially the same criteria as AG Geelhoed. Hence, in regard to Articles 9 and 10 of the Waste Directive, which lay down a permit requirement for waste operators, the ECJ noted that:

- since 1977, Ireland had failed to make a permit system fully operational for municipal landfills;
- the complaints referred to incidents throughout the Irish territory; and
- there was a general tendency among local authorities to tolerate situations which did not comply with those provisions.[76]

[71] Opinion, para 44.

[72] See also the 'global approach' advocated by AG Stix-Hackl in Case C–121/03 *Commission v Spain* [2005] ECR I–7569.

[73] ibid opinion, para 45.

[74] Opinion of AG Stix-Hackl in Case C–121/03 *Commission v Spain* [2005] ECR I–7569, para 120.

[75] ibid opinion, para 47.

[76] Paras 129–33.

In respect of Article 4, the ECJ also referred to the fact that the omissions of local and national authorities had led to a significant deterioration of the environment.[77] However, although the ECJ referred to the existence of environmental damage, it did not appear to view this as a necessary condition for the establishment of a general and persistent breach. Thus, as regards Articles 9 and 10, it found a general and persistent infringement without referring to environmental damage, and in respect of Article 4 it observed that damage had occurred only after having concluded that there existed a general and persistent infringement of the said provision.[78]

In sum, whether there is a general and persistent breach must be examined by taking account of the number of infringements, the extent to which they occur at different localities (ie whether they are widespread), and their duration. More case law will be required further to clarify these conditions. However, it is clear that Member States can be found guilty of GAP infringements for violations of Community law that are less flagrant than those which gave rise to the present case. As for duration, the AG found, based upon an analogy with *Spanish Strawberries*,[79] that it was manifestly clear that 10 years qualifies as persistent, which suggests that shorter periods may also suffice, depending on the nature of Community obligations at stake.[80] In *San Rocco*, for instance, the ECJ found that some eight years of illegal waste dumping in the San Rocco valley amounted to a protracted breach of Article 4 of the Waste Directive.[81] The ECJ has since gone further, and ruled recently in *Commission v Greece* (*Pera Galini*), the facts of which were similar to *San Rocco*, that a failure by national authorities for four years to recover or dispose of the unlawful waste at the Pera Galini site amounted to an infringement of Article 4 of the Waste Directive over a 'protracted period'.[82]

It is also possible for an administrative practice to be 'general' without necessarily covering the entire territory of a Member State. Indeed, the AG phrased this condition in the negative: the infringements should not be restricted to a particular locality.[83] This allows for a GAP ruling in respect of an administrative practice occurring in a particular region, eg in a German *Land*. Hence, in *Commission v Spain* AG Stix-Hackl argued that environmental pollution and legal infractions from a large number of pig farms in the area

[77] Para 175. [78] See paras 174–75.
[79] Case C–265/95 *Commission v France* [1997] ECR I–6959. [80] Opinion, para 45.
[81] Case C–365/97 *Commission v Italy* [1999] ECR I–7773, paras 88–91.
[82] Case C–420/02 *Commission v Greece* [2004] ECR I–11175, paras 24–33.
[83] Opinion in Case C–494/01 *Commission v Ireland* [2005] ECR I–3331, para 44.

of Baix Ter (Gerona Province) reflected a 'generalised defect or structural shortcoming' of the application of the Waste Directive in that area.[84]

3.3 *Procedural conditions*

As noted by the AG in *Irish Waste*, cases where the Commission seeks to demonstrate a general and persistent breach by a Member State are likely to be characterized by an abundance of factual material, and the question of proof is likely to become particularly important.[85] In order for such actions to be viable and effective enforcement instruments, the Commission therefore argued in favour of modifying existing procedural conditions under Article 226 EC to accommodate GAP actions.[86]

First, it submitted that the ECJ should abandon the orthodoxy of examining the alleged infringements only with reference to the situation prevailing at the expiry of the deadline for compliance fixed in the reasoned opinion. Instead, the ECJ should also take into account infringements that were terminated before this deadline had passed. The ECJ concurred and held that:

> [T]he fact that the deficiencies pointed out in one or other case have been remedied does not necessarily mean that the general and continuous approach of those authorities, to which such specific deficiencies would testify where appropriate, has come to an end.[87]

Indeed, when dealing with alleged infringements of Articles 9 and 10 later in the judgment, the ECJ noted that the fact that two of the infringements referred to had been terminated before expiry of the deadline in the reasoned opinion did not alter the fact that, at the time in question, 'there was a general tendency in Ireland . . . to tolerate situations in which those provisions were not complied with'.[88]

The second issue was whether the Commission could, at the stage of judicial proceedings, adduce new evidence about infringements not mentioned in the reasoned opinion. This could serve to back up the alleged general and persistent nature of the disputed administrative practice, which was particularly relevant in relation to a report on large-scale dumping of waste in County Wicklow (96 cases) that had become available at a later stage. The AG dismissed this idea out of hand,[89] but the ECJ again found in favour of the

[84] Opinion in Case C–121/03 *Commission v Spain* [2005] ECR I–7569, paras 3–4 and paras 23–25. The question never materialized since the ECJ found that the environmental pollution fell outside the scope of the Waste Directive.

[85] Opinion in Case C–494/01 *Commission v Ireland* [2005] ECR I–3331, para 40.

[86] Cf sections 2.1 and 2.2 above. [87] Para 32. [88] Para 132. [89] Para 60.

Commission. It noted that this prima facie conflicted with previous case law,[90] but ingeniously construed the *sui generis* nature of the case by arguing that, in the context of a GAP case, bringing new evidence concerning individual infringements did not alter the subject matter of the dispute, ie the general character of the alleged breaches of the Waste Directive.[91] The consequence of this is that private citizens alerted by infringements proceedings against national authorities may continue to feed the Commission with new evidence and complaints until this date.[92]

The third and final issue, deemed crucial by the Irish legal team and subject to much argument, concerned the burden of proof. Adhering closely to the AG's opinion, the ECJ first reiterated that whereas the Commission had to present sufficient information to demonstrate infringements in all of the incidents referred to in the reasoned opinion, it was for Ireland, in the spirit of loyal cooperation, to facilitate this task and to contest specifically the facts alleged in those complaints.[93] If this duty also relates to new evidence brought by the Commission at the judicial proceedings stage, this could obviously place a significant burden on Member States. More importantly, the ECJ extended the application of these findings, which followed from settled case law, to the claim of a general and persistent breach, ie Member States must not only challenge in substance and in detail the information produced as concerns the individual breaches, but also the consequences flowing therefrom.[94] In other words, if the Commission succeeds in establishing individual breaches indicating a general and persistent practice, it is for Member States to establish that these cases are isolated incidents, and that no general deficiencies underpin them. This outcome comes close to a reversal of the burden of proof in this respect.[95]

The importance of the ECJ's ruling on these procedural matters cannot be overestimated. We saw above that the substantive conditions for establishing a GAP case are quite burdensome and that, without modifications to the procedural rules concerning proof, bringing a GAP case would become very difficult, and hence of limited use. Clearly conscious of this dilemma, the ECJ awarded the Commission the necessary tools to be effective as guardian of the Treaty, which is to some extent at the expense of Member States' judicial protection.

[90] See eg Case C–446/01 *Commission v Spain* [2003] ECR I–6053, para 15.

[91] Para 38.

[92] Section 6.2.

[93] Paras 44–46.

[94] Para 47.

[95] The Advocate General referred to a 'shift' of burden of proof onto the Member State once the Commission had presented a prima facie case; see opinion at para 53.

3.4 *Added value*

The efficiency benefits in terms of coordinating efforts both at the Commission and the ECJ in bringing one collective infringement case instead of many isolated cases are obvious.[96] However, in this respect, the Commission could have been satisfied by securing a judgment finding infringements in respect of the 12 complaints, without additionally asking the ECJ to establish a general and persistent breach had occurred. What, then, is the added value of a GAP ruling? Although the AG foresees that GAP cases 'open the way to more effective enforcement of Community law obligations against Member States',[97] neither he nor the ECJ explain why this is so.

In order to answer this question, it is necessary to juxtapose the effects of a 'regular' infringement case, with those of a GAP case. The crucial difference between the two resides in the scope of the judgments. Had the Commission simply asked for a declaration that the 18 incidents were incompatible with the relevant provisions of the Waste Directive, Ireland would merely have had to take the necessary measures to address those specific breaches. If the Commission subsequently would have received fresh complaints about other sites operating without a permit, it would have had to initiate new Article 226 EC proceedings all over again. In contrast, the consequence of the GAP judgment against Ireland is that the national authorities must now not only rectify the specific 18 infringements, but must also correct the general and persistent breaches of Articles 4, 5, 8–10, and 13–14 of the Waste Directive throughout its territory.[98] Hence, the Member State must deal with any existing or subsequent infringements of the relevant obligations *ex officio*, regardless whether these incidents have been subject of an infringement action. One might object that this obligation already flows from the binding force of the relevant Community provisions according to Article 249 EC read in conjunction with Article 10 EC. Whilst this is true, the crucial point here is that a failure in this respect would represent a violation of the Article 226 EC judgment, and the Commission could hence proceed to bring an action under Article 228 EC.[99] This will greatly enhance the deterrent effect of

[96] Opinion, para 5. [97] ibid.

[98] But the judgment still fell short of the even stricter approach devised by AG Geelhoed, who wanted to deduce further that Ireland had generally and structurally breached the Waste Directive altogether; see opinion, para 123. It appears difficult, however, to understand what the effects of such a ruling would have as regards the provisions of the Waste Directive which had not been infringed.

[99] Another benefit of a GAP judgment is that it suffices for the Commission to bring one Article 228 EC case in case of non-compliance, instead of several, individual Article 228 EC cases for each Article 226 EC judgment which has not been complied with. The Seventh Annual Survey on the

Article 226 EC judgments which, as we shall see below, has been further bolstered by the possibility of imposing lump sums in addition to penalty payments under Article 228(2) EC.[100]

In sum, the GAP doctrine allows the Commission to depart from what in German is known as *Kurieren am Sympthom*, and focus instead on the underlying practices, ie general and persistent infringements of Community obligations.[101] Furthermore, by virtue of the GAP instrument, the significance of infringement proceedings is no longer restricted to their *ex post facto* effect but also, and possibly even particularly, in their *ex ante facto* effects.[102]

This conclusion, however, may have to be qualified, depending on the conditions that determine when a Member State is deemed to have failed to comply with a GAP judgment. If, after Ireland has been given a reasonable time to take the necessary measures to amend its flawed practises in accordance with the conditions set out in the judgment, the Commission learns that there is still a general and persistent failure by national authorities to apply the Waste Directive, eg as regards waste operators acting without permits, it may obviously bring Article 228(2) EC proceedings. This situation is analogous to *Commission v France (French Fisheries)* discussed below, where the ECJ imposed economic sanctions under Article 228(2) EC on the basis that the national authorities, several years after being condemned in Article 226 EC proceedings, still failed in a general and persistent manner to monitor and sanction infringements by its nationals of the relevant EC legislation implementing the Community's fisheries policy.

A more difficult issue is whether the Commission could also bring Article 228(2) EC proceedings against Ireland on the basis of one or more prima facie isolated events infringing the operative part of the GAP judgment, eg one or more waste operators still acting without permits in violation of Articles 9 and 10 of the Waste Directive, without having to demonstrate that they are necessarily part of an ongoing general and persistent practice.

The ECJ's case law under Article 228 EC offers limited guidance for this particular question. Of the mere five judgments handed down to date under

Implementation and Enforcement of Community Environmental Law (SEC (2006) 1143) 24, reports for instance that the Commission in 2005 pursued four separate infringement cases under Article 228 EC against Italy for failure to comply with four Article 226 EC judgments concerning landfills operating in breach of Articles 4 and 8 of the Waste Framework Directive (Cases C–382/02, C–516/03, C–375/02, and C–447/93). These violations could instead have formed the basis of a GAP case under Article 226 EC which, if successful, would have allowed the Commission to bring just one Article 228 EC case in response to the subsequent non-compliance.

[100] See section 4.

[101] Opinion in Case C–494/01 *Commission v Ireland* [2005] ECR I–3331, para 4.

[102] ibid.

Article 228(2) EC, only *French Fisheries* is relevant for these purposes, as that case also related to failure to comply with a GAP type judgment.[103] However, the ECJ did not have to deal with this issue since there was general and persistent lack of monitoring and enforcement at the time of the Article 228 EC proceedings, and the question did not arise.

Hence, for lack of any conclusive guidance in the ECJ's case law, it is necessary to assess this question in light of systematic considerations concerning Articles 226 and 228 EC, their objectives, and more specifically the *raison d'être* of the judgment in *Irish Waste*. First, the essential issue is what a Member State must do to comply with a GAP judgment, and more specifically which measures Ireland must take in order to implement the judgment in *Irish Waste*. It seems clear that it is not sufficient simply to improve administrative practices so that infringements may no longer be said to be general and persistent. The national authorities must do whatever is necessary to ensure that there are no further infringements of the relevant obligations. In respect of precise and absolute obligations, eg the requirements in Articles 9 and 10 of the Waste Directive that waste operators must have permits, the judgment against Ireland therefore entails an obligation of result.[104] Strictly speaking, therefore, if the Commission were to identify new waste sites in Ireland operating without a permit, this would amount to a breach of the Article 226 EC judgment even if those infringements could no longer be said to be part of a general and persistent failure to apply the Waste Directive.

Secondly, the *raison d'être* behind the GAP ruling devised in *Irish Waste* was clearly to make enforcement of EC law by the Commission more effective.[105] If the Commission in Article 228 EC proceedings were required to demonstrate that the general and persistent breach has prevailed in the same manner following the Article 226 EC proceedings, the effectiveness of the GAP instrument would be severely restricted, both in its legal effects towards Member States, as well as by placing a heavy burden on the Commission owing to the cumbersome process of establishing a GAP case. This is particularly so in the field of environmental law where the Commission does not have monitoring powers. The fact that the Commission nevertheless succeeded in this in *Irish Waste* is, in my opinion, not an argument for requiring it to do so under Article 228 EC.

The rationale underpinning the GAP instrument seems rather quite the opposite – namely to provide for a broad Article 226 EC judgment which

[103] These cases are commented upon in more detail in section 3.

[104] See, by analogy, Case C–60/01 *Commission v France* [2002] ECR I–5879, paras 25–30.

[105] Opinion, paras 3–4.

would catch any future infringements of the generic kind, and to provide for a deterrent effect through the risk of facing Article 228 EC proceedings.[106]

This leads to the conclusion that, after the national authorities have been given a reasonable time to comply with the *Irish Waste* judgment, the Commission may bring proceedings under Article 228 EC in respect of new infringements of the provisions of the Waste Directive which had been generally and persistently flouted, without the need to prove that those infringements are part of a continuing general and persistent practice. This is not as harsh on Member States as one might instinctively think. As demonstrated by *Irish Waste*, only instances where a Member State ignores the binding effect of Community law over a protracted period may be subject to a GAP ruling. If, against this background, a Member State again fails to comply with the relevant Community obligations after having been alerted by the Commission of new infringements in the pre-judicial stage under Article 228 EC, it seems only fair that economic sanctions are imposed.

The final issue which will be discussed here concerns the legal effects of the specific geographical scope of a GAP judgment. *Irish Waste* concerned incidents that happened throughout the Irish territory, and the general and persistent breach was nationwide. The relevant geographical scope for assessing later infringements for the purposes of Article 228 EC proceedings is thus the whole of the Irish territory. However, GAP judgments may, as indicated above, be of more limited geographical scope, eg on a regional or provincial level.[107] This raises the question whether the relevant territory for assessing an infringement of such GAP cases for the purposes of Article 228 EC is restricted to those areas, or whether the whole national territory may be taken into account.

French Fisheries[108] illustrates this question, although the particular factual circumstances of that case limit its general application. One of the questions which arose in these Article 228 EC proceedings was whether instances of enforcement omissions by the national authorities of the Community's fisheries legislation in the Mediterranean region could be taken into account for the purpose of establishing a breach of the previous Article 226 EC judgment, when the latter only had concerned infringements in the North-Atlantic region.[109] The geographical scope of the first judgment was thus strictly limited to the Atlantic region. An additional complexity of the case

[106] ibid. [107] See opinion in Case C–121/03 *Commission v Spain* [2005] ECR I–7569, paras 3–4 and 23–25.

[108] Case C–304/02 *Commission v France* [2005] ECR I–6263.

[109] Case 64/88 *Commission v France* [1991] ECR I–2727.

was that the relevant Community legislation in force at the time of the first judgment against France did not cover the Mediterranean region, but only concerned fisheries in the North-Atlantic. AG Geelhoed nevertheless held that the infringements in the Mediterranean were relevant as the Commission complaints were aimed at the insufficiency of 'controls as such', and the ECJ's finding in the first case against France 'concerned the lack of monitoring effort in respect of the fisheries provisions then in force, irrespective of the territorial scope of these provisions'.[110] Hence, his viewpoint was essentially that the Article 226 EC judgment against France had established a 'generic infringement' as far as controls omissions were concerned, and that later failures in this regard amounted to a persistent failure of the obligation to 'control as such', regardless of the legislative scope of the relevant provisions and a fortiori the geographical scope of the judgment.

In contrast, the ECJ briefly noted that the infringements in the Mediterranean region were irrelevant for the purposes of establishing a breach of the first case against France, since the judgment necessarily was limited to the geographical scope of the relevant Community obligations in force at that time.[111] The ECJ notably did not comment on the factual geographical scope of the first judgment, which arguably leaves the door open to different results where the applicable legislation is nationwide. Hence, should the ECJ on the basis of, for instance, waste sites operating without permits in southern regions of Italy declare a general and persistent violation of Articles 9 and 10 of the Waste Directive, one could argue – analogously to the reasoning employed by AG Geelhoed – that that judgment established a breach of the permit obligations in Articles 9 and 10 'as such', irrespective of the geographical location of those incidents. The consequence of this view is that any subsequent infringements of those obligations would be relevant for assessing a failure to comply with the judgment in Article 228 EC proceedings, even if they took place in other regions of Italy.

3.5 *Further development*

Shortly after *Irish Waste*, Environmental Commissioner Stavros Dimas said that his staff would be looking carefully to see how the ruling might help 'to focus our enforcement efforts more efficiently in the future'.[112] The scope

[110] Opinion of 29 April 2004 (First Opinion), ibid, para 63. [111] Para 27.

[112] ENDS Environment Daily, 26 April 2005 (Issue 1867). Indeed, there are other environmental GAP cases pending. See the Commission's application in Case C–135/05 *Commission v Italy* ([2005] OJ C132/15) and the Opinion in Case C–334/04 *Commission v Greece* [2004] OJ C228/34, paras 61–62 (unpublished).

and effects of GAP judgments are far-reaching, but could be further broadened in the future.

One could imagine, for instance, the Commission bringing GAP cases in response to infringements of directives which share a certain type of obligation. One example is the frequent obligation to make environmental directives operational by drawing up certain plans and programmes, often referred to as management plans. A GAP case could thus be lodged against a Member State for failing to draw up management plans pursuant to directives on waste[113] and nature conservation.[114] Subsequent failures to comply with the judgment in regard to any of these directives could then trigger Article 228 EC proceedings. Such GAP cases could be broadened even further: the Commission could argue that the failure to draw up management plans represented a general and persistent failure, not just in respect of the relevant directives, but a generic failure to comply with the obligation to draw up management plans in the environmental sector.[115] If the Member State subsequently fails to provide such plans in the context of another directive, for example, Directive 2000/60/EC establishing a Framework for Community Action in the Field of Water Policy,[116] this could be understood as a failure to comply with the initial judgment, and Article 228 EC proceedings may be brought.

It is also theoretically possible to have GAP cases for more general failures to apply and/or enforce environmental directives, which could be construed as a general and persistent infringement of Article 10 EC. But legal certainty and the requirement that the subject matter for Article 226 EC proceedings must be clearly defined obviously set some limits in this regard. However, GAP cases could be brought, in my view, if it is possible to specify a discrete element in the alleged general and persistent failure to apply and enforce environmental obligations, eg systematic failure to provide sufficient information on the implementation and application of environmental directives, or a widespread omission to provide effective and deterrent sanctions for environmental infringements.

[113] See Article 7 of the Waste Directive, above n. 11; Article 6 of Directive 91/689/EEC on hazardous waste [1991] OJ L377/20; and Article 6 of Directive 94/62/EC on packaging and packing waste [1994] OJ L365/10.

[114] Article 6 of Directive 92/43/EC on the conservation of natural habitats and wild fauna and flora [1992] OJ L206/7.

[115] See, by analogy, the reasoning by AG Geelhoed in the opinion in *Commission v France* concerning infringements of the 'generic' obligation to 'monitor', discussed in section 3.4 above.

[116] [2000] OJ L327/1.

The future will tell how far the Commission and the ECJ are willing to stretch the scope of GAP cases, but it appears that the Commission will begin with exploring its potential along the more modest lines indicated above. In the Seventh Annual Survey on the Application and Enforcement of Community Environmental Law the Commission states that it will for the future focus on 'structural problems in Member States through the practice of grouping together cases concerning the same subject matter and launching horizontal cases to address systematic problems of bad implementation (for example horizontal cases on illegal landfills and waste water treatment plans)'.[117]

4 Article 228 EC

4.1 *Introduction*

Article 228(1) EC stipulates that Member States are required to take the necessary measures to comply with an Article 226 EC judgment, which of course already follows from the principle of loyal cooperation embodied in Article 10 EC. However, whilst the Commission could bring proceedings and obtain a declaration that a Member State has failed to fulfil its obligations under Article 228(1) EC, there was originally no possibility to impose any sanctions. This resulted in a lack of deterrence. The Treaty of Maastricht therefore introduced new provisions in Article 228(2) EC which provides for the imposition of penalty payments or lump sums on the defaulting Member State. The Commission was slow to react to this development, however, and until recently only two proceedings, both environmental cases, had been brought under Article 228 EC.[118]

However, as the Commission increased its successful efforts under Article 226 EC, the record of compliance further deteriorated.[119] As recently as 2002 there were 58 judgments which had not been complied with by the end of the year.[120] The Commission consequently started to pursue a much more aggressive use of Article 228(2) EC and had initiated as many as 77 Article 228 EC cases by the end of 2005.[121] These efforts are now becoming visible, as within a short time span the ECJ has handed down three more Article 228

[117] SEC(2006) 1143, 2. [118] See table XIV in Krämer 2004, 133.

[119] See table V in Krämer 2004, 129. [120] Krämer 2004, 129.

[121] Seventh Annual Survey on the Implementation and Enforcement of Community Environmental Law (SEC(2006) 1143) 69.

EC judgments, thus more than doubling its tally to a total of five cases. These cases are examined below with a view to determining the legal framework for imposing financial sanctions under Article 228(2) EC (section 4.2), and the conditions and methods for calculating penalty payments (section 4.3), and lump sums (section 4.4).

4.2 *Legal framework and the ECJ's discretion*

The procedure under Article 228 EC is essentially the same as that under Article 226 EC: the Commission must first issue a formal notice and, if necessary, a reasoned opinion. The Commission in fact issued a second reasoned opinion in *Commission v France (French Fisheries)*, but that is procedurally unnecessary, and should be avoided as it causes further delays.[122] If a Member State has not complied with the reasoned opinion at the time of its expiry, the Commission may bring the case before the ECJ.

The Commission must nevertheless first allow Member States a reasonable time to take the necessary measures to comply with the Article 226 EC judgment, bearing in mind that the process must be started 'at once and completed as soon as possible'.[123] What amounts to a reasonable time in the context of Article 228 EC proceedings, owing to the severe sanctions which may be imposed, was subject to controversy in *Commission v Spain*[124] (*Spanish Bathing Waters*). The case concerned a failure to fulfil the obligations of Directive 76/160/EEC concerning the quality of bathing water, and the deadline to comply with the reasoned opinion was two and a half years after the delivery of the first judgment against Spain. The question was whether this was a reasonable time, given that implementation of the first judgment allegedly required complex and long-term operations, ie to ensure that designated bathing waters complied with limit values in Article 3 of Directive 76/160/EEC.[125] The AG sided with Spain,[126] but the ECJ found the time limit sufficient, even if compliance with the judgment required complex and long-term operations, as it encompassed three bathing seasons.[127]

Leaving aside the somewhat curious guidance provided by employing bathing seasons chronology, the judgment suggests, conversely, that Article

[122] Opinion of 29 April (First Opinion) in Case C–304/02 *Commission v France* [2005] ECR I–6263, para 92.

[123] See eg Case 131/84 *Commission v Italy* [1985] ECR 3531, para 7; Case 169/87 *Commission v France* [1988] ECR 4093, para 14; and Case C–334/94 *Commission v France* [1996] ECR I–1307, para 31.

[124] Case C–278/01 *Commission v Spain* [2003] ECR I–14141.

[125] ibid.

[126] Opinion, ibid, para 69.

[127] Para 30.

228 EC proceedings may in all cases be brought before the ECJ within two and a half years, and probably also sooner where compliance with the judgment is more straightforward, and only requires short-term operations.[128] Indeed, the Commission granted only one and a half years to comply with the previous judgment in *Commission v France*[129] (*French Product Liability*), which concerned incorrect transposition of Directive 85/337/EEC, without France raising any objections.

Article 228(2) EC provides that the Commission must specify the amount of lump sums or penalty payment which it finds appropriate in the circumstances. The Commission has drawn up several communications on the application of Article 228 EC to this end – a general communication in 1996, followed by a 1997 communication on the method of calculating penalty payments.[130] Those guidelines set out the approach the Commission proposes to follow, and the ECJ has accepted their relevance as far as they ensure that the Commission acts in a transparent manner, thus promoting legal certainty.[131] But the ECJ has emphasized that the Commission's suggestions are only a useful point of reference, and that it is for the ECJ, in exercising its discretion, to impose a penalty payment which is appropriate to the circumstances.[132] Indeed, as we shall see below, the ECJ has in three of the five existing cases deviated from the Commission's submissions as concerns the calculation of the penalty payments.

A more controversial question, which arose in *French Fisheries*,[133] is whether the ECJ can impose different sanctions from those proposed by the Commission. The Commission had in that case, as in the previous two, merely proposed penalty payments, but, urged by AG Geelhoed, the ECJ found it appropriate that a lump sum should be handed down in addition. Germany, intervening on behalf of France, argued that the ECJ lacked political legitimacy to impose a financial sanction not suggested by the Commission, but the ECJ held that, in contrast to the administrative phase of the Article 228 EC proceedings conducted by the Commission, political considerations were irrelevant in the judicial procedure before the ECJ.[134]

[128] Considering that the Member States have already failed to implement EC legislation within the applicable time limits, it appears in fact relatively generous to grant them another two and a half years, or three 'bathing seasons', to comply with a judgment declaring the previous breach of EC law; see Janssen 2004.

[129] Case C–177/04 *Commission v France* [2006] ECR I–9981.

[130] The Commission has also adopted a 2002 internal decision on the definition of 'duration' and a 2005 Communication intended to replace those of 1996 and 1997, both of which are discussed further below.

[131] Case C–387/97 *Commission v Greece* [2000] ECR I–5047, para 87.

[132] Case C–387/97 *Commission v Greece* [2000] ECR I–5047, para 90; and Case C–278/01 *Commission v Spain* [2003] ECR I–14141, para 103.

[133] Case C–304/02 *Commission v France* [2005] ECR I–6263.

[134] Para 90.

It added that the appropriateness of the choice of the penalty most suited to the case could only be appraised in the light of findings made by the ECJ, and therefore was outside the political sphere.[135] However, by referring to the fact that it is best placed to determine the most proper sanction, the ECJ missed the fundamental point which rather concerns the doctrine of separation of powers.

The next assertion by the Member States was that the ECJ would violate a general principle of procedural law by going beyond the parties' claim. The ECJ rejected the applicability of this civil law principle, however, with reference to the 'special judicial procedure' laid down in Article 228(2) EC, which was 'not intended to compensate for damage caused by the Member State concerned, but to place it under economic pressure which induces it to put an end to the breach established'.[136] This explanation is somewhat vague, and one might query why the ECJ did not instead rely on the generally accepted dictum – which it itself has applied in relation to national courts' obligation to raise Community law issues *ex officio*[137] – that courts may deviate from their passive role in inter partes proceedings where pressing public interests require it to do so.

Finally, France and other intervening Member States argued that the ECJ's exercise of discretion undermined legal certainty since the Commission's guidelines did not contain provisions on the calculation of lump sums, but the ECJ unequivocally held that the exercise of power conferred on the ECJ by Article 228(2) EC was not subject to the condition that the Commission adopt such rules, which in any event could not bind the ECJ.[138]

As a consequence of the ruling in *French Fisheries*, the Commission has drawn up new guidelines for the application of Article 228(2) EC (2005 Communication) containing provisions on lump sums, and which are intended to replace the 1996 and 1997 communications as from 1 January 2006.[139] However, the 2005 Communication will, just like its predecessors, only serve as a useful point of reference and the ECJ will not hesitate to deviate from it if necessary to ensure sanctions which, in its view, are appropriate and proportional to the circumstances.

4.3 *Penalty payments*

The aim of penalty payments is to induce the defaulting Member State to put an end to the failure to comply with a previous Article 226 EC judgment as

[135] ibid. [136] Para 91. [137] See chapter 3, section 4.2.

[138] Case C–304/02 *Commission v France* [2005] ECR I–6263, para 85.

[139] Commission Communication on Application of Article 228 EC (SEC(2005) 1658).

soon as possible.[140] The relevant time period for determining a failure to comply for the purposes of penalty payments is therefore not the expiry of the reasoned opinion, but the later date of the examination of the facts by the ECJ.[141] If the Member State in the interim has taken the necessary measures to comply, the ECJ may thus not impose penalty payments but can instead impose a lump sum (section 4.4).

The Commission's 1996 and 1997 guidelines provide methods for calculating penalty payments. The basic criteria to be applied include the duration of the infringement, its degree of seriousness, and the ability of the Member State to pay. The calculation is made by employing a unit amount of €500, which is then multiplied with the degree of seriousness (1–20), the duration of infringement (1–3), and a co-efficient determined with reference to the Member State's gross national product and its votes in the Council.[142] The 2005 Communication increases the basic amount in light of inflation to €600, provides for coefficients on the new Member States' ability to pay, and adjusts the coefficients of the old Member States.[143]

The ECJ has in principle accepted this approach, although reserving the right to specify the precise amount of the penalty payment.[144] It has also introduced a fourth variable, namely the effects of a failure to comply on private and public interest and the urgency of obtaining compliance.[145] It would appear that this element is particularly relevant as concerns the determination of the seriousness of the non-compliance.[146] Applying these criteria (perhaps except the last consideration, which was introduced by the ECJ), the Commission proposed a daily penalty payment of €24,000 in the case against Greece, whilst the AG suggested a penalty payment of €15,375 per day.[147] The ECJ opted for the middle road by fixing the fine at €20,000

[140] Case C–304/02 *Commission v France* [2005] ECR I–6263, para 80; and Case C–177/04 *Commission v France* [2006] ECR I–2461, para 59.

[141] Case C–177/04 *Commission v France* [2006] ECR I–2461, paras 20–21.

[142] The co-efficient for the old (15) Member States were as follows: Luxembourg 1.0, Ireland 2.4, Finland 3.3, Portugal 3.9, Greece 4.1, Austria 5.1, Sweden 5.9, Belgium 6.2, Netherlands 7.6, Italy 7.7, Spain 11.4, UK 17.8, France 21.1, and Germany 26.4.

[143] Belgium 5.81; Czech Republic 3.17; Denmark 3.70; Germany 25.40; Estonia 0.58; Greece 4.38; Spain 14.77; France 21.83; Ireland 4.14; Italy 19.84; Cyprus 0.70; Latvia 0.64; Lithuania 1.09; Luxembourg 1.00; Hungary 3.01; Malta 0.36; Netherlands 7.85; Austria 4.84; Poland 7.22; Portugal 4.04; Slovenia 1.01; Slovakia 1.45; Finland 3.24; Sweden 5.28; and UK 21.9 (SEC(2005) 1658) 10.

[144] Case C–387/97 *Commission v Greece* [2000] ECR I–5047, paras 88–90; and Case C–278/01 *Commission v Spain* [2003] ECR I–14141, para 42.

[145] Case C–387/97 *Commission v Greece* [2000] ECR I–5047, para 92.

[146] Case C–304/02 *Commission v France* [2005] ECR I–6263, para 105.

[147] Case C–387/97 *Commission v Greece* [2000] ECR I–5047, para 33, and opinion, para 120.

per day.[148] Although the ECJ noted that the infringement was serious and the duration considerable, it is not clear from the judgment how this translated into the said criteria, and thus how the ECJ arrived at the exact sum of €20,000 (it appears almost to have been set as a lump sum). However, this has become more transparent in subsequent cases, in which the ECJ further elaborated the relevant criteria.

4.3.1 *Seriousness*

The seriousness of the breach is examined objectively, and the ECJ will, as under Article 226 EC, not accept any excuses, save perhaps practical impossibility. This concerns all phases of the implementation process, including application and enforcement.[149] When examining the seriousness of the breach, the ECJ will examine the importance of the Community rules and in particular the effects of the failure to comply on private and public interests.

The ECJ has thus emphasized that rules for the protection on the environment form part of the core objectives of the Community, and are intended to protect human health and the environment. Any infringements must therefore be regarded as particularly serious. However, there is a dichotomy between these grand statements and the coefficients finally determined. In *Greek Waste* the Commission proposed a seriousness of six (out of 20),[150] whilst the ECJ lowered this to five, and the coefficient in *Spanish Bathing Waters* was set at four.[151]

In contrast, the ECJ held in *French Fisheries* that France had committed a very serious infringement by failing to apply and enforce rules concerning the common fisheries policy, in particular as concerned the minimum size of fish. The ECJ noted that the *laissez-faire* constituted a serious threat to the maintenance of certain species and fishing grounds, and ultimately jeopardized a fundamental objective of the common fisheries policy. The co-efficient for seriousness was thus set at 10, which is the highest yet.[152]

However, given the degree of seriousness, a coefficient of 10 out of 20 is still lenient in relative terms, which may imply that higher degrees of seriousness will require fault – for instance a complete failure to take any measures to

[148] ibid para 99.

[149] Case C–278/01 *Commission v Spain* [2003] ECR I–14141, paras 55–56; and Case C–304/02 *Commission v France* [2005] ECR I–6263, para 106.

[150] Case C–387/97 *Commission v Greece* [2000] ECR I–5047, paras 96–97 – by implication.

[151] Case C–278/01 *Commission v Spain* [2003] ECR I–14141, para 58.

[152] Case C–304/02 *Commission v France* [2005] ECR I–6263, para 107.

comply with the Community obligations.[153] However, it should be recalled that there were some particular circumstances to this case, eg that the ECJ of its own motion decided to impose both penalty payments and a lump sum for the first time, which could explain why the ECJ refrained from also questioning whether the seriousness co-efficient proposed by the Commission was appropriate.

The lowest co-efficient yet was set in *French Product Liability*.[154] The case concerned partially erroneous transposition of Directive 85/334/EEC, in so far as French law provided that suppliers of defective products were liable on the same terms as producers. The ECJ noted, however, that recent amendments to French legislation had improved the situation, and the only remaining flaw was that it did not explicitly make clear that the supplier could not be held liable if the producer could be identified. There remained, therefore, no serious interference with the objective of the directive or public and private interests, and the co-efficient of seriousness was set at 1 (out of 20).[155] In this case, the seriousness co-efficient thus becomes nugatory for the purposes of calculating the penalty payment, and the Member State is effectively held liable for the duration of the infringement only.

4.3.2 *Duration*

The relevant period for assessing the duration of the infringement is the time from delivery of the Article 226 EC judgment – or in the case of early judgments (*Greek Waste* and *French Fisheries*), the adoption of the Treaty of Maastricht[156] – until the ECJ assesses the facts in the Article 228 EC proceedings.[157] One would think that the latter is the time of hearing, but the judgment in *French Product Liability* suggests that the relevant time is the delivery of the Article 228 EC judgment.[158]

The duration in *Greek Waste* was thus about eight years, and the ECJ appears to have adhered to the Commission's coefficient of 2 (out of 3).[159]

[153] The French authorities had after all taken some steps to improve controls and the effectiveness of its sanctions against illegal fishing, although the ECJ found that those measures had not been implemented in a sufficiently effective manner to reduce the graveness of the breach that had been established; see para 73.

[154] Case C-177/04 *Commission v France* [2006] ECR I-2461.

[155] ibid paras 65–67.

[156] Case C-387/97 *Commission v Greece* [2000] ECR I-5047, para 98; and Case C-304/02 *Commission v France* [2005] ECR I-6263, para 108. This is because the Treaty of Maastricht introduced financial sanctions, which cannot be given retroactive effect to periods of infringements prior to this date.

[157] Case C-177/04 *Commission v France* [2006] ECR I-2461, para 71.

[158] Case C-177/04 *Commission v France* [2006] ECR I-2461, para 73 read in conjunction with para 71.

[159] Case C-387/97 *Commission v Greece* [2000] ECR I-5047, para 98 – by implication.

The duration in *Spanish Bathing Waters* was almost six years and the co-efficient was set at 1.5,[160] whilst a 14-year long infringement in *French Fisheries* earned a maximum co-efficient of 3.[161]

However, these cases must now be seen in light of *French Product Liability*, which marks a more stringent approach. The duration of the infringement was just short of four years and the Commission proposed a co-efficient of 1.3. The co-efficient had been calculated on the basis of a 2002 internal decision on the definition of duration, according to which the infringement started running from the seventh month after the delivery of the Article 226 EC judgment and a 0.1 co-efficient was added for each month that passed until the expiry of the reasoned opinion.

The ECJ noted first that it was the time of the assessment of facts, not the expiry of the reasoned opinion, which was relevant, and added more importantly that the ECJ's discretion was in any event not limited by the duration scale of 1–3 laid down in the Commission's guidelines.[162] The ECJ emphasized that France had only been required to adopt some transposition measures in order to comply with the previous judgment, which had moreover been clearly defined. Since after nearly four years France had nevertheless only achieved partial compliance with such a straightforward obligation, the ECJ found the duration to be considerable and set the co-efficient at the (previously) maximum of 3.[163]

There are many lessons to be learned from this judgment. First, it seems likely that the ECJ in future cases will set the duration coefficient higher than 3, given that the duration was after all short of four years, as compared with six, eight, and 14 years in the previous cases. Secondly, it seems that the co-efficient for duration is a relative notion, which not only turns on the temporal aspect but also the measures needed to ensure compliance with the previous judgment. In other words, the duration of the infringement is viewed stringently in matters concerning formal transposition, where the requisite measures are clearly defined and can be speedily remedied, and vice versa. Indeed, in *Spanish Bathing Waters* (six years' duration) the ECJ lowered the Commission's proposed coefficient of 2 to 1.5 given that compliance with the previous judgment, ie to ensure that bathing waters complied with the limit values in Directive 76/160, could not be achieved within a short period of time, but required long-term and complex operations.[164]

[160] Case C–278/01 *Commission v Spain* [2003] ECR I–14141, paras 53–54.
[161] Case C–304/02 *Commission v France* [2005] ECR I–6263, para 108.
[162] Case C–177/04 *Commission v France* [2006] ECR I–2461, paras 70–71.
[163] ibid paras 72–74.
[164] Case C–278/01 *Commission v Spain* [2003] ECR I–14141, paras 53–54.

The ECJ has thus in effect imported a fault norm in the determination of the duration, which may seem instinctively reasonable. However, whilst uncertainty, or lack thereof, as concerns the requisite measures to be taken in order to comply with the previous judgment seems relevant for the purposes of determining the co-efficient,[165] I fail to see how the nature of those measures are relevant.[166] The deadlines for implementation of directives already reflects the nature of those obligations, so that Member States have in relative terms short time limits for transposition, and regularly longer ones, often specifically set, in matters concerning long-term and complex operations. Hence, Member States had three years to implement Directive 85/334/EEC (*French Product Liability*) as compared with 10 years in relation to Directive 76/160/EEC (*Spanish Bathing Waters*). It would therefore amount to an arbitrary temporal rebate if Member States failing to comply with the deadlines of directives of the latter type were treated more leniently because of the complexity and long-term nature of the operations necessary.[167]

In fact, one might question whether the duration of the infringement should be considered relevant at all for the purposes of penalty payments. The objective of this sanction is, as mentioned, to induce defaulting Member States to comply with a judgment establishing a failure to fulfil obligations and to ensure that Community law is in fact applied.[168] Whilst impacts on public and individual interests are relevant in determining the level of inducement appropriate, it is difficult to see how past behaviour can have any bearing on this issue. The duration of the infringement should therefore, in my view, only be taken into account when determining punitive sanctions, ie when imposing lump sums (section 4).

The reason for this anomaly is perhaps to be found in the fact that the Commission previously only proposed penalty payments, and seems to have construed this instrument so as also to fulfil the function of lump sums. Since the ECJ has now embraced lump sums, the duration co-efficient should be taken out of the equation for the purposes of calculating penalty payments, which could be compensated by amending the seriousness co-efficient, eg to a scale of 1–60, in order to ensure the necessary level of financial inducement.

[165] Cf the emphasis on the fact that they were clearly defined in *French Product Liability*.

[166] See also 2005 Commission Communication on Application of Article 228 EC (SEC(2005) 1658), 7.

[167] The comments in *Spanish Bathing Waters* should perhaps be read in light of the fact that Spain de facto had less time to implement Directive 76/160 than the other Member States, owing to its late accession to the EC.

[168] Case C–304/02 *Commission v France* [2005] ECR I–6263, para 80; and Case C–177/04 *Commission v France* [2006] ECR I–2461, para 59.

4.3.3 *Time period for compliance*

In *Greek Waste* the ECJ set, on the basis of the above-mentioned criteria, a penalty payment of €20, 000 which was due for each day passing after the delivery of the judgment.[169] In *Spanish Bathing Waters*, however, the ECJ imposed the penalty payment on an annual basis.[170] This was owing to the fact that Article 13 of Directive 76/160/EEC contains an annual reporting duty for Member States, and the court held that any finding concerning compliance with the judgment could therefore only be on an annual basis.

This is not persuasive, since in a case of extremely belated application of Community law one could clearly require ad hoc reporting from the Member State.[171] The reasoning is also peculiar since the expiry date for the annual reporting duty laid down in the directive may not square with the time when compliance with the annual penalty payment is due to be examined, and the Member State may therefore in any event have to report earlier than required by the directive.

A bi-annual penalty payment was required in *French Fisheries*, this time with a different explanation.[172] The ECJ noted that the French authorities had adjusted their practices concerning the application and enforcement of the Community's fisheries legislation, but that it would not be possible to perceive their impact immediately. A half-year period was therefore required before an overall assessment of the results could be undertaken. This observation would appear to apply generally to cases concerning general and persistent flaws in the application and enforcement of Community rules. Conversely, a daily penalty payment would appear appropriate where the infringement concerns omission of formal transposition of Community directives. This has now been confirmed in *French Product Liability*.[173]

Regardless whether a daily, bi-annual, or annual penalty payment is selected, the (potential) penalties owing start running from the delivery of the judgment and the nominal impact of the sanctions are therefore the same. The Member States may of course escape penalties if they manage to ensure compliance within the relevant bi-annual or annual deadline, but otherwise it amounts to the cumulated effects of daily penalties over a period of six months or a year from the delivery of the judgment.

[169] Case C–387/97 *Commission v Greece* [2000] ECR I–5047, para 99.

[170] Case C–278/01 *Commission v Spain* [2003] ECR I–14141, paras 43–46.

[171] Similarly, Janssen 2004.

[172] Case C–304/02 *Commission v France* [2005] ECR I–6263, paras 111–12.

[173] Case C–177/04 *Commission v France* [2006] ECR I–2461, para 77.

I would therefore respectfully disagree with AG Geelhoed's opinion in *French Product Liability*, where he equated the suspension of payment of penalties with a suspension of the time from which the penalty payment should start to run. Hence, he argued with reference to the annual penalty payment in *Spanish Bathing Waters*, that the daily penalty payment in *French Product Liability* should start to run three months after delivery of the judgment.[174] An analogy with *Spanish Bathing Waters* could perhaps have allowed for a three-monthly penalty payment, which is another thing entirely.

His second line of reasoning was more persuasive. He argued essentially that the measures which France had been required to undertake had not been clearly defined in the Article 226 EC judgment, but only definitively determined in the Article 228 EC judgment, and France should also for this reason be given an amnesty from penalty payments for three months.[175] This line of reasoning is reminiscent of the factors relevant for determining a sufficiently serious breach in the context of state liability, and should therefore influence the seriousness co-efficient, rather than warrant a suspension of the penalty payment. That is indeed the position taken in the 2005 Communication from the Commission.[176] The ECJ did not have to deal with the issue since it found, as mentioned, that the obligations had in fact been clearly defined, and it insisted therefore on daily penalty payments due from delivery of the judgment.

It should be added that it is for the Commission to verify whether, and when, the Member State has complied with the Article 228 EC judgment, and the decision taken by the Commission in this respect may be challenged before the ECJ. Hence, France has lodged proceedings against the Commission decision ordering it to pay the first bi-annual instalments in *French Fisheries*, arguing that it has in fact complied with that judgment.[177] This will of course further prolong the Article 228 EC procedure, but it should be kept in mind that Member State takes a risk by bringing such challenges since the financial sanction keep running. A more significant risk from an environmental perspective is that the Commission prematurely finds that compliance has been achieved. The Spanish Bathing Waters[178] provides one

[174] Opinion, ibid, para 70 cf footnote 18. [175] ibid.

[176] See 2005 Commission Communication on Application of Article 228 EC (SEC(2005) 1658) 7, point 16.2.

[177] Case T–139/06 *France v Commission*, pending.

[178] The Commission puzzlingly found that Spain had complied with the judgment when 95 per cent of the bathing waters adhered to the applicable environmental requirements at the end of the year, and no penalty payment was paid – see criticism by Krämer 2006, 412.

example, but the most striking (and ironic) instance concerns Greek Waste.[179] The Commission decided in that case that compliance had been fulfilled once Greek authorities had shut down the illegal Kouroupitos waste site, despite internal disagreement in the Commission as to whether rehabilitation of the site was also required.[180] Four years later the Commission realized its error, and brought Article 226 EC proceedings against Greece on the grounds that the failure to decontaminate Kouroupitos posed risks to human health and the environment.[181] The case is pending before the ECJ, but if the Commission's allegations are correct it follows that the Greek Waste case was closed prematurely – thus letting Greece of the hook financially, allowing risks to human health and the environment to persist, and forcing another round of proceedings which should have been superfluous.

4.3.4 *Flat and relative rates*

A penalty payment is, despite its name, not a punitive instrument but meant to induce compliance. The ECJ has therefore held that it must be set in such a way as to reflect the progress made by Member States. It ruled consequently in *Spanish Bathing Waters* that the annual penalty payment due should be calculated on the basis of the percentage of bathing areas which did not conform with Directive 76/160/EEC at the end of the year.[182] Hence, the penalty payment of €12, 483, 000, based on a 20 per cent non-conformity of Spanish bathing waters, was converted into an annual penalty payment of €624, 150 for each 1 per cent percent of bathing waters which did not conform with Directive 76/160/EEC by the end of the year.

Although this logic should apply similarly to other penalty payments which have a longer time horizon, it will often not be possible to grade compliance in this fashion.[183] This is particularly the case where infringements concern lack of application and enforcement, and the ECJ therefore chose a flat rate in *French Fisheries*.[184]

Furthermore, relative rates do not make much sense where the ECJ imposes a daily penalty payment, which it will do in matters concerning formal transposition, and the ECJ accordingly also chose a flat rate in *French Product Liability*.[185]

[179] Case C–387/97 *Commission v Greece* [2000] ECR I–5047.

[180] Hedemann-Robinson 2006, 330–31.

[181] Case C–112/06 *Commission v Greece* [2006] OJ C121/4.

[182] Case C–278/01 *Commission v Spain* [2003] ECR I–14141, paras 47–50.

[183] See 2005 Commission Communication on Application of Article 228 EC (SEC(2005) 1658) 4–5.

[184] Case C–304/02 *Commission v France* [2005] ECR I–6263, para 113.

[185] Case C–177/04 *Commission v France* [2006] ECR I–2461, para 78.

4.4 *Lump sums*

Penalty payments and lump sums are intended to achieve the same overarching objective, namely inducing Member States to comply with Article 226 EC judgments and to ensure that Community law is in fact applied.[186] The persuasive effects of the sanctions differ, however. Penalty payments are applicable to infringements which persist at the time of the Article 228 EC proceedings, and are therefore effectively intended to provide incentives for the Member States to end the infringement. Lump sums, on the other hand, are according to the ECJ 'based more on the assessment of the effects on public and private interests of the failure to comply with its obligations, in particular where the breach has persisted for a long period'.[187] Although the ECJ's statement is somewhat vague, it seems that the point is that lump sums are intended to sanction past behaviour, whilst penalty payments are directed at future misbehaviour.

Another matter is that both penalties are intended to influence the future behaviour of the Member States in the sense that lump sums are intended to induce compliance with an Article 226 EC judgment, whilst penalty payments provide for the same in respect of Article 228 EC judgments. One might therefore say that lump sums have deterrent effects, whilst penalty payments have coercive effects, or in the words of AG Geeelhoed in *French Fisheries* – dissuasive and persuasive effects, respectively.[188]

It was the complementary nature of the two sanctions which allowed the ECJ to impose both a lump sum and a penalty payment in *French Fisheries*, although the wording of Article 228(2) EC refers to lump sums *or* penalty payments.[189] The reason why a lump sum is required is because Member States may otherwise escape sanctions by ending the infringement at the Article 228 EC proceedings (or at the later date when the actual payment is due), which would undermine the deterrent effect of Article 228(2) EC. The logical consequence of this is that the relevant time for assessing the Member State's infringement for the purposes of lump sums is the expiry of the deadline set in the reasoned opinion, and not when the ECJ assesses the facts as is the case with penalty payments.[190]

[186] Case C–304/02 *Commission v France* [2005] ECR I–6263, para 80. [187] ibid para 81.

[188] Opinion of 18 November 2004 in Case C–304/02 *Commission v France* [2005] ECR I–6263, para 41. [189] ibid paras 81–83.

[190] Opinion of 29 April, ibid, paras 85 et seq. The ECJ omitted to give any clear statements on this issue.

One would think that whether a lump sum is imposed depends on an objective assessment of whether a Member State is in breach of the previous Article 226 EC judgment at the relevant time, as is the case with regard to penalty payments. The factors concerning duration and seriousness would thus only influence the level of financial sanctions. However, *French Fisheries* implies that these factors are in fact determining a fortiori whether a lump sum should be imposed or not. Hence, the ECJ indicated that whether it was appropriate to impose lump sums depended in particular on the duration of the infringement and the effects on private and public interests, and it was only after having verified that these 'conditions' were fulfilled that it imposed a lump sum on France.[191] These conditions could even appear cumulative, since the ECJ refrained from imposing a lump sum in *French Product Liability*.[192] The ECJ did not give any reasons, but since the duration for the purposes of penalty payments had been deemed 'considerable' and set at a co-efficient of 3, it must have been the low seriousness (1 out of 20) which did not warrant a lump sum.

This approach can be criticized on at least three counts. First, from a perspective of coherence it is difficult to understand why duration and seriousness should be relevant for the question whether a lump sum is imposed, and not only the level of sanctions as in the case of penalty payments. Secondly, a failure to comply with a reasoned opinion in the context of Article 228 EC proceedings is, in my view, by definition of such a duration and seriousness as to warrant a lump sum. As for duration, it should be recalled that Member States will often have failed to comply with Community law for a total period of 10 years or more[193] – starting from the first failure to apply Community law, lasting through Article 226 EC proceedings and after expiry of the reasoned Article 228 EC opinion. If the ECJ judges that a Member State has not had sufficient time to comply with the Article 226 EC judgment, it may dismiss the proceedings on the basis that the Commission has violated the Member State's procedural rights,[194] but otherwise it seems that duration cannot be used as an argument for not imposing lump sums.

The relevance of effects on private and public interests appears equally limited in this respect. It should be recalled that in order to establish an infringement of Article 228(1) EC, a Member State must first have infringed specific Community law obligations in violation of Article 249 EC, then

[191] Paras 81 and 114.

[192] Case C–177/04 *Commission v France* [2006] ECR I–2461, para 64.

[193] See section 5.1.

[194] As proposed in the opinion in Case C–278/01 *Commission v Spain* [2003] ECR I–14141, para 71.

omitted to comply with a judgment of the ECJ formally declaring an infringement of those obligations, and finally failed to comply with the Commission's repeated efforts (formal notice and reasoned opinion) to secure compliance from the Member State. The public interest which resides in respect of the Community legal order and its effectiveness is manifestly sufficient to warrant a sanction under such circumstances. It would be tantamount to ignoring the binding effect of Community law to refrain from imposing a lump sum with reference to the fact that the specific public and private interests protected by the relevant Community rules were not sufficiently important to warrant the sanction envisaged by Article 228(2) EC.

The last point of criticism is that a failure to impose sums in cases where Member States have failed to comply with the Article 228 EC reasoned opinion would remove the very deterrent effect which Article 228 EC is intended to ensure. Member States may speculatively delay complying with Article 226 EC judgments until the start of judicial proceedings under Article 228 EC, during which no penalty payment could be imposed.[195]

This scenario has now materialized in the recent judgment in *Commission v Italy*.[196] The Commission had only requested a penalty payment in this case, which Advocate General Poiares Maduro supported. He considered of his own motion whether a lump sum ought to be imposed as well, but opined against it on the grounds that, although the period that had elapsed since the first judgment was substantial (five years), it was not in the same league as the exceedingly long period in *French Fisheries*.[197] The ECJ found that the infringement of the previous Article 226 EC judgment had persisted after the expiry of the time limit to comply with the Commission's reasoned opinion and thus held that Italy had infringed Article 228(1) EC. However, in contrast to the Advocate General, the ECJ did not find that the infringement still existed at the time of the court's assessment. Hence, there were no grounds for a penalty payment and it did not consider *ex officio* imposing a lump sum.[198]

This judgment illustrates the pivotal role lump sums should have under Article 228(2) EC, as Member States may otherwise ignore binding Community law obligations and an Article 226 EC judgment for several years, and still escape any financial sanctions. The Commission should therefore have asked

[195] Similarly, opinion of 18 November 2004 in Case C–304/02 *Commission v France* [2005] ECR I–6263, para 42. This proposition is supported by the Member States' poor record in complying with Article 226 EC judgments. In 2004 there were 81 judgments which had not been complied with at the end of the year; see Krämer 2006b, 412.

[196] Case C–119/04 *Commission v Italy* [2006] ECR I–6885.

[197] Opinion, ibid, para 48.

[198] Paras 45–46.

for the imposition of a lump sum, and the Advocate General was very conservative when he seemingly presupposed that a lump sum is reserved for those manifestly long periods of legal disobedience as happened in *French Fisheries*. Another matter is that the duration of the infringement in *Commission v Italy* was only one year longer than in *French Product Liability*, in which the ECJ found that a lump sum was inappropriate.

However, the Commission has announced in its 2005 Communication that it will ask for lump sums in all cases from now on, regardless of whether the infringement has ended at the time of the judicial proceedings.[199] But in light of *French Product Liability*, and perhaps *Commission v Italy* as well, it appears that the ECJ will not accept this. Some reserve is nevertheless appropriate since the ECJ did not consider the issue of a lump sum in the latter case, whilst there were some special circumstances in *French Product Liability*, which may indicate that it should be interpreted narrowly in light of its particular facts. France appeared to have attempted to implement the Article 226 EC judgment in good faith, but had at least partially failed because of a misinterpretation of the measures necessary, and it also blamed the Commission for not explaining what had to be done. Indeed, the AG went as far as to say that the obligations resting on France had only been definitively determined in the 228 EC judgment.[200] It is perhaps these circumstances which led the ECJ to find that a lump sum was inappropriate. Such circumstances are, in my view, the only relevant reason for not imposing lump sums, since it would serve no deterrent purpose to penalize a Member State acting in good faith, if indeed that is deemed to be the case.

Since the ECJ has only imposed a lump sum once, there is little guidance as concerns the methods for calculating this sanction. Furthermore, the ECJ's treatment of this issue in *French Fisheries* was very brief. It did not apply the Commission's guidelines on the calculation of penalty payments analogously, as the AG did,[201] nor did it devise a method of calculation of its own. It merely noted in sweeping fashion that the failure to comply with the initial judgment had persisted for 'a long period', and that the public and private interests at issue warranted a lump sum. In light of these 'specific circumstances', the ECJ 'fairly assessed' the lump sum at €20, 000, 000.[202] Although it would be easy to make a mockery of this reasoning, or lack thereof, the

[199] 2005 Commission Communication on Application of Article 228 EC (SEC (2005) 1658) 11.

[200] Opinion in Case C–177/04 *Commission v France* [2006] ECR I–2461, para 70.

[201] Opinion of 29 April in Case C–304/02 *Commission v France* [2005] ECR I–6263, para 103.

[202] Judgment, ibid, para 115.

explanation for the ECJ's terse treatment of this question most likely is that it did not want to pre-empt future Commission guidelines on the calculation of lump sums.

Such guidelines have now arrived with the Commission's 2005 Communication, but it should be recalled that they will at most serve as useful points of reference, and that it is for the ECJ, in exercising its discretion, to determine the appropriate lump sums.[203] The most novel aspect of the Communication is that the Commission intends to propose in each case a minimum fixed lump sum, which is determined by the Member State's ability to pay. The lump sums range from €180, 000 for Malta to €12, 700, 000 for Germany.[204]

However, it follows from the ruling in *French Product Liability* that the ECJ is not likely to accept that such minimum lump sums are imposed in each and every case. The Commission guidelines show, furthermore, that it will propose a lump sum calculated on the basis of the number of days the infringement has persisted where this will provide a higher lump sum than the set minimum sum. This method for calculation is broadly the same as for penalty payments. A basic amount of €200 is multiplied with the co-efficients for seriousness and the Member State's ability to pay, and by the number of days for which the infringement has persisted (instead of a co-efficient for duration, as with penalty payments).

It seems that this method of calculation will in most cases lead to a higher lump sum than the preset lump sums, and thus render the importance of the latter nugatory. For instance, if the duration is four years, which is a conservative estimate on the basis of existing case law, any co-efficient for seriousness set higher than 1.7 (out of 20) will lead to higher daily lump sum than the minimum estimates.

5 Structural deficits

In order to determine the effectiveness of the Articles 226 and 228 EC procedures, it is not sufficient merely to examine the legal framework, but account must also be taken of administrative and political factors that influence the practical workings of the infringement procedure. The following section will examine perhaps the two most important aspects, namely the

[203] See, by implication, Case C–387/97 *Commission v Greece* [2000] ECR I–5047, para 90; and Case C–278/01 *Commission v Spain* [2003] ECR I–1414, para 103.

[204] See 2005 Commission Communication on Application of Article 228 EC (SEC(2005) 1658) 12.

temporal dimension of the infringement procedure, and the independence of the Commission in its role as guardian of the Treaty.

5.1 *Duration*[205]

The average duration of the Article 226 EC procedure, ie from serving the letter of formal notice until a judgment has been rendered, was 45 months for the years 2002–2003 and 47 months in 2004–2005.[206] Staggeringly slow as this is, it nevertheless represents a significant improvement in comparison with previous years. The corresponding numbers for 1998–99 and 2000–2001 were 68 and 59 months respectively.[207]

There are significant temporal differences depending on the nature of the Member States' infringement. Transposition omission cases take on average 29 months, whilst incorrect transposition and incorrect application cases last 50 and 53 months, respectively.[208] These numbers reflect the different legal and factual complexity of the cases. It is somewhat curious, however, that incorrect transposition cases take almost as long as flawed application cases, given that the former requires much less factual evidence than the latter. It is also noteworthy that there still exist significant temporal differences between individual cases. Whilst the minimum duration of incorrect transposition and application cases in the years 2002–2003 was 15 and 23 months respectively, there were cases which took as long as 146 and 147 months.[209] The shortest duration in 2004–2005 was 19 months and the longest running case took 168 months.[210] Apart from the fact that such belated cases undermine the effectiveness of EC environmental law, these numbers also suggests that the infringement procedure is still far from being efficient, but functions on an ad hoc basis.

Both in relation to the temporal paralysis and the great fluctuations it seems that the Commission is mainly to blame. The pre-judicial procedure lasts on average 27 months compared with 20 months spent in judicial proceedings, and the corresponding specific numbers for transposition omission, incorrect transposition, and incorrect application cases are 16 and 13 months, 32 months and 18 months, and 28 and 25 months, respectively.[211] The figures may even be understated as the Commission will regularly have had informal communications with the Member State before serving a formal letter of notice.[212] Furthermore, it may be derived from the fact that

[205] This section relies heavily on the statistical data in Krämer 2006b, which has been assembled from the Commission's Annual reports.

[206] Krämer 2006b, Table 9.

[207] ibid.

[208] ibid Table 10.

[209] Krämer 2004, Table VIII.

[210] Krämer 2006b, Table 9.

[211] ibid Table 10.

[212] Hartley, 311.

the duration of ECJ litigation varied between eight and 42 months for the years 2002 and 2003, and that even more significant fluctuations occurred at the pre-judicial stage (since there were, as mentioned, cases which in total took 147 months).[213]

Similar findings of belated enforcement under Article 228 EC may tentatively be deduced from the five cases which have been brought thus far. The judgments were handed down about four, five, six, eight, and 14 years after delivery of the Article 226 EC judgments respectively, bringing the overall time (from the moment the first formal letter of notice was dispatched in the Article 226 EC procedure) to a stunning 7.5, 9.5, 14, 11, and 20.5 years, respectively.[214] It is also noteworthy that the reasoned opinions in the Article 228 EC proceedings were not sent before 15, 22, 29, 52, and 132 months after the respective Article 226 EC judgments were issued.[215]

It appears therefore that the biggest potential for improvement, in regard to both Articles 226 and 228 EC, lies in expediting the administrative phase of the infringement procedure. For instance, it is difficult to understand why the pre-judicial phase under Article 226 EC needs to take 16 months in respect of Member States which have failed to transpose, or to communicate, directives into national law, especially bearing in mind that such cases, according to the Commission's own admission, are opened automatically.[216] Since such infringements are both legally and factually simple, it seems superfluous to serve a letter of formal notice, and even more so in respect of the reasoned opinion. In fact, neither requirements of legal certainty nor the right to defence would seem to preclude that such infringements be brought directly before the ECJ – especially bearing in mind that the ECJ will in any event not accept any justification for belated formal transposition.

Looking at the pre-judicial phase more generally, one might argue that the two-stage procedure is superfluous. It suffices, in my opinion, that Member States are served a reasoned opinion straight away, bypassing the initial letter of formal notice. It is noteworthy that Article 226 EC does not mention the latter instrument at all. It admittedly provides that Member States are allowed to submit observations, but this might be done at the initial informal

[213] Krämer 2004, Table VI.

[214] These numbers correspond to the following order of cases: 1) Cases C–52/00 and C–177/04 (*French Product Liability*); 2) Cases C–212/99 and C–119/04 (*Commission v Italy*); 3) Cases C–45/91 and C–387/97 (*Greek Waste*); 4) Cases C–92/96 and C–278/01 (*Spanish Bathing Waters*); 5) and Cases C–64/88 and C–304/02 (*French Fisheries*).

[215] ibid.

[216] Fifth Annual Survey on the Implementation and Enforcement of Community Environmental Law 2003 (SEC(2004) 1025) 35.

stage which currently precedes the letter of formal notice. Indeed, this was in fact the original practice – the Commission would send an informal letter of inquiry as soon as it started investigations inviting the Member State to submit its views. But following objections from the Member States, a consensus to stop this practice was agreed and today's formal letter of notice was added to the procedure. This agreement was neither recorded in writing, nor adopted on a formal level,[217] which in my view calls into question its legality.

A more significant reform to speed up proceedings was submitted by the Ole Due Working Group, namely that the Commission's claim of infringement by a Member State would be automatically binding on the Member State unless challenged within a certain time limit.[218] The proposal was submitted in preparation for the Nice Treaty amendments, but did not find favour with the Member States.

Another important factor is the well-known fact that the Commission is regularly slow in moving to the next stage of the administrative proceedings, eg from letter of formal notice to reasoned opinion, or to initiating judicial proceedings, and it rarely stringently enforces the deadline prescribed for Member States.[219]

This may partially be explained with reference to a lack of manpower and resources, but there are also structural impediments which add to this problem. One basic problem is that the Commission meets only every six months to take decisions under the Article 226 EC procedure, despite the fact that the normal time limit for the Member State to respond to the letter of formal notice is two months.[220] Member States will therefore regularly have longer than two months to respond. Other serious impediments include the complexity of the Commission's decision-making procedure and the number of different bodies involved, eg technical and policy units, the legal service in DG XI, the horizontal legal service, heads of cabinets and the Commissioners.[221] Significant improvements could be achieved if the number of cooks was reduced, and the decision-making procedure made more streamlined.

5.2 *Independence*

A striking feature of the infringement procedure is that the overwhelming majority of cases are closed before ever reaching the court room.[222] One may

[217] Williams 1995, 365. [218] Macrory 2006, 394. [219] ibid 361.

[220] Krämer 2003, 387.

[221] For an extensive analysis of the procedure, see Williams 1995, 358–73. See also Macrory 1996, 16.

[222] Krämer 2003, 388 reports that only about 10 per cent of all infringement cases that are opened ever reach the ECJ.

presume that this is largely owing to Member States achieving compliance with the relevant legislation before this time, but there is no way of knowing since the Commission's decisions to close cases are confidential. There is accordingly a risk that some of these cases come to a halt for reasons other than that the Member States have secured full compliance. These issues are of course not only relevant to the lodging of proceedings before the ECJ, but applies similarly to the whole procedure from the decision to initiate the pre-judicial stage and onwards.

One particular rule which has caused concern in this respect is the so-called 'one-year rule' laid down in the Commission's internal procedural rules, according to which the Commission strives to issue a formal notice or to close the case within no more than one year from the date of registration of a complaint.[223] This rule was supposed to ensure expediency and to protect the complainant's interests – although, incidentally, the rule itself was not made public before the ombudsman opened an inquiry[224] – but Commission officials have hinted that the rule has in fact been pragmatically invoked as formalistic justification for closing cases.[225]

The lack of transparency of the infringement proceedings – which is discussed further below[226] – and the Commission's composition, competences, and decision-making procedure unfortunately do not alleviate these fears, but, if anything, exacerbate them. The most fundamental problem stems from the fact that the Commission is not only the guardian of the Treaty, but is also empowered with the legislative initiative within the EC. This of course harbours the risk that the Commission may take strategically motivated decisions in its enforcement role in order to accommodate legislative ambitions. The Commission would perhaps be less inclined to initiate infringement proceedings, not to mention proceedings against large Member States which may have an already hostile attitude towards its legislative proposals.

These risks could be avoided if there was a strict separation of powers within the Commission, ie that different persons dealt with enforcement and legislation respectively, but that is unfortunately not the case.[227] At the same time, these problems have probably been reduced with the increasing use of majority voting and the enlargement of the EC.

Another issue which raises fears about neutrality is the fact that there may be national allegiances within the Commission. This risk applies of course in

[223] See Annex to the Commission Communication on relations with the complainant in respect of infringements of Community law ([2002] OJ C244/5).
[224] ibid.
[225] Williams 1995, 369.
[226] See section 6.2 below.
[227] Williams 1995, 354–58.

general, but is particularly acute in respect of the significant number of Commission personnel who are on secondment from national administrations.[228] They may only work in the Commission for a maximum of three years, and their long-term interests therefore presumably lie with the administration from which they came.

6 Rights of private parties

6.1 *Introduction*

The previous section revealed that the independence and neutrality of the Commission's role in the infringement procedure is questionable. This militates in favour of increased transparency and involvement by the public and the ECJ.

Individuals and NGOs play an important role in providing information so that the Commission can properly fulfil its watchdog function, and the bulk of Article 226 EC cases are initiated following private complaints. The latest report (for the year 2003) shows that whilst 1158 cases were initiated following private complaints, only 253 of these were pursued on the basis of the Commission's own investigations.[229] Furthermore, the environmental sector generates by far the highest number of complaints (493 out of 1158), and represented in excess of 40 per cent of the 'active' complaints in 2003.[230]

However, the question is whether the important role played by individuals in respect of the Article 226 EC procedure is similarly reflected in procedural and judicial rights, in particular in respect of those who have filed complaints. This is examined below, on the basis of the three essential pillars of private enforcement – access to information, participation, and justice. The latter part is perhaps especially relevant considering that the overwhelming majority of infringement proceedings are terminated before the judicial phase comes into play,[231] which not only means that there is limited judicial review of Member States' compliance, but also of the Commission's role in enforcing EC environmental law.

[228] Williams 1995, 364 reports (although these are of course outdated numbers which may only give an indication) that 56 of the 400 people working in the Commission's DG Environment Commission were on secondment from the Member State administrations.

[229] 21st Annual Report on Monitoring the Application of Community Law (2003), COM(2004) 839, 4.

[230] ibid.

[231] Krämer 2004, 127.

6.2 *Access to information*

Private enforcement presupposes that individuals and NGOs have access to information relevant to the commencement and course of infringement proceedings. The Commission has begun to publish decisions on infringement cases on the internet,[232] but these publications simply state, in French, that a certain decision has been taken without providing grounds for the decision.[233] Decisions to deliver a reasoned opinion or to refer a case to the ECJ may be published through a press release, but the Commission maintains discretion to decide otherwise.[234] Hence, in order to obtain access to the documents underlying these decisions, individuals must submit requests to the Commission.

Access to information was previously regulated by Decision 94/90/EC,[235] under which individuals had access to Commission documents subject to exceptions where the public interest required confidentiality.[236] In *WWF v Commission* the ECJ decided accordingly that:

> the confidentiality which the Member States are entitled to expect of the Commission in such circumstances [Article 226 EC proceedings] warrants, under the heading of protection of the public interest, a refusal of access to documents relating to investigations which may lead to an infringement procedure, even where a period of time has elapsed since the closure of the investigation.[237]

There exist similar grounds for excluding access to documents under the current regime – Regulation (EC) 1049/2001 regarding public access to European Parliament, Council and Commissions documents[238] – but there are some important differences. The exception relating to investigations and inspections which previously fell under the umbrella of 'public interest' is now an independent ground for refusing access to documents, cf Article 4(2) of Regulation (EC) 1049/2001. However, the confidentiality of such documents is not absolute any more, but subject to the caveat that the public interest does not warrant disclosure. These two changes in conjunction reveal a

[232] See <http://europa.eu.int/comm/secretariat_general/sgb/droit_com/index_en.htm#infractions>.

[233] See Point 12 in Annex to Commission Communication on relations with the complainant in respect of infringements of Community law ([2002] OJ C244/5).

[234] ibid. Krämer 2003b argues that this is incompatible with Regulation 1049/2001/EC on access to documents.

[235] [1994] OJ L46/48.

[236] For a thorough analysis, see Williams 2002, 279–93.

[237] Case T-105/95 *WWF v Commission* [1997] ECR II-313, para 63.

[238] [2001] OJ L145/43; see also Annex to Commission Decision 2001/937 amending its rules of procedure ([2001] OJ L345/94).

reversal of the line of thought under the old regime. Whilst public interest under Decision 94/90/EC was employed as reason for refusing access to documents it may now under certain circumstances trump the confidentiality which Member States and/or the Commission otherwise would be entitled to expect, and the *WWF* ruling is therefore too rigid under the current regime.

One should also bear in mind that the ECJ on several occasions has held that exceptions to access to documents must be interpreted and applied restrictively, so as not to frustrate application of the general principle of giving the public the widest possible access to documents held by the institutions.[239] It would thus seem that where there is a public interest in disclosure of information relevant to infringements proceedings, that interest must be balanced against the Member States' as well as the Commission's interest in confidentiality. What is clear is that the Commission may not simply deny access to information with reference to the fact that this may undermine the purpose of the Article 226 EC procedure in general, but must in each case consider whether there is a public interest in disclosure, and, when appropriate, seek to balance competing interests.[240] The same applies to Article 4(3) concerning access to internal documents.

One important change is that the 'authorship rule' existing under the old regime, ie the principle that the entity which drew up a document decides whether it may be disclosed, was not incorporated in the new system. Article 4(4) of Regulation 1049/2001/EC provides that, when a Community institution is requested to disclose third party documents, it shall merely consult the third party with a view to assessing whether the exceptions in Article 4(1)–(2) apply. However, Article 4(5) allows Member States to 'request' the institution not to disclose the documents. The question in *IFAW*[241] was whether such a request obliged the Community institution not to disclose the documents or whether it nevertheless had to release the information if the exceptions did not apply. The documents in question concerned correspondence between German authorities, including the German Chancellor, and the Commission, following which the Commission authorized declassification of a protected

[239] See eg Case T–84/03 *Turco v Commission* [2004] ECR II–4061, para 60 and, by analogy, concerning Decision 94/90, Case T–309/97 *Bavarian Lager v Commission* [1999] ECR II–3217, para 39, and Case T–191/99 *Petrie and Others v Commission* [2001] ECR II–3677, para 66.

[240] This is implicitly confirmed by the Commission Communication on relations with the complainant in respect of infringements of Community law ([2002] OJ C244/5), in which the Commission commits itself to apply the rules on access to documents in Regulation 1049/2001 in the area of infringement proceedings.

[241] Case T–168/02 *IFAW v Commission* [2004] ECR II–4135.

habitat area under Directive 92/43 EC. The Court of First Instance essentially held that, although the authorship rule had not been incorporated in full by Regulation 1049/2001, it still applied with respect to the Member States by virtue of Article 4(5).[242] Scholars have different views on the merits of this judgment,[243] and it is currently on appeal.[244] It should be added that Article 4(6) allows in any event individuals or NGOs to request access to parts of documents which do not concern information provided by the Member State.

The ECJ has held that the notion of public interest does not include the general principles of openness, democracy, and greater participation of citizens in the decision-making process, since these principles are already reflected in the body of rules laid down in Regulation (EC) 1049/2001.[245] Applications for access to documents invoking the public interest rule must therefore be justified on other, more specific grounds. However, it would seem that the public interest in being informed about important environmental matters, in particular when there is a risk to human health, may qualify as a pressing interest distinct from the mentioned principles.

The *Irish Waste* case in my opinion illustrates one situation where public interest could warrant access to information, since that case concerned a general and persistent breach of waste legislation which was held to threaten both protection of the environment and human health.[246] Access to information could in fact be particularly important in such GAP cases, since the ECJ has allowed the Commission to provide supplementary evidence in court proceedings, and private individuals and complainants may thus continue feeding the Commission with information until this date.[247] Hence, if the public is aware of the reasoned opinion, this may guide them in relevant fact-finding on the basis of alleged legal infringements.[248] This may be the reason why the Irish authorities, in contrast to previous practice, did not make public the reasoned opinion in the *Irish Waste* case.[249]

The Commission has moreover committed itself to provide for specific information rights in relation to complainants. They will be notified in writing, after each Commission decision (formal notice, reasoned opinion, and

242 ibid para 58. 243 Cabral 2006, cf Driessen 2006.

244 Case C–64/05 P *Sweden v Commission* [2005] OJ C115/9: 298.

245 See Case T–84/03 *Turco v Commission* [2004] ECR II–4061, paras 81–83.

246 See section 3. 247 See section 3.3.

248 For an analysis of access to letters of formal notice and reasoned opinions under Regulation 1049/2001, see Krämer 2003b.

249 See <http://friendsoftheirishenvironment.net/main/article.php?sid=494>, posted on 26 April 2005.

referral to the ECJ) of the steps taken in response to their complaint.[250] Complainants will also receive prior notice of any proposal to close a case, including grounds explaining the Commission's position.[251]

6.3 *Right to participation*

Regulation 1367/2006 implementing the Aarhus Convention in relation to the Community institutions has removed the administrative phase of the Article 226 EC procedure from its scope and thereby any rights to public participation in this respect. This has been criticized elsewhere,[252] and will not be repeated here.

The Commission nevertheless allows for certain participatory rights in respect of complainants. Following an inquiry by the European Ombudsman into the infringement procedure, the Commission changed its rules in 1997 and will now hear the complainant before it decides to initiate (the informal stage of) infringement proceedings and allow him to present observations.[253] Furthermore, complainants may at any stage of the procedure ask to explain or elaborate the grounds for the complaint. Finally, if the Commission is considering closing the complaint, the complainant will be invited to submit any comments within four weeks.[254] Investigations will continue where the complainant's submission persuades the Commission to reconsider,[255] which implies a fortiori that the Commission is obliged to take the complainant's observation into account before a final decision is made with regard to the closure of the case.

6.4 *Access to judicial review*

Can individuals oblige the Commission to act, and if necessary require judicial review of a decision not to act or failure to respond to a complaint altogether under Article 230(4) EC and Article 232 EC, respectively? This would seem beneficial, considering that less than 10 per cent of the cases make it from the pre-judicial stage to the ECJ.[256]

[250] See Explanatory note to the Commission complainant form [1999] OJ C 119/5, and point 5 of Annex to the Commission Communication on relations with the complainant in respect of infringements of Community law [2002] OJ C244/5).

[251] Communication, ibid, point 10.

[252] See chapter 5, section 3.4.1.

[253] See 15th Annual Report on Monitoring the Application of Community Law [1998] OJ C250/1, and Krämer 2003, 384.

[254] See footnote 248 above.

[255] ibid.

[256] Krämer 2003, 388.

The ECJ has nevertheless rejected this possibility for various reasons. First, the Commission is under no duty to act under Article 226 EC, but enjoys discretion in this respect.[257] Secondly, individuals are not directly and individually concerned by the decision-making under Article 226 EC.[258] Thirdly, and finally, decisions taken under Article 226 EC are administrative preliminary acts, which are non-binding and thus not subject to judicial review.[259]

These justifications are not altogether persuasive. First, the wording of Article 226 EC clearly states that the Commission *shall* issue a reasoned opinion if it considers that the Member State has infringed EC law. This is admittedly different in respect of initiating ECJ proceedings, where the Commission has been conferred discretion by the word 'may'. However, the Commission must still be deemed obliged to bring proceedings in certain particularly serious cases by virtue of the obligation laid down in Article 211 EC to ensure that Community law is respected.[260] Indeed, the ECJ has on occasion pointed out, eg in cases where a Member State has objected to the expediency of bringing an infringement action and asked for extra time to implement a directive, that 'if the Commission did not act within the normal time-limits laid down by the ECJ, it would be failing to *fulfil its obligations* as guardian of the Treaty'.[261]

The Commission obviously enjoys a certain margin of discretion in this regard, but it is difficult to see why this fact should exclude judicial review altogether, since the exercise of discretion, eg in relation to acts and omissions by Member States, is otherwise often the very subject matter of the ECJ's review.[262] Another matter is that discretionary assessments of course can only be subject to marginal review, limited to situations where the Community institution has manifestly erred in its assessment.

Secondly, it could be argued that the procedural rights the Commission in recent years has granted complainants, eg the right to be heard and to submit observations, makes them individually concerned.[263] Furthermore, if it is

[257] See eg Case 247/87 *Star Fruit v Commission* [1989] ECR 291, paras 11–12; and Case T–126/95 *Dumez v Commission* [1995] ECR II–2863, para 44.

[258] See eg *Star Fruit*, ibid, para 13; and *Dumez*, ibid, para 38.

[259] *Star Fruit*, ibid, para 37.

[260] See, to this effect, opinion of Advocate General Trabucchi in Case 2/73 *Geddo* [1973] ECR 685 and, more recently, the opinion of Advocate General Alber in Case C–260/98 *Commission v Greece* [2000] ECR I–6537, para 72, and Case C–358/97 *Commission v Ireland* [2000] ECR I–6301, para 83. See also the opinion of Advocate General Mengozzi in Case C–523/04 *Commission v Netherlands* [2005] OJ C57/19, para 71 and footnote 49.

[261] See eg Case C–212/98 *Commission v Ireland* [1999] ECR I–8571, para 10 (emphasis added).

[262] See chapter 2, section 3.3. Similarly, Williams 2002, 272.

[263] See chapter 5, section 2.2.1.

clear that the Member State will act in a certain way, or to continue acting in a certain way, as a consequence of the Commission's decision not to initiate infringement proceedings, the condition of 'direct concern' will also be fulfilled since 'implementation' of the Commission's decision is 'automatic'.[264]

There is, however, no disputing that decisions taken during the infringement proceedings are preliminary administrative acts which are non-binding, and thus not subject to review under Articles 230 or 232 EC. The conclusion remains therefore that individuals or NGOs cannot challenge acts or omissions by the Commission under Article 226 EC. This is particularly serious considering that failure to act may not be challenged through the Article 234 EC procedure either,[265] which raises the question whether the EC affords a complete system of judicial control in this respect.[266] The ECJ has nevertheless explicitly held that 'the fact that no effective legal remedies may be available through national courts [does not] constitute elements capable of including the legal classification of the act sought by the complainant'.[267]

6.5 *Community liability*

The fact that individuals cannot seek annulment of a Commission decision to forgo infringement proceedings or obtain a declaration of a failure to act in this respect does not necessarily rule out the possibility of bringing a liability claim against the Commission under Article 288(2) EC.[268] This is because tort liability does not require a binding legal act, but encompasses any administrative action or omission subject to the *Brasserie/Bergaderm* criteria.[269]

However, the second condition of this doctrine is that there must have been a sufficiently serious breach of EC law, which presupposes that the Commission must have a duty to act under Article 226 EC. Hartley[270] has cited *Denkavit* as support for the view that a failure to act under Article 226 EC may warrant liability, but the problem with this case is that the Commission had a duty to act under specific legislation, and the question of whether a similar obligation existed under Article 226 EC did not arise.[271] This question came up in the *Asia Motor* case, however, where the ECJ briefly dismissed the possibility of an Article 288(2) EC action 'since the Commission is under no

[264] See, by analogy, eg Case T–435/93 *ASPEC and Others v Commission* [1995] ECR II–1281, para 60; and Case T–17/96 *Télévision Française v Commission* [1999] ECR II–1757, para 30.

[265] See chapter 4, section 4.3.

[266] See chapter 3, section 2.2.4.

[267] Case T–126/95 *Dumez v Commission* [1995] ECR II–2863, para 38.

[268] See chapter 5.

[269] See chapter 5, section 7.

[270] Hartley 2003, 318.

[271] Case 14/78 *Denkavit* [1978] ECR 2497.

obligation to initiate proceedings under Article 169'.[272] As was noted above, this in my opinion is highly questionable. First, it is clear that the Commission 'shall' issue a reasoned opinion where it finds that the Member State has infringed EC law, which in itself could move the Member State to terminate the infringement. An omission in this respect could therefore be causally linked to damage which subsequently occurs. Secondly, it is difficult to see why the fact that the Commission has discretion to initiate ECJ proceedings under Article 226 EC should preclude the possibility that it might have exceeded its margin of discretion, eg in cases where there is an urgent risk of serious, and perhaps irreversible, environmental damage owing to breaches of EC law. This follows arguably from the purpose of Article 226 EC and more generally from the Commission's obligation under Article 211 EC to ensure that Community law is respected.[273]

It should also be borne in mind that a different conclusion would mean that the Commission is completely exempted from responsibility and judicial control in its role as a guardian of the EC Treaty, which would conflict with fundamental tenets of Community law.[274] Paraphrasing *Denkavit*, there are instances where 'it is necessary to consider whether the Commission, by conduct for which there was no justification, did not improperly contribute to the maintenance of [breaches of EC law] and thereby incur liability'.[275]

7 Horizontal enforcement

The Commission's obligation under Article 211 EC to ensure that the Treaty is applied properly applies not only to the Member States, but also to the Community institutions. However, there are no equivalent provisions to Articles 226 and 228 EC in the latter respect. The Commission may bring

[272] Case 72/90 *Asia Motor* [1990] ECR I–2189, para 13.

[273] It is noteworthy that the ECJ sometimes refers to an 'obligation' to bring infringement proceedings; see eg Case C–212/98 *Commission v Ireland* [1999] ECR I–8571, para 10 discussed above, and Case C–422/92 *Commission v Germany* [1995] ECR I–1097, para 17 where the ECJ made the following comment in respect of an Article 226 EC action brought against Germany despite the fact that Community policy had changed on the relevant issue: 'it is relevant to ask why the Commission thought that it was under an obligation to commence and pursue the present action in such circumstances.' This implies that, under different circumstances, there might indeed be an obligation, as opposed to discretion, to bring infringement proceedings.

[274] See chapter 3, section 2.2.4, and chapter 4, section 4.4.2

[275] Case 14/78 *Denkavit* [1978] ECR 2497, para 8.

actions under Articles 230 and 232 EC, but it will for obvious reasons be apprehensive of bringing such claims owing to the risk of alienating the other institutions, in particular the Council, which could undermine its position both in the short and long-terms.

Hence, the Commission has never brought a case on the basis of genuine environmental concerns, eg because of watering down of its legislative proposals to the detriment of the requirements in Articles 6 and 174 EC. Indeed, the relatively few cases which have been brought by the Commission against other Community institutions have predominantly concerned competence issues, eg choice of legal basis[276] and comitology procedures,[277] where the Commission risked losing powers. It is also noteworthy that these cases have not always coincided with environmentally progressive results – some of the cases have, or would have if the ECJ had followed the Commission's submissions, reduced Member States' discretion to apply higher environmental standards. Without going into further detail, it may be concluded that the Commission is not, for legal and political reasons, likely to serve as an effective watchdog of the Community institutions' practice.

It is also noteworthy that the Commission is to a large extent responsible for adopting implementing rules and decisions, in accordance with Article 211 EC, and in these situations it is left to other Community institutions to assume the role of guardian of the Treaty. The Parliament, in particular, could shoulder this responsibility and bring proceedings against the Commission, but prior to the Treaty of Nice it could only bring actions under Article 230 EC aimed at protecting its prerogatives.[278] This changed with the aforementioned Treaty, and the Parliament has now the same privileged standing rights as the Member States, the Council, and the Commission, following which it has now brought its first case against the Commission for

[276] On the choice between old Article 100a and Article 130s, see Case C–300/89 *Commission v Council (Titanium Dioxide)* [1991] ECR I–2867; and Case C–155/90 *Commission v Council (Waste Framework Directive)* [1991] ECR I–2867. On the choice between Articles 133 and 175 EC, see Case C–281/01 *Commission v Council* [2002] ECR I–12049, para 35; Case C–178/03 *Commission v Parliament and Council* [2006] ECR I–107; and Case C–94/03 *Commission v Parliament and Council* [2006] ECR I–1. On the choice between Articles 29, 31 and 43 EU and Article 175 EC, see Case C–176/03 *Commission v Council* [2005] ECR I–7879; and Case C–440/05 *Commission v Council*, pending.

[277] Case C–378/00 *Commission v Parliament and Council (LIFE)* [2003] ECR I–937; and Case C–122/04 *Commission v Parliament and Council (Forest Focus)* [2006] ECR I–2001.

[278] See Case C–156/93 *Parliament v Commission* [1995] ECR I–2019; Case C–187/93 *Parliament v Council* [1994] ECR I–2857; Case C–303/94 *Parliament v Council* [1996] ECR I–2943; and Joined Cases C–164 and 165/97 *Parliament v Council and Commission* [1999] ECR I–1139. See also commentary by Krämer 2002, 4–6.

failing to protect human health and the environment (as opposed to protecting its prerogatives).[279] The other Community body which has as its objective to examine maladministration by the Community institutions, the ombudsman, is only equipped with soft powers.[280] The Member States may of course also play a role in this respect, but this falls outside the scope of this book.

8 The complementary role of private enforcement

The rationale for the ECJ's recognition of direct effect in *Van Gend & Loos* was to ensure that private parties complement the supervision of EC law entrusted to the Commission (and the Member States). On the basis of the preceding evaluation of the Commission's strengths and weaknesses as the guardian of the environmental chapter of the Treaty, it is now appropriate to consider in which departments private parties can most effectively add to the Commission's enforcement of EC environmental law, and vice versa.

As observed, the Commission has shown considerable reluctance in bringing judicial proceedings against other Community institutions in environmental matters.[281] The fact that the Commission has not initiated proceedings concerning substantive review of levels of environmental protection ensured by Community legislation is hardly surprising, given that it has legislative initiative in environmental matters. The situation is worse in respect of administrative decisions, where the guardian of the Treaty and the perpetrator of infringements are often one and the same institution – the Commission. Hence, for the purposes of judicial review of acts and omissions by Community institutions, private enforcement is paramount to ensure judicial control. This may involve seeking preliminary rulings on the validity of Community acts through Article 234 EC – although a failure to act is noticeably not subject to review under this procedure – or by way of direct actions brought under the auspices of Regulation 1367/2006.[282]

The situation is different in relation to enforcement of EC environmental law against Member States. The Commission brings currently about 40 environmental Article 226 EC cases per year, more than in any other field of EC law.[283] The question is therefore essentially in what types of cases

[279] Case C–14/06 *Parliament v Commission* pending. [280] Article 195 EC.
[281] Section 7. [282] Chapter 4, section 4; and chapter 5.
[283] See references in section 1.

against the Member States private parties may most usefully complement the Commission's efforts. This issue may be addressed by first recalling the Commission's monitoring powers in relation to the various types of infringements: lacking or belated implementation, wrongful normative implementation, and lacking practical application and enforcement of environmental directives.[284] The Member States' duty to notify national implementing measures to the Commission allows it effectively to identify the first two types of infringements, and cases of non-transposition are automatically opened once the deadline for implementation has expired. This suggests a modest role for enforcement by private parties as regards these types of infringements.

Having said that, it ought to be recalled that the Commission is not obliged to open infringement proceedings against the Member States, and there are various reasons why it may choose not to do so.[285] In politically sensitive cases, in particular, it is therefore important that private parties bring proceedings in national courts if the Commission fails to take action. This is in fact the only way individuals and organizations may address such stalemates, since omissions by the Commission under Article 226 EC are not open to judicial review. Furthermore, the delay incurred by the obligatory administrative phase preceding the legal phase of the Article 226 EC procedure means that it is hardly a timely remedy.[286] The effectiveness of infringement proceedings is further compromised by the fact that the Commission cannot obtain interim relief during the administrative phase of the Article 226 EC procedure.[287] In situations of urgency, where lack of implementation of environmental rules poses a risk to human health or irreversible environmental damage, eg in relation to habitats and species, individuals, and environmental organizations would therefore be well-advised to bring cases directly before national courts.

It is nevertheless in cases of non-application and lack of enforcement by public authorities that private enforcement is likely to bring most added value. Although environmental directives regularly contain provisions requiring national authorities to report on the practical application of environmental rules, the Commission's lack of monitoring powers on the Member States' territory in environmental matters makes it difficult to verify whether the information is correct and complete, in particular as concerns individual and local infringements. In these instances the Commission is largely dependent on private complaints and information from individuals and environmental organisations. This begs the question in which types of

[284] Section 2.2. [285] Section 6.4. [286] Section 5.1. [287] Section 2.4.5.

non-application cases individuals and environmental organizations should bring the matter before national courts, rather than lodge a complaint with the Commission. If the infringements concern complex issues requiring scientific evidence and possibly lengthy legal proceedings, the Commission will usually possess superior resources and expertise. Furthermore, if there are several infringements of the same type which indicate a general and persistent (GAP) flouting of the relevant environmental rules, it seems more effective to lodge private complaints with the Commission, which then can bring a single GAP case, rather than bringing several isolated cases before national courts.[288] Importantly, the ECJ has interpreted the Article 226 EC procedure in such a way so as to provide procedural benefits for the Commission in assembling and bringing GAP cases, benefits that do not exist at the national level. Finally but significantly, failures to implement GAP judgments may pave the way for an Article 228 EC case and hefty economic sanctions. The Article 228 EC procedure of course provides a general argument in favour of infringement cases by the Commission, but it is a particularly powerful instrument in relation to GAP cases.

In summary, it may be concluded that individuals and environmental organizations may most usefully enforce environmental rules in national courts in individual and prima facie isolated cases of lacking application and enforcement, which do not require significant scientific expertise and complex legal proceedings. In addition, environmental plaintiffs may complement the Commission's efforts by bringing cases directly against private parties, a possibility which is not open to the Commission.

The above-mentioned conclusions square with the Commission's strategic approach announced in its Seventh Annual Survey on Implementation and Enforcement.[289] In an enlarged Europe of 25 Member States the Commission has realized that it needs to become more selective in its priorities, and has chosen for the future to focus on transposition and conformity issues, as well as structural and systemic cases of non-application.[290] Individual cases of non-application and lack of enforcement will therefore increasingly have to be tackled by individuals and NGOs. Another matter is that this division of labour could be seen as an appropriate corollary of the tools which the ECJ has made available to individuals and NGOs in order to enforce EC environmental law. But if this scenario is to materialize, it seems beneficial that the ECJ clarifies that its general case law on procedures and remedies is fully

[288] Section 3. [289] SEC(2006) 1143. [290] ibid 5–6.

applicable in public interest cases, as has been argued in this book, in order to make potential environmental plaintiffs aware of the possibilities for enforcement of EC environmental law. Furthermore, it would be necessary that the ECJ – or the Community legislature, but that seems unlikely – further develops minimum requirements tackling the practical and economic difficulties of bringing environmental suits, eg as concerns national rules on time limits, legal costs, and so forth.[291]

Assuming that environmental plaintiffs indeed have the necessary instruments effectively to complement the Commission's supervisory role in these matters, some have questioned whether the Commission should have to act unless all national remedies have been exhausted – by analogy with the European Commission on Human Rights.[292] Such an analogy seems a bit premature, however. Although environmental plaintiffs enjoy wider procedural and remedial rights than before it would probably be stretching the argument to claim that they enjoy the same access to justice as applicable in the field of human rights. Furthermore, whilst it might have some merit to require individuals to exhaust the applicable remedies made available for the protection of their own fundamental rights, a majority of environmental cases concern infringements that do not directly violate rights of individuals, eg in the case of habitat and bird protection as well as more general infringements affecting the public at large. Under such circumstances it seems neither practical nor reasonable to require that individuals and NGOs act on behalf of the general public before the Commission is required to intervene.

One could instead conceive of different reforms providing for closer co-operation between decentralised and centralised enforcement as well as enhancing the effectiveness of the complaint procedure. Such mechanisms have been enacted in competition law through Regulation 1/2003.[293] Another example is the SOLVIT network set up in the internal market sphere.[294] Independent national authorities or specialized centres could similarly be allocated initial responsibility for assessing complaints concerning infringements of EC environmental law. This would overcome the linguistic barrier currently hampering the efficiency and effectiveness of the Commission's efforts, and allow for a more expedient verification of the factual situation referred to in complaint.[295] The decentralized complaint institutions could then effectively filter cases by opining on the merits of the complaints and if

[291] See chapter 3, section 4. [292] The issue was raised during the peer review of this book.
[293] [2003] OJ L1/1. [294] [2001] OJ L331/79. [295] Krämer 2003a, 93.

appropriate, recommending the Commission to bring legal proceedings. Effective cooperation between decentralized bodies and the Commission would presuppose information exchange, and the Commission should retain powers to take over the case where this is deemed appropriate.[296] Conversely, if the complainant after the initial review procedure decides to bring legal proceedings, national courts could, similar to competition law cases, allow the Commission to submit written or oral observations.

[296] See, by analogy, Article 11(6) of Regulation 1/2003 ([2003] OJ L1/1) and the Commission Recommendation on principles for using SOLVIT ([2001] OJ L331/79).

7

Conclusion

1 Introductory remarks

The background for this book was a prevailing perception among commentators that EC environmental law is 'different' from other sectors of EC law in terms of rights and remedies. According to this view, many of the judicial tools devised by the ECJ to ensure that individuals may enforce Community law have limited application in the field of environmental law.[1] This in turn undermines access to the preliminary reference procedure, whilst direct challenges before the ECJ are ruled out because of lack of standing. These views inspired the hypothesis that restricted access to judicial means may explain the relatively minor role of private enforcement in environmental matters, compared with fields such as the internal market, competition, and state aid. In order to test this hypothesis, we asked the question whether environmental plaintiffs have in fact access to the basic judicial means to enforce EC environmental law and, if so, whether these instruments are sufficient to allow for effective enforcement in national and Community courts, taking into account the particular features defining this field of law. This chapter takes stock of our findings and provides recommendations for the future enforcement of EC environmental law.

2 Private enforcement against national authorities and private parties

2.1 *Rights and remedies*

Those who have argued that EC environmental law provides for limited opportunities for private enforcement have focused on two arguments. First,

[1] See references in chapter 1, section 1.

environmental rules normally do not confer rights on individuals. Secondly, such rights are prerequisites for relying on Community provisions in national courts and access to the procedural and remedial guarantees established by the ECJ. The findings of this book indicate that the first assumption is incorrect and that the latter must be modified.

Starting with the issue of rights in EC environmental law, it is instrumental for an understanding of the debate to recall the distinction between subjective rights and objective rights.[2] In countries operating this distinction, only subjective rights are normally enforceable in national courts and thus 'rights' proper. However, this approach has consistently been rejected by the ECJ in favour of an autonomous and broad interpretation of rights that does not distinguish between objective and subjective rights.

Hence, the ECJ has held that environmental rules that protect public health confer rights on individuals, and must be implemented in a sufficiently clear and precise manner so that the persons concerned can ascertain the full extent of their rights and rely on them before national courts.[3] The fact that the public concerned is a large and not specifically delimited group has not prevented this conclusion. Since a significant proportion of environmental legislation has a link to human health, in accordance with Article 174(2) EC, it follows that EC environmental law often confers rights on individuals. The remaining question flowing from this liberal yet anthropocentric case law, is whether environmental provisions that do not relate to human health may still confer rights on individuals.

However, this question has been rendered largely moot for the purposes of relying on Community provisions in national courts, as it has become increasingly clear that conferral of rights is not a precondition for direct effect but its result: directly effective conditions confer rights on individuals.[4] These rights are hence procedural rights, ie the right to rely on unconditional and sufficiently precise provisions in national courts and the corresponding duty of the national judge to make them operational in the domestic legal order.

Some commentators who have accepted that direct effect does not presuppose the conferral of rights on individuals still argue, however, that this is a precondition for access to the ECJ's judicial protection doctrine. This doctrine has been broadly understood here as encompassing, inter alia, the *Rewe* principles, the *Simmenthal* principle of full effectiveness of Community law, and the *Johnston/Borrelli* principle of effective judicial protection and

[2] Chapter 1, section 2. [3] Chapter 2, section 2.1. [4] Chapter 2, section 2.1.

control. This assumption would for instance exclude the applicability of these principles to actions based on Community provisions for the protection of birds, species, and habitats.

However, this view has been refuted in this book for various reasons.[5] First, the ECJ has held in relation to Directive 92/42/EC (Habitats Directive) that proper implementation is necessary, inter alia, in order to allow individuals and environmental organizations to assert their interests in nature conservation before national courts. This implies that the judicial protection doctrine can be invoked against national restrictions hindering suits brought against infringements of the Habitats Directive, and it is also noteworthy that the ECJ refers to 'interests' as opposed to rights in these cases. Secondly, the ECJ has found *Rewe* applicable in cases concerning Directive 85/337/EEC (EIA Directive), which is not only concerned with human health, but applies to decisions which may have an adverse impact on the environment or human health. Thirdly, in one of these cases the ECJ held more generally that 'it is for national courts to ensure the legal protection which persons derive from the *direct effect* of provisions of Community law'. The ECJ has hence taken the view that it suffices for the legal protection doctrine and *Rewe* to come into effect that the plaintiffs are relying on procedural rights which they derive from directly effective provisions.

The detailed findings in respect of the jurisprudence on procedures and remedies for enforcement of EC environmental law in national courts need not be repeated here, and it suffices to observe that the judicial protection doctrine lays down minimum requirements pertaining to a wide range of legal issues, eg on standing, time limits, judicial review, effects of infringements in the domestic legal order, interim relief and reparation.[6]

The final fundamental issue in the context of rights and remedies is whether the principle of state liability nonetheless requires that the infringed provisions confer specific rights on individuals.[7] A majority of commentators and some national courts have answered this question affirmatively. Even if this was the correct view, a substantial body of environmental provisions qualify on the basis of their link to protection of human health. The anthropocentric notion of rights as it relates to state liability is therefore in any event fairly broadly interpreted.

However, this book has shown that environmental provisions which are only remotely related to human health and individual rights in the subjective sense may also confer rights for the purposes of state liability suits. For instance,

[5] Chapter 3, section 2.3. [6] Chapter 3, sections 4–9. [7] Chapter 3, section 10.

the ECJ has held that infringements of the EIA Directive may result in state liability. It appears therefore that subjective rights are not a precondition for state liability, but that the notion of rights in this context is commensurable with procedural rights derived from the binding effect of directly effective provisions. This is not to say that direct effect in the narrow sense is a requirement for state liability, which was demonstrated in *Francovich* and *Wells*. The point is that since the *raison d'être* for the state liability doctrine is to complement the direct effect doctrine, for purposes of which individual rights are irrelevant, it must follow that infringements of subjective rights are not a precondition for state liability. Indeed, the court has on occasion indicated that the purposes of compensation in Community law is not limited to protecting individuals' rights, but is also a means of ensuring that infringements of Community rules incur a sanction and ultimately that the binding effect of the *acquis communautaire* is respected. As AG Jacobs has succinctly observed:

> The Court's approach, historically at any rate, has not been to promote the rights of individuals for their own sake or as a matter of ideology; its approach has been essentially pragmatic and the recognition of individuals' rights has been almost instrumental, being necessary to ensure the effectiveness of the legal order.[8]

Arguably therefore, the ECJ should depart from its rights terminology since this is liable to cause much confusion when applied in national legal systems that employ a different and above all narrower concept of rights. However, there might be political reasons for the ECJ's persistent reference to rights:

> It may well be that by invoking the language of individual rights, the ECJ tries to benefit from the mystique of the term in order to ensure that the requirements which it formulates are more readily accepted in national legal order. After all, in the supranational context the protection of individual citizens' rights seems a much more laudable project than merely stipulating that Member States must be controlled.[9]

In sum, and returning to our initial question, environmental plaintiffs are not constrained by formally different access to tools allowing them to enforce EC environmental law in national courts than plaintiffs in other sectors of Community law. Another matter, discussed in the next section, is that other unique features of EC environmental law may in practice render application of these remedies more difficult than in other areas of Community law.

[8] Jacobs 2004, 308. [9] Prechal and Hancher 2002, 105.

2.2 *Effectiveness*

Most environmental legislation comes in the form of directives. This means that – unlike other fields, such as internal market and competition, which to a large extent are governed by directly applicable Treaty provisions and regulations – private plaintiffs are in principle unable to enforce EC environmental law as against private parties, or as against national authorities where this amounts to imposing obligations on private parties. National authorities are similarly prohibited from invoking unimplemented directives directly against private parties.

However, the ECJ has watered down these principles in practice. This it has done by way of liberal interpretation of the notion of public entities, acceptance of incidental horizontal direct effects, extensive use of the principle consistent interpretation, and a narrow interpretation of the notion of 'direct obligations'.[10] Environmental plaintiffs can therefore, in fact, often enforce environmental rules against individuals or other private entities.

Article 249 EC stipulates that directives are binding as to the result to be achieved, but leave national authorities the choice and forms of methods for achieving it. Environmental directives accordingly rarely contain unconditional and sufficiently precise obligations in respect of the means for attaining environmental goals. This does not rule out direct effect (in the broad sense), but it means that environmental plaintiffs can relatively rarely require national authorities to fulfil obligations in a specific manner. Instead, they may require review of legality on the basis of the results stipulated. However, this may not be a timely and effective remedy where directives, as often is the case, provide for an extensive period before the result must be realized. In these situations one must fall back on the form of precautionary direct effect which the court has outlined in some cases, eg *Inter-Environnement Wallonie*.[11]

Furthermore, although environmental directives are binding as to the result to be achieved, there are great variations in the manner in which such results are specified. Failure to fulfil in fact clearly defined results, eg numerical emission and quality limit values, allows national courts to infer that Member States have failed to take the measures required by the directive. Conversely, the ECJ has ruled that failure to achieve objectives, which are usually less clearly prescribed, merely provides an indication that a Member State has acted in breach of the directive, and only if it persists over a protracted period of time.

[10] Chapter 2, sections 2.3 and 3.3.3.

[11] Chapter 2, section 2.2.3.

This case law has been criticized, and it has been submitted that the distinction between objectives and results should only have relevance for the finding of a breach, but not the legal consequences of such failures.[12] Once a Member State has failed to respect the aims of a directive, irrespective whether these are expressed in numerical values or in broader terms such as 'endangering the environment or human health', national courts must conclude that that Member State has failed to take the necessary measures, without having to wait for the passage of a protracted time. This conclusion is especially important in light of the growing emphasis in EC environmental policy on 'flexibility' and 'differentiation', which has promoted the articulation of broad environmental objectives instead of numerically defined standards.

Another factor which restricts the intensity of review is that environmental legislation often concerns issues which require complex assessments of a scientific, economical and technical nature. The frequent use of best available technology (BAT) as a regulatory reference point, and sometimes not even just used as a means but as a goal in itself,[13] is only one example. In such instances, national courts need to go no further in their review of the legality of national implementation than the Community judicature in similar types of proceedings against Community institutions. In practice, however, it appears that the ECJ has conducted a more stringent review of national authorities' exercise of discretion, and the principle of coherence provided for in *Upjohn* requires national courts to do the same.[14]

If judicial proceedings have passed all these hurdles and a national measure has been held incompatible with EC environmental law, the principle of supremacy dictates that it has to be set aside. However, some recent environmental cases suggest that in cases of infringements of procedural Community law the matter is not as straightforward as this. Where the effects of an infringement may not be ascertained on the basis of the provisions at issue, as is the case with the EIA Directive for instance, it appears that national procedural law not only governs the forms in which the illegal act is to be set aside, but also whether it should be set aside at all, albeit subject as always to the *Rewe* doctrine.

This is liable seriously to undermine the effectiveness of EC environmental law, since a large part of that law is made up of procedural requirements, whilst procedural defects in many Member States do not necessarily result in invalidity. In light of the fact that procedural law is as binding upon the

[12] Chapter 2, section 2.2.5. [13] Chapter 2, section 2.2.6. [14] Chapter 3, section 6.

Member States as substantive law, the ECJ should in my view adopt the position that the principle of supremacy dictates the setting aside of any measure suffering from a procedural defect, whilst Member States only have procedural autonomy, subject to *Rewe*, in relation to the forms in which this happens.[15] The ECJ should alternatively more often interpret environmental procedural directives as also governing the effects of infringements, thus entailing an obligation to set aside acts suffering from procedural defects.

Infringements of EC environmental law will often lead to environmental impairment in some form, which brings us to the issue of reparation.[16] In some cases, environmental damage may be identified with reference to the discrepancy between the factual situation and the results stipulated in a directive, eg as concerns quality values for air, water, and soil. Plaintiffs may then rely on the direct effect of obligations of result in order to obtain 'reparation'. Other environmental provisions are, as observed, not as precisely drafted with regard to the result to be achieved. However, even general obligations usually lay down a minimum result to be achieved, which may be enforced against the national authorities.

The instances where recourse to *Francovich* is necessary are typically where the obligations in the directive are conditional and require further implementing measures, or where national procedures and remedies in some way have shortcomings which do not allow environmental plaintiffs to enforce the directly effective obligations in full. However, on the basis of the current case law it may be argued that state liability only applies to economic loss, and that pure environmental damage may consequently not be addressed using the *Francovich* doctrine. However, this is a circular argument, since the ECJ has until now only been faced with cases concerning economic loss, and the issue therefore as yet remains unresolved. Examination of the underlying justification for state liability, ie to ensure the binding effect of Community law and that infringements are sanctioned, implies that *Francovich* may also entail an obligation to provide reparation for ecological damage. The proposition that state liability is a 'course of action rather than a specific remedy' is moreover supported by the general nature of the underlying principle first laid down in *Humblet*, namely to nullify the consequences of unlawful actions.[17] Furthermore, when referring to *Francovich* in *Wells*, the ECJ formulated it as a responsibility for the national authorities 'to undo harm caused'. These broad and general formulations indicate that state liability is not confined to providing economic compensation.

15 Chapter 3, section 7.3.

16 Chapter 3, sections 10–11.

17 Chapter 3, section 11.2.

Having summarized our findings in relation to the main elements in judicial proceedings, it is appropriate to consider some basic procedural restrictions to environmental proceedings.[18] Studies have shown that the most significant barriers to environmental litigation before national courts is in fact not lack of standing, limited judicial review, or inadequate remedies, but mundane rules on issues such as legal costs and time limits. Such rules are of course not specific to environmental cases, but in practice they often have a more restrictive impact in the environmental sector than in many other areas. Environmental plaintiffs, particularly individuals but also environmental organizations, cannot afford the same level of legal expenditure as commercial companies. There is also a lack of financial incentives in non-commercial environmental cases. Environmental plaintiffs are in addition often less professional than commercial actors, which means that they will have difficulty in responding to infringements and assembling the necessary material for law suits involving complex scientific evidence within short time limits. There is also the issue of delayed damages that do not become apparent within the time limits.

The ECJ has been sensitive to such concerns in principle, eg in the closely related field of consumer affairs, and has emphasized that whether a given restriction makes it 'excessively difficult' to enforce Community law in national courts must be assessed on a sector-by-sector basis.[19] The ECJ has demonstrated the effectiveness of this approach in relation to time limits, but the problem is that *Rewe* can only be applied with difficulty to detailed matters such as the appropriate level of legal costs. For such matters there is an urgent need for harmonization initiated by the Community legislature.

3 Private enforcement against Community institutions and bodies

The ECJ's approach to private enforcement at the Community level has been significantly different from its progressive case law on procedures and remedies in the national order of Member States. The avenue of direct actions before the ECJ has been severely restricted ever since in *Plaumann* it embraced the notoriously strict interpretation of individual concern under Article 230 EC.[20] This is quite ironic when compared to the stringent

[18] Chapter 3, section 4. [19] ibid. [20] Chapter 5, section 2.

demands the ECJ has imposed on the Member States' procedural law in the name of effective judicial protection and control. The requirement of individual concern serves to exclude most actions brought by private parties, but it is especially prohibitive in relation to environmental cases, as demonstrated by *Greenpeace*. Environmental directives normally protect public interests, and the measures will therefore not affect individuals' position 'by reason of certain attributes peculiar to them, or by reason of a factual situation which differentiates them from all other persons and distinguishes them individually in the same way as the addressee'. Environmental plaintiffs are therefore for practical purposes excluded from having recourse to judicial review under Articles 230 and 232 EC.

One might explain the discrepancy between the ECJ's progressive attitude to national law and its very conservative approach at the Community level by the fact that the wording of Article 230(4) EC simply prevented the ECJ from granting locus standi for public interest law suits. Commentators, Advocates General and the CFI have not proscribed this formalistic explanation, however, especially given the ECJ's record of applying teleological interpretation of other Treaty provisions. The underlying reason seems rather that the ECJ has felt that there is less need for private parties instigating judicial review of actions of the Community institutions than those of Member States. Another matter, to which we turn below, is that the preliminary reference procedure allows for some judicial relief in actions against Community institutions, so that arguably the requirement of a 'complete system of judicial control' is satisfied.

The ratification of the Aarhus Convention by the Community was set to change the prevailing situation in two ways:[21] first, by requiring public participation rights in decision-making which under the ECJ's case law would make the entities involved 'individually concerned' and, secondly, through stipulating access to justice rights. Regulation 1367/2006 on the application of the Aarhus Convention on Access to Information, Public Participation in Decision-making and Access to Justice in Environmental Matters to Community Institutions and Bodies[22] (Regulation 1367/2006 or the regulation) is flawed in the first regard, however, since contrary to Article 6 of the Aarhus Convention it does not confer any public participation rights in relation to decision-making at Community level. It does, on the other hand, grant access to justice by allowing certain entities to request Community institutions and bodies to conduct an internal review of acts or alleged omissions. The persons concerned will in turn obtain

[21] Chapter 5, sections 3–4. [22] [2006] OJ L264/13.

locus standi under Article 230 EC by having the written reply addressed to them, or under Article 232 EC in the event of a failure to reply.

There are nevertheless various significant shortcomings in Regulation 1367/2006 in this regard. The personal scope is restricted to environmental organizations fulfilling certain requirements, which means that individuals and ad hoc organizations are excluded. Furthermore, the scope of acts subject to internal review under the regulation appears very limited, which consequently restricts access to judicial control. The effectiveness of Regulation 1367/2006 therefore hinges in particular on how the ECJ will interpret the notion of acts of 'individual scope', bearing in mind that the ECJ is obliged to interpret this term in conformity with the Aarhus Convention.

The standing rights which Regulation 1367/2006 bestows on environmental organizations will allow plaintiffs to seek interim relief under Articles 242 and 243 EC, as well as reparation under Article 288(2) EC. However, the ECJ's stringent case law under Articles 242 and 243 EC as concerns urgency and the balance of convenience suggest that it will be difficult to obtain interim relief in practice, in particular if the ECJ also requires financial guarantees.[23] As for Community liability, it is noteworthy that the conditions applicable under Article 288(2) EC correspond to those laid down in relation to state liability. The discretion enjoyed by Community institutions in respect of the internal review is restricted in various ways, and it should therefore not necessarily be too onerous to fulfil the condition of sufficiently serious breach.[24] Furthermore, it should be recalled that the Community institutions are required to nullify unlawful consequences of an internal review decision which is annulled by the ECJ, and recourse to Article 288 EC will therefore in many cases not be necessary.

As was noted in relation to private enforcement at national level, there are procedural restrictions concerning time limits and legal costs which may significantly hamper the effectiveness of Regulation 1367/2006. The most prominent limitation is that plaintiffs only have six weeks to lodge requests for an internal review. This is less than the time afforded by Article 230(5) EC, which is arbitrary, most likely in conflict with Article 9(4) of the Aarhus Convention, and represents an example of dual standards in light of requirements imposed on national law in similar circumstances. If a failure to react within this time limit also excludes the possibility of preliminary rulings on the basis of an analogy with *Deggendorf*, Regulation 1367/2006 may actually undermine judicial control.[25]

[23] Chapter 5, section 5, cf chapter 4, section 4.6.

[24] Chapter 5, section 6.

[25] Chapter 4, section 4.3.

For all remaining cases which fall outside the personal, substantive, and temporal scope of Regulation 1367/2006, plaintiffs must seek recourse to national courts with a view to obtaining a preliminary reference on the validity of the disputed Community act.[26] The ECJ has claimed that this remedy ensures that there is a complete system of procedures and remedies for judicial control of the Community institutions, but this proposition is debatable. First of all, one might query the sincerity of this claim given that the plaintiff's right to have preliminary questions referred is conditional on the exercise of discretion by national courts. Furthermore, it is also the national court that decides what the relevant questions (grounds for review) are and the way in which these are phrased.

Having said that, it is noteworthy that, unlike preliminary questions concerning interpretation of Community law, all national courts are in principle obliged to refer questions to the ECJ where they entertain doubts of the legality of Community acts. However, national courts will often be reluctant to refer questions to the ECJ in light of the administrative burden and delay this involves. This situation is further exacerbated by the fact that the ECJ has laid down stringent conditions for interim relief against the Community institutions, the absence of which undermines the effectiveness of preliminary references. This may also partly explain why there are so few environmental references on issues of either validity or interpretation.[27]

In addition, there exist substantive gaps in the scope of Article 234 EC. For instance, national courts may not refer questions concerning failure to act since the wording of Article 234 EC relates to validity of 'acts', as opposed to 'omissions'.

One important way in which the preliminary reference procedure does complement Regulation 1367/2006 and Article 230 EC, however, is by providing for judicial review of general administrative acts as well as legislative acts. The effectiveness of the Article 234 EC procedure in this respect has been further boosted by the possibility of seeking declarations on the validity of such acts without the need to await national implementing measures. This has significantly reduced the time within which actions may be brought. Another matter is that it might not be possible under national law to challenge Community measures directly in the absence of any implementing measures, but *UPA* has now clarified that national courts must in any event as far as possible interpret national law so as to allow for such actions.[28]

[26] Chapter 4.4.

[27] See data in chapter 4, section 1.

[28] Chapter 4, section 4.3.

However, the ECJ will only conduct a minimum review of generally applicable acts where the Community institutions typically enjoy a wide margin of discretion. Although the ECJ has held that Community acts are susceptible to substantive review on the basis of the environmental standards and environmental principles laid down in the Treaty, it is questionable whether these norms are sufficiently precise and unconditional to allow for effective judicial review in practice.[29] It therefore seems that review of general administrative and legislative acts for practical purposes is mainly limited to a review of formal legality, eg for infringements of essential procedural requirements.

4 The Aarhus Convention

The dual standards employed by the ECJ in relation to rights and remedies at the national versus the Community level means that the level of compliance with the Aarhus Convention differs accordingly. The ECJ's effectiveness driven inroads into national procedural autonomy has had the consequence that Member States to a large extent are already subject to requirements comparable with – and in some aspects more stringent than – the Aarhus Convention. Even if the proposed Directive on Access to Justice in Environmental Matters (the proposed directive) should fail, the ECJ's case law should in most respects be adequate to ensure compliance with the Aarhus Convention on a national level (which is ironic, considering that several Member States oppose the proposed directive on the grounds that it allegedly falls within their remit of competence to ensure compliance with the Aarhus Convention on a national level).

The main benefit of the proposed directive implementing the Aarhus Convention, should it be adopted, therefore resides largely in its codification of existing procedural and remedial guarantees. More than the complex and inaccessible case law of the ECJ, this will serve to make environmental plaintiffs aware of their procedural and remedial rights, and bring increased legal certainty and transparency to this field of Community law.

The Aarhus Convention might also serve as a catalyst for more progressive case law in two departments. First, Article 9(3) of the Aarhus Convention places enforcement of environmental law against private parties on equal footing with actions against national authorities. This would of course not

[29] Chapter 5, section 4.

change the ECJ's view on horizontal direct effect, but it might sway it to review national restrictions on procedures and remedies for such enforcement more stringently than it has in the past. Secondly, it could be argued more generally that the requirement of 'adequate and effective remedies' laid down in Article 9(4) of the Aarhus Convention is more stringent than the minimum requirement in the second limb of *Rewe*, which as will be recalled is phrased negatively to the effect that national rules must not make the application of Community law 'excessively difficult or virtually impossible'.

The situation is quite different at the Community level, however. As noted above, there is hardly any possibility to obtain judicial relief directly before the ECJ in environmental matters under Articles 230 and 232 EC, while at the same time the preliminary reference procedure is not in all respects adequate to ensure a complete system of procedures and remedies notwithstanding claims by the ECJ to this effect.

But despite the adoption of Regulation 1367/2006 there remain doubts whether this will be sufficient to ensure full compliance with the Aarhus Convention. The first questionable issue stems from the fact that the Regulation excludes the public concerned from public participation rights on the Community level (and thus procedural rights which would have given them locus standi). Secondly, individuals do not have access to internal review and thus neither to judicial review, despite the fact that Article 9(3) of the Aarhus Convention clearly requires judicial relief for individuals as well as environmental organizations. Finally, Regulation 1367/2006 cannot, of course, amend the system of procedures and remedies that are provided by the Treaty, and in some respects it may be queried whether the Treaty provisions ensure 'adequate and effective remedies' as required by Article 9(4) of the Aarhus Convention. Some of these shortcomings are compensated for by the preliminary reference procedure, eg the conditions for standing for individuals, but others are not, eg the conditions for interim relief.[30] It is also justified to query whether the preliminary reference procedure in any event fulfils the condition of a 'timely remedy' as required by Article 9(4) of the Aarhus Convention.

[30] The rules on standing in national courts fall within the remit of the court's progressive judicial protection and control doctrine, whereas the conditions for interim relief against acts by the Community institutions are the same in preliminary references as in actions brought directly before the ECJ; see chapter 4, section 4.7.

5 Recommendations

Implicit recommendations on various issues have already been articulated in the sections above, and it suffices here to point out the main issues which should be addressed.

Our findings indicate that the enforcement deficit in relation to EC environmental law on the national level, perhaps surprisingly, resides not so much in inadequate procedures and remedies, but has its origin in the form, drafting, and substance of environmental legislation. For purposes of horizontal enforcement it would be beneficial if regulations were to be more widely used. For the sake of vertical enforcement it is important that the obligations of result, if not the forms and methods for attaining those results, are clearly and unconditionally defined. It is inconsistent for the ECJ to go to great lengths to equip private plaintiffs with the necessary judicial tools for enforcing environmental legislation, and at the same time for the Community legislature increasingly to sponsor environmental legislation that lends itself to enforcement only with great difficulty. It should be added that this enforcement deficit hampers not only private enforcement, but also the Commission's enforcement under Articles 226 and 228 EC, which adds to the oddity of the situation considering the significant Community resources employed in this respect.

The time seems ripe, therefore, for a thorough analysis and debate at Community level regarding the real benefits of 'efficient legislation', in the shape of increased levels of flexibility and differentiation, if the costs in the form of the resulting enforcement deficits are taken into account.[31] In view of persisting deficiencies in terms of implementation and application of EC environmental law – which is not likely to improve following recent enlargement – it is my view that the Community needs to adopt environmental legislation that accommodates effective enforcement as a discrete value to a much higher degree than currently is the case.

As for impediments that remain in terms of judicial means for enforcement of environmental law in national courts, focus should now be shifted from basic procedural and remedial elements governing private enforcement, eg standing, direct effect, judicial review, and remedies, to restrictions stemming from the practical realities of bringing environmental actions. The most important issues that should be tackled are prohibitive time limits, legal costs – including

[31] Chapter 2, section 2.2.6.

cross-undertakings for interim relief – and the duration of preliminary references. The compatibility of time limits may be tackled by the ECJ, the legitimate level of costs ought to be harmonized through secondary legislation, and the structural impediments concerning the Article 234 EC procedure probably presupposes institutional reform.

For actions against Community institutions and bodies, however, there is still a need for significant improvement of the judicial tools for enforcing environmental law. The most obvious recommendation is that the ECJ ought to abandon its narrow interpretation of the standing requirements under Article 230 EC, but any such hopes have been dashed after the ECJ held in *UPA* that any liberalization must be effected through amendment of the Treaty. The amendment introduced in Article III–365 of the Treaty Establishing a Constitution for Europe is minor, and is not likely significantly to improve access to justice in environmental matters. Another matter is that the future of the Constitutional Treaty looks bleak. The only realistic recommendation is therefore to urge the ECJ to interpret Regulation 1367/2006 in conformity with the Aarhus Convention, in particular as concerns the scope of acts susceptible to review.

As for the functioning of the Article 234 EC procedure in relation to review of Community acts, the need for institutional reform so as to expedite proceedings is also relevant in this context. This requires changes in the workings of the ECJ, and could involve the establishment of environmental panels.[32] The ECJ should also address other deficiencies, for instance by allowing for interpretations on obligations to act (and thus accommodate indirect review of failures to act), and by liberalizing the onerous conditions for interim relief in order to make this an effective remedy in environmental cases.

6 Final conclusion

This study has shown that environmental law is not fundamentally different from other areas of Community law in terms of rights and remedies. The ECJ has formulated a wide notion of (procedural) rights which to a large degree affords environmental plaintiffs similar access to remedies in national

[32] See analysis in Krämer 2003b, 87–88; and, on the national level, Lord Justice Carnwath 2004, 326–27.

courts as plaintiffs in traditional rights-oriented sectors. The main reason for this environmentally progressive case law stems from the fact that the ECJ has been less preoccupied with protection of subjective rights than with promoting the effectiveness of Community law, and in this perspective all sectors of EC law are equal. This, in my view, is the correct approach since the ECJ's jurisdiction, as will be recalled from Article 220(1) EC, is not limited to protecting individuals' rights (in the narrow sense), but to ensure that 'in the application of this Treaty the law is observed'. At the same time, in the design and the application of some of these remedies the ECJ has taken into account practical and factual differences between various sectors of EC law in order to ensure effective enforcement in practice, eg in its application of the *Rewe* doctrine. However, in relation to enforcement in actions directly before the ECJ, it has defined a notion of rights, in the shape of individual and direct concern, which in practice discriminates against environmental plaintiffs.[33] The dichotomy between judicial control of the Member States and the Community institutions is partly as a result of divergent views on how the two actions promote the effectiveness of EC law, and partly to different discretionary powers for the ECJ to craft the appropriate tools.[34] However, the difference is to some extent alleviated through the preliminary reference procedure, and will become less pronounced following the entry into force of Regulation 1367/2006.

Some academics have criticized the ECJ's case law, arguing that it should have differentiated between various sectors of EC law in its harmonization of national procedures and remedies:

> In some sectors, (such as state aid and competition law), uniformity remains a valid goal of Treaty policy, and the harmonisation of domestic remedies and procedural rules might well be justified. In other sectors (such as environmental, consumer and employee protection), the Treaty does not appear to harbour ambitions of achieving any genuine degree of regulatory uniformity, and the principles of subsidiarity and proportionality suggests we should adopt a correspondingly more restrained interpretation of the need for remedial approximation.[35]

What proponents of such views tend to overlook is that uniformity is not the only relevant aim underpinning harmonization of procedures and remedies. At least as important is the effectiveness of EC law. The fact that the Treaty

[33] See the ECJ's brief dismissal of the principle of 'equity of arms' in T–94/04 *EEB and Others v Commission* [2005] ECR II–4919, para 65.

[34] Cf Article 10 EC with the precise procedural and remedial rules in Articles 230 EC et seq.

[35] Dougan 2005, 390.

and the Community legislature in general afford more substantive discretion to Member States (and the Community institutions, for that matter) in environmental law compared with state aid and competition does not imply that private parties should not have similar opportunities effectively to police the exercise of discretion – regardless of how narrowly or broadly those boundaries are drawn. This fact has thankfully not been lost on the ECJ, and one may only hope that it continues in its stride and will not surrender to voices suggesting a decline of rights and remedies in fields such as EC environmental law. As noted by former Advocate General Jacobs:

> [T]he Court has performed a difficult task, if not always coherent, nevertheless imaginatively, boldly and with broadly satisfactory results . . . [T]he Court's case law is exceptionally and perhaps uniquely effective in terms of enforcement.[36]

Hence, it remains for environmental plaintiffs to take advantage of the judicial means made available by Community law, and assist in protecting the European environment.

[36] Jacobs 2006, 205.

BIBLIOGRAPHY

Alberts-Llorens, A. (1998) Case Commentary 35 CMLRev 227

Apter, S. (2003) Interim Measures in EC Law: Towards a Complete and Autonomous System of Provisional Judicial Protection Before National Courts? EJCL Vol 7.2

Arnull, A. (1997) 'Rights and Remedies: Restraint or Activism?' in Lonbay, J. and Biondi, A. (eds) *Remedies for Breach of EC Law* (Wiley & Sons)

Arnull, A. (2000) *The European Union and Its Court of Justice* (Oxford University Press)

Arnull, A. (2001) Private Applicants and the Action for Annulment Since *Codorniu* 38 CMLRev 7

Arnull, A. (2002) 1995–2002 Plus Ça Change 27 ELR 509

Barav, A. (1997) 'State Liability in Damages for Breaches of Community Law in National Courts' in Heukels, T. and McDonnel, A. (eds) *The Action for Damages in Community Law* (Kluwer Law) 363

Barbier de la Serre, E. (2006) 'Accelarated and expedited procedures before the EC courts: A review of the practice' 43 CMLR 783

Bebr, G. (1983) 'The Rambling Ghost of "Cohn-Bendit": Acte clair and the Court of Justice' 20 CMLRev 439

Bebr, G. (1996) Case Commentary 33 CMLRev 795

Bengoetxea, J., MacCormick, N., and Moral Soriano, L. (2001) 'Integration and Integrity in the Legal Reasoning of the European Court of Justice' in de Búrca, G. and Weiler, J. (eds) *The European Court of Justice* (Oxford University Press) 43

Bergkamp, L. (2001) *Liability and the Environment – Private and Public Law Aspects of Civil Liability for Environmental Harms in an International Context* (Kluwer Law)

Bergkamp, L. (2004) Case Commentary 4 EL 171

Bergkamp, L. (2005) 'The European Environmental Liability Directive and its Effects on Industry and the Economy' in Mellenberg, R. and Uylenburg, R. (eds) *Aansprakelijkheid voor schade aan de natuur* (Europa Law Publishing) 95

Besselink, L. (2004) Case Commentary 41 CMLRev 1429

Betlem, G. (2002) 'The Doctrine of Consistent Interpretation – Managing Legal Uncertainty' in Prinssen, J. and Schrauwen, A. (eds) *Direct Effect – Rethinking a Classic of EC Legal Doctrine* (Europa Law Publishing) 79

Betlem, G. and Nollkaemper, A. (2003) 'Giving Effect to Public International Law and European Community Law Before Domstic Courts. A Comparative Analysis of the Practice of Consistent Interpretation' 14 EJIL 569

Biondi, A. (2003) '2001 in Luxembourg: Recent Developments in the Case law of the Community Courts' 9 EPL 39

Biondi, A. (2003a) Case Commentary 40 CMLRev 1241

Biondi, A. (2005) 'The Rule of Reason and National Procedural Limitations: Is it Really Reasonable?' in Schrauwen, A. (ed) *Rule of Reason – Rethinking Another Classic of European Legal Doctrine* (Europa Law Publishing) 131

de Búrca, G. and Ryall, A. (2002) 'The ECJ and Judicial Review of National Administrative Procedure in the field of EIA' in Ladeur, K.-H. (ed) *The Europeanization of Administrative Law* (Ashgate/Dartmouth)159

Burnett-Hall, R. (1995) 'The Enforcement of EC Directives against Suppliers of Public Services' EELR 42

Buxton, R. (2002) 'Third Party Challenges – An Individual's Perspective' JPEL 47

Cabral, P. (2006) 'Access to Member State Documents in EC Law' 31 ELR 378

Cane, P. (2004) *Administrative Law* (Oxford University Press)

Caranta, R. (1995) 'Judical Protection Against Member States: A New *Jus Commune* Takes Shape' 32 CMLRev 703

Carnwath, R. (2004) 'Judicial Protection of the Environment: at Home and Abroad' 16 JEL 315

Coppel, J. (1994) 'Rights, Duties and the End of Marshall' 57 MLR 859

Craig, P. (1997) 'Directives: Direct Effect, Indirect Effect and the Construction of National Legislation' 22 ELR 519

Craig, P. (2003) 'Standing, Rights and the Structure of Legal Argument' 9 EPL 493

Craig, P. (2006) *EU Administrative Law* (Oxford University Press)

Craig, P. and de Búrca, G. (2003) *EU Law* (Oxford University Press)

Craufurd Smith (1999) 'Remedies for Breaches of EU Law in National Courts: Legal Variation and Selection' in Craig, P. and de Búrca, G. (eds) *The Evolution of EU Law* (Oxford University Press) 287

Davies, P.G.G. (2004) *European Union Environmental Law* (Ashgate)

Dhondt, N. (2003) *Integration of Environmental Policies into Other EC Policies* (Europa Law Publishing)

Doyle, A. and Carney, T. (1999) 'Precaution and Prevention: Giving effect to Article 130r Without Direct Effect' 8 EELR 44

Doppelhammer, M. (2000) 'More Difficult than Finding the Way Round Chinatown? The IPPC Directive and its Implementation' 9 EELR 199
Dougan, M. (2000) 'The Francovich Right to Reparation: Reshaping the Contours of Community Remedial Competence' 6 EPL 103
Dougan, M. (2000a) 'The "Disguised" Vertical Direct Effect of Directives' CLJ 586
Dougan, M. (2003) Case Commentary 40 CMLRev 193
Dougan, M. (2005) *National Remedies Before the Court of Justice* (Hart Publishing)
Driessen, B. (2006) 'Access to Member State Documents in EC Law: a comment' 13 ELR 906
Dross (2005) 'Access to Justice in the EU Member States' 2 JEEPL 22
Ebbesson, J. (ed) (2002) *Access to Justice in Environmental Matters in the EU* (Kluwer Law)
Edward, D. (1997) 'Foreword' in Holder, J. (ed) *The Impact of EC Environmental Law in the United Kingdom* (Wiley & Sons)
Edward, D. (1998) 'Direct Effect, the Separation of Powers and the Judicial Enforcement of Obligations' in *Scritti in onore di Giuseppe Federico Mancini, II, Diritto dell Unione Europea* (Guiffré) Vol II, 423
Edward, D. (2000) 'Reform of Article 234 Procedure: The Limits of the Possible' in O'Keeffe, D. and Bavasso, A. (eds) *Judicial Review in European Union Law, Liber Amoricum in Honour of Lord Slynn of Hadley*, 119
Edward, D. (2002) 'Direct Effect: myth, mess or mystery?' in Prinssen, J. and Schrauwen, A. (eds) *Direct Effect – Rethinking a Classic of EC Legal Doctrine* (Europa Law Publishing) 3
Eilmansberger, T. (2004) 'The Relationship Between Rights and Remedies in EC Law: In Search of the Missing Link' 41 CMLRev 1199
Epiney, A. (2005) 'Environmental Principles' in Macrory, R. (ed) *Reflections on 30 Years of EU Environmental Law – A High Level of Protection?* (Europa Law Publishing) 19
European Environment Agency (2006) 'The European Environment – State and Outlook 2005' Executive Summary
Faure, M. (2005) 'De Europese Richtlijn Milieuaansprakelijkheid: kritische inledende bedenkingen' in Mellenberg, R. and Uylenburg, R. (eds) *Aansprakelijkheid voor schade aan de natuur* (Europa Law Publishing) 3
Geddes, A. (1992) 'Locus Standi and EEC Environmental Measures' 4 JEL 29
van Gerven, W. (1995) 'Bridging the Gap Between Community and National Laws: Towards a Principle of Homogeneity in the Fields of Legal Remedies?' 32 CMLRev 679

van Gerven, W. (1998) *Cases, Materials and Texts on National, Supranational and International Tort Law: Scope of Protection* (Hart Publishing)

van Gerven, W. (2000) 'Of Rights, Remedies and Procedures' 37 CMLRev 501

van Gerven, W. (2004) 'Remedies for Infringements of Fundamental Rights' 10 EPL 261

Grimeaud, D. (2001) 'Reforming EU Water Law: Towards Sustainability' 10 EELR 41–51, 88–97, 125–135

Hardcastle, I. (1994) 'Interim Measures in Proceedings Concerning EC Law: New Departures' 5 EBLR 95

Harlow, C (2002) 'Proceduralism in English Law' in Ladeur, K.-H. (ed) *The Europeanisation of Administrative Law, Transforming National Decision-making Procedures* (Aldershot: Ashgate/Dartmouth)

Hartley, T.C. (2003) *The Foundations of European Community Law* (Oxford University Press)

Harwood, A. (2004) 'EIA, Development Consent and Duties on the Member State' 16 JEL 269

Hattan, E. (2003) 'Implementation of EU Environmental Law' 15 JEL 273

Hedemann-Robinson, M. (2006) 'Article 228(2) EC and the Enforcement of EC Environmental Law: A Case of Environmental Justice Delayed and Denied? An Analysis of Recent Legal Developments' 15 EELR 312

Heukels, T. and Tib, J. (2000) 'Towards Homogeneity in the Field of Legal Remedies: Convergence and Divergence' in Beaumont, P., Lyons, C., and Walker, N. (eds) *Convergence and Divergence in European Public Law* (Hart Publishing) 111.

Hilson, C. (1997) 'Community Rights in Environmental Law: Rhetoric or Reality?' in Holder, J. (ed) *The Impact of EC Environmental Law in the United Kingdom* (Wiley & Sons) 51

Hilson, C. and Downes, T. (1999) 'Making Sense of Rights: Community Rights in EC Law' 24 CMLRev 121

IMPEL Network (2000) Complaint Procedures and Access to Justice for Citizens and NGOs in the field of the environment within the European Union

Jacobs, F.G. (1997) 'Enforcing Community Rights and Obligations in National Courts: Striking the Balance' in Lonbay, J. and Biondi, A. (eds) *Remedies for Breach of EC Law* (Chichester: John Wiley & Sons) 25

Jacobs, F.G. (2001) 'Some Remarks on Community and Member State Liability' in Wouters, J. and Stuyck, J. (eds) *Principles of Proper Conduct for Supranational, State and Private Actors in the European Union: Towards a Ius Commune* (Intersentia Publishing)

Jacobs, F.G. (2004) 'The Evolution of the European Legal Order' 41 CMLRev 303

Jacobs, F.G. (2006) 'The Role of the European Court of Justice in the Protection of the Environment' 18 JEL 185

Jans, J.H. (2000) *European Environmental Law* (Europa Law Publishing)

Jans, J.H. (2000a) 'Proportionality Revisited' 27 LIEI 239

Jans, J.H. and de Jong, M. (2002) 'Between Direct Effect and Rewe/Comet: Remarks on Dutch Administrative Law, Procedural Defects and the EIA Directive' in Ladeur, K-H. (ed) *The Europeanization of Administrative Law*, 68

Jans, J.H. and Prinssen, J. (2002) 'Direct Effect: Convergence or Divergence? A Comparative Perspective' in Prinssen, J. and Schrauwen, A. (eds) *Direct Effect – Rethinking a Classic of EC Legal Doctrine* (Europa Law Publishing) 107

Jans, J.H. (2005) 'Did Baron von Munchhausen ever visit Aarhus? Some Critical Remarks on the Proposal for a Regulation on the Application of the Provisions of the Aarhus Convention to EC Institutions and Bodies' in Macrory, R. (ed) *Reflections on 30 Years of EU Environmental Law – A High Level of Protection?* (Europa Law Publishing) 475

Jans, J.H. (2005a) *Doorgeschoten? Enkele opmerkingen over de gevolgen van de Europeanisering va het bestuursrechts voor de grondslagen va de bestuursrechtspraak* (Europa Law Publishing)

Jans, J.H., de Lange, R., Prechal, S., and Widdershoven, R.J.G.M. (2006) *Europeanisation of Public Law* (Europa Law Publishing)

Janssen, J. (2004) Case Report 13 EELR 130.

Jendroska, J. (2005) 'Aarhus Convention and Community Law: the Interplay' 2 JEEPL 12

Kakouris, C.N. (1997) 'Do the Member States possess judicial procedural "*autonomy*"?' 34 CMLRev 1389

Kapteyn, P.J.G. and VerLoren van Themaat, (1998) *Introduction to the Law of the European Communities: From Maastricht to Amsterdam* (Deventer: Kluwer)

Krämer, L. (1996) 'Differentiation in EU Environmental Policy' 5 EELR 133

Krämer, L. (1996) 'Direct Effect of EC Environmental Law' in Somsen, H. (ed) *Protecting the European Environment: Enforcing EC Environmental Law* (Blackstone Press) 99

Krämer, L. (2000) 'Differentiation in EU Environmental Policy' 9 EELR 133

Krämer, L. (2002) *Casebook on EU Environmental Law* (Hart Publishing)

Krämer, L. (2002a) 'Liability For Damage to the Environment and the European Union' in *Approximation: The Never Ending Story* (Published by Institute of Environmental Policy, Prague)

Krämer, L. (2002b) 'Thirty Years of Environmental Law: Perspectives and Prospectives' 2 YEEL 155

Krämer, L. (2003) *EC Environmental Law* (Sweet & Maxwell)

Krämer, L. (2003a) 'The Future Role of the ECJ in the Development of European Environmental Law' in Jans, J.H. (ed) *The European Convention and the Future of European Environmental Law* (Europa Law Publishing) 85

Krämer, L. (2003b) 'Access to Letters of Formal Notice and Reasoned Opinions in Environmental Law Matters' 12 EELR 197

Krämer, L. (2004) 'Data on Environmental Judgments by the EC Court of Justice' 1 JEEPL 127

Krämer, L. (2006) 'Thirty Years of Environmental Governance in the European Union' in Macrory, R. (ed) *Reflections on 30 Years of EU Environmental Law – A High Level of Protection?* (Europa Law Publishing) 555

Krämer, L. (2006a) 'Environment, Crime and EC Law' 18 JEL 277.

Krämer, L. (2006b) 'Statistics on Environmental Judgments by the EC Court of Justice' 18 JEL 407

Kumm, M. (1999) 'Who is the Final Arbiter of Constitutionality in Europe?' 36 CMLRev

Ladeur, K.-H. (ed) *The Europeanisation of Administrative Law, Transforming National Decision-making Procedures* (Aldershot: Ashgate/Dartmouth)

Lang, J.T. (2000) 'The Principle of Effective Protection of Community Law Rights' in O'Keefe (ed) *Liber Amoricum Slynn* (Kluwer Law International) 235

Lang, J.T. (2003) 'Actions For Declarations That Community Regulations Are Invalid: The Duties of National Courts under Article 10 EC' 28 ELR 102

Lang, J.T. (2004) 'Declarations, regional authorities, subsidarity, regional policy measures and the Constitutional Treaty' 29 ELR 94

Lee, M. (2005) *EU Environmental Law* (Hart Publishing)

Lenaerts, K. and Arts, D. (1999) *Procedural Law of the European Union* (Sweet & Maxwell)

Lenaerts, L. and Corthaut, T. (2006) 'Of birds and hedges: the role of primacy in invoking norms of EU law' 31 ELR 287

Lenz, M., Tynes, D.S., and Young, L. (2000) 'Horizontal What? Back to Basics' 25 ELR 509

Macrory, R. (2004) 'Principles of Judicial Review on Environmental Assessment' 16 JEL 285

Macrory, R. (2006) 'The Enforcement of EU Environmental Law; Some Proposals for Reform' in Macrory, R. (ed) *Reflections on 30 Years of EU*

Environmental Law – A High Level of Protection? (Europa Law Publishing) 385

Mancini, G.F. and Keeling, D.T. (1991) 'From *Cilfit* to *ERT*: the Constitutional Challenge Facing the European Court' 11 YEL 1

Mastroianni, R. (1999) 'On the Distinction Between Vertical and Horizontal Direct Effects of Community Directives: What Role for the Principle of Equality?' 5 EPL 417

Murgatroyd, S. (1993) 'State Liability and the European Environment: Francovich, Maastricht and the Question of Compensation' 1 EL

Nash, M. (1997) 'Remedies for Breach of EC Environmental Law in UK Courts' in Lonbay, J. and Biondi, A. (eds) *Remedies for Breach of EC Law* (Chichester: John Wiley & Sons) 117

Oliver, P. (1992) 'Interim Measures: Some Recent Developments' 29 CMLRev 7

Oliver, P. (1997) Case Commentary 34 CMLRev 635

Oliver, P. (1998) 'State Liability in Damages following Factortame III' in Beatson, J. and Tridimas, T. (eds) *New Directions in European Public Law* (Hart Publishing)

Onida, M. (ed) (2004) *Europe and the Environment – Legal Essays in Honour of Ludwig Krämer* (Europa Law Publishing)

Pagh, P. (2006) 'The Battle on Environmental Policy Competences; Challenging the Stricter Approach: Stricter Might Lead to Weaker Protection', J. in Macrory, R. (ed) *Reflections on 30 years of EU Environmental Law* (Europa Law Publishing) 1

Papadias, L. (1994) 'Interim Protection under Community Law before National Courts: The Right for a Judge with Jurisdiction to Grant Interim Relief' LIEI 153

Peers, S. (1998) 'Taking Supremacy Seriously' 23 ELR 146

Pescatore, P. (1983) 'The Doctrine of Direct Effect: An Infant Disease of Community Law' ELR 155

Prechal, S. (1995) *Directives in European Community Law* (Oxford University Press)

Prechal, S. (1998) 'Community Law in National Courts: The Lessons From Van Schijndel' 35 CMLRev 681

Prechal, S. (2000) 'Does Direct Effect Still Matter?' 42 CMLRev 1445

Prechal, S. (2001) 'Judge-made harmonisation of national procedural rules: a bridging perspective' in Wouter, J. and Stuyck, J. (eds) *Principles of Proper Conduct for Supranational, State and Private Actors in the European Union: Towards a Ius Commune* (Intersentia) 40

Prechal, S. (2002) 'Direct Effect Reconsidered, Redefined and Rejected' in Prinssen, J. and Schrauwen, A. (eds) *Direct Effect – Rethinking a Classic of EC Legal Doctrine* (Europa Law Publishing) 17

Prechal, S. (2005) *Directives in European Community Law* (Oxford University Press)

Prechal, S. (2005a) 'Commentary on Case C–397/01 *Pfeiffer*' 42 CMLRev 1445

Prechal, S. and Hancher, L. (2002) 'Individual Environmental Rights: Conceptual Pollution in EU Environmental Law' 2 YEEL 89

Prieur, M. (1998) 'Complaints and Appeals in the Area of Environment in the Member States of the European Union' (European Environmental Law Council, Study for the Commission of the European Community, DG XI)

Rasmussen, H. (1984) 'The European Court's Acte Clair Strategy in *Cilfit* (Or: Acte Clair, of course! But What does it Mean?)' ELR 342

Rasmussen, H. (1998) *The European Court of Justice* (Gadjura)

Ruffert, M. (1997) 'Rights and Remedies in European Community Law: A Comparative View' 22 CMLRev 316

de Sadeleer, N. (2002) *Environmental Principles: From Slogans to Legal Rules* (Oxford University Press)

de Sadeleer, N. (2003) 'Procedures for Derogations From the Principle of Approximation of Laws under Article 95 EC' 40 CMLRev 889

de Sadeleer, N., Roller, G., and Dross, M. (eds) (2005) *Access to Justice in Environmental Matters and the Role of NGOs* (Europa Law Publishing)

Schermers, H. (1997) 'No Direct Effect for Directives' 3 EPL 527

Schermers, H. and Waelbroeck, D. (2001) *Judicial Protection in the European Union* (Kluwer Law International)

Schrauwen, A. (2005) Case Commentary 42 CMLRev 851

Scott, J. (1998) *EC Environmental Law* (Longman)

Scott, J. (2000) 'Flexibility in the Implementation of EC Environmental Law' 1 YEEL 37

Sebba, I. (1995) 'The Doctrine of "Direct Effect": A Malignant Disease of Community Law' LIEI 35

Sevenster, H.G. (2000) 'The Environmental Guarantees After Amsterdam: Does the Emperor Have New Clothes?' 1 YEEL 291

Sharpston, E. (1993) *Interim and Substantive Relief in Claims under Community Law* (London: Butterworths)

Sharpston, E. (1997) 'Interim relief in the National Courts' in Lonbay, J. and Biondi, A. (eds) *Remedies for Breach of EC Law* (Chichester: John Wiley Sons)

Shockweiler, F.A. (1992) 'La Responsiblité de l'Autorité Nationale en Cas de Violation du Droit Communautaire' 28 Revue Trimestrielle de Droit Européen 44

de la Sierra, S. (2004) 'Provisional Court Protection in Administrative Disputes in Europe: The Constitutional Status of Interim Measures Deriving from the Right to Effective Court Protection. A Comparative Approach' 10 ELJ 42

Somsen, H. (1996) 'Francovich and Its Application to EC Environmental Law' in Somsen, H. (ed) *Protecting the European Environment: Enforcing EC Environmental Law* (Blackstone Publishing) 135

Somsen, H. (1998) 'Dynamics, Process and Instruments of Environmental Decision-making in the European Union' in Jewell, T. and Steele, J. (eds) *Law in Environmental Decision-making* (Oxford University Press) 190

Somsen, H. (2000) 'The Private Enforcement of Member State Compliance with EC Environmental Law: an Unfulfilled Promise?' 1 YEEL 311

Somsen, H. (2002) 'Discretion in European Community Environmental Law: An Analysis of the ECJ Case Law' 40 CMLRev 1413

Somsen, H. (2003) 'Current Issues of Implementation, Application and Enforcement of EC Environmental Law; A Critical Analysis' in Krämer, L. (ed) *Recht um Undwelt: Essays in Honor of Prof Dr Gerd Winter* (Europa Law Publishing) 415

St Clair Bradley, K. (1999) 'Institutional Aspects of Comitology: Scenes from the Cutting Room Floor' in Joerges, C. and Vos, E. (eds) *EU Committees: Social Regulation, Law and Politics* (Hart Publishing) 71

Steiner, J. and Woods, L. (2000) *Textbook on EC Law* (Blackstone Press Limited)

Timmermanns, C.W.A. (1979) 'Directives: Their Effect Within the National Legal Systems' CMLRev 533

Timmermans, C.W.A. (1998) 'Community Directives Revisited' YEL 1

Toth, A.G. (1990) Case Commentary 27 CMLRev 573

Tridimas, T. (1994) 'Horizontal Effect of Directives: A Missed Opportunity?' 19 ELR 621

Tridimas, T. (1999) *The General Principles of EC Law* (Oxford University Press)

Tridimas, T. (2001) 'Liability for Breach of Community Law: growing up and mellowing down?' 38 CMLRev 301

Tromans, S. (1996) 'EC Environmental Law and the Practising Lawyer' in Somsen, H. (ed) *Protecting the European Environment: Enforcing EC Environmental Law* (Blackstone) 265

Vandamme, T. (2005) *The Invalid Directive; The Legal Authority of a Union Act Requiring Domestic Law Making* (Europa Law Publishing)

Vershuuren, J. (2005) 'Shellfish for Fishermen or for Birds? Article 6 Habitats Directive and the Precautionary Principle' 17 JEL 265

Vos, E. (1999) 'EU Committees: The Evolution of Unforeseen Institutional Actors in European Product Regulation' in Joerges, C. and Vos, E. (eds) *EU Committees: Social Regulation, Law and Politics* (Hart Publishing) 19

Waelbroeck, D. (1997) 'Treaty Violations and Liability of Member States: The Effect of the Francovich Case Law' in Heukels, T. and McDonnel, A. (eds) *The Action for Damages in Community Law* (Kluwer Law International) 311

Ward, A. (2000a) *Judicial Review and the Rights of Private Parties in EC Law* (Oxford University Press)

Ward, A. (2000b) 'Judicial Review of Environmental Misconduct in the European Community: Problems, Prospects and Strategies' 1 YEEL 137

Ward, A. (2004) 'Locus Standi under Article 230(4) EC of the EC Treaty: Crafting a Coherent Test for a "Wobbly Polity" ' 22 YEL 45

Wates, J. (2005) 'The Aarhus Convention: a Driving Force for Environmental Democracy' 2 JEEPL 2

Wattel, P.J. (2004) 'Köbler, CILFIT and Welthgrove: We Can't Go On Meeting Like This' 41 CMLRev 177

Wennerås, P.E. (2003) 'Fog and Acid Rain Drifting from Luxembourg over Art. 95(4) EC' 12 EELR 169

Wennerås, P.E. (2004) 'State Liability for Decisions of Courts of Last Instance in Environmental Cases' 16 JEL 329

Wennerås, P.E. (2005) 'A Progressive Interpretation of the Environmental Liability Directive' 4 JEEPL 257

Wennerås, P.E. (2005a) 'Permit Defences in Environmental Liability Regimes: Subsidising Environmental Damage in the EC?' 4 YEEL 149

Wennerås, P.E. (2006) 'A New Dawn for Commission Enforcement Under Articles 226 and 228 EC: General and Persistent Infringement (GAP) Cases, Lump Sums and Penalty Payments' 43 CMLRev 31

Williams, R. (1995) 'The European Commission and the Enforcement of Environmental Law: an Invidious Position' 14 YEL 351

Williams, R. (2002) 'Enforcing European Environmental Law: Can the European Commission be Held to Account?' 2 YEEL 271

Winter, J. A. (1972) 'Direct Applicability and Direct Effect: Two Distinct and Different Concepts in Community Law' 9 CMLRev 425

Winter, G. (2003) 'Environmental Principles in Community Law' in Jans, J.H. (ed) *The European Convention and the Future of European Environmental Law* (Europa Law Publishing)

de Witte, B. (1991) 'Community Law and National Constitutional Values' 2 LIEI

de Witte, B. (1999) 'Direct Effect, Supremacy and the Nature of the Legal Order' in Craig, P. and de Búrca, G. (eds) *The Evolution of EU Law* (Oxford University Press) 179

Wyatt, D. (1998) 'Litigating Community Environmental Law – Thoughts on the Direct Effect Doctrine' 10 JEL 9

Wyatt, D. and Dashwood, A. (2000) *European Union Law* (Sweet & Maxwell)

Zuleeg, M. (1992) 'Umweltschutz in der Rechtsprechung des Europäschen Gerichtshofs' 46 Neue Juristische Wochenschrift 31

INDEX

Aarhus convention
  access to information 90–1, 117–18
  access to justice 90–1, 100–1, 107–8, 137, 183–4, 215–7, 224–8, 230–2, 234–5, 237
  general 5, 75, 90–2
  public participation 91, 123–4, 224–6, 299
  shortcomings 170, 317–18, 320–321
access to information
  Community level 177, 241
  infringement proceedings 296–9
  national level 117–18, 129–30
access to justice, *see* interest and standing
acte clair 164, 166, 175, 249
acte éclairé 163, 174
actio popularis 108, 114
acquis communautaire 2, 44, 213, 312
administrative appeal boards 173
admissibility 81, 106, 174–6, 187–8, 244, 256–7
agriculture 192, 201, 233
air 43, 144–6
Amsterdam Treaty 9, 192

best available techniques (BAT) 43, 314
birds 33–4, 36–7, 39 143, 229

Charter of Fundamental Rights 5, 80–1, 87
Commission enforcement Article EC 226
  consequences 259–60
  development 2, 262–74
  discretion 300–1
  duration 291–3
  see General and Persistent (GAP)
  grounds of review 259
  horizontal enforcement 302–4
  independence 293–5
  interim relief 260–2
  judicial stage 256–261
  monitoring 253–6
  pre-judicial stage 256
  procedural requirements 256–7
  rights of private parties 295–302
  role of private enforcement 304–8
  subject matter 258–9
Commission enforcement Article 228 EC
  discretion 275–7
  legal framework 275–7
  lump sum 286–90
  penalty payment 277–85
compensation, *see* damage
comitology 196, 240, 303
competition 3, 12, 27, 94–5, 119, 148, 193, 216, 231, 307, 324–5
consistent interpretation
  Aarhus convention 92, 235, 323
  added value 57
  basis 56
  Contra legem 63–6
  criminal law 66–7
  horizontal application 63–68
  non-binding acts 58
  substantive application 57–60
  temporal application 60–63
consumer law 95–6, 98, 101, 151, 233, 316
contaminated land 1, 70–1, 144, 148
contra legem 63–6
cost-benefit analysis 43, 196, 200, 322
costs
  general 100–2, 316, 322–3
  interim relief 103–4, 211, 323
criminal law 58, 66–7, 167–8, 170, 179, 191–2
cross-guarantees 103–4, 211, 323; *see also* costs and interim relief

damage, *see also* liability
  ecological/environmental 98, 141–3, 149, 152, 155–6, 203, 208, 246–7, 265
  economic/pecuniary 155–6, 220, 315
  punitive/exemplary 149, 157, 212
declaratory relief 134, 136–7, 143–4, 187–8, 202, 243, 259, 301
defences
  permit 199, 206
  practical impossibility 39, 42, 129, 279
  state of the art 206
designation of protection areas 33–4, 39, 105, 255, 263
deterrence
  costs 96, 102
  infringement proceedings 2, 214, 228, 268–9, 271, 273

deterrence (*cont.*):
liability 156, 159, 169–70
lump sum 286, 288–9
penalty payment 286
preliminary references 212, 214
sanctions 82, 87
direct and individual concern 217–26; *see also* standing
direct applicability 15, 25–6, 54, 118, 187–8, 222, 229
direct effect
conditions 25–44
estoppel 16, 35, 37, 45
exclusion 51–4, 65, 67
genuine discretion 33, 36, 59
horizontal 44–55
implemented rules 28, 119, 142, 148
incidental horizontal 49–55
indefinite legal concepts 33
interest 21–5
inverse vertical 48–9
notion 27–30
objectives 40–2, 143–4, 313–4
precautionary 31
raison d'être 15–16
reparation 141–9, 315
results 27, 32
retroactive 141
rights 15–25
substitution 51–2
sufficiently precise 16–18, 20, 25, 27, 28–30, 38–42
temporal effect 30–2, 60
unconditional 32–8, 58–9
vertical 45
directives
application 2, 28, 255, 291, 305–6
communication 253–4
enforcement 2, 28, 40–42, 255, 271–2
deadline 31–2, 40–2, 258
framework 40, 43
implementation 2, 28, 38, 255, 305
operationalisation 28, 255, 264
transposition 27, 291, 305
discrimination, *see* principle of non-discrimination *and* Rewe
distinctiveness, *see* environmental law
Due report 293
duration
Commission enforcement 291–3
preliminary references 204

ECHR 83, 87
effective judicial control 80–3, 87–8, 106, 166, 317
effective judicial protection 80–3, 87–8, 109, 112, 166, 221, 317
effective (judicial) remedy 80, 136–8, 166, 313
effectiveness, *see* Rewe and Simmenthal
effet utile 16, 24, 67, 69, 79, 152, 250
emanation of state 45–8, 150
emission standards 43, *see also* limit values
enforcement, *see* Commission, national authorities, and private enforcement
enlargement 294, 322
environmental action programmes 58, 186, 232
environmental impact assessment (EIA) 35, 48–9, 54, 126–7, 132–4, 145, 153, 155, 162–3
environmental law
Aarhus Convention 117, 233
competence 26–7, 168, 179, 191–6, 254, 303, 320
distinctiveness 9, 323
evolution 9–14, 43–4, 322
objectives 196–7
policy 196–7
principles 196–201
requirements 200–1
equity of arms 324
estoppel 16, 35, 37, 45; *see also* direct effect
Eurobarometer 13
European Constitution 5, 81, 222–3, 236, 322
European Environmental Agency 231, 254
ex officio
national authorities 69–71
national courts 68–9, 93–6,
Community courts 176–7, 277

fisheries 201, 207–8, 210, 233, 254, 271–2, 279
Francovich, *see* liability of state
free movement, *see* internal market
functional subjectivisation 153

General and Persistent (GAP doctrine)
added value 268–72
further development 272–4
procedural conditions 266–8
substantive conditions 263–6

habitats 18, 23, 33, 36–7, 103, 123, 143
harmonization
  jurisprudential v legislative 91–2
high level of protection 9, 12, 89, 187, 195–8, 200–2, 207

IBA 39
indirect effect, *see* consistent interpretation
injunctions 90, 118, 134–7, 143–4
interest
  access to justice directive (proposal) 115, 117–8
  direct and individual concern 217–220
  direct effect 21–5
  direct interest 22, 110
  ecological 38, 114
  effective interest 23
  environmental 85, 109, 113, 171
  general 96, 113, 210, 219–20, 258
  individual interest 21–2, 72, 159, 169, 209–10, 282
  infringement proceedings 258
  multiple 113, 151, 310
  personal scope 22
  public 93–4, 101, 108, 127, 154, 183, 220, 287–8, 296–8
  protective interest 23
  Regulation 1367/2006 227–9
interim relief
  Community level 244–5
  infringement proceedings 261–2
  national level 137–41
  preliminary references 204–11
internal market 3, 12, 83,193, 195, 211, 233, 251, 313
internal review
  grounds 237–8
  personal scope 227–9
  substantive scope 230–7
  time limits 229–30
interpretation, *see* consistent interpretation and preliminary references
IPPC 43–4, 91, 109

judicial review of acts by private parties
  Community level 231
  national level 107–8, 118–19, 135, 147–9
judicial review of Community acts
  acts 185–9, 217, 230–7
  competence 173–4
  consequences 202–4, 243–4
  failure to act 186–8
  grounds of review 189–202, 241–3
  incidental review 242–3
  infringement proceedings 299–301
  intensity 120, 195
judicial review of national acts
  Aarhus convention 117–8, 123–4
  acts 104–7
  consequences 124–131
  failure to act 134–7
  grounds and intensity of review 120–3

kurieren am sympthom 269; *see also* GAP

Lappel banks 103, 204
law and economics 4
legal certainty 48, 52, 57, 62–4, 68, 78, 88, 97, 132–3, 163, 182, 184, 230, 273, 276–7
legitimate expectations 68
liability of the Community
  causation 247–8
  damage 246–7
  rights 246–7
  sufficiently serious breach 248–9
liability of private parties
  direct effect 147–9
  Directive 2004/35 34–5, 49, 98, 142–3, 171, 199–200, 206
liability of the state
  causation 160–3
  damage 150–7
  entities 150
  fault 158
  mitigate loss 161–2
  rights 150–7
  sufficiently serious breach 157–60
limit values 39, 42–4, 73, 143, 160, 275, 281, 313
locus standi, *see* interest and standing
lump sum
  calculation 289–90
  communications 277, 289–90
  conditions 287–8
  discretion 276–7
  objectives 286

Maastricht Treaty 2, 9, 274, 280
mandatory requirements 11, 88–9
manifest breach 133, 163–5, 177, 248, 300

manifest error 12, 39, 159, 120, 160, 195, 246
mixed agreements 179, 185

national authorities
  concept 45–8, 68–9, 150
  discretion 32–3, 159
  liability 149–69
  obligations 68–9
national courts
  concept 172–3
  discretion 120–3
  liability 163–7
  obligations 68–9, 166, 173–5
Nice Treaty 80, 222
non-binding acts 56, 58, 71, 104–6, 108, 179, 185–6, 196, 224, 232–3, 300–1
non-governmental organisations (NGO) 114–6, 210, 227–9, 238
notification
  Community acts 184, 230, 240
  national acts 18–19, 23, 50, 54, 125, 126
nullify unlawful consequences
  Community institutions 203, 238, 318
  direct effect 71, 145–6, 315
  infringement proceedings 259
  preliminary reference 182
  state liability 146–7, 149, 153, 155, 315

Ombudsman 231, 294, 299, 304

penalty payment, *see also* Commission enforcement
  Commission guidelines 279
  discretion 276–7
  duration 280–2
  flat and relative rates 285–6
  seriousness 279–80
  time period for compliance 283–5
pillars of the Treaty 56, 178–9, 191–2
plans and programmes 40, 104, 105, 107–8, 118, 127–9, 190, 224, 273
polluter pays principle 12, 196, 199, 206
precautionary principle 12, 198–201, 206, 208, 243
preliminary reference
  acte clair and éclairé 174–5
  acts 178–80, 185–9
  admissibility 175–6
  consequences 180–3, 202–4
  ex officio 176–7
  failure to act 186–7
  interim relief 204–11
  interpretation 177–8
  judicial review 183
  liability 181–2, 203, 212
  obligation to refer 173–5
  precedents 181–2
  sanctions 211–2
  temporal effect 182–3, 202
  time limits 184–5
primacy, *see* supremacy
principle of coherence 83, 88, 92, 105, 122–3, 153, 203, 314
principle of complete system of procedures and remedies 83–4, 88, 112, 138, 183, 187, 205, 210, 213, 221, 227, 301
principle of effective judicial protection, *see* effective judicial protection
principle of judicial control, *see* effective judicial control
principle of integration 11–12, 201–2, 233
principle of loyal cooperation 84, 153–4, 176, 203, 207
principle of non-discrimination (substantive) 50, 54, 59, 81–2, 85, 110
private enforcement 2–6, 304–8
procedural autonomy 76, 83, 109, 111, 131–2, 141, 146, 174, 182
proportionality, *see also* rule of reason
  Community acts 193–5
  national acts 11–12, 194–5
  procedural law 88–90
public participation
  Community level 223–6
  infringement proceedings 299
  national level 117–8, 129–30

recommendations, *see* non-binding acts
regulations 25–6, 45, 118–9, 210
remedies in national courts
  against illegal acts 130–4
  failure to act 134–7
  procedural infringements 125–30
  see also interim relief and liability
reparation, *see* damage and liability
res judicata 98–100, 173, 182, 185
restitution 146–7, 259
review, *see also* judicial review
  Kraaijeveld 28, 122
  legitimacy test 121
  procedural 123–4, 190–1, 241

substantive 123–4, 191–202, 242
Wednesbury 121–2
Rewe doctrine
equivalence/non-discrimination 68–9, 83, 85, 97, 100, 102, 110, 149, 157
effectiveness/excessively difficult 97, 102–3, 131, 133, 157, 166, 316
general 77–8
relevance 84–6
rule of reason 88–90
sector specific assessment 97, 101, 316
rights
academic perception 3–4, 6–7, 14, 17, 19, 23, 28, 83, 150–1, 154
Community liability 246–7
direct effect 15–25
directly conferred 110, 152
environmental 6, 170
fundamental 5, 80–1, 83, 87, 307
infringement procedure 295–302
judicial protection doctrine 86–8
objective 7, 310
preliminary references 172, 213
procedural 85, 110, 124, 178, 223–4, 226, 246, 287, 300
result 20–1
Rewe 84–6
Simmenthal effectiveness 84
state liability 150–7
subjective 8, 19, 72, 85, 109, 153, 310, 312
rule of reason
procedural 88–90
substantive 89
rules
procedural v remedial 76, 78, 80, 133, 171, 324

sanctions 82, 87, 167–9, 211–2, 286
schutznorm 7, 115, 166
separation of powers 277, 294
Simmenthal principle of effectiveness 79–80, 82–5, 88, 103, 130, 132, 135, 138, 166, 310
Single European Act 9–11
specific performance 20, 141, 143–5, 148
standing, *see also* interest and rights
Community level 216–26
national level 108–120
state aid 12, 231, 234, 259–60, 309, 324–5
state liability, *see* liability of the state
statement of reasons 81, 126, 129–30, 136, 242–3, 250
statistics
infringement proceedings 212, 251, 291–3
preliminary references 3, 204, 212, 251
Stavros Dimas 272
subsidiarity 43, 193–4, 324
sui generis 15, 267
supremacy 20, 79, 110, 125, 127, 130–2, 166, 314–5

teleological interpretation 27, 222, 293, 303
time limits
direct actions 184–5, 230
national courts 96–8
preliminary reference procedure 184–5
Regulation 1367/2006 229–31
tort, *see* liability
transport 233

uniformity 72, 140, 193, 205, 324

validity 130–1, 180–1, 202

waste 27, 32–3, 40–2, 127–9, 148–9, 199–200, 224, 262–72
water 39–40, 44, 119, 143, 145, 160, 194
Wednesbury review 121–2